£1.20p ^{od} Oct 1/47

H R Williams

IRELAND HER OWN

PRINTED AT PARKGATE PRINTING WORKS
DUBLIN BY CAHILL AND CO. LIMITED.

IRELAND HER OWN

AN OUTLINE HISTORY OF THE IRISH STRUGGLE
FOR NATIONAL FREEDOM AND INDEPENDENCE

T. A. JACKSON

Ireland her own, and all therein, from the sod to the sky.
JAMES FINTAN LALOR.

*Ireland one, and Ireland free,—is not this the definition
of Ireland, a Nation?* PATRICK PEARSE.

LONDON
COBBETT PRESS
2 SOUTHAMPTON PLACE, W.C.1
1946

TO

THE MEMORY OF

MY FRIEND AND COMRADE

CON O'LEHANE

one-time Secretary of the Cork Branch, Irish Socialist Republican Party ; a representative of that long line of Irishmen who have done valiant service in the working-class, democratic, and socialist movement in England, Scotland, and the U.S.A. without ceasing for a moment their fight for Ireland's national freedom.

What do they make of Ireland,
Of Fianna girls and Fianna boys?
De Valera, Lemass and Brooke
What do they make of Ireland?
>   *Said the man in the militia jacket*
>   *That he got in the war in Spain.*

Do they break the stone in Ireland
As when they cheered Parnell?
Are the factories closed against them
For whom Jim Connolly fell?

No sound I hear but silence
Speaking louder than any band,
And Irishmen as channel spray
Labouring in neighbour England.

But neither Gael nor Saxon
Have found their liberty,
Nor will unless they build a bridge
Of unity, by unity.

So proudly then might Ireland
Send her children oversea,
And Fianna girls and Fianna boys
Dance on England's pleasant lea.

And they'll wear the English posies
The Kent and Surrey may,
And English lads wear Irish green
For ever and a day
>   *Said the man in the militia jacket*
>   *That he got in the war in Spain.*

—EWART MILNE (1944).

FOREWORD

In this book I try to tell the story, first of how Ireland came to be a part of the British Empire, then of how the Irish people struggled to undo that conquest and so regain possession of the soil and the sovereign rule of Ireland.

The reason for telling this story is that, contrary to common belief, the process is not yet complete. I have thought it necessary to show the causes of the Anglo-Irish conflict, since only when these are known will the common people of England, the final arbiters, be able to tackle this long-outstanding *Irish Question* with a comprehension of the real issues involved.

The most valuable parts of this book should be those which show with what anxiety and diligence the rulers of England have had to labour to avoid being caught in a " pincer attack " between two distinct but converging emancipation struggles—those of the English and of the Irish common people respectively. The relations between the English rulers and the Irish ruled have been, throughout, *imperialist* relations, consequently, the history of the 800 years of Anglo-Irish conflict—with its examples of every variety of imperialist aggression and of every form of resistance thereto—supplies an invaluable introduction to the critical study of Imperialism in general.

The writings of Englishmen upon Anglo-Irish relations only too often call to mind an often-quoted remark by the Earl of Essex to Queen Elizabeth :

" 'Twere well for our credit that we had the exposition of our quarrel with these people and not they themselves."

Irish writers upon the subject have commonly been

satisfied with destroying such shreds of credit the
English expounders of the quarrel have contrived to
save. Thus they have, usually, missed the real tragedy
involved in Ireland's history—the manner in which the
English and Irish common people, each of them
struggling for freedom, have been time and again
jockeyed into becoming weapons used by the exploiters,
each for the enslavement of the other.

The outstanding exception is JAMES CONNOLLY, whose
work LABOUR IN IRISH HISTORY is a work of
genius. This work I have taken as my guide ; but
Connolly, writing as an Irishman for Irishmen, could
suppose that his readers knew many things which are
not at all well known to the ordinary Englishman.
I, who write as an Englishman, primarily for Englishmen, have to explain these things, as well as to continue
the narrative beyond the point at which Connolly left
off. If I have succeeded in what I have tried to do, my
outline will provide English readers with an introduction
to the study of Connolly's work, and that of other
specialist writers on Irish History. It will, at the same
time, provide Irish readers with an introduction to
the history of the English democratic and labour
struggle.

The English and the Irish common people, each with
its own splendid record of unyielding resistance to
oppression, should, by rights, understand each other
better than they do, and be more ready than they have
been to act in concert. Both together should find
reasons for solidarity with the democratic and working-
class struggles in other lands.

It was, as it chanced, on " Wolfe Tone Sunday "
(June 22nd, 1941) that the Nazi-Reich launched its
attack upon the Soviet Union. The spirit of WOLFE
TONE and of the UNITED IRISHMEN forms so fundamental an ingredient in Irish Nationalist tradition that
one looks with confidence for an Irish enthusiasm for

the Soviet Union parallel to that of Tone for the revolutionary people of France.

The very words with which Irishmen, in 1791, acclaimed the French, would apply with treble force to the people of the Soviet Union to-day :—

"Go on, then—great and gallant people! You are in very truth the hope of the world—of all except a few men in a few Cabinets who thought the human race belonged to them, but who, now, taught by awful example, tremble and dare not confide in armies arrayed against you and your cause."

Tone died struggling to win the RIGHTS OF MAN for Ireland. Those who follow him could not honour him better than by claiming for Ireland her rightful place in the battle-line of those who fight to win the Rights of Man for the whole world.

I write frankly as a partisan. I have done my best to be candid; but impartiality is beyond my scope. My concern is to help forward the cause I uphold. If this book does that, even by a little, I shall have attained my object.

T. A. J.

CONTENTS

PART I

THE ENGLISH CONQUEST OF IRELAND.

CHAPTER ONE

ANCIENT IRELAND

WHEN they invaded Ireland in 1169, the Anglo-Normans found in being a SOCIAL ORDER—one radically different from their own—which resisted for centuries their efforts to break it up.

In this chapter we examine the nature of this GAELIC SOCIAL ORDER.

Geographical Determinants

Measured from the Mediterranean Regions in which modern civilisation arose, England and Ireland lay together at the end of the earth. Each was protected by the sea against mass migrations; but neither was impervious to cultural infiltration, or immune from conquest by a determined invader.

Each preserved the primitive social organisation which the West Mediterranean region had long outgrown. In England this was thrown into confusion by the Roman occupation, and into further disintegration, centuries later, by the barbarian invasions which followed the Roman withdrawal. During all these years Ireland developed without interruption. As the barbarians over-ran the Roman Empire, "saints and scholars," fleeing from their ravages, found a refuge in Ireland. And it was from Ireland that a large part of Western Europe was ultimately re-civilised and re-Christianised.

To its escape from inclusion in the Roman Empire and involvement in its collapse, Ireland owes its early differentiation from England's development; and this in turn caused Ireland to react differently to those experiences the islands went through in common.

England was better placed for communication with

the Mediterranean over land ; but Ireland was the better
placed for communication by the long sea route.   Ireland
received Christian influences from Greece and Alexandria
long before England received them from Rome ; and
at a later date Ireland through its southern and western
ports was able to maintain trade contacts with France,
Spain and Italy while completely cut off by England
from contact with the over-land trade-routes.

A point of internal geography is that Ireland's mountain masses lie mostly upon, or parallel to, its coast-line.
This is rocky except for a gap on the east coast where
the great central plain reaches to the sea—which
central plain is traversed by rivers and interspersed
with bogs, some of considerable extent.   This dis-
position of the mountains played an important part in
the history of Ireland.   In ancient times the central
plain was densely wooded, so that the aboriginal
settlements took place in isolated parts of the hill
country.   This delayed materially the development of a
centralised state.   Later on these separate mountain
regions provided refuges from the Anglo-Norman
invaders, and similarly checked their efforts at unification.

Gaelic Society
   Of the racial origins of Gaelic Ireland little is known
with precision though much is inferentially established.
The GAELS, who reached Ireland in comparatively small
parties, at different times, came from various points—
Spain, Western France, and Belgium—after a prolonged
period of wandering in the grassland-belt of Europe.
Detached parties of their stock made their way into
Greece and Asia Minor and also into Italy, France and
Spain.   It is quite inconceivable that they should have
preserved their "racial purity" during all these, possibly,
thousands of years ; and very doubtful whether they
had any to preserve.   A federation of tribal-groups of

mixed origin, which, through long association, had evolved a common speech, gives the most probable starting-point for the history of the GAELS.

In Ireland they found an aboriginal population which was likewise of mixed descent. The Gaels did not exterminate the aborigines; in time they fused with them. Any theory, romantic or fascist, which supposes a " pure " Gaelic " blood " as a determinant of Irish history, is completely worthless. Not only have the Irish people " racial " affinities, at one point or another, with most of the nations of southern and western Europe; the seemingly " unique " features of Gaelic-Irish society can be shown to be akin to those of the *kinship society* which everywhere in Europe preceded the establishment of the class-differentiated *Territorial State*.

The special interest of Gaelic society is that it preserved into modern times an archaic social organisation which had not changed, in principle, since the Bronze Age, but which, notwithstanding, proved to be compatible with a high degree of cultural development or " civilisation."

The economy upon which Gaelic society rested was basically a " natural " economy—production for immediate consumption by the producing community. Its principal feature was cattle-breeding, supplemented by tillage and handicrafts. There was, in general, a surplus of production in excess of immediate requirements which was disposed of to a limited extent in exchange, but more normally by the " ostentatious consumption " of the chiefs of *Septs* and *Clanna*.

The unit of exchange-value was the *cumal* (" coo-al ") which means literally a slave-woman, but in practice denoted three cows. Wealth was reckoned in terms of cattle, and an aristocracy of wealth was replacing, where it had not already replaced, an aristocracy of descent. Milk and milk-products with oatmeal porridge and barley-bread constituted the staple diet, and this was supplemented from the game with which the country abounded.

In structure Gaelic society was hierarchical both in its economic and its political aspects. The *economic unit* was the *Fine* ("finna") which resembled the *familia* of the Romans but was of wider scope. The *political unit* was the *Clann* which corresponded to the Roman *tribe*. Intermediary between the *Clann* and the *Fine* was the *Sept* whose functions were both political and economic.

The territory occupied by a *Clann* was deemed its collective possession; it was variable in extent, since an area of no-man's-land invariably separated the territories of adjacent *Clanna*. The upper limit of expansion was fixed for each *Clann* at the point where further advance would be regarded by its neighbours as an encroachment. Its limit of contraction was set by the fixed quantity of land possessed by the *Septs* of which it was composed.

The area belonging to each *Sept* was by undeviating practice fixed in extent and location. This area as a whole was an inalienable possession of the *Sept* collectively. The portions allotted to meadow and arable, and the share allotted to each *Fine* in each of these, varied in quantity and location. Thus, while the *Clann*-territory might vary in extent and the *Fine*-allocation might vary in location, the *Septland* remained fixed in both respects; and this gave Gaelic society its stability through the fluctuations of circumstance and mischance. In the gradual break-up of Gaelic society under the impact of invasion and conquest the *Sept* was the last unit to succumb. A question which has exercised Gaelic scholars is whether this society was "communist" or "individualistic". The dispute has little relevance since in different aspects it was both, and neither. This is seen from the structure of the *Fine* and its relation to the *Sept*.

In its completest form the *Fine* consisted of " seventeen men " disposed in four grades. The *Geilfine* (or " true family ") consisted of a *Flaith* (" Flah ") and his four sons, or other males next of kin. These constituted, with their dependants and slaves, a single productive unit, and claimed a full member's share in the allocation of the *Sept* lands. The four males next of kin to the foregoing constituted the *Deirbhfine*, the four next the *Iarfine*, and the four next again the *Innfine*. These grades made a " family " for two purposes. They shared in the division of the disposable property of the *Flaith* at his death in a proportion which lessened with each succeeding grade. Broadly the " true family " took two-thirds, the second grade two-thirds of the residue, and so on. Similarly when the *Flaith* became involved in a feud, or liable to an *eric* or bloodfine, or other penalty imposed by judicial authority, the responsibility was *collective* but in a degree differentiated in a way which corresponded to the gradation of the family.

A cardinal point, and a clue to its functioning, is found in the rule that as the sons of a *Flaith* reached manhood they entered the *Geilfine*. If it had previously its full quota, the new-comer automatically pushed out its senior member (under the *Flaith*). For economic purposes the senior so extruded became qualified to share in the Sept lands as a full member. For other purposes he descended to the next grade, pushed out its senior, who repeated the process so that with a full " seventeen " the arrival of a new-comer at one end released a kinsman from family obligations at the other.

Thus the *Fine* gives a fine example of an historically conditioned transitional stage between collective and " private " property and responsibility. It is remarkable as combining the maximum of stability with the maximum of fluidity.

The territory of a *Sept* was disposed of in three ways :

(1) To each *Fine*, land was allocated as a *permanent* possession. On this " mensal " land the family dwelling was erected with the huts of the dependants, etc. Only if the *Fine* became extinct did this land revert to the *Sept*. (2) A portion of the land was cultivated in large open fields as arable or meadow, and in each field the *Fine* shared in prescribed proportions. The remainder was left undivided ; but custom set limits to its use by each *Fine* according to its standing. Common affairs were decided upon by a Council of *Flaiths* who appointed one of their number Chief of the *Sept*. An old Gaelic law tract says : " It is one of the duties of a *Sept* to support every member, and the *Sept* does this when it is in a proper condition."

The Political Structure

Gaelic society on its political side never attained to the complete unity of a Territorial State. It approximated thereto but was more of a multiplicity than a unity despite the fact that a so-called " High King " (*Ard-Ri*) was recognised for centuries before the Norman invasion, as also was a number of subordinate but independent " province kings".

The unit of this agglomerate structure was the *Tuath* (" too-ha ") or petty-state, which comprised, under a common head, the *Ri* (" ree "), a number of neighbour *clanna*.* The title *Ri* is cognate to the Latin *rex*, which possibly derives from it. Within recognised limits the office was elective, and the holder could be deposed by the Council of Chiefs whose sanction installed him in office. Even when at a later date the office became virtually hereditary this sanction was necessary and could be refused.

The right to depose a *Ri* was jealously guarded to

---

*The *clanna* were also grouped in kinship aggregates called *Cinel* (" kinnel ") which occasionally coincided with the *tuatha* but were usually dispersed between differing *tuatha*. Here again a rudimentary transition from a purely kinship organisation to a purely territorial one is observable.

the end. Its exercise provided a pretext for the Norman invasion ; and later still occasioned one of the bloodiest of the Elizabethan wars in Ireland. The fact that a *Ri* became disqualified by physical blemish, congenital or acquired, proves his function to have been basically magical—that of a public mascot. This is supported by the fact that the office of war leader, called *Toiseach* ("Tee-shock") was quite distinct. A corollary of the elective nature of the office of *Ri* is seen in the appointment of a *Tanist*, a "next in succession," who could take over in an emergency.

The functions of the *Ard-Ri* and of the "province kings" are less clearly defined. Originally they represented a differentiation among the various *Ri-tuatha* of a regional or an All-Ireland predominance, based on the possession of some spot—generally a hill—deemed to be endowed with special *mana* or "sanctity." Thus the *Ard-Ri* was for long the *Ri* in possession of the hill of Tara. The term " province king " is a complete misnomer. They were not " kings " and they did not rule " provinces." The familiar territorial division of Ireland into four provinces was made originally by the Church for purely ecclesiastical purposes. The names attached to them are those of federations of *Cinnel* or of *Tuatha*, with in three cases a Danish termination (" ster " —stand, or abiding place) added to a Gaelic tribal name. Thus *Ulaidh* (Ulla), *Laighin* (Lay-in), *Muman* (Moo-an) and *Connachta* were each originally the names of tribal federations, whose territories were liable to variation at their points of contact. In each case the *Ri-mor* who was accepted as the federal chief was vested with a ceremonial primacy rather than any authority to rule. Here again a transitional form in between kinship society and the territorial state is evident.

According to tradition Ireland was always divided between Five of these federations. In historical times the extra " province " was created by dividing *Laighin*

into North and South.   Later a portion of the territory
of the Northern Laighin, with portions from *Ulaidh*
and *Connacht*, constituted the "province" of *Midhe*
(Meath) with Tara as its centre.

Unity and Opposition in Gaelic Society

That an All-Ireland community-consciousness existed,
which contrasted sharply with the political division of
Ireland into scores of independent *Tuatha*, is testified by
the antiquity and importance of periodical festivals at
which, in theory, every free man and woman in Ireland
attended.   They bore notable affinities to similar assemblies among the Hellenic Greeks, and, like them,
derived from collective rituals deemed of magical
efficacy.   They also served the purpose of a periodical
market ; and showed the learned professions (Brehons,
Bards, etc.) as constituting each a species of "guild"
which laid down rules, fixed an order of professional
precedence, and admitted, or refused, candidates to
the profession.

The only surviving function of the *Ard-Ri* was to
preside at the magical-religious part of this ceremony,
and to pronounce judgment in law-cases submitted for
his final jurisdiction.

A basic social division was that between the "free"
and the "unfree"—"freedom" in this case being
that to share in the allocation of *Sept* land as of right.
Originally this division corresponded to that between
the conquering kindred and the conquered aborigines
who were tolerated on the *Sept* land in return for the
performance of servile functions.   It became extended
by the admission into the *Sept* area of "strangers,"
sometimes merchant-craftsmen, sometimes men ejected
from other Septs for various reasons.   Where these
strangers possessed wealth they were admitted to the
Sept land on payment of a "rent" to the Chief. Usually
they occupied a portion of what had been unappropri-

ated land ; but they might on occasion be admitted to
rent a portion of the *mensal* land of a Chief or other
Flaith.

As distinct from household slaves—who were usually
purchased as young boys and girls from English traders
—the lowest grade of the unfree, the *Fuidhir*, supplied
most of the heavy manual labour required by the *Fine*
to which they were attached. They were paid with
food for themselves and their families and with a small
share in the mensal land of the *Fine*. A superior grade
of " old retainers " was admitted to a share in the arable
and meadow land allotted to the *Fine ;* four of this grade
usually received between them the share of a single
member of the *Fine*.

There were provisions enabling a *Fuidhir* to reach the
category of an Old Retainer, and for an old retainer to
be admitted to the *Sept* by adoption into a *Fine*. Correspondingly there were provisions whereby a *Sept* member
might lose his rights and become "unfree." This
arose occasionally from the commission of a crime.
More usually it arose from the practice of cattle-lending
—a form of hire-purchase in which the rate of payment
was fixed at one-third of the value loaned each year
for seven years. If a cattle-borrower made default he was
subject to distraint ; and, in certain circumstances, to
the loss of his *Sept* membership.

A point here is that cattle-borrowing would be
resorted to only when a man's near kinsmen were
unable, or unwilling, to make him a free gift. The
cattle would be borrowed, therefore, usually from one
of the wealthy strangers whom the Chief or the *Clann*
had allowed to establish themselves on *Clann* land not
the property of any *Sept*. When a *Sept* member lost
his rights he did so very often by default to such a
stranger, who, acquiring the defaulter's rights, thus
acquired entry into the Sept.

Within the communal-collectivity of Gaelic society

appeared therefore (1) inequalities of descent; (2) inequality of wealth; and (3) lines of class-division developed from the germinal forms of the employer-labourer, landlord-tenant, and debtor-creditor relations —all of which existed in Gaelic society as in the society of Greece and Rome on the eve of the transition to the Territorial State.

These tendencies were accentuated by two important historical impacts : (1) The Establishment of the Christian Church ; and (2) the Danish Invasions.

The Church in Gaelic Ireland

The Christian Church was instituted in Ireland by Patrick the Saint in the thirty-three years which closed with his death in 465.

There had been isolated Christians in Ireland long before the mission of Patrick. Like Augustine in England he *organised* the Church, and he did so with the approval and support of the *Ard-Ri* and of the "province" *Ri-mor*. The support of the Church and its authority was invaluable to them in their struggle to bring the *ri-tuatha* into subjection. A parallel process went on in England, and indeed all through Europe.

"The Establishment of the Western State was curiously coincident with the triumph of a new type of religion, the chief characteristic of which was *universality*. It may sound at first hearing ridiculous to associate the meek religion of Christ with the aggressive military institution of the *State*. Yet it is quite certain that Christianity had a great deal to do with breaking down tribal prejudices and with establishing great political communities . . . Though Christianity in its early days had been a mission to the poor and lowly, its great conquests in Northern and Western Europe were due to the conversion of Kings and Princes. The conversion of Aethelbirt of Kent was the

signal for the conversion of England. Christianity
passed from Court to Court. . . . And Christianity
well repaid the favour of princes. Under the cry
of " One church and one King " the older tribal
divisions were ultimately wiped out and England
became one nation, with *Church* and *State* in
intimate alliance."

—EDWARD JENKS : *History of Politics.*

In Ireland a similar process was well-advanced when
it was interrupted and aberrated first by the Danish,
then by the Norman invasion. An interesting other-
side of the process is found in the manner in which the
Church was accommodated to, and was itself modified
by, *Clann* society :

"Each *clann* had its own bishop, and its own
priests, the diocese was merely the district occupied
by the *clann.* There was naturally a great number
of bishops . . . and it was not until the 12th
century that the present system of definite dioceses,
grouped into provinces, was introduced. The
Clann allotted to its clergy for their support certain
lands . . . looked after by an official who was
generally a layman. The clergy of a *clann* mostly
lived in communities under their bishop, so that
the church was both tribal and monastic."

—HAYDEN–MOONAN : *Short History of the Irish People.*

These communities performed an important function by
becoming centres for the cultivation of arts and crafts,
for the development of industry as distinct from agriculture, and for the development of trading-relations.
The completion of this process was aided by two
centuries of Danish invasion.

The Danish Invasion (795–1014).

The forays of the Scandinavian pirates who are
known traditionally in Ireland as the " Danes " left

indelible marks upon the history of Ireland. They did not establish themselves permanently as they did in Normandy, or make themselves kings of the country as they did for a time in England and in Sicily. They effected a great deal of destruction and completed the elimination of the *tuath* as an independent entity—it being replaced by the enforced aggregation of *septs* under a *Ri-Mor* or Chief of a composite " *clann.*" The driving of many *Clanna* from their ancestral locations——their *Septs* being driven often in different directions—caused the *clanna* in many cases to disappear as such ; while the dispersed *Septs* of differing kindred united under a common *Ri-mor* to establish new aggregates in the territory to which they had been driven.

A more positive effect was the establishment by the Danes of some of the chief sea-ports of Ireland. The Danes had been traders before they turned pirates, and continued to combine the occupations—piracy procuring the materials for a profitable trade. They had been farmers and fishers before they became traders ; and the cities they established at the mouths of rivers and on inlets gave them first-class facilities for practising all their specialities at once. Dublin, Wexford, Waterford, Youghal, Cork, Bantry and Limerick were all founded and built up into walled cities by the Danes ; and, in the intervals of peace during the two centuries of their era, they developed into permanent institutions the market relations which the Church had begun to establish. In their cities they provided a refuge for the individual craftsmen and traders scattered by their violent destruction of the monastic communities. On the other hand, some monastic communities survived—by means of the ingenious invention of the Round Towers—to become, when peace was restored, nuclei for trading towns in the interior.

Under the impact of invasion, the various *Ri-Mor* had to develop into military chiefs, with strong bands of trained men under their command, or go out of existence. They recruited professional soldiers—trained in war against the Danes—in England, and these *Gall-oglaich* (foreign-soldiers) survived as an institution to mystify later ages under the name of " gallow-glasses." Thus equipped with armed bands the rival chiefs commenced a furious struggle for the title and office of *Ard-Ri*.

The prize was won by a North Munster Chief, Brian called *Boroimhe* (" bor-roo "), meaning " of the Tributes," meaning again that he achieved the first step toward a unified state by extorting tribute from every *Ri* in Ireland.

A measure of peace began to emerge when, in 1014, the Danes made a final rally to come to the aid of the Danish King of Dublin from whom Brian the Brave had extorted tribute. A battle fought within sight of Dublin on the shore at Clontarf ended in the total rout and partial extermination of the Danes. Brian, then an old man, was killed by a fugitive Dane. As the *Njal Saga* says : " Brian lost his life ; but he saved his Kingdom."

After Brian's death the anarchical strife for possession of the title of *Ard-Ri* was resumed. General exhaustion caused, in the end, the recognition, by most contenders, of the superior claims of Ruraidhe O'Connor, *Ri-Mor* in Connacht.

It was at that point, when all Ireland was settling down to enjoy a long-wished-for peace, that Diarmuid MacMurrogh, *Ri-Mor* in Laighin, fell into feud with the chief of the O'Rourkes—over some " trifle " of wife-stealing. The chiefs of the Laighin *Septs* promptly ejected Diarmuid from office. They wanted peace ; and were not going to be mixed up in his family quarrels.

Diarmuid fled overseas to the court of Henry II, King of England, swore fealty to him as his vassal, and asked for aid to " recover his rights." Henry, for reasons explained in the next chapter, gave Diarmuid permission to recruit any of his vassals who were willing to try their luck.

All Ireland wanted was peace ; all Ireland got was an Anglo-Norman invasion.

CHAPTER TWO

THE SUBJUGATION OF IRELAND—I

REDUCING Ireland to the status of a fief of the King of England proved a tedious and an interminable business. It was " always a-doing, yet never done." Centuries passed, the Middle Ages ended; but the struggle to conquer the still unsubdued Irish went on and on.

The NORMAN CONQUEST became a TUDOR CONQUEST which continued into the reign of the first Stuart before it reached an approximate end.

In this chapter we outline the NORMAN CONQUEST from 1169 to 1485, then the TUDOR-STUART conquest from 1485–1610.

The Political and Economic Background

Henry's prompt compliance with Diarmuid's petition calls for some comment.

The basic explanation is that the feudal system was still in its ascendant phase and an equilibrium between the powers of the King, the barons and the church respectively, had not been attained. It was the Papal policy of the period to work for a settlement along the lines of " One Church and One King "; which meant in practice that the Papacy as a temporal power aimed at a political rule—effected through a few powerful monarchs acting as its vassals—which would form the complement to the unified authority it had already established in the spiritual sphere. With that object, the Pope had granted Henry II an authorisation to make himself Lord of Ireland, twenty years before Diarmuid appealed to him for aid.

Though a most powerful monarch in theory—being not only King of England, and Duke of Normandy,

B

but also Lord of Brittany, Anjou, Maine and Aquitaine—
Henry II was in practice faced with trouble arising
from the predatory rivalry of the barons, his vassals,
in every part of his dominions. These barons united
only to resist his efforts to unite them into an ordered
state.

What this had led to was described by a monkish
scribe on the eve of Henry's accession :

> " It was a time when any rich man made his
> castle and when they filled them with devils and
> evil men. They were days when wretched men
> starved with hunger. In those days the earth
> bore no corn, for the land was all foredone by
> such deeds, and men said openly that Christ and
> his Apostles had gone to sleep."

Ireland was as good a place as any in which to dump
that potent cause of mischief—the unemployed problem
peculiar to feudalism—the problem of disposing of the
younger (and the illegitimate) sons and the redundant
dependants of the feudal lords.

The company Diarmuid recruited illustrated Henry's
problem vividly. The leaders were most of them the
bastard sons of Norman lords. The followers were all
professional " toughs,"—Norman, Welsh, French and
Flemish mercenaries, greedy for pay and plunder. All
were at a loose end in consequence of their failure to
carve out lordships for themselves in Wales. Diarmuid
must have appeared to them like a fairy godmother,
while Henry must have been more than glad to see the
backs of them all.

The Submission of 1171

The expedition had little difficulty in effecting its
object. It got possession of Wexford and Waterford,
advanced to Dublin and sacked it. Diarmuid was
reinstated as " king " of Leinster. In gratitude he
married his daughter to the leading gangster, " Strong-

bow," and advanced a claim to the title and office of *Ard-Ri* of Ireland. At that moment (1171) he died; and "Strongbow" as his heir by marriage, claimed, along with Diarmuid's Kingship, the reversion of his claim. There seemed nothing to stop him making this claim good.

This was anything but what Henry II wanted. In next to no time he was in Ireland with a strong army led by reliable supporters, and accompanied by a Papal Legate, who summoned a Church Synod, while Henry summoned every *Ri* and chief in Ireland to come in and make his submission. The clergy submitted to Papal authority, and persuaded most of the chiefs likewise to submit immediately. O'Connor held out for a bit, but came in later. Strongbow came to heel without a murmur.

Having installed himself as Lord of Ireland, Henry II proceeded to apportion his new dominion between his leading followers—leaving to them the job of effecting an actual occupation. The walled cities he retained as direct crown possessions. In each a castle was built and a royal seneschal installed. Dublin and the "County" around it he made into a special appanage of the Crown. He repeopled the city (which Strongbow had destroyed) with Englishmen—mostly from Bristol—who were given special inducements to restore the town and its trade; and he apportioned the County in small estates between minor "lords of manors" who were permitted to grant sub-tenancies only to actual tillers, on English-feudal tenures, mostly in villeinage. Only those Irish were admitted who were willing to become "English" in dress, speech and allegiance. This was the first "English" plantation in Ireland, and the most nearly successful. The special area, surrounded by a dyke, or palisade, became known as "within the Pale," or for short *the Pale*. Any Irish caught in the area were hunted with as little mercy as wolves.

Such was the Anglo-Norman Conquest of Ireland
as feudal law envisaged it. It constituted the only
quasi-legal claim English kings had to Lordship in
Ireland from 1171 until, in 1541, a hand-picked " Parliament " in Dublin invited Henry VIII to assume the
title of King of Ireland.

The Progress of the Conquest

From this " submission " onwards, for three centuries,
the history of Ireland outside the Pale presents a monotonous succession of variations on a single theme.
The Anglo-Norman lords, with their private armies,
advanced across the great central plain, and up (or down)
the great river valleys. The Irish retreated with their
cattle to the hills, the woods, and hiding places in the
bog-country.

On the level plains the clansmen stood no chance
against the armoured Norman spearmen and their
professional archers. In the hill country the reverse
was the case, and every defile was a death-trap. As for
the bogs—the spearmen might as well try to charge
from Wexford to Milford Haven.

Thus as a first result the Normans got possession
of large tracts of empty land ; but in nearly every
case the Irish, hidden in their lurking places, were
only a night's march away, ready to pounce on cattle,
barns, or outlying parties. The expected flow of
emigrants from England dried up early ; thereafter,
to get any profit from their lands, the Normans, willy-
nilly, had to come to terms with the Irish *Septs*. Soon
the Irish were back where they had been, paying tribute
to the newcomer it is true, but in all other respects
living as they did before he came.

This brought the second result. The backsliding
Norman lords were impeached as " traitors " by the
Lord Deputy, the King's seneschal or by those of their
number who had contrived to import settlers and plant

their estates on English feudal tenures. The result was a series of bloody feuds among the Anglo-Norman nobles, in the course of which their harried English tenants skipped off either to the towns, or back to England again. The English kings could only at rare intervals give any assistance to their agents in Ireland; accordingly the feuds, in time, burned themselves out.

To get into good standing with the clan chiefs the Norman lords married Irish wives, or contracted marriages between their daughters and Irish chiefs or their sons. (Their followers, most of them, had done likewise already.) As the old generation died away they were succeeded by half-Norman, or quarter-Norman heirs. Brought up by Irish nurses, with none but Irish or part-Irish playmates, speaking nothing but Irish except on rare occasions, these heirs *thought* in Irish, and became " more Irish than the Irish themselves." From tolerating the BREHON law, they passed on to complying with it. Save for their titles they had become Irish clan chiefs.

The Pale and the towns held out against this. They drove a profitable trade with England, of which they had a monopoly, and it was to their interest that the demand for English products should not fail. But even their position was weakening, as the Irish steadily filtered in. The ruin and wastage of war produced a thin stream of refugee clansmen who, for convenience, were ready to comply outwardly with English usages. The Lords Deputy and the Pale Parliament (set up in imitation of the English original shortly after that was instituted) railed bitterly against the " Irish enemy "; but the process went on.

The Statute of Kilkenny

How far the process of Gaelicising the conquerors had gone was revealed in a Statute of the Parliament called by the Duke of Clarence, son of Edward III, then

Viceroy, and held in Kilkenny in 1367. Among other
things this Statute decreed that:

(1) Intermarriage with the Irish, and entering into
    binding personal ties with them, such as
    gossipred, incurred penalties as High Treason.

(2) Englishmen adopting Irish names, dress, customs
    or speech, incurred forfeiture of all lands and
    tenements.

(3) Tolerating the *Brehon* law, still more submitting
    to it, was High Treason.

(4) Permitting Irish tenants to hold by Gaelic
    tenures, or permitting Irish *Septs* to graze
    their cattle on estates granted by the Crown
    incurred forfeiture.

(5) Anyone harbouring or encouraging Irish
    minstrels, rhymers, or taletellers incurred heavy
    fines.

(6) Admitting Irish priests to benefices, or to
    monastic establishments was forbidden.

(7) The practice of *coyne and livery* was declared
    an abuse.

(8) Etc., etc., etc.

The correct way to interpret this historic Statute of
Kilkenny is to treat it as a Hymn of Hate by the Pale
against the Anglo-Irish lords. The Parliament had no
power to enforce a single one of these decrees. Nor
could the Viceroy enforce them without a large-scale
war for which he was not prepared.

The Statute recognised, in the language of the law-
lords of the Pale, the existence of a " middle nation "
separating the " English " Pale from the " Irish enemy,"
a middle nation composed of " degenerate English "
and partly-anglicised Irish. It admitted that the Normans
had made only a formal conquest over some of the
Irish, while the Irish had made a real cultural conquest
of most of the Norman-English.

The Statute of Kilkenny gave itself away by making it treason to make war upon the Irish, or to *conclude peace with them*, without authorisation from the King's Deputy.

Its provisions were aimed at known and notorious offenders. The descendants of Henry II's leading follower, Hugo de Burgh (Gaelicised as " Burke ") had " gone Irish " so far that Richard de Burke had accepted the status of a *Ri-mor*, and his tenantry had reciprocated by becoming Clann Rickard. The sons of his son William had gone further. They had divided the inheritance and taken the name of MacWilliam. Theirs was far from being the only instance. The provision against harbouring minstrels, etc., was aimed especially at the Geraldines, both the Kildare and the Desmond Fitzgeralds, all notorious offenders.

The provision against *coyne and livery* arose from a then-recent incident. The Lord Deputy having reason to fear an Irish raid upon the Pale had called upon the Earl of Desmond* for aid. Desmond had come with 10,000 men, nearly all Irish or three-quarters Irish, and had quartered his troops upon the gentry and inhabitants of the Pale. He claimed it was an old Irish custom, *coinmed* (" coyney ") which the English translated as " livery " or board-wages. It was, as Desmond claimed, an old Irish custom, but with a qualification he was careful to forget. In Irish law the amount a chief might levy in this way was strictly limited. Not knowing this the Lord Deputy was left wondering whether it was worse to be ravaged by the Irish or saved by Desmond.

The final futility of the Statute was revealed less than twenty years later when Richard II, who had come to Ireland to enforce submission all round, suffered a crushing and ignominious defeat at the hands of the

*Desmond=South Munster as Thomond=North Munster.

Wicklow clans — a defeat which sent him back to England, without an army, totally discredited and ripe for deposition.

Preoccupation with dynastic changes, French war, and the civil war of the Roses which followed, kept the English kings from paying attention to Ireland until after the accession of Henry VII in 1485.

The Prelude to the Tudor Conquest

The reign of Henry VII (1485-1509) was one of the major transition periods in English history. The transition involved was that from feudalism as a system of graded local sovereignties to feudalism centralised and fixed in its final—and therefore ossified and degenerating —form of *Absolute Monarchy*.

The first essential of the change consisted in destroying the separate military powers of the great feudal lords and absorbing all their sovereignties into that of the King as *sole sovereign and Lord*. The change was necessitated by the anarchy into which the older system had degenerated, and by Henry Tudor's precarious position as technically a " usurper ". It was facilitated by the self-destruction of the nobles in the civil war of the Roses and by the support of the burghers, who gained from the change a much greater freedom to develop their bourgeois mode of production. The nobility accepted the change when they realised that the loss of their political independence gave them greater freedom to exploit their domains economically. As a rent-eating landocracy and as profit-grasping sheep-farmers they became less ostentatious but greedier than ever. Eventually they became slavish adulants of the New Monarchy when, to complete its Absolutism, it turned to rob and degrade (politically) the Church, and then to set sharp barriers before any further political progress of the bourgeoisie which had helped to bring the changes about.

An important technological factor in this transition was the possession by the Crown of the only train of heavy artillery in the country, and its ability—aided by the wealth of the burghers—to hire an army of continental mercenaries equipped with, and skilled in the use of, the new firearms.

The process as outlined falls into three stages : (1) The disarming of the territorial lords by the destruction of their castles and the dispersal of their private armies ; (2) The " Reformation " struggle against the Papacy and the Church ; (3) The imposition of restraints upon the bourgeoisie by the Crown and the landocracy in alliance. During the first of these phases the Kings of England (Henrys VII and VIII) had to temporise in Ireland by tolerating there, in the persons of the Earls of Kildare, the political aggrandisement of the territorial nobility they were systematically destroying in England. During the second phase in England it became possible to carry through the first two stages simultaneously in Ireland. This constituted the Tudor Conquest which passed over into the Stuart conquest which involved the application of the third stage in both countries.

The Tudor Conquest : First Phase

While England was racked by the War of the Roses, the policy of the Norman Conquest in Ireland revealed its final bankruptcy. Its essential feature had been that of *conquest through intermediaries*. The Pale, directly under the control of the Crown, was established to supply a base for, and also to exercise control over, the Territorial Nobility, who, in turn, were expected to establish their sway over the Irish Chiefs, who were expected to carry through the actual subjugation of the Irish people.

The policy broke down because the Territorial Lords (by becoming largely Gaelicised) came to an understanding with the Irish Chiefs and so grew far too powerful for the Pale to control. In fact, with the

English Kings draining away its man-power instead of adding to it, the Pale, ravaged by the Geraldine Lords and largely reoccupied by the clans, became reduced to its smallest dimensions, and kept itself in being only by paying *blackmail* both to the Clans, and to the Territorial Lords.

At the same time the Norman policy succeeded to the extent that the conditions it had brought about favoured a large degree of *feudalisation* of the Gaelic " Nation ". The Chiefs became in practice hereditary. They greatly increased their power over their Clansmen in consequence of the fact that the shifts and migrations impelled by centuries of strife had broken up the older clan *unities* and combined under the surviving Chiefs a somewhat fortuitous aggregation of unrelated *Septs*. Thus as the Territorial Lords grew Gaelicised the clans grew feudalised. A possibility was established for a re-union of Ireland into a frankly feudal state which, absorbing the Pale, would become completely independent of England.

Two things operated as a check upon this tendency.

(1) The Territorial Lords and the greater clan chiefs, each pursuing a policy of family aggrandisement, were perpetually at feud with each other. Their situation differed in fact from that of their English counter-parts in the War of the Roses only in that there was a free-for-all fight instead of a simple Red-versus-White struggle.

(2) The trading towns in the Pale, and in the *Gaeltacht* were more concerned to develop intercourse with England that to interrupt it. Similarly, the Territorial Lords, who in many cases owned estates in England, gained as landlords from the changes introduced by the New Monarchy. Thus there existed a power to separate from England, but *no will to do so*. That alone saved English dominion in Ireland at this point.

The extent to which economic development had

gone in the area outside the Pale was far greater than is commonly realised :

> " In all the Irish territories *great fairs* were periodically held, and were attended by Irish and foreign traders. So well attended were these fairs that the townspeople of the Pale complained of the injury they suffered because English and other traders deserted their own markets in favour of them. The records of European ports also show that Ireland carried on a *great foreign trade* . . . from the Mediterranean to the Baltic."

—HAYDEN-MOONAN : *Short History of the Irish People.*

The cultural progress of Gaelic Ireland, though severely set back at first by the Norman invasion, made a recovery commensurate with this economic advance.

In these circumstances it was impossible for the English King to rule in Ireland except through the instrumentality of the leading family of the " middle nation "— the Kildare Geraldines. Three Earls of Kildare, father, son and grandson, held the position of Lord Deputy in succession, virtually monopolising between them the Government of Ireland from 1468 to 1533, with only temporary interruptions.

This virtual *Ard-Ri*-ship of the Geraldines, THOMAS, GARRETT MOR and GARRETT OG, involved a virtual scrapping of the whole Norman policy turning upon the supremacy of the Pale.

The Geraldines were supreme *over* the Pale and as good as absorbed it into the " middle nation ". At the same time they were intermarried with the O'Neills and the O'Connors (as their junior branch, the Desmond Fitzgeralds, was with the O'Briens) and so in part closed the gap between the " middle nation " and the " mere Irish ". They were, however, closely related also to the leading Yorkist families and lent them assistance during

the Civil War. Their power was so great that Henry
VII on his accession recognised the need to ignore their
Yorkist affiliations and confirm GARRETT MOR in the
post of Lord Deputy. But for the fact that the Henrys,
VII and VIII, knew enough statecraft to " play " the
Geraldines, Garrett Mor and Garrett Og, as a skilled
angler plays a trout a break might easily have come.

When, however, the time was ripe, their virtual
monopoly of office, and the zeal with which they had
sought to bring Ireland under their rule as a single unit,
were turned into weapons against them. All the rivalries
and jealousies they had aroused—particularly their feud
with the Ormond Butlers—were secretly fostered and
then crystallised into charges. GARRETT OG was summoned to London, but as he was allowed to appoint
his son " SILKEN " THOMAS to act as his substitute,
and as he, his father, and his grandfather had all survived
similar summons, he thought little of it. This time,
however, the mine was sprung. Arrived in London,
Garrett Og was arrested and thrown into the Tower.
Silken Thomas was tricked by a bogus letter into
believing his father had been executed. He accordingly
renounced his allegiance and called out his supporters
for war.

It was what was wanted. This was not a " *nationa.*
revolt " : the Geraldines in the exercise of their office
had made too many enemies for that, and the " mere
Irish " were only indirectly concerned anyway. But it
was powerful enough to call for the full strength of the
Royal power. Once again the Royal train of artillery
came into action, and a Royal army of German and
Italian mercenaries. When the Geraldine stronghold
of Maynooth was battered down and all its garrison
exterminated, Silken Thomas surrendered. His father,
Garrett Og, had died in the Tower. When Silken
Thomas and five of his uncles were all hanged together
at Tyburn on a single gallows, in 1537, the whole senior

line of the Geraldines became extinct save for an infant who had by a fluke been overlooked in the sack of Maynooth.

With their central leadership destroyed the entire " middle nation " with their Irish allies were at the mercy of the Royal power. The Pale which a few years before had been all-but absorbed into the " middle nation " was now all-but liquidated in an opposite direction. Being now extended virtually to all Ireland— save for pockets of Gaelic clan-influence—it ceased to exist as a " Pale " and became " official " Ireland.

Irish Chiefs, English Lords

The technique which had been employed against the Geraldines was, from this point onwards, employed with modifications against the Irish clan chiefs. It was very simple. The Chief was first flattered with titles, honours, and a subsidy into becoming an agency of anglicisation. If he fell in with the plan he was made straightway, by a legal " magic ", the *owner* of all the clan-territory ; and his clansmen, if they submitted, became his tenants, either for life, on lease, or at will. If he accepted the title but did not introduce English-feudal tenures he was attainted as a traitor, his lands were confiscated and the English-feudal tenures were imposed on the clans by force. If the clans revolted either with the new lord-chief or against him, a punitive expedition achieved the same result. All through the process the one object was steadily pursued : as in England, every " lord " whether English, Anglo-Irish, or plain Irish had to choose between (1) becoming a rent-hungry *landlord* on the English model, or (2) being attainted as a traitor, hanged as a " rebel ", driven into exile, or disposed of by private assassination.

The process continued with monotonous persistence from 1533 into the next century. The revolts involved grew bigger, the Irish lords involved more powerful,

the repressions more wholesale and bloodier. Eventually toward the end of the " spacious days of Great Elizabeth" the local revolts so ran into each other that something near to general revolt raged all through the *Gaeltacht**
and what was left of the " middle nation ".

The issue was complicated by the *quasi-religious* war between England and Spain. The rebel lords appealed for aid to Spain and to the Pope, who sent small expeditions which landed at Dingle, in 1579, and at Kinsale in 1580. The only difference they made was to give the English commanders an excuse for ferocity to the limit of extermination.

In order to force the rebels to surrender, cattle were impounded, and the standing-crops were destroyed systematically. In one campaign alone crops to the value of £20,000 (equal in current values to £1,000,000) were destroyed. The result was a famine of appalling intensity. An Irish chronicler laments that " the low of cattle could not be heard from the rock of Cashel to Dingle Bay ". An English observer, the " poet's poet ", Edmund Spenser, describes what he saw :

> " Ere one year and a half they (the rebels) were brought to such wretchedness as that any stony heart would have rued the same. Out of every corner of the woods and glens they came creeping forth upon their hands, for their legs could not bear them ; they looked like anatomies of death ; they spoke like ghosts crying out of their graves ; they did eat the dead carrions, happy where they could find them : yea, and one another soon after, insomuch as the very carcasses they spared not to scrape out of their graves ; and if they found a plot of water-cresses or shamrocks, there they flocked as to a feast for a time, yet were not able long to continue there withal ; that in short space there

* *Gaeltacht* : that part of Ireland in which Gaelic was (or is) the everyday speech of the people.

were none almost left, and a most populous and plentiful country suddenly left void of man and beast."

—ED. SPENSER : *View of the State of Ireland* (1595).

Confiscation and Plantation

Overlapping this culmination of Tudor policy was a development which continued into the reign of James the First Stuart, the policy of " clearance and plantation".

Impelling the policy of tricking Irish Chiefs into incurring the confiscation of their estates was the general desire to establish English *Landlordism* in Ireland. Impelling the particular policy of *clearance* followed by *plantation* was the same motive which gave the Reformation the distinctive form it took in England—the desire for a *reservoir* of estates from which to reward the pliant tools of the Crown, which estates in turn would absorb as tenants some of the army of vagrants infesting the English countryside, as a result of " clearances " to make room for profitable sheep-walks owned by the new nobility.

All that Ireland ever saw of the Protestant Reformation was this aspect—of an excuse for robbing the Church of its treasures and its lands. There was literally nothing in Ireland to correspond to the popular ideological-political movement which on the Continent and in England made the Reformation " the first general uprising of the European bourgeoisie ".

As if to point this difference, the first state experiment in large-scale *clearance* was made during the reign of Mary the Catholic. The lands cleared were made into " shire-land " and divided into " Queen's County " and " King's - County " with " Maryborough " and " Phillipstown " as their respective county towns. The land was auctioned off in large estates for which there was no lack of bidders. When it came to *planting* them with new settlers a great lack was found of Englishmen ready to risk their lives and their capital in farms in Ireland. In the end the original clansmen returned, to occupy as tenants under a landlord (usually an absentee) the lands they had once owned without question or doubt.

A similar clearance was attempted in the same reign in South Wicklow and North Wexford; and here a few English *Catholics* were induced to settle—until the O'Dwyers, O'Faollain's and MacMurroughs from the hills gave them a sufficient reason for returning to England. Thereafter the clans returned as before.

An exactly similar result attended an attempt to *clear* and *plant* the large area in Munster which had been desolated by war and famine. Here again large estates were granted, and they in turn were cut up into large-size farms. Walter Raleigh the "Empire builder" was one of the grantees; Edmund Spenser had one of the farms and was busily at work upon the *Faery Queen* when those of the O'Driscolls, O'Lehanes, O'Carrols and O'Donovans who had survived came out of the woods and burned his farmstead about his ears. Once again, the Clans came back—*with a vengeance.*

The Plantation of Ulster

At this time (1598) was planned the most-known Plantation of all, that of Ulster, which was, eventually, carried out in 1609.

All the estates of the Earls of Tyrone (O'Neill) and Tyrconnell (O'Donnell) and those of their chief supporters, comprising some half a million estimated acres of arable land (waste, woodland and bog thrown in uncounted) in the counties of Donegal, Tyrone, Fermanagh, Cavan, Coleraine (Derry), and Armagh, were confiscated:

"The land was divided into lots of 2,000, 1,500, and 1,000 acres, and these lands were assigned to be occupied by persons of three classes. The

Undertakers on whom the largest lots were bestowed were ordinary colonists English or Scots. They were forbidden to take Irish tenants. The *Servitors* (those who had held office under Government in Ireland) who might, if they chose, let a portion of their land to the Irish. But if they did so, the rent which they themselves had to pay to the Crown would be increased from £5 6s. 8d. per 1,000 acres to £8. On the other hand, persons of the third class, the *Natives*, must not receive as tenants anyone but their own countrymen. . . . As a rule only small estates were given to the Irish, and the total they received was scarcely one-tenth of the whole. They were required to pay . . . £10 13s. 4d. per 1,000 acres."

—Hayden-Moonan : *Short History of the Irish People.*

From the limited size of the holdings, and the fixed rents stipulated, it is clear that the object of this plantation differed from its predecessors in that the crown's greed for revenue was subordinated to its *imperialist* need for a reliable garrison of planted colonists who would hold the Irish nation in check. To get round the difficulty of finding suitable colonists, part of the problem was shifted to the Corporation of London which was asked to " Undertake " the planting of the County of Coleraine (now called Londonderry) and the restoration of the cities of Derry and Coleraine.

The city undertook the work somewhat grudgingly. There was clearly little or no prospect of profit ; but on the other hand it was good policy to oblige the King. A special company—the Irish Society—was formed to manage the plantation, and the actual planting was divided between groups of city companies in proportion to the amounts subscribed towards the cost. Farms of specified size were erected ; Derry and Coleraine and their respective harbours were put into repair.

c

To find suitable tenants was not easy. Few Englishmen or Scots were willing to expatriate themselves unless for some reason, creditable or otherwise, they feared facing the wild Irish less than risks of staying at home. Some were persecuted Dissenters. Some were secretly Catholics. Many wished to bilk their creditors or the mothers of their illegitimate offspring, or for other reasons to get beyond the reach of " avenging justice ". A contemporary Scottish writer said that the settlers were " generally the scum of both countries . . . abhorred at home ".

It is in fact a complete fallacy to attribute to this Plantation the peculiar characteristics of political " Ulster ". That four out of the six counties planted were never part of " Orange " Ulster (until the Partition) and that the two most " Protestant " counties, Antrim and Down, were never included in this plantation are facts which destroy the myth.

Actually the difficulty of finding tenants caused even the London Corporation to wink at breaches of the terms of their grant. In 1624 they had 4,000 Irish tenants when they should have had none.

The Ulster Plantation—from whose area the clans were simply ejected—laid the foundation for an explosion and a new conquest. For the time being, however, the object of English policy seemed to have been attained.

CHAPTER THREE

THE SUBJUGATION OF IRELAND—II

THE third great wave of conquest beneath which Ireland
was submerged—the CROMWELLIAN CONQUEST—differed
from the preceding conquests in that it was less of a
prolonged process, and more of a sudden, calamitous
impact. For that reason it has left bitter memories
which survive in popular memory while the older
conquests are remembered only vaguely.

Another distinctive feature of the Cromwellian Conquest is that it arose as a by-product of a revolutionary
crisis and uprising in England into whose orbit Ireland
became drawn on the counter-revolutionary side; with
consequences disastrous both for England and for Ireland.

Background : English Revolution 1640

The Revolution of 1640 arose from a cause we have
already indicated. The establishment of the *New*
(*absolute*) *Monarchy* was bound to reach a point at which
stabilisation could be brought about only at the expense
of the bourgeoisie, and particularly of its freedom to
trade and accumulate capital.

Identifying the English Revolution as a *bourgeois*
revolution does not mean, as reactionaries and sentimentalists have supposed, that its motives were entirely
selfish and base, or that the King and the Cavaliers
fought to protect the common people from Capitalist
exploitation. Very far from it !

> " The interests for which Charles' Monarchy
> stood were not those of the common people at all.
> It represented the bankrupt landowning nobles,
> and its policy was influenced by a Court clique

of aristocratic-commercial racketeers, and their
hangers-on, sucking the life-blood from the whole
people by various methods of economic exploitation
. . . . And free capitalist development was of much
more benefit to the masses of the population than
the maintenance of an outmoded unproductive and
parasitic feudalism."—CHRISTOPHER HILL : *English
Revolution*, p. 13.

The Tudor monarchy had been, on the whole, popular
in England because it opened up (temporarily) new
fields for expansion to the producing classes. The
Stuart Monarchy dissipated this popularity because
these classes learned at its hands that this expansion
would be permitted only so far ; that thereafter productive expansion would be tolerated only on condition
that it yielded a " rake-off " to the King and the Court
clique of racketeers.

Finding that this roused the bourgeoisie and the lower
orders generally to a fury of revolutionary resentment,
Charles I and his advisers cast around for ways and means
of dragooning the Commons generally into submission,
alike in England and in Ireland. The Revolution of
1640 was precipitated by the going astray of a plan
concocted between the King and his chief advisers—
Archbishop Laud and the Earl of Strafford (previously
Sir Thomas Wentworth, and Lord Wentworth)—a plan
for a counter-revolutionary *coup d'état* called by the
conspirators among themselves the " Thorough " plan.

Ireland and the " Thorough " Conspiracy

As part of the project Strafford went to Ireland as
Lord Deputy. Here his plan was broadly (1) to so reduce
the country to disciplined submission to the Crown that
it would yield the King a revenue which would make him
independent of the English Parliament ; (2) to placate
the resentment of the Irish by making concessions to

the Catholics and winning them over to the King's side ; (3) to raise an Army in Ireland (largely composed of Catholics) which could be used at a pinch to coerce the English into submission. In a word the plan was designed to do for its period what every variety of " fascism " has attempted in our own time ; and the Irish Catholics were to be tricked into becoming the gangsters and thugs through whom the plan was to be imposed.

Strafford went to work in a businesslike style. He called a Parliament, but took care to pack it well before-hand by creating sixty new boroughs for each of which he nominated two members. These, with office-holders under the Crown whom he could dismiss at will, gave him a majority straightaway. A majority of the Lords thought it safest to stay away and send their proxies for Strafford to use at pleasure.

His next concern was to complete the conquest by planting Connacht—or, rather, threatening to plant it. He demanded that every landowner in Connacht should surrender " voluntarily " one acre in every four to create farms upon which he could plant reliable men. Simultaneously he " put the wind up " every landowner in Ireland by appointing a Commission to inquire into the validity of all titles to estates. It soon appeared however that the Connacht landowners could escape if they paid down a cash fine, and that a similar payment would " remedy " any defect in any title, however glaring.

He and his fellow-conspirator Laud worked the same trick on the City of London. The Court of Star Chamber, presided over by Laud, revoked the City's Ulster Charter on the express ground that they had failed to exclude Catholic tenants. A new Charter cost them £70,000.

The Dublin Parliament was " worked " by the trick of asking Catholics and Protestants to draw up statements of the " graces " they desired the King to grant (in

return for a subsidy). The King got his subsidy :
Catholics and Protestants were each told that the King
would "consider" their petitions.

When any landowner would not submit to the
"racket", a "defect" was found in his title.   If he went
to law Strafford either packed the jury, or, as in one
instance in Galway, when the jury gave a verdict against
the Crown, imprisoned the entire jury until every member
had paid a heavy fine.

He is credited with having promoted the linen industry ; but this is a complete error.   What he did was to
sell a Charter of Monopoly to a Linen Company which
would have ruined all the domestic spinners and weavers
in Ireland, if the Company itself had not gone bankrupt.
It was part of the "Thorough" plan to establish similar
monopolies for every industry in England as well as in
Ireland.   Being himself interested personally in the
Yorkshire woollen manufacture Strafford set the example
of banning the export of woollen cloth from Ireland,
and subsidising the export of raw wool.

He paid particular attention to the raising, training
and equipping of an Army.   Its rank and file was almost
exclusively Catholic, its officers were mostly English
Protestant aristocrats.   (The analogy to the "native"
regiments in India is obvious.)

Finally he circulated diligently both by word of mouth
and by ambiguously worded letters a rumour that, as
soon as he had reduced the English Commons to
"reason," the King would grant liberal concessions to
the Irish Catholics.

At this stage Strafford was summoned post-haste to
England.   His fellow-conspirator Laud had "upset the
apple-cart" by trying to impose the English liturgy on
the Scottish Kirk.

Religion in the English Revolution
So much of the controversy attending the Revolution

of 1640 turned on questions of Religion that a note or two on the issues really at stake is necessary. The crux of the matter is that, at that date, men understood by " religion " something much wider than a system of private belief and its expression in practice. They thought of " religion " as an indispensable *public* institution and function. The Church was part of the apparatus of the State. It was, in its local expression, a unit of local government and magistracy, as well as a dispenser of public assistance. It was also a revenue-yielding *property*; a property-owning corporation in itself, and a source of revenue directly and indirectly to the lay-impropriators of the tithes, as well as to the nobles and squires who had the right of presentation to Church livings. The Church in Ireland was, in this way, a valuable supplement to the revenues of the English landlord class which as absentee owners of land in Ireland " possessed " these Church emoluments, or the right of installing dependants to enjoy them.

From the point of view of the State, the Church not only provided a *moral* " police " and a supplement to the magistracy; it fulfilled the indispensable function of *moulder and guide of public opinion.* From the pulpit once a week at least the people were told what to believe, not only about Heaven and Hell but still more about earthly matters. It was self-evident that in such a crisis as was then brewing the Church would be an indispensable instrument for royalist and counter-revolutionary propaganda.

It is also self-evident that in such circumstances those who were opposed to the political policy of the Court and its clique would resent this use of the Church and denounce it. They would, in more advanced cases, make provision for *pulpits* through which their own anti-royalist views would find expression. In a word they would set up *Nonconformist* or *Dissenting* " sects " which would supplement their political hostility to the Crown and Court with a theological hostility to the Bishops, their doctrine and their ritual.

The Reformation, in England, as a popular movement, had been basically a revolt against an alien *Italian* Church and its *foreign* propaganda. It had been an intensely *Nationalist* revolt, and the same spirit was carried over to and intensified in the Nonconformist sects.

From the point of view of the "Thorough" plan these Nonconformist sects had to be stamped out as rigorously as Hitler and his *gauleiters* stamped out all listening to unauthorised and "enemy" broadcasts. But Laud was hampered in this by the existence of the Presbyterian Kirk in Scotland which he could not control. As it was a State Church in Scotland he could not ban it in England, and the revolutionaries took full advantage of his dilemma.

He tried to get over the difficulty by persuading a section of the Scottish clergy to adopt the Anglican liturgy as the first step towards bringing the two Churches into conformity. The result was an explosion of Scottish revolt, the mass signing of the Solemn League and Covenant, and the march of the Scottish Army to, and beyond, the Border.

It was this revolt that Strafford was sent for to repress.

It may be added here that the Reformation passion of hostility to the Papacy and Papalism generally was still intense both in England and in Scotland. Laud's insistence upon liturgy and ceremonial seemed to the masses "Papistic", and, as the King was notoriously under the thumb of his ostentatiously Catholic wife, the popular opinion swayed to the conclusion that the Royal plans included a restoration of the Papal Church, and with it (of course) "the Inquisition".

As the struggle developed, the more *ultra*-Protestant sects—those which most completely rejected all *Authority* in religion save that of the individual conscience—naturally came increasingly to the front, since they had

most to gain from the defeat of the King and his reactionary schemes. In this way an anti-" Papist "
element was introduced into the struggle from the
outset, a sentiment which grew more bitter as the
struggle progressed.

The Long Parliament ; and the Rising of 1641

When Strafford reached England and faced the situation he saw that Laud had bungled badly. The King's
soldiers were few, and none too ready to fight the
Scots. The English militia were openly mutinous, and
were more likely to join the Scots than to fight them.
The best policy, as Strafford saw, was to play for time ;
to call a Parliament, fob it off with promises, get
supply, and, when the excitement had died down, get
to work another way. He, in the meanwhile, would
push on the work of raising, quietly, a really powerful
army in Ireland.

Strafford's advice was accepted. A Parliament was
summoned in England, while Strafford himself returned
to Ireland, summoned his packed Parliament, and got
a vote of £180,000.

In England the matter was not so simple. All efforts
to pack a Parliamentary majority failed. When Parliament met in November, 1640, its first Act was to decide
that it could not legally be dissolved without the consent
of both Houses. When Charles gave his assent to this
Act—which he was in no position to refuse—the initiative
passed to the revolutionaries, and *the English Revolution
had begun.*

A few days later the Courts of Star Chamber and
High Commission were declared unconstitutional and
a grievance. Everyone connected with them, from Laud
downwards, was ordered under arrest. When Strafford
arrived from Dublin he too was impeached, arrested,
and thrown into the Tower. Charles tried to save his
fellow conspirators by arresting the five leaders of the

Commons. Warned in time, the members escaped, and the Commons as a body took refuge in the City of London which called out its trained-bands and closed its gates.

Charles gave way. The Commons, finding Strafford might wriggle out of a formal trial, passed a special Act declaring him guilty and sentencing him to death. On the night of the day (May 12th, 1641) on which Strafford was executed all England blazed with bonfires of rejoicing.

Optimists thought the struggle was over and the Revolution won : sceptics thought things were going too well to last. As if in answer to their doubts came the startling news that the Irish clans had risen *en masse* on the night of October 23rd, 1641, and " massacred every Protestant in Ireland."

Things were not, in fact, as bad as that; or as good as the Irish had hoped. The central pivot of the whole rising—the capture of Dublin Castle—had failed to materialise. But the O'Neills, O'Donnells, O'Dohertys, O'Cahans and Maguires had " cleared " the planted area of Ulster and driven the population in panic flight before them to take refuge in the towns and castles.

How many Protestants were killed, in fair fight and otherwise, and how many died of exposure during the flight and pursuit has been debated with partisan acrimony on both sides ever since. An estimate of those killed may be fixed, on a balance of probability, at under 3,000 ; perhaps as many as 7,000 died of exposure. This is bad enough in all conscience, and proved that the clansmen showed as little consideration as they had received. But contemporary estimates—the belief which determined the conduct of the English revolutionaries—put the figure at 300,000 and even 400,000 " massacred in cold blood." That JOHN MILTON, an experienced man of affairs, who stood in the front rank of the cultured of his time, and was in touch with the best-informed official opinion of his day, as also the last man to be swayed by any passing wave of popular credulity, should have accepted as a fact the highest of these estimates is decisive as to what was actually believed. Actually there were not so many as 300,000 Protestants in all Ireland in 1641 ; while the succeeding years showed the Protestant community in being without noticeable diminution.

The effect of the "atrocity" story upon English affairs was immediate and searching. The King reported the rebellion to Parliament and asked for supply and a Parliamentary authority to raise an army for the suppression of the rebels.

The Commons received the message with deep suspicion. An army he could rely upon was the one thing the King could not be trusted with. Then there was the manifesto issued by the Irish rebels themselves which avowed they were not hostile to the King or his authority, but were only seeking a remedy for intolerable grievances.

Englishmen in 1640 had not been conditioned into the belief in *Handy Andy* as the *norm* of Irish National character, consequently they did not dismiss this manifesto as an Irish "bull". They took it at its face-value and argued that if assaulting the King's garrisons, capturing his castles, and chasing the King's officers and his Protestant subjects into places of refuge or out of the country was not done in defiance of the King it must have been done, if not by his authority, at any rate with his collusion. They remembered Strafford, and so much as had come to light of the "Thorough" plan ; and with it that the Irish were "Papists" while the King was credited with a design to restore Papacy.

It all seemed to fit in. Accordingly, after deliberation, they passed an Act authorising the raising of an army, but they inserted into the Act *the names of those who were alone empowered by the Act to recruit soldiers, to appoint officers, and to dismiss them along with the troops when they thought fit.* The names they inserted were all those of men upon whom the revolutionary chiefs thought they could rely.

The King's reception of this Act confirmed their worst suspicions. If his desire had been, *bona fide*, to suppress the Irish rebels with no ulterior motive, he had no reason to object to the safeguards adopted by the Commons. If he objected to them, a probability was at once established that he wanted the army for some work nearer home than in Ireland. A great suspicion arose that the Irish Rebellion had been engineered to provide Charles with a pretext for raising just the army he required.

The King did more than object. He left London for Nottingham, and there raised his Royal Standard and summoned the nobility and gentry to aid him against his " rebellious " Parliament.

The English Revolution thus passed into the phase of *Civil War*.

The details of the Civil War in England do not concern us. It is sufficient to note that the course of the struggle necessitated the " new modelling " of the army in such a way that it became recruited wholly from sturdy petit-bourgeois, peasant and near-proletarian elements, all zealots for the revolution and fanatically hostile to royalism and episcopacy in all their forms—in short it became a *democratic* republican army.

Rebellion and Civil War in Ireland

While the Civil War raged in England (1641–1649) Ireland was the theatre for a succession of political combinations, divisions, and recombinations so tangled that it almost defies analysis.

Confusion began even before the Rising of 1641. Strafford had kept the threads of things so entirely in his own hands that his arrest—which took him completely by surprise—left nobody to make provision for the pay or the provisioning of his Irish Army. There is no doubt that he, and Charles I, had intended that this army should follow Strafford to England as soon as the weather was favourable ; but the arrest and impeachment of Strafford made the ship-owners, Irish as well as English, unwilling to take the risk of transporting the troops. Left without pay or provisions the army took to plundering and had to be disbanded. Many of its elements took part in the Rising ; others provided nuclei for the various armies which contended in the later struggles.

The Rising itself was planned by a group of clan-chiefs who, although they had submitted to the English, and had accepted knighthoods and titles, were not comfortable in their new position of Anglicised land-lords. The ultimate cause of the Rising was the dis-content and anger of the clansmen who were constantly urging their chiefs on to recover possession of the clan lands. General dissatisfaction ; the doubt and uncertainty excited by Strafford's administration ; the hope that the King and Strafford would do something for them ; the fear that they would do nothing—or worse, might carry out their threat of planting all Connacht—; hopes and fears centred upon the King, and hopes and fears of a victory for the Parliament ; all these combined to make an occasion for the Rising and to ensure at the same time that the objects of the rebels should be hopelessly in conflict. The only settled purpose was that of the clans and of Owen Roe O'Neill, then in effect the head of the O'Neill clan, a distinguished soldier in the service of Spain who had promised the conspirators that if they could get an army together he would come from Spain to lead it.

O'Neill and the clansmen were of one mind from the start. They wanted a restoration of the clan-lands and of the independence of Ireland ; and the example of the Scots seemed conclusive as to what might be achieved by a *united* nation. But a united nation was just what did not exist in Ireland, though a semblance of unity was forced upon the Catholic community by its common fear of both the contending factions in England.

The King through his officials in Dublin denounced the Rising of 1641 as a " Papist " plot, and threatened condign punishment on all concerned. The English Parliament proclaimed a long list of proprietors as " traitors " and raised money to fight the King on the security of their estates—which were declared forfeited. Threatened by both sides the Anglo-Irish Catholics, led by their landlords, and ex-chiefs, joined the original conspirators ; but with many misgivings.

There were thus from the outset *three* distinct parties, each with its army in the field in Ireland—(1) The *English Parliamentary Party* held Derry City and part of the Counties of Derry, Antrim and Down ; (2) The *King's Party* led by Ormond held Dublin, Louth, part of Meath, and, through Lord Inchiquin (Murrough O'Brien), part of Cork ; (3) The *Catholic Confederation*, formed in Kilkenny, in May 1642, held the rest of the country.

The *Catholic Confederation* set up an elaborate Council in which each province and every county was represented, but from the start it disavowed any sort of separatism. It affirmed its allegiance to Charles ; and stuck his head on its coinage. It showed a tolerant spirit towards other religions, but it courted trouble from the Ormond Royalists when it decreed the restoration of Church lands to the Catholic Hierarchy. It refused to do the obviously correct thing and appoint Owen Roe O'Neill its Commander in Chief. Instead, it appointed THOMAS PRESTON, nephew of Lord Gormanstown, an Anglo-Irish Catholic. Preston had served with distinction in Spain, but he was in every respect inferior as a soldier to O'Neill with whom he had quarrelled.

The Confederation, in short, took as its basic stand-

point the *landlordism* which the English conquerors had
introduced, and only tolerated O'Neill and his clansmen
so far as they were necessary to their resistance to the
Parliamentarians led by COOTE and MUNRO in the
North, to the Royalist ORMOND in the Pale (who held the
" Papist rebels " in the utmost abhorrence) and to the
turncoat INCHIQUIN in the South—who joined and sold
every party in turn, but who at the outset earned the
name of " Murrough of the Burnings " by the desolation
he worked in East Munster and South Leinster.   But
for Owen Roe the Confederation would have been
overwhelmed more than once ; but all the time it bent
its chief energies upon negotiating a treaty with Charles
which would give satisfaction to Catholic claims.   There,
however, the Confederation split into fragments.   The
Anglo-Irish Catholics of the Pale would have been
satisfied with toleration and a free parliament ; the
Clerical party wanted more than this—a restoration of
church lands, the possession of all churches recaptured
from the Protestants in the Rebellion, and so on.

The political confusion in the Catholic camp was
increased by intrigues in the Royalist camp.   While
Ormond and Inchiquin in concert were campaigning
fiercely against the Catholic Confederates, an emissary
of Charles was negotiating a secret treaty with the Council of the Confederation.   Charles was willing to
promise anything in return for an Irish Army ; but he
dared not let it be known in England that he was negotiating with the Irish rebels.   Half his English Army
would have been ready to desert if they had known of it.
When this secret treaty was discovered, Charles repudiated it, and imprisoned the man (Lord Glamorgan)
who negotiated it.

Meanwhile Ormond for the Anglo-Irish Protestant
Royalists was negotiating a peace of his own.   The
King had suffered the crushing defeats of Marston
Moor (1644) and Naseby (1645), and Inchiquin had

gone over to the Parliamentarians, when Ormond, in 1646, negotiated a peace which a majority of the Confederate Council agreed to. Those who opposed it were, however, the more powerful since they included the Pope's Nuncio and Preston (who both wanted a peace the Queen was negotiating on her own authority) and Owen Roe who wanted no treaty with the King at all.

Owen Roe and Preston marched on Kilkenny, scattered the old Council, and appointed a new one which repudiated the treaty. Ormond, in disgust, threw up the struggle, surrendered Dublin to the Parliamentarian General MICHAEL JONES (1647) and retired to France.

The departure of Ormond simplified the situation somewhat by eliminating the Royalists as a separate force. Some of his followers joined the Catholic Confederation; some joined Inchiquin and the Parliament. Shortly afterwards (1647–8) Inchiquin, who had over-run all Munster, opened negotiations with the Confederates and made offers for a peace and an alliance. A majority of the Council accepted his offer; and Owen Roe, indignant, broke with the Council and took the field with an independent army. The Nuncio excommunicated everyone who had signed the treaty with Inchiquin, but Ormond at that moment came forward with fresh offers, and the second Ormond Peace was concluded January 17th, 1649. The Nuncio in disgust sailed from Ireland a few weeks later, just after Charles I had been executed in Whitehall as " a man of blood, false to his word, and an enemy of the people of England".

Ormond returning to Ireland as the representative of Charles II, at once dissolved the Catholic Confederation, converting its followers into a Royalist party pure and simple. He had great hopes of Scottish assistance since the Scots had broken with the English Parliamentarians and a Scottish army was besieging the Parliamentarian General Coote in Derry.

Owen Roe would have nothing to do with Ormond, Preston, Inchiquin, or any of the Irish and Anglo-Irish gentry. He drove the Scots away from Derry and entered into negotiations with the English Parliamentarian General MONK.

This, which is passed over in orthodox histories as a mere episode of no significance, was in fact by far the most fateful moment in the whole struggle, as we shall see when we look at it from the English angle. Meanwhile we note only that the English Parliament issued peremptory orders to Monk to break off all negotiations instantly.

Owen Roe, there being nothing else for it, agreed to a treaty with Ormond and prepared to march to his aid. He was, however, already a sick man, and in November, 1649, he died. It was commonly believed he was poisoned; there is next to no evidence to support the belief, except the character of Inchiquin, who was, indeed, quite equal to anything.

Meanwhile, at the end of August, 1649, Oliver Cromwell had landed in Dublin at the head of an army of veteran troops.

The Episode of the Levellers

The situation in which the newly-born English Republic stood in the spring of 1649 was highly precarious.

That the *New Model Army* and its supporters were only a minority of the population is probably true. But it is equally true that they were the strongest single political force in the country and the only united and organised body. That they had executed the King was not, as sentimentalists and reactionaries have argued, any sign or cause of weakness. On the contrary, it proved a thing that many then living needed to be taught—that a King's head would come off just as easily as that of any other man, and that a King could be in

D

fact called to account for crimes committed in the exercise of his public trust.

It was because they taught the world that salutary lesson that the men of the New Model Army who brought the King to trial, and insisted upon their Parliamentary representatives executing justice upon him, were hated and reviled by the reactionaries in every court in Europe, and have been traduced, slandered, and misrepresented by sentimentalists and reactionaries ever since.

The real weakness of the position arose from a fact common to all bourgeois revolutions. Necessarily, to carry through its fight against feudalism and the Absolute Monarchy, the bourgeoisie had to carry with it into the struggle all the virile elements in the lower ranks of society. The yeoman farmers, the small manufacturers, the independent craftsmen, journeymen, and so forth, who formed the rank and file of the New Model Army, had developed in their camp meetings and debates a high grade of political understanding and consciousness.

Up to the point at which the King was finally disposed of, and the Monarchy and the House of Lords abolished the interest of the progressive bourgeoisie coincided with that of its petit-bourgeois rank and file. Here, however, the turning point was reached, since here the bourgeoisie wished, in principle, to bring the revolution to an end and begin the work of conserving the victory won.

The rank and file wished to go further and complete the revolution by breaking the power of the squirearchy as well, and that of the parson also. They wanted at any rate a *political levelling*; and some of them wanted an *economic levelling* into the bargain.

The vital crux was the demand for the confiscation of the estates of the King and the royalist landowners and their distribution among the land-hungry in the army and the countryside. With this went a demand

for the restoration of the people's rights in the common-
land which the landlords had stolen. And it was just
at this point, when the *Leveller* sentiment had spread to
most of the rank and file of the army, and their kinsfolk
and supporters among the civilian population, that Owen
Roe O'Neill and George Monk—who was suspected of
Leveller leanings himself—opened negotiations in Ireland.

Did Owen Roe know that a strong party in England
entertained designs upon the estates of the aristocracy
and gentry of England which were on all fours with his
own designs for Ireland? He was too good a general
not to be well-informed about what was going on in the
enemy camp. And he was an experienced politician
who could tell the way the wind was blowing as well as
any man. We can only guess. But the promptness
and vigour with which Monk was ordered to break off
all negotiations with the " rebels " is very eloquent
when read in conjunction with the equal promptness
and vigour—not to say violence—with which Cromwell
at the same time crushed the incipient mutiny of the
Levellers before it had time to come to a head.

Moreover it is suspiciously suggestive of a deliberate
side-track that Cromwell and the Parliament promised·
the Leveller Regiments ordered for service in Ireland
that they would be rewarded with a share of the land
confiscated from the *Irish Royalists*—who now as a result
of Ormond's skilful intrigues and the political weakness
of the Confederates—included virtually all the landowners in Ireland.

When the English Levellers let themselves be side-
tracked ; and when Owen Roe, stalled-off, succumbed to
Ormond's temptations, both the English and the Irish
revolutions were aborted. From that moment the
Restoration of the Monarchy was merely a question of
time.

The Cromwellian Conquest of Ireland

When Cromwell landed in Dublin he knew clearly what he had to do. The Irish armies had to be smashed utterly before either the Scots, or any Continental aid Prince Rupert and Charles Stuart the younger could muster, could get into action. Provided he could deal with these enemies one by one there was little reason to doubt the result. Therefore he acted with a speed and a ferocity that gave a measure of his estimate of the urgency of the situation.

The military details of the campaign need not detain us. Cromwell attacked Drogheda first, and ordered an assault as soon as the wall was breached. As is notorious, the order of " no quarter " was given and obeyed—the fact that the garrison consisted mostly or largely of *English Royalist* troops did not incline the men of the New Model to show mercy anyway. The same process was repeated at Wexford. In each case a certain number of civilians got mixed with the garrison and were slaughtered along with them.* All " friars " and priests were " knocked on the head as soon as seen."

The business was barbarous, bloody, and inexcusable. And the fact that the Elizabethan conquerors had done equally barbarous deeds, or that giving " no quarter" to a garrison which refused to surrender on summons was a military custom of the period does not lessen the enormity. An Englishman concerned for the honour of the English Revolution, and the good repute of the New Model and its Leveller rank and file, has a right to protest that a standard set by the exterminators of the German Peasants' War, by Alva in the Netherlands, and by Tilly and Wallenstein in the religious wars in Germany is a standard of condemnation not of exoneration.

The only excuse for Cromwell's " frightfulness " was

---

* The story of the " massacre of hundreds of women and children around the market cross at Wexford " is a fiction invented by counter-revolutionary Royalists, without a shred of contemporary evidence to support it.

that he was genuinely pinched for time and, further, that the policy worked. Inchiquin, double-crossing to the last, deserted to the Parliament. Garrison after garrison surrendered at summons. A rump of the Anglo-Irish Catholic nobility sent an appeal for aid to the Duke of Lorraine. A few towns—notably Waterford and Limerick—put up a stout resistance. But the only real check the New Model met—apart from delays caused by weather and outbreaks of epidemic disease—was when they met and were repulsed by the O'Neills and their fellow-clansmen in the breaches of Clonmel.

In that mutual slaughter of the last representatives of the communism of primitive society and the first representatives of the communism of the future, lies the essential tragedy of the English Revolution and of the Cromwellian conquest of Ireland.

Called away to meet and defeat the Scots, Cromwell left the completion of the conquest to his lieutenants Ireton, Fleetwood, and Ludlow. It was ended in May 1652, when the last Irish armies—mostly clansmen—accepted the Articles of Kilkenny. All who surrendered, and were not guilty of murder, were allowed to transport themselves beyond the seas. Thirty-four thousand Irish soldiers took the opportunity to take service in the Armies of Continental Kings.

The Cromwellian Settlement

In 1652 Ireland had been in a state of war for eleven years. With bloodshed, destruction, and the interruption of normal pursuits, plague and pestilence and famine had stalked hand in hand. "Whole counties had been de-populated," says one witness. "A man might travel twenty miles and not see a living creature, either man or beast or bird," says another, an English officer. "As for the poor commons," says a third, "the sun never shined upon a nation so completely miserable." These were the conditions in which the English

Parliament, moving with great deliberation, set to work to effect a " Settlement " of the population.

In principle they merely followed the " clearance and replanting " plan of their predecessors ; but the scale upon which they did it would have taken Elizabeth's breath away—and she was " as tough as they make 'em ". Cromwell must take his share of the blame—Royalist reactionaries have combined with Irish sentimentalists to put all the blame upon him—as must also the rank-and-file soldiers who made the settlement possible and shared in the plunder. But it is only fair to point out that Parliament had decided in principle what it intended to do immediately after the Rising of 1641.

The principle of the Settlement was simple. The Commonwealth was in debt to sundry creditors, and to its soldiers for arrears of pay. Ireland, considered as a *property*, had to bear the whole of this burden.

In essence the whole of Ireland was deemed to be confiscated from its legal owners. Then a scale of degrees of criminality was drawn up. Those who had shown " constant good-affection " to the Parliament and its Cause, which meant those who had fought for the Parliament all through, or who had aided those that fought, were adjudged to be entitled to the number of acres they then held. Those who had organised the Rising of 1641 were to lose all the acres they possessed ; if they were guilty of murder they were hanged also. Those whose criminality was less, were to lose *two* acres in every three. Those whose criminality was least were to lose *one* acre in three.

When every landowner who had possessed more than 50 acres had been classified, the Catholics among them were ordered on a certain date to betake themselves with their belongings beyond the Shannon into Connacht, where room would be found for them on the acres confiscated from the proprietors there domiciled.

The villainy of the business lay in a matter the

Commissions had overlooked. It had not been intended to interfere with small leaseholders, tenant farmers, cottagers, or artisans. The commissioners knew from experience that tenants and labourers from England were hard to get, and nobody wanted the land just to look at. What they had to face was that the Irish Catholic landlord in the majority of cases stood to his tenants in the relation of a chief to his kinsmen. In many instances this was actually the case. In others it was a tradition-based custom. In most cases where the landlord went, there his tenants followed, regardless of the fact that they might have stayed. In many of these cases the humble tenant had a purely customary tenure based on a verbal understanding ; such a tenant feared to remain lest the new landowner should eject him as a trespasser or impose upon him conditions not to be borne.

In the end the authorities found the situation they themselves had created was an impossible one. Legal juggling was set to work and soon the tide was setting the other way. The " Transplanters " were allowed, in many cases, probably a majority, to creep back. It cost them dearly. They had to surrender more acres ; or to pay a " rake-off " ; or even to return as tenants to lands they had once owned. With them returned their dependants, and things were as before, except that virtually the whole Irish population now carried on their backs the burden of alien landlords.

This reshuffling was greatly to the advantage of a swarm of speculators who followed the Land Commissioners like vultures swooping over a battlefield. The army's claim for accumulated arrears of pay was met by a distribution of " tickets " entitling the soldiers to share in the allocation of land by lot. Speculators who had lent money to the Government received the equivalent in acres, but in scattered parcels. Many soldiers did not want to settle in Ireland. There was a grand opening for a speculator with ready cash to buy soldiers' "tickets" (at a liberal discount) and then negotiate exchanges until he had got together a fine compact estate of tens of thousands of acres. More than one "noble" family estate was thus thriftily got together.

An incidental by-product of the period was that swarms of orphan children, and youths of both sexes, were to be found on every hand. Their parents had died, their employers had cast them off, or they had strayed and got lost in the confusion. To get rid of them the Government rounded them up and sold them to agents who shipped them to the West Indies or to the Carolinas where they fetched a good price as "indentured labourers." The profits were so great that the agents came back for more; and, when the supply of Irish vagrants ran out, took to kidnapping to supply their market. The agents got so bold that they kidnapped Englishmen, not only in Ireland, but also in England. Then the traffic was prohibited.

The Restoration Finale

When the Monarchy was restored in England there were great hopes among the dispossessed proprietors that their fidelity to the Stuart cause would be rewarded.

Some little was done in the case of a few Anglo-Irish lords whom the Commonwealth had deported, but little more.

The Irish found themselves up against the difficulty that virtually every one of them had been technically in rebellion against the Crown at one time or another. And as any real restoration of confiscated acres would have to be made at the expense of Englishmen of wealth whom Charles—not wishing "to go on his travels again"—had no intention of disobliging, he gave the Irish his blessing, and let it go at that.

CHAPTER FOUR

THE SUBJUGATION OF IRELAND—III

THE fourth and final conquest of Ireland—the WILLIAMITE CONQUEST (1690-2)—grew, as its predecessor had done, out of a revolutionary conflict in England into whose orbit Ireland became drawn; again, on the counter-revolutionary (" loyalist ") side.

This time the crisis was that of the WHIG* REVOLUTION (1688). Once again a revolutionary advance in England involved in Ireland a further subjugation and an intensification of enslavement.

The Whig Revolution (1688)

After the Restoration of the Monarchy (1660) the English common-people had time in which to regret that they had been headed-off from their true line of revolutionary advance. They had thwarted the designs of Charles I, Laud, and Strafford; but the cream of the gains from their victory had been skimmed-off and enjoyed by an oligarchy of wealthy (and ennobled) bourgeois allied to aristocratic (and bourgeoisified) landlords and a clique of Court parasites.

In these new political circumstances even the great and growing advances in trade and commerce (for which the Revolution of 1640 had prepared the way) were no adequate compensation for their steadily intensifying dread of a new and more subtly-contrived attempt to re-establish the Absolutism they had fought to destroy, and with it, possibly, a return to " Papacy " also.

There were agitations, and insurrectionary conspira-

* *Whig and Tory:* These party nicknames came into use between 1660 and 1685 as denoting respectively those who wished to restrict the Crown and the succession by specific Constitutional law, and those who thought this a personal insult to the King and an illegitimate curtailment of the Royal prerogatives.

cies ; but the main body of the bourgeoisie had been content (while grumbling) to pick up the material gains of trade while their aristocratic upper strata and the Court clique held the lower orders drastically in check.

The accession in 1685, of James II, a Catholic zealot, threw this tacit coalition entirely out of balance. It threatened a considerable section of the oligarchy with a deprivation of political power and a loss of the emoluments of public office, as well as of its monopoly of patronage. It threatened the Church with loss of status and of revenue ; and it threatened the bourgeoisie with the restraints (and the parasitism) it had escaped from in 1640.

In these circumstances the common-people of the West of England—then the chief manufacturing area— where Leveller traditions were still strong—believed they could count upon support from the merchants of the City of London, and the Whig nobility and gentry in the North. Accordingly they responded to the call of James, Duke of MONMOUTH, a bastard son of Charles II, and rose in revolt ; choosing significantly the *sea-green* of the Levellers, as their party badge.

Their rising was double-crossed in two ways. (1) The Whig lords and gentry fearing the strong *Leveller* element in the rebellion, held aloof. (2) Monmouth, to placate these Whigs, rejected the demand of his followers for an immediate proclamation of a Republic, and tried the compromise line of claiming to be the legitimate heir to the throne. Thus he alienated the Leveller elements in London who might have forced the hand of the City merchants. On the whole it paid the Whigs best politically to let James II incur the extra odium of suppressing the rebellion with ruthless ferocity, since this would destroy any hold he might have on the country at large, and at the same time minimise the risk of a Leveller Movement in the revolution they were contemplating on their own account.

Things worked out as the Whigs had planned. The West Country rising was suppressed with a barbarity that revolted all England. James, both obstinate and stupid, showed his intention to corner all the chief state offices and emoluments for Catholics—real and pretended —in so glaring a fashion that even a docile and subservient Church took alarm. A Whig junta representing an alliance of landowners, wealthy merchants, and ecclesiastics, sent an invitation to the ruler of Holland, WILLIAM OF ORANGE—who as a grandson of Charles I on the maternal side, and as the husband of James's eldest daughter had a direct interest in the succession— to come to England with an army to " restore the Liberties of England and the Protestant Religion ".

Accordingly when William of Orange complied, and landed with an army at Torbay, on November 5th, 1688, James II found himself confronted, not only with an invasion but a universal desertion by Army, Navy, Court functionaries, the Law, the Church, the City, and even his own family. Fearing for his life at the hands of a raging London mob, James fled for refuge to the Court of Louis XIV of France.

When a convention Parliament had formally installed William and Mary as joint monarchs, and they had given their assent to a Bill of Rights and an Act of Settlement, limiting the succession to the throne exclusively to Protestants (even marriage to a Catholic constituting a disqualification) the Whig or " glorious " Revolution was accomplished.

Ireland and the Whig Revolution

In Ireland, the accession of James the Catholic had aroused intense excitement because of its possible bearing upon the Cromwellian settlement which Charles II had refused to upset, or to modify, except to a negligible extent.

The extent of the problem involved may be gathered

from an estimate made after Charles II had modified the settlement (slightly) in favour of the Catholics.

The categories named hereunder possessed (in 1665) the number of acres specified :—(1) owners installed by the Cromwellian settlement, 4,560,037 acres. (2) Old English Colonists 3,900,000 acres. (3) " Innocent " Irish, including some Transplanted, 2,323,809. (4) Irishmen of " good affection " 600,000. This left, out of an estimated total of 12,208,237 acres, only 824,391 acres not appropriated by any large landowners, a good proportion of this category being town dwelling-sites, etc.

There were then some 200,000 Protestants in Ireland to over 1,000,000 Catholics, therefore if we ignore the " unappropriated " category, which was largely in the hands of planted Cromwellian soldiers or their Protestant descendants, we get the result that over two-thirds of the good arable and meadow land was owned by less than one-sixth of the total population, the large-owning minority being almost exclusively Protestants. The proportion of Protestants to Catholics in the various provinces was : *Ulster* 5 to 2 : *Leinster* 2 to 13 : *Munster* 2 to 20 : *Connacht* 2 to 25.

From these figures can be estimated the height of Catholic expectation and the depth of Protestant fears excited by the accession of James II in 1685.

Hopes and fears were equally intensified when James appointed an Anglo-Irish Catholic, the Earl of Tyrconnel* (otherwise " Lying Dick " Talbot) Commander in Chief, and later, Lord Lieutenant of Ireland. And Tyrconnel, unwittingly, contributed to James's downfall by raising Catholic regiments in Ireland, and sending some of them to England to support the Crown at the

---

* *Tyrconnel :* Talbot must not be confounded with the O'Donnell, who claimed this title. This Talbot Tyrconnel was alluded to in the song

"There was an old prophecy found in a bog,
That Ireland be ruled by an ass and a dog.
Now is that prophecy come for to pass,
For Tyrconnel's the *dog* and James is the *ass*."

crisis of the trial of the *Seven Bishops* for sedition—the
" sedition " being a written protest against James's
attempt to suspend by arbitrary decree the laws against
Catholic worship.

The Irish regiments arrived in the neighbourhood
of London, just in time for the immense, popular rejoicing at the acquittal of the Seven Bishops (1688).
Their coming excited a frantic panic when a rumour
spread that they were marching to sack London and
massacre the population. The rumour was baseless ; but
it indicated the state of feeling in the English Army as
well as in the civil population. The attempt to introduce
Irish Catholic regiments into England ensured that not
a single English soldier would be ready to so much as
fire a shot in defence of James. Bundling the Irish troops
back to Ireland did nothing to better the situation.

Meanwhile the withdrawal of the troops from Ireland
had given the towns of Derry and Enniskillen a chance
to close their gates and defend themselves against the
troops of Tyrconnel and James.

In 1689 Tyrconnel refused to accept the Settlement
of the Throne enacted by the Convention Parliament.
He declared for James, and invited him to come from
France (with an army) to take possession of his " lawful "
kingdom. James landed in March, 1689, with some
officers, French and Irish, a few troops, but little or no
artillery. His concern for Ireland was small ; his real
hopes being fixed upon Scotland, where " Bloody
Grahame of Claverhouse " (alias " Bonnie Dundee ")
was raising the clans on his behalf. Checked by the
stubborn resistance of Derry and Enniskillen, James
summoned a Parliament to meet in Dublin.

The " Patriot " Parliament of 1689

The Parliament which assembled on May 7th included
six Protestant bishops among the Peers—James had
thought it expedient not to summon the Catholic bishops

—and something under a score of Protestants among
the 232 members of the House of Commons. In the
circumstances it was bound to be revolutionary; but
once again revolution for Ireland clashed with and
countered the revolution in England.

The " Patriot " Parliament (1) declared the English
Parliament incompetent to pass laws for Ireland; (2)
made the Irish House of Lords the court of final appeal
in law cases; (3) declared for complete religious toleration; (4) enacted that tithes while remaining compulsory
might be paid by the land-holder to the Church of his
choice. So far even the English Whigs had little to
complain of. But when it went on to (5) revoke the
Cromwellian Settlement, and (6) threaten all emigrant
land-owners with confiscation if they did not " return
to their allegiance " (to James) by a specified date, it
stirred up a nest of hornets some of which still buzz.

The chief failure of the Patriot Parliament—its
willingness to leave the mass of Irishmen as landless as
it found them—is seldom noted.

From James's standpoint the Patriot Parliament was
disastrous. Revoking the Cromwellian Settlement
alienated at a stroke all the Tory landowners in England
upon whom he was counting for aid; and his worst
fears were realised a week after the Parliament had
adjourned, when, first, Dundee was killed in action at
Killiecrankie, and then Derry was relieved after standing
a siege of 105 days.

The Williamite War

Following the relief of Derry, WILLIAM OF ORANGE,
began (somewhat tardily) military operations to obtain
possession of Ireland; but the war which followed was
only in part an incident in the Whig Revolution.

Both England and Ireland were pawns in a balance-of-
power game fought out on the Continent between Louis
XIV and his Allies, on one side, and a European Coalition,

(which *included the Pope*, as a temporal monarch, as well as William of Orange) on the other. It was England's good luck that the maintenance of its independence coincided with William's continental interest. It was Ireland's bad luck that it stood to lose whoever won. James II and his backer Louis were even less concerned for the independence of Ireland than was William III. Apart from the incidental question as to which of two rival Kings of England should rule Ireland, the issue which the mass of Irishmen fought to decide was whether they would be robbed by an English protestant landlord, or a Catholic Irish one.   Robbed they were certain to be either way.

It is illuminating to remember that the English Whigs were so loath to give William the army he needed—" he had plenty of Dutchmen anyway "—that when he did advance to force the crossing of the Boyne on July 1st, 1690, William's army included—as well as a few English, Scottish, and Ulster regiments—Dutch, Danes, Swedes, Prussians, and French Huguenots.   Incidentally, William's army wore *green* badges to distinguish them, some of the Ulster troops choosing the Leveller *sea-green*. James's army wore the *white* cockade of the Bourbons and the Stuarts.

As a battle the Boyne-crossing was an affair of little significance. William's army was slightly the superior in numbers, and much the superior in training, equipment and artillery. *Patrick Sarsfield* the best soldier on James's side, advised against accepting battle at the Boyne. Knowing the relative strength of the two Armies Sarsfield advised a retreat behind the line of the Shannon until the Irish troops had become better trained and equipped. James over-ruled Sarsfield's objections and insisted upon a battle, which he promptly proceeded to lose by massing his best troops to face what proved to be a feint on his left, and so leaving his centre and right too weak to prevent the forcing of the fords. The only dash and skill shown by James was in securing the lead of the retreat to Dublin! The total casualties on both sides were under 2,000.

A story, probably true, runs that Sarsfield, covering the retreat, exchanging banter with English officers whom he knew personally, shouted: " Change kings with us, and we'll fight it all over again ! " Incidentally also, we note that a Pontifical High Mass and *Te Deum* were sung in Rome in thanksgiving for William's victory at the Boyne.

After rhe Boyne, with James out of the way, the Franco-Irish army fell back, as Sarsfield had advised, to defend the line of the Shannon. The year closed with Sarsfield's successful defence of Limerick, which was set off somewhat by Marlborough's capture of Cork and Kinsale from the sea.

In 1691 the line of the Shannon was forced at Athlone by a desperate Anglo-Dutch assault upon a weakly-guarded ford. The French general, St. Ruth, decided to risk a stand (July 12th, 1691) at Aughrim, near Ballinasloe, Co. Galway, but in the middle of a bloody struggle St. Ruth was killed and a pass for the English advance was treacherously deserted by an English-Jacobite cavalry commander Henry Luttrell. Taken in the flank and rear, with no one in command, the Irish were routed in confusion.

After Aughrim only the cities of Galway and Limerick were left to be conquered. Galway surrendered early in August, and Limerick, seeing the situation hopeless, accepted terms.

The Treaty of Limerick

The articles of Capitulation, commonly called the Treaty of Limerick, signed on October 13th, 1691, derive importance from the difference revealed between the attitude of William III who approved them and that of the Irish Parliament which rejected them.

There were two treaties. Under one the Irish soldiers who surrendered were given the option of taking service with the King of France (which some 10,000 of them did) or of returning to their homes unmolested. Under the other the civilian Catholic population was promised, in return for taking an oath of allegiance to William, " not less toleration " than they had enjoyed prior to the accession of James.

The Dublin Parliament, from which all Catholics were excluded, refused (1692) to ratify the Treaty, until in 1697 a number of laws penalising Catholics had been passed, and a legal stipulation had been accepted that the Treaty meant that the *least* favourable conditions for Catholics prior to 1685 were to become the *most* favourable condition for Catholics in the future.

The Treaty of Limerick became in this way a classic instance of " English " bad faith.

In 1692, along with its refusal to approve the Treaty, the Dublin Parliament adopted an English Act which imposed confiscation upon all Irish landowners who had taken part with James. The Catholics appealed to William on the ground that this involved a flagrant breach of the Treaty of Limerick. Eventually the matter was compromised by the surrender of some three quarters of a million acres by the incriminated Catholics. Those who lost entire estates were mostly English Jacobites. The estates of James II in Ireland were granted by William to his mistress, the Countess of Orkney.

The Penal Code

Beginning in 1692, a number of Acts were passed by the Dublin Parliament, all levelled against the Catholics, which are known collectively as the *Penal Code*.

Catholics were debarred from the vote, and from entry into Parliament, the municipal corporations, the learned professions (except medicine) and from commissions in the Army, Navy, and Civil Service. No Catholic

E

might open or teach in a school ; or take any part in the sale or manufacture of arms. No Catholic might possess or carry arms without a magistrate's licence, nor might one own a horse worth more than £5. Except in the linen trade, no Catholic might have more than two apprentices. Protestants might not take Catholic apprentices at all. Catholics were barred from the manufacture and sale of newspapers and books. Marriages between Catholics and Protestants were prohibited as far as possible.

Catholics were subjected to special taxes, and to special restraints if they were landowners. No Catholic estate could be entailed : it must be divided at death between all the children. Catholics could not take leases for longer than thirty-three years and a Catholic's profits from sub-letting might not be more than one-third of the rent he paid. A Protestant landowner lost his civil rights if he married a Catholic ; a Protestant heiress, marrying a Catholic, lost her inheritance.

By conforming to the Protestant Church, a Catholic son could make his father a mere tenant for life on his own estate, which the son could inherit entire. Catholic orphans must be brought up as Protestants. A Catholic wife by conforming to the Protestant Church acquired the right to live apart from her husband and make him support her.

With regard to the Catholic Church itself all arch-bishops, bishops, etc. were ordered to leave the country under the penalties for high treason if they remained or returned. Only one priest was permitted per parish, however large, and he must register, and might not set foot outside his parish except with special permission. No priest might enter the country from anywhere.

These provisions were designed to make the work of the Church, and its continued existence, impossible. They had the effect of turning it into an " underground " organisation endeared to the people. Unregistered priests and banned ecclesiastics carried on the work in the huge country parishes in which only one priest was permitted by law. Mass was celebrated in secluded spots, in all weathers, while scouts watched for the approach of enemies.

English trade-unionists who know how firmly the tradition of trade-unionism was laid in England when the unions were banned as " seditious conspiracies " by law, can understand why adherence to the Catholic Church came to be a point of honour with the common people of Ireland.

Protestant Ascendancy

An aspect of this iniquitous Code which has survived into our own time is that it conceals the *political* subjection of a distinct people to special *super-exploitation*, combined with social segregation and humiliation, all under a cloak of zeal for a particular religion. That this religion was the Established Religion of the *imperial* country shows this pretended zeal as the imperialist hypocrisy it was.

In England the Anti-Papal tradition, since it arose in the course of *national* struggles against an *alien* church, and counter-revolutionary kings, had at first a strong revolutionary content. It is not noted as often as it should be that for analogous reasons the Catholic tradition in Ireland has always had (despite the Hierarchy) a strong democratic and revolutionary tradition likewise, and that it is against this *revolutionary democratic content* that the malice of the Protestant Ascendancy faction was, and still is really directed.

In England, the " No Popery " tradition as it lost its revolutionary significance degenerated into the equivalent of the reactionary slogan " Down with the Jews ". In Ireland from the days of the Penal Code it has equated with the imposition of the " colour bar " and the " Jim Crow " laws of the Plantation States of the U.S.A.

The reactionary *political* essence of the Protestant
Ascendancy slogan is proved by the fact that at that
period, and for long after, the term "Protestant" included
only adherents to the established Church, and excluded
the Dissenters who were likewise subjected to special
penalties as the politically suspected descendants and
representatives of the revolutionaries of 1640, and
especially of the Leveller element in the New Model
army.

The Dissenters were mostly located in North-Eastern
Ulster where they were small farmers, merchants and
manufacturers. On a most favourable computation the
Dissenters and " Protestants " together were never more
than one-third of the total population, and the Protestants
were seldom, if ever, equal in numbers to the Dissenters.
Thus the Penal Code was designed and imposed as an
instrument for the aggrandisement of a privileged caste,
which with its flunkey and sycophant hangers-on never
totalled more than one-sixth of the population of Ireland.
In their interest the Pale, which had ceased to exist as a
territorial division, was revived as a line of social-
economic and political exclusion.

The Penal Code and Irish Nationality

Such a policy as that embodied in the Penal Code was
bound to have far-reaching effects, most of them evil,
especially upon the characters of the respective categories
of rulers and ruled, superiors and inferiors. Irish writers
of our own time have summarized its consequences thus :
> " The Protestants developed the vices of slave-
> owners, becoming idle, dissipated, and neglectful
> of their duties. The Catholic population grew, as a
> serf-population always does grow, cringing, shifty,
> untruthful. They were lazy because they had nothing
> to work for ; lawless because they knew the law
> only as an enemy to be defied or evaded wherever
> possible. Not such had been the Irish of the old

times, praising truth as the highest of virtues; obeying strictly a law supported by no force save that of public opinion. Nor were such qualities observed in the soldiers and statesmen whom Ireland at this very time was giving to the nations of Europe and of America.

" That bad effects must have followed from these pernicious enactments as regards proficiency in professional and artistic work, in industry and in agriculture is evident. The Catholic's abilities were lost to the country, since he had no means of exercising them. The tenant whose improvements the landlord might confiscate at the end of his short lease, if indeed he had a lease at all, naturally did not improve. If a tenant at will he did not dare even to show any sign of prosperity in his dress or in the equipment of his house or farm. The purchase of a new coat or a new plough might result in a raising of his rent next gale day."

—HAYDEN-MOONAN : *Short History of the Irish People.*

This summary, though true as a generalisation, needs qualification. The Code had a different effect upon different classes of the subjected Irish population. For the Catholic landowners there were ways of escape. They could make a formal submission to Protestantism. They could convey their estates in trust to sympathising Protestants who could as the nominal owners shelter them from the law while leaving them in continued possession in fact. With Protestant connivance they could provide education for their children in England or on the Continent. A sense of class-solidarity made the bulk of the Protestant landowners collaborate with them in evading all the more offensive personal restrictions of the Code.

From any such easy way out the great mass of the Irish people were debarred by their poverty. The

immense majority of them were small-scale tillers of the
soil whom necessity kept tied to scanty holdings and
conditions of tenure which could have no result but one
or other form of wretchedness. For their children, the
only education available—apart from a few ill-intentioned
and worse-managed institutions designed to turn Catholic
children into monstrosities of sycophantic servility
miscalled Protestants—was such as they could pick up
from wandering scholars who taught the children of the
poor under hedges in the fields, while scouts watched
out for spies and informers.

The penalty for these " hedge-schoolmasters ", if
caught, might be hanging, or transportation on a charge
of treason, or a flogging on the charge of vagabondage.
The payment for their labour was—a seat by the fire,
a lodging in the hay, a share in the family meal, and such
oddments in the way of clothing and ha'pence as the
neighbours could scrape together. But they were sure
of a welcome at any time in any thatched cabin because
they were the last survivors of an integral feature of the
old Gaelic social order. Many of them were the actual
descendants of the hereditary chroniclers, pedigree-
keepers, brehons, bards, and tellers of legendary tales
of one or other of the clans ; and it is due entirely to
them and those who sheltered them that the living
stream of Gaelic culture never wholly failed. With the
parish priests, who remained faithful to their vocation
in circumstances which make the lot of a missionary to
cannibals luxurious by comparison, the hedge-schoolmaster, and the wandering poet or musician kept glowing
a spark of Gaelic fire among those humblest tillers of
the soil who seemed in English eyes less to be regarded
than the beasts of the field.

These tillers, the lowest strata of the conquered Irish—
segregated by poverty, by language, by creed, by law,
and by the supercilious arrogance of the class which, in
Grattan's phrase, " knelt to England on the necks of

eir countrymen "—these people of the thatched cabins
ad one inestimably precious compensation.   Around
eir turf fires they could hear retold again and again the
gendary stories of the Gaels, and be solaced by poem,
ong and music preserved from days which far out-dated
e oldest of their miseries—far-off days when the sun
lways shone and the blackbird's whistle never failed
1 the glen.

It was thus, and in these cabins, that the seed was
ept alive which in due time would burst forth in the
ch profusion of a regenerated Irish Nationality.

PART II

From Grattan to the United Irishmen

O may the wind of Freedom
  Soon send the Frenchmen o'er
To plant the Tree of liberty
  Upon our Shamrock shore.
O, we'll plant it with our weapons
  While the English tyrants gape
To see their bloody flag torn down
  To Green on the Cape.
        O, the wearing the Green!
        Yes! the wearing the Green!
God grant us soon to see that day
        And freely wear the Green.

Antrim's Defenders' Song, 1796.

CHAPTER FIVE

ENGLAND'S COLONY—IRELAND

So far we have traced the ENGLISH CONQUEST: from now on we are concerned with the RE-CONQUEST of Ireland by the Irish Nation. And first of all this entails considering how a new IRISH NATION was evolved historically in the developing process of struggle against the agencies and consequences of English Rule. In Part II we deal with the first epoch in that process— one which begins with the rise of GRATTAN and the VOLUNTEERS (1778-82) and ends with the rise and fall of the UNITED IRISHMEN (1791-98). In this chapter we deal with the economic and political relations which led to the rise of GRATTAN, and the VOLUNTEER episode.

England's Colonial Policy

English official policy in the 17th and 18th centuries treated a colony as a child which had a claim upon, but also owed a duty to, its parent country. This policy originated in the Navigation Acts designed to break the Dutch mercantile monopoly and to make London the chief centre of the commerce of the world. Goods were refused entry to England unless carried in English ships, or in those of their country of origin. Exports were permitted only in English ships or those of the country to which the goods were invoiced.

In effect this policy restricted the Colonies to producing raw materials in exchange for English manufactures, all the carrying being done in English ships. Applied strictly, it would have prevented all sea-borne trade between one American colony and another except in English ships; and, though laxly enforced, it remained a rule that the American Colonies must not trade directly with foreign countries or with the possessions of foreign powers in America. In the end the friction these rules generated was the basic cause of the revolt of the American Colonies, and the War of Independence (1776-82).

Restraints upon Irish Trade

In America this policy restricted manufactures and trade as they arose. In Ireland it involved *destroying deliberately trade and manufactures that had already arisen* and were competing successfully with English rivals. A few examples will illustrate the process.

In the 17th century a profitable Irish trade in *fat cattle* exported to England grew up. English graziers protested ; the trade was prohibited. Irish cattle-breeders exported, instead, *lean cattle* for English graziers to fatten. English cattle-farmers protested ; the trade was stopped. Ireland exported *slaughtered carcasses ;* English butchers protested, and the trade was banned. Finally, *salt beef (and pork) in barrels* became the outlet for Irish live-stock breeders ; and this trade, being useful to the English Navy and the mercantile marine, was allowed to pass without protest. It became one of Ireland's staple industries.

Irish-grown wool was of exceptionally fine quality, and the manufacture of Irish woollen cloth developed rapidly after 1690. It was of sufficient importance to induce the Irish Parliament to tax woollen exports to produce a revenue. The *English* Parliament placed a prohibitive import-tax upon woollens imported from Ireland. Finding that continental buyers bought Irish woollens in preference to English, the *English* Parliament prohibited all woollen export *from Ireland*, including raw wool, except to England and Wales—where the cloth had to pay a prohibitive duty. The raw wool useful to English manufacturers was admitted duty-free.

Irish manufacturers, unable to support themselves upon Ireland's internal market, emigrated and set up woollen manufactures in Germany, Holland, Belgium, France, and Spain,—relying in each case largely upon raw wool and woollen yarn smuggled from Ireland.

These are type examples; similar restraints were applied in every branch of Irish industry, with the solitary exception of *linen manufacture*. This was fostered by royal and State subsidies because Irish manufacturers were better able than the English to compete successfully with French and Dutch producers. It was, as it happened, fostered in a *Protestant* area; but equivalent encouragement would have established it equally well in a *Catholic* region.

A contributory motive for this trade policy was that it diverted to investment in *English* manufactures all the *capital accumulations* wrung by the Anglo-Irish landlords from their *Irish* tenantry.

Administration and Parliament in Ireland

The Irish Administration consisted of the Viceroy, the Chief Secretary, and Ministers appointed by the Viceroy. The Viceroy and the Chief Secretary were, in practice, nominated by the *English* Cabinet to which the Chief Secretary was directly responsible. From this followed a radical difference between the English and Irish Parliaments. Irish Administration was changed, if at all, from London. No adverse vote of the Dublin Parliament need affect it : an adverse vote at Westminster altered it immediately.

As in England, but in a greater proportion, many of the seats in the Irish Parliament were for Boroughs which had no real existence. With Catholics debarred from voting, most of the counties were also controlled by territorial magnates. The borough franchise was usually so restricted that most of them became, virtually, nomination boroughs. Out of 300 seats, it was estimated, in 1778, that 219 were the property of patrons. Of the 81 " contested " seats many were shamelessly corrupt.

Four great landowners by combining their interest could command a majority of the House, even against Crown influence. The " management " of the House thus became merely a business of awarding places, pensions, etc. Nearly two-thirds of the Members were placemen, pensioners, or both. And this state of things had endured for more than fifty years.

The Irish Parliament was further restricted by " Poyning's Law ". No Bill might be introduced until its " heads " had been approved by the two Privy Councils, either of which might delete clauses from Bills *after* they had been passed. In addition, by an Act of 1720 the English Parliament claimed the right to pass laws for Ireland at its pleasure. This arose from the desire to prevent the use of Ireland by the Crown as a base for resistance to the people and Parliament of England, which was an additional reason for checking the growth of trade and manufactures in Ireland. Collaterally, the Irish Civil List was a convenient means of making provision for Court favourites (King's mistresses, etc.) whom it was inadvisable to saddle upon the English establishment.

The Irish landed oligarchy, who could invest their revenues in England, had no direct interest in promoting Irish trade or manufactures. As they controlled the Irish Parliament, there was little or no resistance from that quarter to English legislation against Ireland's trade and manufactures.

Economic Conditions in Ireland (1690-1778)

England in 1690-1760 was passing through the mercantile-manufacturing prelude to the Industrial Revolution. Ireland's economy was being arrested in its development and turned aside into producing, as well as subsistence for the Irish population, food-stuffs or English workers and raw materials for England's manufactures.

The bulk of Irish land was owned in large estates by titled landowners, many of them English absentees. A large proportion was leased on long terms either to resident gentry or to speculators who sub-let in smaller estates. There was a fair number of substantial freeholders, mostly Protestants of " planted " stock; and a fair number of Catholic leaseholders on short terms. Much the most numerous class was that of the cottagers whose position was a compromise between that of a wage-labourer and that of an allotment farmer.

When a labourer was hired he was allotted a plot (an acre or half-acre) upon which to erect a cottage, sometimes with materials supplied in part by his employer. From this " potato-ground " he produced the subsistence for himself and family. In addition he was allotted grazing for a cow or cows. He paid rent for both potato-ground and cow's grass by deductions from wages due. Any surplus was paid in cash or kind.

The tenant of a small farm frequently needed to supplement its yield by wage-labour for the landowner. Thus his position approximated to that of the cottager-labourer, while the landlord stood to both much as a tribal chief stood to his clan-kinsmen. The practice of permitting the labourer and the smaller tenants the free services of the landowner-employer's bull or stallion was another vestigial relic of the clan relation.

The main productive activity of the Irish population (1690-1760) was *subsistence tillage*. The diet-staple of the peasantry of every grade was *potatoes* and *butter-milk*, supplemented in the off-season by *oatmeal*. Bread-corn was grown primarily for sale to the towns. Barley was grown for brewing and distilling; which, in this period, grew rapidly from domestic crafts into important manufactures. Dairy products—butter, cheese, poultry, eggs, and bacon—were too valuable as articles of

exchange for them to enter, more than occasionally
into the dietary of the peasantry.

Certain consequences followed : (1) The Landlord's
rent was provided *not* by advancing *production* beyond the
point at which the tillers' wants had been satisfied ; it
was provided by depressing the *consumption* of the tillers
to the lowest level compatible with continued existence.
(2) The grass-farmer who needed a minimum quantity
of labour for a maximum number of acres was the
natural enemy of all tillage-farmers and especially the
cottagers. (3) Any failure of the potato crop brought
immediate disaster to the mass of the population. (4) If
such a failure coincided with a rise in grass-farming, a
trade slump, or any other curtailment of the demand
for labour, literally the only choice for the peasantry was
between begging, stealing, and absolute starvation.

In that masterpiece of blazing indignation disguised
as smooth-faced irony—his *Modest Proposal* to use the
children of the poor as butcher's meat for the rich—
JONATHAN SWIFT envisages just such a state of things

> " I have already computed the charge of nursing
> a beggar's child (*in which list I reckon all Cottagers
> Labourers, and four-fifths of the Farmers*) to be about
> two shillings per annum, *rags included*, and I believe
> no gentleman would repine to give Ten Shillings
> for the carcass of a good fat child, which as I have
> said, will make four dishes of nutritive meat when
> he hath only some particular friend or his own
> family to dine with him. Thus the squire will learn
> to be a good landlord and grow popular among his
> tenants, the mother will have eight shillings net
> profit and be fit for work till she produces another
> child."

Swift, it will be noted, so defines the " Beggars " as to
include five-sixths of the rural population. He goes on
to drive the point home :

" I grant this food will be somewhat dear and therefore *very proper for landlords* who as they have already devoured most of the Parents seem to have the best title to the children."

He turns the point against England :

" This kind of commodity will not bear exportation, the flesh being of too tender a consistence to admit a long continuance in salt, although perhaps *I could name a Country which would be glad to eat up our whole nation without it*."

Swift, no doubt, exaggerated ; but not so much—only enough to make his thrust go right home.

F

CHAPTER SIX

GRATTAN'S REVOLUTION

ENGLISH Colonial policy begot an inevitable result in the revolt of the American colonies, who declared themselves INDEPENDENT, July 4th, 1776. The war which resulted gave the Anglo-Irish colony its chance to enforce (*a*) FREEDOM TO TRADE (1780), and (*b*) LEGISLATIVE INDEPENDENCE (1782). This enforcement constitutes GRATTAN'S REVOLUTION.

The crisis was led up to by popular agitations (*a*) among the urban trading community, and (*b*) among the rural population.

Urban Agitations

In the first third of the 18th century, no combined action including both the Anglo-Irish colony and the subjected Irish agrarian community was conceivable. Within the colony there was furious discontent among the manufacturers and traders at the restraints upon trade, and at the acquiescence therein of the oligarchy. The agrarian (Irish) community was, at first, too disorganised by defeat to offer any general resistance. Struggle began in spontaneous local protests at particular hardships. Since, however, both the urban and rural struggles were, in practice, directed against one and the same ruling oligarchy, their continued development begot in the end a sense of *community* in struggle against a common enemy.

Much experience had to be gone through before the champions of the colony and of the *Gaeltacht* could think of each other as " fellow-countrymen ". The champions of the " colony " against the English Government no more thought of themselves as " Gaels " when they called themselves "Irish" than Benjamin Franklin or George Washington identified themselves with the Sioux or the Iroquois when they called themselves "Americans". As a proportion of the Gaelic Irish became drawn into trade and manufactures by the penal obstructions to land-owning by Catholics, they became drawn likewise into echoing the traders' protests against English exactions and interference.

One of the earliest champions of the "colony" was JONATHAN SWIFT (1667-1745), then Dean of St. Patrick's, Dublin. He joined in the protest against a flagrant job—the giving to an English iron-founder of the job of minting a new copper coinage for Ireland—and helped to work the agitation up to fever pitch.

Writing ostensibly as a "Drapier", Swift in his first *Letter* attacked the project on *utilitarian* grounds— adopting the (fallacious) popular belief that the currency in Ireland would be permanently debased. In his second *Drapier's Letter*, Swift attacked those who granted the patent on *public* grounds—that it was a "job". He excited so much agreement that the Dublin Parliament was forced to join in his protest. When the English Parliament scornfully refused to take notice of "clamour", Swift in his *Third Letter* took *patriotic* ground and asked—would anyone in England dare so to describe a protest by both Houses of the *English* Parliament? "Are not the Irish people, then, as free as the English? Is not their Parliament as representative?"

This raised the issue from a squabble about the relative values of two brass farthings into a question whether the Irish Parliament did or did not possess the right to control and mint its own coinage. In his *Fourth Letter*, addressed to "the whole people of Ireland", Swift took a definitely *Nationalist* ground:

"'Tis true indeed that within the memory of man the Parliaments of England have sometimes assumed the power of binding this Kingdom by laws enacted there, wherein they were first opposed openly (so far as Truth, Reason, and Justice are capable of opposing) by the famous MR. MOLYNEUX an English gentleman born here, as well as by several of the greatest patriots and best Whigs in England. But the love and torrent of power prevailed.

"Indeed the arguments on both sides were invincible. For, in Reason, *All Government without the consent of the Governed is the very definition of slavery ;* but, in Fact, eleven men well armed will certainly subdue one single man in his shirt."

The issue is joined squarely : Ireland has the *Right*, but England has the *Might*. The logical deduction was too obvious to need statement.

Swift's *Modest Proposal* written a year later openly identified the landlord class with England and stigmatised both jointly as the implacable enemy of Ireland. Swift's Nationalism was exclusively " colonial " ; but he cannot be denied his title of Father of Nationalism in Ireland. From the time of his *Drapier's Letters* a patriot opposition was never lacking in the Irish Parliament.

Agrarian Unrest and Revolts

We have noted earlier the complete dependence of the peasant upon his potato patch and cow. A word is necessary about the operation of the " middle-man "— the speculator who leased land only to sub-lease it. An extension of this system begot a hierarchy of " landlords " broadening down from the great owners-in-chief at the apex to a mass of tenants at the base, all holding tiny plots as yearly tenants, tenants by labour service, or plain tenants at will. The wretched peasantry at the base carried on their backs a hierarchy of middle-men, three and four deep, with the great lord himself to cap all.

To add to their miseries a practice was introduced of

putting tenancies, as they fell in, up to auction. The insecurity this created was a powerful lever for exacting the last possible farthing from the tenantry. And if, as frequently happened, the middle-man saw a chance to let his land in large parcels for grass farming, the resultant eviction of the occupiers, and loss of employment, made the change-over as disastrous to the poor man as was the death of his cow or the failure of his potato crop.

Such a change-over on a large scale produced the first-recorded general uprising of the peasantry (1761) known as the "WHITE-BOY" conspiracy.

It first appeared, near Limerick, as a reply to an attempt by the landlords to enclose stretches of waste land which had been treated as common from time immemorial. This "waste" was indispensable to scores of peasants as grazing for their cows, sheep, goats, etc. Faced with this calamity the peasants turned out by night, threw down the walls, filled the trenches, ploughed up the meadows and restored the whole "waste" to its original condition. The landlords abandoned their attempt. From this successful beginning the Whiteboy movement spread through Munster into Connacht and Leinster.

From sporadic and occasional resistance to attempts to substitute grass-farming for tillage, the movement developed into a permanent resistance to rack-renters, evictors, land-grabbers, and tithe-proctors. Finally it offered resistance to landlord-employers who offered (and labourer-tenants who accepted) employment at less than a standard rate.

The methods of the WHITEBOYS were frequently terroristic. Threatening letters were followed up by domiciliary visits and physical vengeance. Murder was rare; but bludgeoning, and such punishments as being flung naked into a pit filled with thorns, were common. More highly-placed offenders suffered the maiming of their cattle.

Whatever might be said against the barbarity of their

methods, it remains a fact that the Whiteboys (so called
from wearing shirts outside their garments as a disguise)
did function as a Tenants' Protection Society and an
Agricultural Labourers' Union, and did establish a code
of agrarian solidarity which became generally observed

From the circumstances in which they operated, the
Whiteboy organisation never advanced far beyond a
loose aggregation of self-contained local secret societies.
They developed in time a species of " free-masonry "
with signs and passwords whereby the members of one
local society could make themselves known as confederates to those of other localities ; and, in the form of a
dispersed aggregate of " Ribbon Lodges ", the organisation survived down to the end of the 19th century.

From 1761 to 1778 the landlords and the Authorities
waged perpetual war against the Whiteboys. Military
expeditions were led against them. Suspects were taken
and hanged in scores. Acts were passed imposing
frightful penalties—including death—for administering
or taking the Whiteboy oath of fidelity. All of them
failed. As often as Whiteboyism was reported " exterminated " in one locality it reappeared in another. Even
the cynical Lord Chesterfield, when Viceroy, was moved
to observe that if the military had shot half as many
landlords as they had hanged Whiteboys it would have
been twice as good for the peace of the country.

The spontaneous origin of the Whiteboy movement
from economic causation is proved by the appearance
of parallel movements in Ulster. As a Protestant tenantry
was involved these were usually less ferociously repressed
than were the Whiteboys.

The " OAKBOYS " appeared in Monaghan in 1762—
spreading thence into Tyrone and Armagh—as a revolt
against the exaction of forced labour for the repair and
upkeep of roads. Catholics and Protestants joined in
this movement which was finally suppressed only after
a bloody battle in Armagh in which the Oakboys were

defeated. This notwithstanding, they won their point. Thereafter a money-rate was levied instead of forced labour.

The "STEELBOYS" were Protestants of Antrim and Down who put up (1764) a mass resistance to fines for the renewal of tenancies, to rack-rents, to tithes, and to an attempt to introduce grass-farming. They were strong enough to march into Belfast, break open the gaol, and liberate some of their number who had been captured. Juries in Belfast refused to convict Steelboys and, when the venue of trial was changed to Dublin, juries there also refused to convict.

In the end, however, the landlords were strong enough to drive most of them to emigrate to America.

These Agrarian struggles testified to an unrest which gave added force to the opposition waged in Parliament against the landed oligarchy on other grounds. They prepared the way for a *National* movement.

The Volunteers

In the American War of Independence the sympathies of Irishmen were almost unanimously on the side of the Americans, whose grievances were very similar to those of the " colony ". The war, too, brought distress to Ireland by automatically cutting off a profitable linen-trade, and this was intensified when the English Government banned all exports of " provisions " (barrelled beef and pork). When the Irish Parliament agreed to place all the troops in Ireland at the disposal of the Crown, and voted money to raise regiments specially for service against the Americans, it brought a hail-storm of indignation about its ears.

This indignation was given its lever to work with when France and Spain took the opportunity (1778) to join in the war on the side of the Americans ; and when the Administration had to warn Belfast that a descent by a combined French and American fleet upon the

North of Ireland might be anticipated at any moment
The Administration confessed that, as it had sent all it
troops to England or to America, it had none to plac
at Belfast's disposal. It recommended the citizens t
provide for their own defence.

The citizens of Belfast rose to the occasion. Within
surprisingly short time several regiments of VOLUNTEER
were raised. All were uniformed, armed, equipped, and
supplied with cannon by public subscription. The
Volunteers elected their own officers and started intensiv
training at once.

Belfast's example proved contagious. Town cor
porations and County Grand Juries took the lead and
by the middle of 1779 fifty thousand volunteers were
embodied; by the end of the year there were a hundred
thousand with 130 pieces of cannon.

This Volunteering enthusiasm transformed the
political situation. The will and ability of the citizens
to defend themselves contrasted sharply with the
confessed inability of the Administration; and, in turn,
it derived added significance from the failure of the
English Government to hold its own against the American Colonies. The war being nearly as unpopular in
England as it was in Ireland, the possibility of the Irish
Administration's getting military support from England
could be disregarded.

The altered situation gave an opening for the free
expression of every Irish grievance. In imitation of the
Americans, " non-importation associations " began to
be formed, whose members were pledged neither to use
themselves nor to associate or trade with those who
used, or traded in, goods *imported from England*. Every
meeting to raise recruits for the Volunteers became an
agitation meeting; every meeting of Volunteers to elect
officers became an organisation meeting; every meeting
of officers to plan drills, parades, etc., became a caucus
meeting of the *mass opposition party* in which the Parlia-

mentary leaders of the Patriot Opposition figured prominently from the start.

The Government could do nothing. It tried to start a scare that, under cover of Volunteering, the Catholics were securing arms. The Opposition leaders countered this by requesting the Catholics to refrain from Volunteering. The Catholics complied ; and in addition raised large sums of money to buy equipment for the Protestant Volunteers. The Government thus, in trying to divide Protestants and Catholics, promoted their union. The laws which debarred the more well-to-do Catholics from large-scale landowning and from the professions had caused the more well-to-do Catholics to put their sons to trade and manufacture, and when the test came bourgeois *class-solidarity overrode sectarian divisions*. This enthusiasm of the Catholic bourgeoisie for the common cause—for the common struggle against the restraints upon trade, and against the English Government and Parliament which imposed them—communicated itself to the Catholic countryside ; and so was created the ground-plan for a *united Irish Nation* in modern form.

In places, the ban upon Catholic entry into the Volunteers was disregarded. In Dublin, a popular small-proprietor and trader, JAMES NAPPER TANDY, a Protestant democrat, whose championship of the Catholics on the Dublin Corporation had earned him the title of " Tribune of the *Plebs* ", got round the difficulty ingeniously. He formed a corps of Volunteer *Artillery* into which he recruited Catholic artisans freely, arguing that they could not be said either to *possess* the cannon (which legally belonged to him as Treasurer) and still less to *carry* them. Tandy's humorous ingenuity was a joke enjoyed by all Ireland outside Dublin Castle.

Henry Grattan and his Leadership

HENRY GRATTAN (1750-1820), a young Dublin barrister and small proprietor, had risen by his eloquence and

zeal for the Volunteers to the recognised leadership of
the Patriot Opposition in Parliament. In October, 1779,
he voiced the growing National demand by moving an
amendment to the Address demanding a " free export
trade ".

The time was well chosen. The disastrous course of
the American War had reduced the power and political
credit of the English Government to a minimum. All
England was a ferment of discontent. With no possibility of aid from England the Irish Administration was
totally unable to face a front-to-front trial of strength
with the Opposition. Several of the leading borough-
mongers had deserted them. The lower ranks of the
aristocracy and most of the gentry were on the popular
side. Consequently the debate on Grattan's motion
resolved itself into a competition, in which placemen
joined, to see who could best amend the amendment into
the strongest possible expression of the popular demand.
It passed, finally and unanimously, as an unequivocal
demand for FREE TRADE.

Unable to resist openly, the Administration played
for time : the Viceregal reply was evasive. The popular
retort was not. Parading a few days later at the customary
celebration of William of Orange's birthday (Nov. 4)
around his statue on College Green, Captain Napper
Tandy's Artillery carried placards depending from the
muzzles of their cannon reading : " *Free Trade ; or
else——— !* " .* The House of Commons underlined
the point by granting supplies for six months only.

The English Government gave way. In December,
1779, and January, 1780, Acts were rushed through
the English Parliament abolishing nearly all restraints
upon Irish trade.

Flushed with their victory, the Opposition, backed
by the Volunteers, pressed forward with new demands.

---

* Legend tells of an exchange between two great Irish *Rí-mor* : " Pay me
my Tribute, or else——— ! " " I owe you no Tribute, and if——— ! "

In April, 1780, GRATTAN moved a resolution denying the right of the English Parliament to legislate for Ireland. The Administration secured a postponement of the vote. The Opposition then introduced a *Mutiny Bill* in identical terms with the English Army (Annual) Act which was held, in England, to apply in Ireland. The intention was to put the English Government in a dilemma. If they rejected the Act, they would bring on a direct conflict with the Irish Parliament. If they accepted it they accepted in principle the claim of the Opposition to the Legislative Independence of Ireland. The Privy Council threw the dilemma back upon the Irish Parliament by accepting the Bill with the clause limiting its operation to one year struck out. The Opposition, under protest, accepted the mutilated Act and returned to the attack with a *Habeas Corpus Act*. This the Privy Council accepted without alteration.

The English Government had, in fact, lost all power of resisting. Its last army of any size had surrendered to WASHINGTON; the American War had as good as ended in total defeat. It was merely a question of how long Premier LORD NORTH could delay the inevitable coming to power of the Whigs.

The Patriot Opposition filled in the interval with a CATHOLIC RELIEF BILL which repealed the Penal prohibitions which debarred Catholics from bequeathing, inheriting, or purchasing estates, and from taking leases of 999 years. The coming to power of the Whigs in England ensured the Bill's acceptance by the Privy Council.

Meanwhile, the Volunteer agitation proceeded. On February 15, 1782, a CONVENTION of 243 delegates from every Volunteer corps in Ulster met in DUNGANNON, County Tyrone, and carried with virtual unanimity the following resolutions, among others:

"(1) The claim of any body of men other than the King, Lords, and Commons of Ireland to make laws to bind this Kingdom is unconstitutional, illegal, and a grievance.

"(2) The Powers exercised by the Privy Council . . . under pretence of the Law of Poynings, are unconstitutional and a grievance.

"(3) As men, as Irishmen, as Christians, and as Protestants, we rejoice in the relaxation of the Penal Laws against our Roman Catholic fellow-subjects, and we conceive the measure to be fraught with the happiest consequences to the union and prosperity of the inhabitants of Ireland."

Similar resolutions were adopted by similar conventions in the other three provinces.

Thus mandated, GRATTAN in Parliament moved (Feb., 1782) a DECLARATION OF IRISH RIGHT. The Administration once again contrived a delay; but it was only momentary. Led by CHARLES JAMES FOX, a friend of Grattan and his policy, the English Whigs were of one mind with the Irish Opposition. Accordingly the Irish Parliament met on April 19th, 1782, specially summoned "to consider Irish grievances".

GRATTAN made his way to the House through streets lined with Volunteers in parade uniform, who presented arms as he passed, while their cannon roared a salute. For the third time he moved his Declaration; and this time there was no resistance. The Declaration was adopted by acclamation, and the English Government and Parliament at once complied with Acts (May, 1782) which conceded all Grattan's demands.

The Irish Parliament celebrated its new-won freedom by limiting the Mutiny Act to two years. As an appreciation of the REVOLUTION he had accomplished, Parliament voted Grattan £50,000 to purchase an estate. He could have had double but was satisfied with this.

Flood: and the Convention of 1783.

At this critical stage in the struggle, the Opposition

was split and Grattan's leadership was frustrated by a
" Leftist " drive headed by HENRY FLOOD.

Grattan had known perfectly well that, if the English
Government had resisted his demands, his next step
would have been necessarily to overthrow the Irish
Administration by the armed force of the Volunteers.
This step he was prepared to take, though he knew
that it carried with it the risk that the movement would
grow beyond his power to control it. The timely
surrender of the English Government gave him the
chance to shift the struggle to a new plane and begin
a purely Parliamentary struggle for instalments of
reform which would leave political power in the hands
of the smaller landed gentry in alliance with the wealthier
traders and merchants. Like all his class Grattan had a
horror of *democracy* ; but he was eager to broaden the
base of the property interests represented in Parliament
by including Catholics as voters, and among those
qualified for sitting in Parliament. To achieve reform
while keeping the movement within moderate bounds
it was necessary to keep the more radical elements
in the Volunteers under the leadership of a political
alliance of the progressive aristocracy and the moderate
bourgeoisie.

FLOOD upset this plan by affecting to believe that a
simple repeal of the Act which had asserted the right
of the English Parliament to legislate for Ireland was
not enough. He demanded an express RENUNCIATION
of that claim.

This line, as Flood knew, was bound to be popular
with the Volunteer rank and file because of their
ingrained suspicion of English statesmen ; and it had
the further advantage that it enabled Flood and his
aristocratic allies to pose, without risk, as being far
more " revolutionary " than Grattan himself, or his
bourgeois supporters.

Grattan thought the demand for Renunciation bad

in principle and worse in practice. It made Ireland'
Right dependent on an *English* Act of Parliament; an
it imperilled the Party Grattan was building up witl
such care. Soon the rival Harrys were treating th
House to a display of Billingsgate, after which the
would have gone out to pistol each other if they had no
been restrained by force. In the end Grattan was beate
by a rally to Flood of the extreme Right as well as th
extreme Left. Within a few months of receiving publi
thanks for his services Grattan found himself deserte
by the Volunteers and by the bulk of the Opposition.

The English Parliament showed what it thought o
the dispute by passing the RENUNCIATION ACT (1783
with hardly a word of debate.

FLOOD followed up his victory by manœuvring t
get control of the crucial VOLUNTEER CONVENTION
which met in Dublin in November 1783. Like Grattan
Flood was the son of a legal dignitary; unlike Grattan
he was a man of wealth with connections with th
upper strata of the aristocracy. He and his friend
Lord CHARLEMONT, the Volunteer Commander-in-Chief
were able to pull sufficient wires to secure the electio
of a majority of delegates favourable to their point o
view.

The Convention was virtually unanimous in favou
of a programme of Parliamentary reforms—Ministeria
responsibility to the House; the exclusion of placemer
and pensioners; and an extension of the suffrage with
elimination of " rotten " boroughs. The real crux cam
with the question whether the Catholics should be
admitted to the vote and to Parliament. The genuine
Radicals, led by the Belfast delegation, were ardently
in favour of Catholic Emancipation. Flood and the
" fake"-Radicals were as determinedly hostile. In the
end Flood gained a majority (with the aid of notorious
Castle hacks and placemen who had contrived to get
elected as delegates).

Having won his point Flood worked a characteristic "stunt". He proposed that while he and the other M.P.s then present should carry the Convention's Reform demands to the House, as they were, *in Volunteer uniform*, the Convention should continue permanently in session *to await an answer*.

There was literally no point in the proposal unless Flood was prepared to reply to a refusal by calling for, and leading, an immediate resort to armed insurrection by the thousands of Volunteers then assembled in Dublin. A large proportion of the delegates were ready for this; but the House knew perfectly well that Flood had no such intention and, accordingly, refused flatly to consider proposals "presented at the point of the bayonet". Flood despite his "revolutionary" posturing could do nothing but return to the Convention and propose an adjournment to "consider the situation". The Convention met several times more, but its spirit had evaporated. After prolonged wrangling it dispersed—disillusioned, disorganised, and demoralised.

The Volunteers and the Radical movement they had fostered declined rapidly from that moment. And with the collapse of the Volunteers Flood lost his momentary significance. He introduced his Reform Bill as a private member's motion; but, while it was given a debate, it was heavily defeated,—as everybody had foreseen.

As Flood sank swiftly into obscurity, Grattan patiently set to work to rebuild the Party Flood had shattered. The Reform agitation did not really revive, however, until entirely new men had set on foot an entirely new movement.

CHAPTER SEVEN

THE RISE OF THE UNITED IRISHMEN

What the AMERICAN REVOLUTION was to Gratta
and the Volunteers, the FRENCH REVOLUTION was t
the SOCIETY OF UNITED IRISHMEN (1791-1798) led b
THEOBALD WOLFE TONE (1763-1798). The grea
achievement of the United Irishmen was that c
combining Catholics and Protestants. Thus they secure
the largest single instalment of CATHOLIC EMANCIPATIO
ever known. How they did it, and what followe
thencefrom is told in this chapter.

Ireland in 1790-1

Though balked in their main desires the Grattanit
Whigs secured some reforms of advantage to th
economic development of Ireland. They secure
PROTECTION for Irish manufactures and a CORN LAV
which—by checking imports and encouraging export
by a bounty when the price was low, and reversing th
procedure when the price was high—secured a stabl
market for Irish-grown wheat at a satisfactory price
This made grain-growing profitable on all but th
smallest holdings, and made for the general prosperit
of the farming community; which prosperity in tur
provided a brisk market for home manufactures. Th
prosperity was, of course, unequal. The trend toward
grain-growing and away from grass-farming was a gai
for the labourers and cottagers, but the intensifie
competition for good arable land caused a general ris
in rents. The repeal of the restrictions on Catholi
landowning caused some increase of Catholic proprietor
on the land; at the same time the new prosperity o
manufacturers caused an influx of the Protestan

" gentry " into that field. In town and in country the intermingling of Catholics and Protestants was promoted.

In the south of Ireland, in 1760, it was asserted that the bulk of the business of money-lending was in Catholic hands. In the North, the craftsmen and manufacturers were predominantly Dissenters ; but Catholics also were well represented. In short, economic development had destroyed a great deal of the segregation which the Penal Code had been designed to create. This was seen in the frequent combination of Catholics with Protestants in agitations for reform. Even the Munster Whiteboys, it was rumoured, were beginning to find Protestants to lead them.

Such was the general background for the rise of the SOCIETY OF UNITED IRISHMEN in 1791 under the leadership of THEOBALD WOLFE TONE.

Theobald Wolfe Tone

Tone was born in Dublin, on June 20, 1763, the son of a coachbuilder whose father had been a substantial freeholder in Co. Kildare. The family came of Cromwellian " planter " stock. Tone, the eldest son, had been educated for a barrister. The law had few attractions for him ; but, having contracted an early marriage, he was drudging at his profession when the thunderclap of the French Revolution aroused him as it did everybody else :

"Two years before," he writes in his *Autobiography*, " the nation was in lethargy . . . As the revolution advanced, and as events expanded themselves, the public spirit of Ireland rose with a rapid acceleration. The fears and animosities of the aristocracy rose in the same or in a higher proportion. In a little time the French Revolution became the test of every man's political creed, and the nation was fairly divided into two great parties, the Aristocrats and the Democrats . . . It is needless,

G

I believe, to say I was a Democrat from the beginning."

His friend, THOMAS RUSSELL, an Army officer then stationed in Belfast, wrote, early in 1791, telling Tone of a proposal to celebrate the second anniversary of the taking of the Bastille, and asking him to draft resolutions suited to the occasion. Tone responded with a resolution embodying three propositions :

(1) That English influence in Ireland is the great grievance of the country.

(2) That the most effective way to oppose it is by a reform in Parliament.

(3) That no reform would be just or efficacious which did not include the Catholics.

Learning that his third proposition had met with opposition, Tone at once set to work upon a pamphlet, entitled *An Argument on Behalf of the Catholics of Ireland by a Northern Whig.* He aimed, he tells us, at convincing the Dissenters :

"That they and the Catholics had but one common interest and one common enemy ; that the depression and slavery of Ireland was produced and perpetuated by the divisions existing between them ; and that consequently to assert the independence of their country, and their own individual liberties it was necessary to forget all former feuds, to consolidate the entire strength of the whole nation, and form for the first time but one people."

Tone confesses that he was " not a little proud " of his work which, in a few weeks, produced remarkable results. He was called to Belfast to assist in forming (October, 1791) the SOCIETY OF UNITED IRISHMEN, for which he wrote its statement of objects. Then, more unexpectedly, he received an invitation from the CATHOLIC COMMITTEE in Dublin to take up the post of salaried agent for that body.

Both these events were to prove momentous.

The Society of United Irishmen declared itself as—
"constituted for the purpose of forwarding a
Brotherhood of Affection, a Communion of Rights,
and a Union of Power among Irishmen of every
religious persuasion, and thereby to obtain *a
complete Reform in the Legislature*, founded on the
Principles of civil, political and religious liberty."
Thus the Society took as its point of departure what
had been the high-water mark of the Volunteers' agitation defeated in 1783. But, although the founders had
contacts with the few Volunteer regiments then
surviving, it is noteworthy that they went beyond the
Volunteers and aimed at *a political party organisation*
recruited directly among the people at large. It pre-dated
by a year the formation of its nearest English counterpart,
the LONDON CORRESPONDING SOCIETY, which, by general
consent, was the starting-point of all *organised* working-
class radical-democratic and revolutionary political
struggle in England.

While the immediate object of the Society was Parliamentary Reform, it was well understood, by those
nearest to TONE, that he desired that reform as a means
to a wider end :

"To subvert the tyranny of our execrable
Government ; to break the connection with England,
the never-failing source of all our political evils ;
and to assert the independence of my country—
these were my objects. To unite the whole people
of Ireland, to abolish the memory of past dissensions,
and to substitute the common name of *Irishman* in
place of the denominations of Protestant, Catholic,
and Dissenter—these were my means."
For that reason the invitation from the CATHOLIC
COMMITTEE—the recognised mouthpiece of all the
Catholics in Ireland—was doubly welcome. It was
welcome, in itself, as offering TONE lucrative employment
at a congenial task. It was still more welcome as eviden-

cing a profound change in the political temperature
of the Catholic Committee.

Till then the Committee had pursued the policy of
currying favour with the Crown through the Viceroy,
hoping in that way to secure protection against the
bigoted animosity of the ruling oligarchy, in Parliament
and out of it. Their invitation to Tone proved a complete
change of attitude. Previously they had begged for
favours as a *sect*. Now they were preparing to demand
their *rights as citizens*. That, in itself, was a revolutionary
change which delighted Tone beyond words. He had
expressed his opinion of Grattan's " Revolution " in
his *Argument* in words which the Catholic Committee
had read and noted :

> " The Revolution of '82 was a revolution which
> enabled Irishmen to sell at a much higher price
> their honour, their integrity, and the interests of
> their country ; it was a revolution which while at
> one stroke it doubled the value of every borough-
> monger in the Kingdom, left three-fourths of our
> countrymen [the Catholics] slaves as it found them,
> and the Government of Ireland in the base, wicked
> and contemptible hands who had spent their lives
> plundering and degrading her . . . Who of the
> veteran enemies of the country lost his place, or his
> pension ? Not one. The power remained in the
> hands of our enemies, again to be exerted for our
> ruin, with this difference, that, formerly, we had our
> distresses *gratis* at the hands of England, but now
> we pay very dearly to receive the same with aggra-
> vations at the hands of Irishmen—yet this we
> boast of and call a Revolution."

To have seen this fact so clearly showed penetration ;
to have stated it so boldly showed courage ; but to have
got Belfast Protestants and Dissenters to applaud the
statement, and to take action upon it, and simultaneously
to have produced an equivalent response from the

leaders of the Catholic community showed that Tone possessed political genius of a very high order.

The Rights of Man in Ireland

Tone himself, as modest as he was fearless, attributed the result wholly to the French Revolution ; and, indeed, it is difficult to over-estimate the delivering power of that Titanic event. To it must be attributed the immediate and rapid spread of the Society of United Irishmen. Within a month (November, 1791) Tone, Russell, and Napper Tandy were assisting other notables to found a Dublin Society ; and thereafter the two Societies of Belfast and Dublin were the twin parent-societies of a rapidly proliferating organisation. Belfast made contacts most readily with Protestants; Dublin most readily with the Catholics. Between them they began to spread a network of affiliated individuals and local societies throughout the country.

They propagated their views, 18th century fashion, in after-dinner discussions among an invited company, or in meetings specially summoned to discuss addresses and resolutions on topics of the day. Their primary contacts were among professionals, merchants, and manufacturers, with a sprinkling of the more progressive gentry; but from the first they had a profound effect upon the substantial working-farmers, the independent artisan-craftsmen, and the work-people employed by the leading members of the Society.

At its foundation the Society stood broadly on the principles of PAINE's Rights of Man (first published, 1792) which work, Tone notes with glee, at once became the " Koran " of Belfast. Its programme soon grew specific ; and eventually included the points (also approved by the English and Scottish " Jacobin " Societies) of : (1) Manhood suffrage ; (2) Equal electoral districts ; (3) No property qualification ; (4) Annual Parliaments ; and (5) Payment of Members. That is to say the United

Irishmen anticipated the programme of the English Chartists by half a century and secured for this programme a mass support which far exceeded the support obtained, until much later, by the English Radicals.

The UNITED IRISHMEN did not confine themselves to purely political demands. They declared for the abolition of church establishments, and of tithes; for resistance to rack-rents; and, ultimately, for sweeping measures of agrarian reform. Through their organ, the *Northern Star* (founded by SAMUEL NEILSON in Belfast early in 1792) they gave a cordial welcome on their first appearance to MARY WOLLSTONECRAFT's *Vindication of the Rights of Woman* and to PAINE's *Age of Reason*.

Their internationalism was not less pronounced than their nationalism. They corresponded cordially with the JACOBIN SOCIETY in Paris, and reported its proceedings regularly in their journal. They sent a delegation to the British National Convention (1792) and when THOMAS MUIR, the Scottish Jacobin, was sentenced to fourteen years' transportation the Belfast Society made him an honorary member. The progress of the revolution in France—the overthrow of the monarchy, the foundation of a Republic, the victories of the conscript armies—all received enthusiastic applause from the United Irishmen.

Tone (a good barometer) notes in his diary on August 19, 1792:

> " *The King of France dethroned;* very glad of it, for now the people have fair play. What will the Army do? God send they stand by the Nation. Everything depends on the line they will take."

He records the execution of Louis XVI almost with indifference:

> " The King of France was beheaded (Jan. 21, 1793). *I am sorry it was necessary.*"

Taken altogether it is clear that the object aimed at by the Society of United Irishmen was well summed up by Tone in his phrase : " *the establishment of the Rights of Man in Ireland.*"

Tone and the Catholic Committee

Before Tone took up his work with the Catholic Committee it had undergone an internal revolution. Tired of the timid, cringing policy of the Catholic lords and ecclesiastics who, till then, had dominated its counsels and dictated its policy, a wealthy Dublin merchant, JOHN KEOGH, advocated a bolder course. He proposed an Address to Parliament direct, calling attention to Catholic grievances, and demanding redress as a *right*.

The peers were horrified ; the bishops were scandalised; timid laymen predicted every calamity. Tone compares the struggle to the victorious uprising of the Third Estate in France :

> " Their peers, their gentry (as they affect to call themselves), and their prelates, either seduced by the Government or intimidated, gave the measure all possible opposition. At length, after a long conflict . . . the question was decided on a division by a majority of at least six to one in favour of the intended application."

The defeated Catholic aristocrats and prelates withdrew. Timid as hares in the face of English authority, they were raging lions against the " mutinous " Catholic laymen. When the Committee's petition was presented to Parliament (with a supporting petition from the United Irishmen of Belfast) it was confronted with a counter-petition from the seceders denying the right of the Committee to speak for the Catholic community. Reactionaries in Parliament were delighted to have so plausible an excuse for rejecting the plea with studied insult.

On Tone's advice the Committee adopted a plan to secure a properly representative Committee. Delegates elected by parishes would meet to elect county and town representatives who when assembled in Dublin would be in effect a " Parliament " of the Catholics of Ireland.

The Reactionaries fell into a panic. Led by Lord Chancellor JOHN FITZGIBBON, Earl of Clare (a rancorous bigot and anti-democrat), all the Judges on Circuit laboured mightily to induce all the Grand Juries to adopt resolutions denouncing the scheme. The Catholic bishops, alarmed, added their condemnation ; parish priests followed suit.

Again acting on Tone's advice, the Committee sent its most influential members to tour the provinces, to win over bishops, priests, and laymen to the project. Tone himself, who had toured Ulster to gain support for the United Irishmen, now toured Leinster, Connacht, and parts of Ulster to secure support for the Catholic Convention; generally with John Keogh. So well did they work that the bishops withdrew their ban, the priests came over, and the elections proceeded with enthusiasm.

To us, delegate conventions are commonplace things ; in the autumn of 1792 they were " portents dire ".— In fact the very name " Convention ", which popular usage fastened upon the assembly, underlines the fact that, while the delegates were being elected in Ireland, the NATIONAL CONVENTION was being elected in France. For world-background the Catholic Convention had— the upsurge of the Jacobin Republic in France, the storming of the Tuileries, the purging of the prisons, the rush of the conscript levies to clear the frontiers, the cannonade at Valmy; and all to the crashing rhythms of the *Carmagnole* and the *Marseillaise*.

A passage in Tone's diary, though expressed in terms of jest, gives a revealing glimpse of the public excitement engendered by the discussions, public and private, incidental to the elections of delegates to the Convention :

"Nov. 9th '92. At court [i.e. the Four Courts, Dublin]. Wonderful to see the rapid change in the minds of the Bar on the Catholic question. Some for an immediate abolition of all penal laws. Certainly the most magnanimous mode and the wisest. All sorts of men, and especially lawyer Plunkett [afterwards Irish Lord Chancellor] take a pleasure in girding at Mr. Hutton [Tone] '*who takes at once all their seven points in his buckler, thus.*' Exceeding good laughing. Mr. Hutton called *Marat*. Sundry barristers apply to him for protection in the approaching rebellion. Lawyer Plunkett applies for Carton [the Duke of Leinster's country seat, near Maynooth]. Mr. Hutton refuses inasmuch as the Duke of Leinster* is his friend, but offers him Curraghmore [the Marquis of Waterford's seat]. This he does to have a rise out of Marcus Beresford [brother of the Marquess] who is at his elbow listening. Great laughter thereat. The Committee charged with causing the non-consumption agreement against Bellingham beer. Mr. Hutton at the risk of his life asserts the said charge to be a falsehood ! Valiant ! All declare their satisfaction thereat ! Everything looks as well as possible. Huzza ! " †

And again the next day, without jesting :

"Hear that Government is very much embarrassed what to do . . . The Chancellor talks big. If he attempts to use violent measures I believe a

---

* *Duke of Leinster :* elder brother of Lord Edward Fitzgerald, and cousin to Charles James Fox.

† Tone's diary was written for the information and amusement of his family-circle,—his wife, his sister, and his friend Russell. The name " John Hutton " was a family joke ; the real owner of that name being a coachbuilder, a trade rival of Tone's father.

war will be the inevitable consequence. My own conviction is that the Government must *concede*."

The Catholic Convention

On the day appointed (Dec. 3rd, '92) 244 delegates assembled : representing every county in Ireland, forty large provincial towns, and the City of Dublin. No assembly even nearly so representative had met in Ireland since the " Patriot " Parliament of 1689.

The spirit of the assembly was in proportion. The first resolution declared the Convention " the sole body competent to voice the opinions of Catholic Ireland." After this repudiation of the aristocratic and ecclesiastical seceders, the Convention settled down to debate the kind of petition to be adopted. It was decided to have done with all half-measures and demand, boldly, that Catholics should be restored to a " position of equality with Protestants ".

The next question was : to whom should the petition be presented ? Amid thunderous applause, a delegate proposed to pass over all the " middlemen " and present the petition to the King himself. A query was raised whether this course might not be deemed " disrespectful to the Administration ". Amid redoubled enthusiasm the mover answered : " It is intended to be so." The proposal was adopted unanimously.

A delegation was appointed to carry the petition to the King ; and then, before adjourning, the Convention first adopted and approved a *Vindication of the Catholic Committee* drafted by Tone, and then carried a unanimous vote of thanks *to the citizens of Belfast*, " to whom," said a delegate, " we owe it that we meet here in safety."

This was no figure of speech ; and it was more than a formal compliment to the contingent of Belfast Volunteers who had mounted guard over the Convention. It was a recognition that it was the resolute attitude of Belfast, led by the United Irishmen, which alone had

prevented the Chancellor from attempting " violent
measures ".

The Catholic Relief Act (1793)

Tone accompanied the delegation to the King. The
state of the winds and tides induced the delegates to
travel *via* Donaghadee and Stranraer. This entailed
passing through Belfast, and there they met a royal
reception. Met at the City boundary, they were entertained at the leading hotel, and then escorted on their
way amid enthusiastic plaudits from all the democrats
in Belfast. The horses were removed, and wealthy
merchants vied with artizans in competition for places at
the drag-ropes. At the boundary they were sped on
their way with cheers and loud wishes for their
success.

Belfast is often enjoined to " Remember 1690". *Wm War*
When it again recovers a pride in *remembering* 1792,
Ireland's day of final deliverance will be at hand.

Arrived in London the delegates would not allow
themselves to be swayed from their purpose. They saw
the King, were " received graciously ", and returned
convinced they had not had their work for nothing.
They were right. They had barely reached Dublin again
when the Viceroy informed Parliament that the King
" recommended a consideration of the situation of the
Roman Catholics ". The English Government, fore-
seeing war with France, had decided to force the hands
of the Irish Administration.

Grudgingly the Administration gave way ; but even
then they wriggled out of conceding the complete
emancipation which would have been " both magnanimous and wise ". By backstairs methods they induced
Keogh and a majority of the Committee to accept less
than " equality with Protestants ".

Tone was so furious that he nearly broke with Keogh.
He gave in at last—there was no help for it—and

contented himself with noting in his diary : " Merchants, I see, make bad revolutionaries."

With all its faults the CATHOLIC RELIEF ACT (1793) remains the largest single instalment of emancipation ever gained for the Catholics of Ireland. It virtually swept away all that was left of the Penal Code, except that, while it conceded the vote, it denied Catholics the right to sit in Parliament and to enter the higher grades of the law, the Civil Service, the Army and Navy. Incidentally it also removed the Sacramental test which had banned Dissenters as well as Catholics from public service. It coupled every concession, it is true, with petty restrictions ; but on the whole it gave so much relief that Keogh and the Committee felt satisfied they had got as much as it was reasonable to expect at one blow.

Before it finally adjourned the Committee voted £1,500 and a gold medal to Tone as a mark of esteem and gratitude for his invaluable help.

Tone was greatly pleased. But he would have been more pleased still if they had stood out to the last and made a fight of it.

CHAPTER EIGHT

THE WAR UPON THE UNITED IRISHMEN

N February, 1793, before the Catholic Relief Act became
law, WAR WAS DECLARED WITH THE FRENCH REPUBLIC.
The Government took this as a chance to wage war
also with the United Irishmen. As a result, the Society
was (May, 1794) proclaimed illegal and driven " underground". TONE was driven into exile. Open counter-
revolution made its appearance with the ORANGE
SOCIETY (Sept., 1795).

This chapter describes the stages of this struggle.

The Programme of Reaction

The chance to declare war upon France (created by
the execution of Louis XVI, Jan. 21st, 1793) was also
a chance for the counter-revolutionary bigots in the
Administration, with their hangers-on, to obtain revenge
for the concessions they had been forced to make to the
Catholics. The English Prime Minister WILLIAM PITT
(1759-1806) favoured a policy of winning the well-to-do
Catholics by concessions; but wartime exigencies
compelled him to allow the " Protestant Ascendancy "
bigots at the head of the Irish Administration a much
freer hand than he would otherwise have done. This
faction saw their chance to achieve their old end by a
different road. By treating the United Irishmen and
their allies as a " desperate *Jacobin* conspiracy " to be
repressed at all costs, they hoped to win from the *fears*
of the Catholic property-owners all that Pitt hoped to
gain from their *gratitude* and *expectations*.

The risk involved in this policy was that the United
Irishmen, till then a constitutional party, would become
in fact what the Government alleged they were—a

JACOBIN CONSPIRACY—and this is what resulted. In the
end, as we shall see, Pitt had to come to the rescue of the
Irish Administration.

The Administration foreshadowed its programme in
three Bills introduced concurrently with the debates
on the Catholic Relief Act : (1) a CONVENTION ACT
(2) an ARMS ACT and (3) a MILITIA ACT.

The first, which made all *assemblies of delegates* illegal
was designed to prevent the United Irishmen and the
progressive Catholics from developing a political party
by organising the newly emancipated Catholic voters
The second, by prohibiting the importation, manufacture
and sale of arms and gunpowder, was designed to
cripple in advance any attempt at insurrection. The
third was designed to provide a counter-revolutionary
force with which to suppress any movement by the
Volunteers or similar bodies. In this way all further
advance by the United Irishmen was to be barred.

The Convention Act and the Volunteers

The Convention Act was prompted in part by the
great success of the Catholic Convention ; but it was
also prompted by a fear of a repetition of the historic
Dungannon (Volunteer) Convention of '82.

While the elections for the Catholic Convention were
proceeding there had been notable signs of a Volunteer
revival and of a movement towards re-creating '82 on
a more radical plane.

As we have noted, there was, after the abortive Convention of 1783, a rapid decline in the numbers and
significance of the Volunteers. The aristocrats and
gentry who had commanded, and, in some cases,
maintained corps of Volunteers, their end having been
attained in '82, grew conservative thereafter ; and, as
far as possible, put an end to Volunteering and parading.
The more popular corps which survived underwent a
social change, as the more aristocratic officers and the

more moderate members withdrew, and their places were taken by more democratic-bourgeois officers and a more plebeian rank and file. Grattan expressed the change forcibly : the Volunteers, he said, had been the ' *armed property* " of Ireland : they were fast becoming its " *armed beggary* ".

There were, it is true, still a *Lawyers'* corps in Dublin and *Merchants'* Corps in both Dublin and Belfast. But Grattan's point was made by the fact that these ' respectable " corps held together expressly to provide a counter-poise against such non-respectable corps as Tandy's famous Dublin Artillery.

The outbreak of the French Revolution and the rise of the United Irishmen prompted somewhat of a revival in Volunteering in Belfast and Dublin. Many corps in other parts which had been in a state of suspended animation showed signs of reviving when, in September, 1792, NAPPER TANDY supported by TONE and others recruited a new corps in Dublin, frankly modelled on the French " National Guard ". The uniform adopted was similar, except that dark green was used instead of blue, and a " National " cockade of *green* replaced the French tricolour. The buttons bore a *cap of Liberty on a pike*.

The new corps set an example the other Dublin corps followed. It refused to parade, decorated with *orange* ribbons, at William III's statue on November 4. Instead, all corps held an ordinary parade at their customary meeting-places, where, after discussion, it was agreed to hold a ceremonial parade a week later in honour of the French victories of Valmy and Jemappes. Citizens were also asked to illuminate their windows in honour of the occasion. The United Irishmen, for the same night, called a meeting to adopt an address of congratulation to the French Republic, and an address of exhortation to the Volunteers.

By a proclamation (in which penalties were threatened

to all " seditious " associations) the parade and th
meeting were both prohibited. The Authorities coul
not prevent the citizens from illuminating their window
—which most of them did—and the United Irishme
held a " private " meeting in a Volunteer drill hall a
which the Address to the Volunteers was read.

The central point of this Address (which to the scanda
of all reactionaries opened with the words ' CITIZE
SOLDIERS ') was a reminder to the Volunteers of th
momentous consequences which had followed th
Dungannon Convention of Feb. 15, 1782:

> " The 15th of February approaches, a day eve
> memorable in the annals of the country as th
> birthday of a New Ireland. Let parochial meeting
> be held as soon as possible. Let each parish retur
> delegates. Let the sense of Ulster be again declare
> from Dungannon, on a day auspicious to Union
> Peace, and Freedom, and the Spirit of the Nort
> will again become the Spirit of the Nation . .
> Fourteen long years have elapsed since the rise o
> your Associations [1778] and in 1782 did yo
> imagine that in 1792 this Nation would still remai
> unrepresented ? How many Nations in this interva
> have gotten the start of Ireland ? "

For the publication of this Address the Chairma
(WILLIAM DRENNAN) and the Secretary (ARCHIBALI
HAMILTON ROWAN) were both prosecuted on a charg
of " sedition ". Their trials were, however, postponed
they did not take place until more than a year later.

Meanwhile the anxiety of the Authorities was deepene
by this call to revive the Volunteer agitation of 1782
A Convention, not confined to volunteers, but electe
by parishes, did, in fact, assemble at Dungannon on th
historic date. Being a Sunday all the delegates—Catholics
Dissenters, and Episcopalians—attended the paris
church and heard a sermon of cordial welcome an
spirited exhortation from the rector of Dungannon

Next day the Convention assembled, and, after deliberating, issued a call for an All-Ireland Convention.

It was then that the Authorities introduced the CONVENTION ACT and rushed it into law.

The Suppression of the Volunteers

When the Government had secured, along with the Arms Act, an augmentation of its Army from England, it proceeded to the next step—the suppression of the Volunteers.

Here the United Irishmen were patently caught napping. They had called the Volunteers, rhetorically, " to arms ! " But they had made no preparations for doing so, in fact. Hence their position fell to a Governmental assault without a blow.

The Dublin Volunteer Corps all received (without warning) a peremptory order to deliver their cannon and stores of powder and ball to the Government " for safe keeping ". The result was described by Henry Grattan, Junior, in a single, sufficient sentence :

> " The Government seized by surprise the Artillery of the *Liberty Corps*, made a private arrangement by which it got possession of that of the *Merchants' Corps ;* and induced the *Lawyers' Corps* to give up theirs—first making a public procession before they were surrendered."

Dublin being thus disposed of, it was the turn of Belfast. On the afternoon of Saturday, March 9, 1793, parties of the English dragoon-regiments stationed in nearby camps swarmed into Belfast. Being ostensibly off-duty they made, first of all, for the taverns. Then, refreshed, they dispersed through the town in small parties and began to attack everything they thought offensive. Shop signs with the heads of BENJAMIN FRANKLIN and GEORGE WASHINGTON, and anything *green* in any window, each and all provoked a furious assault. It was apparent that the dragoons were provided with

H

lists of the addresses of leading United Irishmen. Their homes, and the printing-office of the *Northern Star*, were attacked without scruple. Eventually the military rioters retired to the taverns for the night.

A town's meeting, hastily summoned, assembled at daybreak with the local Volunteers under arms as a guard. A collison between the dragoons and the Volunteers was averted by the arrival of the officer commanding the Dragoon Regiment. He agreed to march off the dragoons if the Volunteers were similarly withdrawn.

The Mayor sent protests to the Government and to the military authorities ; but he got no sort of satisfaction. In succeeding weeks several renewals of the rioting occurred, including another attack on the *Northern Star*. The Mayor, protesting again, told the Government that the homes of leading citizens would have suffered " serious outrage " if they had not been guarded by Volunteers. The Government replied by suggesting, with brazen impudence, that the Volunteers had caused all the trouble. It removed all troops from the vicinity of Belfast ; but it also ordered the Volunteers to *surrender their arms and disband*. One " respectable " corps protested that this was hard usage after their zeal in protecting a noble lord's eviction party which regular troops had refused to guard. But, as they were not prepared for an armed struggle with the authorities, all the Belfast corps submitted. They were disarmed and disbanded. So ended the Volunteers.

The Resistance to Militia Conscription

The Militia Act empowered the Government to raise a force of 15,000 men by the method then practised in England—the method of drawing lots, called " balloting ".

Even if the war had been popular, this highly haphazard method of selection would have excited protests.

Great hardship was inflicted when breadwinners were taken away without compensation to their helpless dependants. As it was, with the peasants' sympathy wholly on the side of the French, resentment, protest, and resistance were almost universal.

The officers, too, were all drawn from the local Protestant landlords, squireens, and rack-renting middle-men. Nothing would persuade the peasants otherwise than that the balloting was faked to make the lots fall upon those who had been boldest in defying these local tyrants; particularly in respect of electing delegates to the Catholic Committee, which these tyrants had tried to prevent. Once in the militia, it was believed, these victims would be spirited away to " Botany Bay".

The very fact that they were to be called upon to fight the French was a grievance. Like themselves, the French were Catholics and a peasant people. That these French Catholic peasants had stormed, looted, and burned their landlords' chateaux, and chased the landlords from the country, might horrify London or Dublin Castle. It was glorious news for the Irish peasant, in whom each fresh French revolutionary " outrage " excited mounting admiration and envy.

Resistance to conscription became general. Regular military operations were required to break up the bands of peasants who took to the hills and defended themselves with desperate courage.

In Sligo, large companies forced their way into the homes of the gentry, took all the arms they could find, and drank " success to the French " in the gentry's own wine. Pitched battles were fought at Ballinafad, Sligo; at Enniskillen, Fermanagh; and at Athboy, Meath; in which latter place the troops were beaten up. In Wexford, conscripts were rescued by force, and the rescuers themselves were attacked and dispersed with many killed.

Near Baltinglass, Wicklow, the assembled peasants

sent notice to the military-magistrate that his quota
of conscripts was waiting for him to collect them—
if he *cared to take the risks entailed.* He "prudently
declined to obey the requisition".

The resistance was overcome after months of struggle,
partly by terrorism, partly by concessions. The commander of the troops, Lord Carhampton, the head of
the Luttrell family—whose surname was a synonym for
treachery among the Irish—led the way in trying the
captured peasants by "courts martial" composed of
the local gentry and squireens at which scores were
sentenced, in defiance of all law, to terms of penal
service in the King's Navy. The victims had no
chance of legal assistance; they were flung in irons, into
wagons, carted to the seaports, and put on board a
man-of-war before they, or anybody, knew where they
were going. Once entered upon the ship's books, and
there was, in practice, no remedy. At a later date
Parliament obliged with an Act of Indemnity absolving
Lord Carhampton from the consequences of his barbarous illegalities.

Combined with coercion went concessions. Men
with dependants were excused service; a fund was
subscribed by the gentry to provide a bonus for every
volunteer; the pay, and the dependants' allowance,
were both increased. Gradually the resistance subsided,
and the militia became embodied.

The United Irishmen and the Defenders

During this minor civil war in the West and parts of
the South, it seemed evident to the Administration that
the peasants' resistance was such as presupposed an
organised leadership and direction. An understanding
of the peasantry and their point of view would have
forced the obvious inference that this was ready to hand
in the "Whiteboy" quasi-freemasonry of the countryside and the survival of clan-traditions. But an under-

standing of the peasants' point of view was as alien to the mentality and conventions of Dublin Castle as an understanding of the point of view of the Australian blackfellows was, at that date, to a Police Commissioner newly-arrived in Botany Bay. Authority jumped to the conclusion that the peasants' resistance was directed either by " the French " or by the United Irishmen. A House of Lords Committee was set up to fish for evidence, and several fierce legal tussles with the United Irishmen resulted.

Actually there was, at this date, very little connection between the United Irishmen—whose organisation was primarily located in the towns—and the self-contained, historically-evolved, peasants' secret-societies. Such contacts as there were had arisen quite casually as incidental by-products of the organisation of the elections of delegates to the Catholic Committee ; and where they had arisen they had been of a totally different character from what the Authorities wished to suppose.

There had been, for example, bickering between Catholic and Protestant peasants in Co. Armagh, which had evolved into a feud between rival sectarian agrarian organisations in Armagh and Down, before the Society of United Irishmen was founded. It had arisen, in Armagh, through an influx of Catholic tenant-farmers seeking an escape from land-hungry Connacht. The newcomers, acting in ignorance, had rented farms which Protestants had abandoned rather than pay the increased rents and the exorbitant " fines " demanded for the renewals of leases. The action of the Catholic newcomers was resented as " black-legging "—as a breach of the traditional code of honour of the peasantry.

This dispute had been adjusted with satisfaction all round ; but it had lasted long enough to give local bigots an excuse for attacking Catholic farmers not implicated in the original dispute, and raiding their farms under a pretext of searching for concealed arms.

This practice spread from Co. Armagh into Co. Down; and from their habit of making their raids at break of day, the Protestant terrorists came to be known as Peep-of-Day Boys. Soon the Catholics responded with a counter organisation, the "*Defenders*," who, being unable, legally, to buy arms, took a leaf out of their enemies' book and raided the homes of the gentry to procure arms.

So far we have a notable example of how, in special circumstances, a spontaneously-arising defence-organisation of the peasantry—which, normally, would make for solidarity and mutual aid throughout the whole countryside—becomes differentiated into a bitter antagonism of rival organisations. To understand its further development there must be borne in mind the generally disturbing and antagonising effect produced by the *middlemen* who, intervening between the landlord at the top and the actual tiller at the bottom, imposed upon the latter conditions of increasing insecurity and fierce competition for good farming land. Needless to say, the more embittered the strife between Catholic and Protestant peasants—the more ready each side became to disregard the old "Whiteboy" code and bid against each other for farms—the better pleased these middlemen *squireens* became. The more often the farms changed hands the more they profited. Analysed to the bottom, the root cause of the feud between Peep-of-Day boys and Defenders is found in *the middlemen*, and in the spread of their disintegrating rapacity from 1778 onwards. There can be no possible doubt that these *squireens* more than once revived the feud deliberately when it had lapsed and when, if left to itself, it would have died out. We shall have a classic example of this to deal with shortly. Here we note an instance of the opposite kind produced by the intervention of the United Irishmen and the Catholic leaders.

While engaged in organising the elections for the Catholic Committee, Tone and Keogh came upon a local feud between Defenders and Peep-of-Day Boys in County Down into which the local gentry had been drawn on both sides. They were able to induce both sides to agree to join in forming a Volunteer Corps which would act impartially to repress every would-be disturber of the peace. Urged forward by the United Irishmen and the Catholic leaders acting in conjunction, the policy had a striking success. In one place Peep-of-Day Boys supplied a drill sergeant to teach the Defenders how to handle their weapons. In another place the situation was reversed—the Catholics lent their weapons to the Protestants and stood by applauding while a Catholic drill-sergeant put them through their exercises.

The success of the policy was so great in Ulster that the irreconcilables had to go outside of Ulster into County Louth to keep the feud alive. And when Defender organisations sprang up in Louth, the Authorities took a hand in the game by prosecuting their leaders under the Whiteboy Acts.

At this point only did the Authorities find any evidence connecting the United Irishmen with the illegal side of the Defenders' activity. NAPPER TANDY, himself a Co. Louth man, was called upon for consultation by the Louth Defenders. But before they would divulge any details they made him take their customary oath of secrecy. This, under the Whiteboy Act, made him liable to the penalty of hanging. And in May, 1793, Tandy learned, in the nick of time, that a Government informer had sworn information against him on this ground, and that a warrant for his arrest had been issued. Tandy had only just time to get on board a ship and escape to the Continent.

The Society of United Irishmen Suppressed

By the beginning of 1794 the Authorities were

ready—and eager—to suppress the United Irishmen by force. The Society up to this point had confined itself to the advocacy of Parliamentary reform ; and, although it was a fairly open secret that some of the leaders of the Society hoped to use a reformed Parliament, when gained, as a base from which to struggle for separation from England, this was not, in itself, a ground for legal proceedings.

Nor was the fact that the members of the Society were all sympathisers with the French and hostile to the conduct and continuance of the war. To a milder degree the Whigs, led in England by Fox and in Ireland by Grattan, were also French sympathisers hostile to the Government's foreign policy, and they also advocated Parliamentary Reform, though not favouring the radical-democratic reform advocated by the United Irishmen.

Tone regarded the Whigs as rather more to be despised than " the common prostitutes of the Treasury Bench " and their supporters. They limited the Government's freedom of action somewhat, but they hampered much more the United Irishmen's freedom of opposition. The Government had secured the Convention Act with Whig aid ; and this prevented the Society from developing from the stage of an aggregation of local societies into a unified national political organisation. And the Government had secured, also with Whig aid, the Arms Act and the Militia with which to thwart anything in the nature of an insurrection. The Government thought it safe, therefore, to proceed to a legal persecution of the leaders of the United Irishmen.

In January, 1794, they at last proceeded to put Hamilton Rowan upon his trial for the " Citizen Soldiers " Address to the Volunteers—the trial of William Drennan being still further postponed.

Rowan was defended by the greatest popular advocate then living, JOHN PHILPOT CURRAN. Born in Munster, a descendant of a planted Cromwellian soldier, Curran from the poverty of his family circumstances had associated on familiar terms with the Catholic peasants, farmers, and shop-keepers since childhood. Though, for the reason indicated, Curran would be classed by " racialists " as of *English* descent, his physique, features, eloquence, wit, and the general cast of his mind made him stand out as a Gael among the Gaels. Through the whole of the terrors of the time upon which we are entering, no man's name stands out with a greater lustre, for fearless steadfastness in the teeth of every terror, than that of Curran—unless it be the name of Tone himself.

Curran's defence of Hamilton Rowan was a magnificent effort ; and, though it availed nothing with a carefully hand-picked jury, it ensured that, thereafter, no State trial was complete without Curran leading for the defence.

Found guilty of sedition, Rowan was sentenced to a heavy fine and to two years' imprisonment.

Rowan had been convicted of " publishing " the Address by reading it to an assembly of Volunteers (among whom it had been circulated as a leaflet). The desire of the Government to shackle the press was shown when they elected to proceed against Drennan on a charge of " procuring its publication " in a Dublin newspaper. The proprietors and printers of the *Northern Star* were also prosecuted, at the same time, for publishing the same address. A conviction was secured (May, 1794) against the printer of the *Northern Star*, but the jury refused to find a verdict against Drennan.

It was on the eve of these press-prosecutions that the Government passed to the direct suppression of the United Irishmen. On May 4, 1794, a party of soldiers, headed by one of Dublin's military magistrates, forced their way into the Tailors' Hall, in Back Lane, the regular meeting-place of the Dublin United Irishmen, and ordered the meeting then proceeding to disperse. All papers were seized, and the building was retained in military occupation. A proclamation was issued suppressing the Dublin Society, and the Attorney General announced in Parliament that any similar association anywhere in Ireland would be dealt with in the same way. He charged the United Irishmen categorically with "treasonable association with the King's enemies".

The evidence on which this charge was based had been secured a week earlier by the arrest of the Rev. WILLIAM JACKSON and his valet-associate COCKAYNE.

Jackson, a clergyman of the Church of Ireland, had been domiciled in Paris from before the Revolution. He had been present at a meeting in Paris attended by all the well-to-do Englishmen, Scots, and Irishmen then resident in Paris—which meeting applauded the setting up of a Republic in France, and applauded also the offer of the National Convention to move to the aid of any people struggling to attain their freedom. Jackson had come from this meeting all agog to discover how far the peoples of England and of Ireland respectively would welcome a French Army coming to their aid.

Whether he had or had not a commission from the French Foreign Office is not known. What is known is that Pitt's secret service was so good that he knew of Jackson's trip from before his landing in England, and had planted Cockayne, one of his agents, in Jackson's path. Jackson fell for Cockayne's hard-luck story, and took him with him to Ireland as his secretary-valet.

In Ireland Jackson sought out the leading United Irishmen and asked their opinions. Tone, at first, would have nothing to do with him; but, finding him trusted by others, including Hamilton Rowan (who was allowed to have all the visitors he pleased in prison) Tone agreed to draft a memorial on the state of Ireland.

In it Tone emphasised the complete contrast between England and Ireland :

"Any invasion of England would unite all ranks in opposition to the invader. . . . The Government of Ireland is only to be looked upon as a government of force; the moment a superior force appears it would tumble at once as founded neither in the interests nor the affections of the people."

A copy of this memorial was despatched by Jackson (through Cockayne) to an address in London, with instructions to forward it to a banker in Hamburg—whom Pitt knew to be in touch with agents of the French Republic. It was this intercepted despatch which was the basis of the charge against Jackson personally and also against the United Irishmen generally.

A week after the raid on the Dublin United Irishmen, the English Government swooped down upon THOMAS HARDY, HORNE TOOKE, and the other leaders of the English " Jacobin " Societies.

The news of the " discovery " of treasonable communications between the United Irishmen and the French Jacobins created a state of public excitement bordering upon panic-hysteria. Reactionaries howled for blood; faint-hearts began to fall away from the United ranks. Hamilton Rowan bribed his gaoler and escaped to France. John Reynolds, a leader of the Ulster Freemasons and a member of the United Irishmen—who had, incautiously, entertained Jackson and introduced him to others—also fled the country. The leading Whigs—Grattan it is sad to say among them—begged Keogh and the Catholic Committee to sever their connection with their deeply-compromised agent, Tone.

Greatly to their credit Keogh and the Catholic Committee refused: Tone, in his memoirs, records his undying gratitude. There can be no question that if

the Catholic Committee had cast him off, Tone's lif
would not have been worth a twelve months' purchase
While he remained the salaried agent of the Catholi
Committee (whom the Government desired to placate
he was safe at any rate from arrest on suspicion.

Here the Irish Administration was influenced by
political change in England. Faced with continue
failure abroad—the continued military success of th
French at the expense of the Allies—and with dangerou
opposition at home, WILLIAM PITT had decided t
broaden the base of his administration by making a
alliance with the moderate Whigs who followed th
lead of the Duke of PORTLAND. This left Fox and th
anti-war Whigs reduced to a small faction, unabl
seriously to resist the Government.

As the price of their support, the Portland Whig
demanded the direction of Irish affairs ; and a new
Viceroy, Earl FITZWILLIAM, an ardent reformer, wa
sent across to initiate a new policy of moderate reform
based on conciliating the Catholics, and admitting then
to Parliament. In this way it was hoped to make
breach between the Catholics and the " Jacobin "
United Irishmen, and to establish with Catholic suppor
a new, moderate, Whig Administration of which Grattai
would be the head.

This scheme included, however, an important detail
which proved its undoing. To make room for the
new Administration, the " old gang "—the clique of
Fitzgibbons and Beresfords who made patronage unde
the Administration a family preserve for years—had
to be cleared out, not only to create vacancies, and to
effect the transfer of authority, but because this clique
was the directing centre of the most virulent Protestant-
Ascendancy bigotry in Ireland.

Infuriated at the threat to his Party's places and power,
Fitzgibbon, the Earl of Clare, slipped secretly to England, where he so worked upon the King and the inner

Court-clique that George III's Protestant religious mania was inflamed; and, using this as a convenient tool, the clique forced Pitt and Portland to retreat.

The Catholic Relief Bill (which would have completed the work accomplished in 1793) was withdrawn; Fitzwilliam was recalled; Clare and the Beresfords were re-established; and Grattan was permanently excluded from all hope of office. Ireland was handed back, without reserve, to the rabid counter-revolutionary faction; while Pitt, for his part, began, from that moment, to concert plans for the Union he saw to be the only alternative to the overthrow of the " old gang " by a democratic-republican upheaval from below.

Fitzwilliam's régime had never actually been instituted. It had lasted nominally from the beginning of July, 1794, to the middle of March, 1795; but while it had lasted, the drive of repression against the United Irishmen had been virtually suspended. As Fitzwilliam departed, so the drive began again.

Jackson was put on trial on April 24th. In part, the delay in bringing him to trial had been due to the Government's hope that he would turn informer and directly incriminate Tone, against whom they had only hearsay evidence. When this hope failed Jackson's conviction followed as a matter of course from the evidence of the English informer, Cockayne. He made a dramatic exit by dropping dead in the dock (having taken poison) before the Judge could sentence him.

With Jackson convicted, Tone's position became untenable; and, accordingly, he accepted as a compromise (negotiated, it would seem, by Grattan) the proposal to go voluntarily into exile. Six weeks after Jackson's conviction, Tone and his family sailed from Ireland for the United States.

The Orange Society Founded

The Fitzwilliam episode taught the more corrupt and

reactionary strata of the Governing caste that it was
faced with a double danger. It was threatened in
front by the rising wave of democratic-republican
enthusiasm stirred up by the United Irishmen and the
Catholic Committee in alliance—an enthusiasm which
imperilled this caste along with the whole body of the
landed oligarchy and gentry. But it was no less
threatened by the proposals of the English Moderate-
Whigs to stave off this frontal attack by concessions
to the upper stratum of the Catholic Community, since it
was with *their* political privileges, and with the places
of profit *they* had hitherto monopolised, that the English
" Liberals " proposed to buy over the wealthier and
more moderate Catholics.

English Whigs proposed to break up the popular
unity by buying over the wealthier Catholics ; the
threatened Castle clique retorted by stirring up the more
ignorant, debased, corrupt, and reactionary stratum of
the Protestants to create disunity and disturbance under
a pretence of zeal for the Protestant religion.

Under the influence of the United Irishmen, sectarian
divisions were fast being replaced in Ulster by political
unity ; and, inspired by this, the more Catholic provinces
were responding with public-spirited zeal. The last
weapon left to the reaction was the traditional fear of
the Papacy and hostility to the Catholic religion, which
was strongest in the social strata, and the location where
zeal for republican-democracy was greatest, namely,
among the Dissenters. In Ulster, therefore, and among
the most ignorantly prejudiced, the most corrupt, and
the most debased of all classes of the Protestant population, the Castle clique sought and found a weapon
against the United Irishmen.

As we have seen, County Armagh, where the population was fairly evenly divided between the sects, had
been for years the scene of sporadic faction fighting
between Peep-of-Day Boys and Catholic Defenders.

This had died down to nothing under the influence of United Irish agitation. When the "pro-Catholic" Fitzwilliam was appointed Viceroy, the Peep-of-Day Boys suddenly resumed activity *after nearly two years of quiescence*. It is impossible to miss the connection between this fact and the lie deliberately circulated by the Clare-Beresford faction—that Fitzwilliam was coming to replace Protestant ascendancy with Catholic ascendancy. And if this point could have been missed it would have been made clear when the most reactionary Protestant magistrates in County Armagh took advantage of these renewed disturbances to search Catholic homes for "*seditious literature*". The Peep-of-Day Boys took the hint and began again to "search" Catholic homes for "concealed arms". That it was now legal for Catholics to possess arms did not trouble the Peep-of-Day Boys.

Soon the Defenders' organisation was again in action, beating off Protestant attacks; and every successful defence, trumpeted abroad as a "Catholic outrage", brought a fresh magistrates' search for evidences of "sedition" followed by a spread of anti-Catholic violence to areas previously peaceful. In a few weeks a regular *pogrom* was in full swing in Armagh and the counties adjoining. The victims, fleeing from their burning homes, spread panic all through Catholic Ireland.

The motive actuating this "Protestant" villainy became unmistakable when it was seen that it was the most improved farms, on the best land, which were first attacked, and whose occupants were first offered the alternative of "Hell or Connacht". Poor and struggling Catholic farmers scratching a living from a stony hill-top farm rarely, if ever, excited Protestant zeal even in the heart of Antrim. To this day the richer soil in the valley-bottoms in Eastern Ulster is Protestant to the last half-acre while Catholics survive on every barren hill-top.

This artificially worked-up *pogrom* culminated, o
September 21st, 1795, in an incident—the " battle o
the Diamond "—which has taken a front place i
Orange mythology ever since.

The myth-version is that a body of " peaceful '
Protestants was set upon by a multitude of " cowardly '
Catholics whom the brave Protestants routed witl
great slaughter. The truth, vouched for by contem
porary *Protestant* testimony, is that a semi-secret assembl
of Catholics in the hills was sniped persistently b
Protestant sharpshooters ; that this brought on desul
tory fighting, which continued off and on for severa
days, but was ended on the joint intervention of ;
Protestant magistrate and a Catholic priest.

The Catholics, it should be noted, were almos
entirely unarmed, while the Protestants were an organised and armed force.

Just as peace had been concluded, and the Protestants
were formed up ready to march away, a new body of
Catholics arrived, hastening to the aid of their fellow-
Catholics. These newcomers, misunderstanding the
situation, attacked the Protestants and had suffered some
loss before the situation could be explained to them and
the incident brought to an end.

Peace was restored. But that same night a body of
magistrates, squires, squireens, and parsons in County
Armagh met together and formed the Mother Lodge
of the Orange Society. Under a pretext of zeal for
law, order, and the Protestant religion an oath-bound
secret society on the Masonic model was organised,
which, in practice, proved a fomenting centre, as well
as a cloak of protection, for the organised knavery into
which the Peep-of-Day Boys had degenerated. The
Orange Order became an organised conspiracy of all
the most degenerate reactionaries of every social strata—
an instrument whereby the *lumpen* strata were used as
tools to break up the solidarity engendered by the

United Irishmen, and to replace the struggle for democratic advance by disintegrating it into an embittered war of sect against sect, from which the only ones to profit were the Clare-Beresford clique in Dublin Castle and their hangers-on of every social grade.

In evaluating the Orange Society it must not be forgotten that the bodies it was founded to disrupt and destroy—the United Irishmen and the Defenders—functioned, the one as a great liberating force, and the other as a tenants' protection league and an agrarian trade union. The Orange lodges functioned as a " union-smashing " force, operating in the interest of an oligarchical clique threatened with overthrow by a revolutionary-democratic advance. They constituted the first " Fascist " body known in history.

CHAPTER NINE

" THE FRENCH ARE IN THE BAY "

The key moves in the Anglo-Irish struggle from the end of 1795 to the end of 1797 all centred around the endeavour of WOLFE TONE to secure a successful *French landing* in Ireland. The counter-moves of the Irish Administration were aimed primarily at smashing up the *underground organisation* of the United Irishmen, and making it impossible for them to co-operate effectively with a French invasion. This chapter deals in detail with TONE's MISSION IN FRANCE and with the Administration's DRAGOONING OF ULSTER.

Wolfe Tone in France

Before he sailed for America, TONE's mind was made up : he was determined to get from France the arms, officers, and military support necessary to ensure success for an Irish insurrection. His friends (Russell, T. A. Emmet, and others) were warmly in agreement. On Cave Hill, Belfast, he and they

> " took a solemn obligation . . . never to desist from our efforts until we had subverted the authority of England over our country and asserted our independence."

In Philadelphia he met a check. The French Minister received him so coolly that his hopes fell to zero. He was lifted from his gloom a few months later by letters from RUSSELL, KEOGH, and others, all urging him " in the strongest manner " to carry out his pledge and to—

> " move heaven and earth to force my way to the French Government in order to supplicate their assistance."

Next day the French Minister met him with cordiality and arranged the business at once. On January 1st, 1796, Tone sailed from Sandy Hook. Fellow-exiles, JOHN REYNOLDS, HAMILTON ROWAN, and NAPPER TANDY, made special trips to wish him good luck. He reached France without mishap or delay and at once set to work. How he set about his enormous task we can only indicate baldly, using as far as possible TONE's own description, given in his diary—the most movingly human of all autobiographies.

His honest commonsense shines out from the first. Asked by a French statesman if the Irish could do anything unaided, Tone told him:

"Most certainly not. If a landing were once effected everything would follow instantly, but *that* was indispensable. I begged him to state that as my opinion . . . if 20,000 French were in Ireland we should in a month have an army of 100,000, 200,000, or, if necessary, 300,000 men; but the *point d'appui* was indispensable."

Personally, he explained, he would go with "a Corporal's guard"; but to do the thing properly 20,000 trained men were the minimum required.

His good sense, his frankness, firmness and disinterestedness compelled respect. He won over CARNOT (the "organiser of victory") and he had an instantaneous success with the intrepid Jacobin general LAZAR HOCHE. As the prospect brightens, Tone grows whimsical:

"I am a pretty fellow to negotiate with the Directory of France, pull down a monarchy, and establish a Republic; to break a connection of 600 years' standing and contract a fresh alliance . . . What would my old friend Fitzgibbon [the Chancellor] say if he could read these memorandums? ' *He called me a dog before he had cause*! ' I remember he used to say I was a viper in the bosom of Ireland. Now that I am in Paris I will venture to say he lies, and that I am a better Irishman than he and his whole gang of rascals—as well as the gang that are opposing them—*as it were.*"

French fears that a liberated Ireland might prove monarchist, aristocratic, or clericalist, took a lot of dissipating :

"We then for the hundredth time beat over the old ground about the priests without starting any new ideas ; and I summed up all by telling him that as to religion we would content ourselves with pulling down the Establishment, without setting up another ; that we would have no State religion, but let each sect pay its own clergy voluntarily.

"As to royalty and aristocracy they were both odious in Ireland to such a degree that I apprehended much more a general massacre of the gentry and a distribution of the entire of their property than the establishment of any sort of government that would perpetuate their influence ; that I hoped this massacre would not happen and that I for one would do all in my power to prevent it . . . At the same time the pride, cruelty and oppression of the Irish aristocracy was so great that I apprehended every excess from the just resentment of the people."

Tone's contempt for the aristocracy and gentry is equalled by his faith in the common people :

"Our independence must be had at all hazards. If the men of property will not support us they must fall. We can support ourselves by the aid of that numerous and respectable class of the community *the men of no property.*"

His scorn for the Whigs is profound :

"The Whig Club, I see, are taking up the condition of the labouring poor. They are getting frightened and their guilty consciences will not let them sleep. I suppose they will act like the gentry of Meath, who from fear of the Defenders raised their workmen's wages from eightpence to a shilling a day, but took care at the same time to raise the rent of the hovels and the grass for their cows in the same proportion so that at the end of the year the wretched peasant was not a penny the richer. Such is the honesty of the squirearchy of Ireland. No! No! it is we who will better the condition of the labouring poor if ever we get into that country ; it is we that will humble the pride of that execrable and contemptible corps, the country gentlemen of Ireland. I know not whether I most hate or despise them, the tyrants of the people and the slaves of the Government."

The point comes up again later when he and a friend (LEWINES) are negotiating with the Dutch Government. A statesman who had travelled in Ireland observes that " from the luxury of the rich and the extreme misery of the poor, no country in Europe had so crying a need for a revolution."

" To which LEWINES and I replied, as is most religiously the truth, that one great motive of our conduct in this business was our conviction of the wretched state of our peasantry and our determination if possible to amend it."

The European Situation

To appreciate fully the conditions in which Tone laboured from 1795 to the end of 1798 one must possess a detailed grasp of the vast complex of historical reactions set in train all over Europe by the immense upheaval of the French Revolution. It is impossible, here, to do more than note that from July, 1789, to July, 1796, the Revolution rose through a succession of spectacular successes which destroyed the absolute Monarchy and the powers of the semi-feudal aristocracy and the ecclesiastical Hierarchy. That of itself was sufficient to scare the feudalistic Absolutists, in all the great monarch-

ies and principalities of Europe ; who accordingly band
together to destroy the Revolutionary French Republ.

In self-defence the Revolution was forced to wa;
war in all the states adjacent to its frontiers. The victori
of the armies of the Republic gave the Revolutic
freedom to complete itself in France ; but from Jul
1794, it entered upon a *conservative* phase in whic
through a succession of political defeats inflicted upc
the lower classes, power came to rest in the hands of tl
upper stratum of the bourgeoisie—the money-lords, lan
speculators, and Army contractors—supported by tl
main body of *the peasantry* who had gained greatly fro
the liquidation of their feudal burdens.

The Republic however still needed armies to prote
itself from the vengeance of the princes, kings, an
Emperors whose political systems had been thrown int
confusion by the upheaval. Hence NAPOLEO
BUONAPARTE, his armies, his conquests, and his quas
Republican Empire—which was *revolutionary* to the king
and emperors while it was *conservative* and even *counter
revolutionary* in France itself—were all historicall
necessitated so long as France was faced with the need t
fight for its life against a feudalistic-monarchist Europea
coalition.

That is where England and the policy of its rulin;
class, as expressed by WILLIAM PITT, comes into th
picture. But for Pitt, and the financial and naval aid h
put at its disposal, the Coalition of Kings and Prince
could never have survived the victories of the Republic
However plausibly it may be argued that it was a politica
necessity for England to make a stand against the
Napoleonic Empire, it remains a fact that *but for Pitt'
policy*—which was that of the King, the Court, and the
ruling-oligarchy of England—*there would have been n
Napoleonic Empire.*

So far as the French Revolution involved the overthrow of the Bourbon Monarchy—with which England

ad been repeatedly at war since 1690—and the overthrow
f the Bourbon Empire—which was England's greatest
val—the English bourgeoisie and ruling-class could
iew the French Revolution with complacency; and so
ar they put no obstacles in the way of the spontaneous
xpression of sympathy by the progressive bourgeoisie
nd petty-bourgeoisie of England with the victory of
heir class counterparts in France.

When, however, the *lower orders* looked like triumphing
ermanently in France, the ruling oligarchy in England
aw the justice of the alarms expressed by the Emperors,
Kings, etc. The war upon France, in alliance with the
Coalition of Kings, etc., was also a disguised form of
var upon the *lower orders* in England, and still more
and without disguise) upon the people in Ireland.

When the continental victories of the French Armies
reated a fear that the Republican Empire might grow
o be an even greater menace to England's Empire than
he Bourbon Empire had been—and particularly a fear
hat England's trade and manufactures might be shut
ut completely from the valuable European market—the
English bourgeoisie found their abstract sympathy for
he French Revolution dwindle and disappear in face
f the realities of economic rivalry. Thus, in the end,
Pitt was able to rally behind him all the property-owning
nterests of England in his war to the death with revolu-
ionary France.

This in England, and still more in Ireland, involved
n intensification of the domestic war against the lower
orders, whose aspirations had been quickened by the
riumph of Revolution in France.

Here emerges the radical difference between England
nd Ireland. Tone was never so right as when he saw
hat while a French invasion of Ireland could count
vith confidence on the mass support of virtually all
classes below the level of the Ascendancy-oligarchy, in
England an exactly opposite result would be produced.

The lower orders in England were exploited, an
resented it, as the Irish people also resented the explo
tation *they* suffered. But the English lower orders we
exploited as *classes*; and a successful invasion, instead
easing their position, would worsen it by imposing
national subjection which would hamper at every poi
their *class-struggles* for emancipation.

That which the English lower orders feared as
possible calamity was something which *had alrea
happened in Ireland.* The Irish people were alread
enslaved *as a nation.* An invader would come to them
a welcome ally against the enslavers from whom the
yearned to be freed. Thus, what was a nightmare boge
to the English masses was the thing of things to b
desired by the Irish masses.

It is against this background that we must envisag
TONE drudging away doggedly at persuading first th
Minister and then another until at last he extorts
definite promise of an Army of Liberation for Ireland—
drudging on until the expedition is actually bein
assembled; until preparations are complete; until, *at las,*
he and the expedition are actually at sea, bound fo
Ireland !

It is against the same background that we mus
envisage the UNITED IRISH LEADERS labouring i
Ireland to perfect their organisation; to obtain store
of arms and powder; to see that, failing muskets
every man had at least a pike. And, above all, labouring
to keep their followers patient under every provocatio
until the day when the French should actually hav
landed in force.

It is against the same background that we must view
DUBLIN CASTLE as a centre in which a company o
aristocratic conspirators plot, scheme, and plan to
anticipate every move of the United Irishmen; to
break their connections, raid their stores, arrest thei
leaders, and in every way to try to provoke enough

resistance to provide a pretext for the barbarous repression they desire in their hearts to see and will soon accomplish in deeds.

And it is against the same background that we must envisage WILLIAM PITT and his Cabinet in London, sending out subsidies to keep this King or that Emperor steadfast in the struggle against the French; sending out proclamation after proclamation to the fox-hunting Tory squires, and their bottle-companions the parsons, keeping them all up to their job of holding the country-side in order; suspending the *Habeas Corpus* Act; facing mutinies in the Militia, mutinies in the Fleet, food-riots and other manifestations of a will, half-formed in the lower orders, *to start a revolution and fight the French at the same time !*

French Attempts to Invade Ireland, 1796-97

It was with hopes keyed up to the highest pitch that Tone sailed from Brest with the French Fleet towards the end of December, 1796. It was in a condition bordering upon absolute despair that he returned on the ship he had sailed on, a fortnight later, with nothing done. It was, he noted, a year to the day since he had landed in France, fresh from America, with a hundred guineas in his pocket and a determination to move the earth, if need be, to free Ireland.

The expedition had carried 15,000 trained men, and arms for 20,000 more. LAZAR HOCHE was in command. The rendezvous was Bantry Bay. They passed the English blockade squadron in a fog; and all seemed set fair for success. Then misfortunes began. A gale scattered the fleet; those who first arrived off the Irish coast had to wait for the rest to struggle up in ones and twos. Then, when the Fleet was nearly complete again, one of the few ships still missing was the ship which carried LAZAR HOCHE. As they waited the stipulated three days the wind freshened into a terrific gale from

just the one quarter which made a landing impossible.
And so they continued while the gale blew with unaba-
ting fury for eight days. One by one the ships were
blown from their anchorage; until, at last, facing the
fact that success was now impossible, the Admiral
ordered the few ships that remained to slip their cables
and make their way back to France.

Tone had gone through the heart-rending experience
of being for ten days within clear sight of the Irish shore
—at times near enough to toss a biscuit on to the rocks—
and yet as far from setting foot on Irish soil as if he were
still in Paris. Any man less of a hero than Tone would
have been nerve-shattered and will-broken for life after
such a strain. It testifies, as with trumpets, to his un-
conquerable spirit that he was hardly on shore again
before he was again at work preparing a new expedition.

Hoche, whose ship had been chased by English
cruisers—and then, half-wrecked in the gale, blown
leagues out of its course—had contrived to struggle
back to Paris *via* Bordeaux. He was all agog for another
try; and Spain being France's ally, the Spanish Fleet
was called upon to slip out of Cadiz, make its way to
Brest, and there help to cover the French Fleet with
Lazar Hoche on board as it made another dash for
Ireland. It was a pretty scheme and, but for " the devil ",
it might have come off. The devil, however, intervened—
in the form of the English Fleet led by Sir John Jervis
and including Commodore Horatio Nelson among its
captains. On February 14th, 1797, off Cape St. Vincent,
the Spanish Fleet got such a mauling that it went back
to Cadiz and stopped there.

Failing the Spaniards, there were the Dutch; and, to
them, Hoche and the indefatigable Tone made their
way to prepare another expedition. Preparations went
forward without haste—as things were wont to go with
the Dutch. Tone had to face the appalling exasperation
of being totally unable to profit by the unique chance

presented by a succession of mutinies in the Home
Fleet of England. Plymouth, Spithead, the Nore,
Yarmouth, all were involved. For the better part of two
months the English Home Fleet was immobilised. But
what was the good of that when the fleets blockading
Brest and Cadiz kept holding on like bulldogs? And
while, in the Texel, one administrative delay after another,
French as well as Dutch, made it impossible for the
expedition to sail? Then, when all things were ready once
again, the wind deserted to the English.

It was, it seems, only possible to get out of the Texel
roads when there occurred in conjunction (a) a high tide,
and (b) a wind from a certain direction. Normally ships
seldom had to wait more than five days for this conjunction to occur. This time the wind remained foul for
seven weeks straight off, and by then the season was
too far advanced for the attempt to be made.

The expedition was put off until the following spring;
but before then all hope of it vanished when the Dutch
fleet was destroyed by the British fleet under Duncan at
Camperdown on October 11th, 1797.

Nearly desperate now, Tone returned to Paris, and
there secured a promise that another expedition would
be prepared which would definitely sail in the following
spring,—that of 1798.

The Dragooning of Ulster

When the French Fleet lay tossing in Bantry Bay, the
Castle "gang" were in an agony of suspense. There
were not 3,000 troops that could be relied upon in the
South of Ireland; and those in the North could not be
moved for fear of what the United Irishmen would do
in their absence. If the wind had dropped for so little
as three hours, Ireland would have been lost to the
British Empire.

The saying that a "reign of terror" is usually the
"reign of the terrified" is not wholly true; but it truly

describes the reign of terror which was instituted in
Ireland as Dublin Castle's response to the portent of a
French Fleet in Bantry Bay. The Irish Parliament met
and, in a session which lasted only from January 21st to
April 15th, occupied itself with only two measures : an
Act of Indemnity for " all such persons as had, in the
previous half-year, exceeded their legal powers in the
preservation of the public peace ", and with it an
Insurrection Act—" one of the most severe and com-
prehensive in Irish history ".

The first of these covered with legal oblivion the
state of things which had supervened in Ulster as soon
as the Orange Society had settled down to work. It
began with a campaign of terrorism in Armagh which
devastated the county and extended through the border
counties into Connacht : it culminated with the Orange
magistrates refusing to convict Orangemen even when
plainly guilty of murder ; with the same magistrates
(quite beyond their legal powers) awarding sentences of
transportation for life to Catholics who procured arms
to defend themselves against the Orange gangs. Even
friends of the Ascendancy were forced to protest. Lord
Gosforth, the Lord Lieutenant of County Armagh, in
an address to the county magistrates, spoke with indignation of the " persecution " and the " ferocious cruelty "
which was driving thousands from their homes. " Of
late no night passes that houses are not destroyed and
scarce a week that dreadful murders are not committed."
The Catholics, aided by United Irishmen, fought back
wherever they could ; but this only brought in a
Government Terror to supplement the Orange Terror.
The Indemnity Act was designed to cover the villainy
of the magistrates who had abetted the Orange Terror,
and to put difficulties in the way of the victims who
claimed compensation. The Insurrection Act was
designed to complete the work ; and, in addition, to
cope with the awkward fact that Orange persecution

ad driven the Defenders in the North and the Whiteboys
1 the South over to the United Irishmen in a body.

The state of the North may be inferred from a single
ircumstance : the Indemnity Act was popularly believed,
y the victims as well as by the terrorists, to guarantee
mmunity for everything done, or to be done, in the
ame of the Orange order. On top of that the Insurrec-
ion Act gave the Government powers to suspend the
Iabeas Corpus Act and impose martial law upon any
rea proclaimed as " disturbed ". It imposed death as
he penalty for administering a " seditious " oath, and
ransportation as the penalty for taking one. It ordered
he registration of all arms, which the magistrates could
onfiscate at will, and imposed transportation, or
mprisonment, as the penalty for possessing or concealing
nregistered arms ; for " tumultuous assembly " ; or
or possessing, distributing, or selling " seditious "
apers. Magistrates were given large powers of arrest
n suspicion.

Almost before the Act was passed the Administration
iad appointed General Lake Military Commander for
Jlster, and he had issued a proclamation imposing
nartial law over the greater part of the province. The
roclamation ordered the surrender of all arms by a
ertain date.

Being none too certain of the troops—especially
n view of the mutinies which began to be reported
rom England—and more than doubtful about the
nilitia regiments, Dublin Castle had given permission to
he country magistrates and gentry to form corps of
" Yeomanry " on the English model. Like some of the
arliest Volunteer corps these were, at first, corps formed
oy the gentry and the *squireens* from their family connec-
ions, their dependants, and such tenants as they thought
hey could rely upon. Later, infantry companies were
idded. In practice these " Yeomanry " corps were little
lse than Orange Lodges and Peep-of-Day Boy gangs

put into uniform and given an official licence to wo
their will upon the countryside in the name of law an
order.   To secure a parallel end Orange Lodges we
established in each militia battalion, and a systemat
purge was instituted, beginning with the officers, t
weed out every man suspected of unwillingness to g
to any length in Orange terrorism.   Yeomanry an
militia regiments were brought over from Englan
which were, as in the case of the evilly-notoriou
" Ancient Britons ", commanded by Sir Watkin William
Wynn, little else than Church-and-King mobs supplie
with weapons, pay, and rations, for displaying th
ignorant brutality which in England they displayed fron
a love of savagery, stimulated by bribes of guineas an
beer.

When the date fixed in General Lake's proclamatio
had expired, a general house-to-house search for arm
was ordered through all the proclaimed area in Ulste
For tactical reasons it was deemed expedient to keep th
troops (and most of the militia) concentrated in th
towns.   The actual raiding for arms was conducted
therefore, by the Orange Yeomanry.   Soon the whol
country was ringing with tales of their barbarity an
outrage.

In the first surprise impact of the raids a considerabl
quantity of arms was discovered.   5,000 muskets wer
found in Co. Armagh alone.   Thereafter few were found
Convinced that arms were being concealed, the Orang
Yeomanry proceeded to show what they could do
From simple assault and robbery they proceeded t
arson, rape, and murder.   A competition develope
between the " Ancient Britons " and the Orang
Yeomanry as to which could inflict the greatest barbarity
in the name of " the Law " and " loyalism ".   To extor
confessions of concealed arms, they resorted to flogging
but this, even when the victims died under the lash
soon jaded the palates of these upholders of the law

icketing—a variety of crucifixion in which the victim
vas fastened, back to the ground, his wrists and ankles
lrawn to full stretch by cords tied to picket pegs—
half-hanging and pitch-capping—crowning the victim
vith a linen cap filled with hot pitch—these, with
oasting the soles of the victim's feet at a turf fire, were
he methods fashionable with the yeomanry engaged in
dragooning Ulster. When the terrified inhabitants fled
t their approach, they could do nothing worse than
ourn the house down.

To this Orange terror the magistrates added an
accompaniment of arrests on suspicion. When the
gaols could hold no more, they were cleared, on a
simple magistrate's order, by the expedient of " impress-
ing " all the prisoners for service in the Fleet.

The rumour circulated by Pitt's Government, that the
Naval Mutinies of '97 at Spithead and the Nore were the
work of " Jacobin agents " working through the
United Irishmen and the London Corresponding Society,
has been proved to have been a plain lie, invented to
excuse the savagery of the yeomanry in Ireland, and the
suppression of all democratic societies and trade-unions
in England. But in face of what was happening in
Ireland it was the sort of thing that could be only too
easily believed.

Waiting for the French to come

To justify their dragooning of Ulster, the Irish
Government recited a long list of " outrages ". Arms
had been collected and concealed in large quantities.
Ash trees had been cut down (without leave) on gentlemen's estates to make pike-handles ; magistrates had
been fired at ; informers had been murdered in broad
daylight in the middle of Belfast ; a quantity of gunpowder had been looted from a Government store ;
seditious literature was in every home ; detached parties of
yeomanry had been attacked by armed bands ; and so on.

Nor was this all. Anyone who joined the yeomanry
was met with insult and ostracism by " disaffected "
employers as well as by work-people. People gathered
in " great masses " to stack the hay, cut the corn, and
lift the potatoes of men detained in gaol. If the military
dispersed these " seditious assemblies " by day, they
came back and did the work by moonlight. There
were, of course, secret drillings. The " wish that the
French would come " was expressed openly and every
where. And, to cap all, an honourable member assured
the House that there existed a " generally-expressed
determination to abolish all taxes and all tithes, and
reduce rents to a standard of 10s. an acre for the best
land, and so downwards in proportion". Another
honourable member added the last word : They were
facing " *a war of the poor against the rich*".

The dragooning of Ulster was, in fact, only a very
qualified success for the Administration. It secured
some arms, and in various ways threw the United
Irishmen's organisation into confusion. It created an
excuse for the final suppression of the *Northern Star*
and the wrecking of its machinery. It had the effect, too,
of scaring out of the United ranks a number of well-to-do
waverers who, in some cases, turned informers to save
their necks. But as a set-off against these gains there
were losses.

The places of the deserters from the United ranks
were taken by more resolute spirits roused to furious
indignation by the Government's methods. The panic
spread by the victims of the Orange *pogroms*, and those
of the official terror in Ulster, drove the most sluggish
of the peasantry in all the other provinces to take
measures for self-defence. The partial disarming of
Ulster was set off by a zealous, secret arming of the rest
of Ireland. By the Government's own policy the United
Irish system was helped to spread into the remotest
points.

The troops, too, began to be affected. The militia, mostly composed of Catholics, had to be purged and re-purged. Even the establishment of Orange Lodges did not always accomplish anything beyond inflaming the national and Catholic zeal of the rank and file; often the new recruits were more " disaffected " than the discharged ones had been. One English regiment was found to be definitely " corrupted " and had to be bundled back to England; another was " very doubtful". In May, 1797, at the time when mutiny had immobilised the Fleet at the Nore, courts-martial were sitting on cases of " disaffected " soldiers in Cork, Limerick, and Belfast. When a number of Cork militiamen were found to have taken the United Irish oath, and were sentenced to death, a Scottish regiment refused in a body to take any part in the execution. Only with difficulty could a " reliable " regiment be found.

Brawls which grew to the dimensions of pitched battles broke out between parties of yeomanry and militia over the wearing of partisan badges of Orange and of Green.

All Ireland was one great question—*When, and where, will the French land?*

CHAPTER TEN

THE RISING OF ' NINETY-EIGHT

The struggle between the forces of REVOLUTION and COUNTER-REVOLUTION passed into the phase of actual war and bloody repression in May, 1798. In this chapter we examine the stages whereby this culmination was reached and what followed as its immediate consequences.

The Case of William Orr

The policy pursued by the Administration as a sequel to the dragooning of Ulster was illustrated in an event to which enormous importance was attached at the time, though to us it seems of minor significance.

Among the Ulster leaders arrested in 1796 (along with Thomas Russell) was a young Antrim farmer WILLIAM ORR. Detained with the rest without specific charge, he was, without warning, put on trial in October, 1797, on a charge of *administering an illegal oath*.

The offence was graver legally from the fact that it was a serving soldier whom Orr was alleged to have sworn in as a United Irishman. The soldier himself and a comrade of the same regiment were the witnesses.

The prosecution made the most they could of this " proof " of the " Jacobinical " and " treasonable " designs of the United Irishmen to " seduce from their allegiance " the " men who are the Kingdom's only safeguard against the foreign foe ".

The people at large took more notice of these things :

(*a*) The offence, even if proved, was more than twelve months old. If the evidence had only just been unearthed, of what value was it after so long an interval ? If the evidence had been known to the

authorities all the time, what excuse had they for
their delay? If they had ignored the charge for
twelve months, why act upon it now?

(*b*) The penalty imposed under the Insurrection Act
was *death*. This penalty had been denounced as
barbarous when the Act was passed; as nearly two
years had elapsed without its being enforced
men had come to regard it as a dead letter. Did
the bringing to trial of William Orr mean that
the Government intended to enforce the penalty
in every case? Did that mean that the hundreds
of prisoners then in the Government's hands (all
uncharged) were each and all threatened with
the fate of William Orr? The fear was general,
and was not wholly without justification.

The actual trial did not differ greatly in its incidentals
from any normal State trial of the period. The United
Irishmen knew in point of fact that Orr had not administered the oath on the occasion sworn to. We have the
evidence of an eye-witness (JAMIE HOPE) for that. The
soldier witness perjured himself; he was proved to be
a bad character; he retracted his evidence in a sworn
affidavit, and then retracted his retraction. But that
does not differ greatly from the usual course of the
informers of the period.

The jurymen swore that a whiskey-jar was illegally
passed into the jury room, and that those who for hours
stood out for a verdict of acquittal gave in finally under
the influence of drink. Even that was not wholly
unprecedented.

The real crux of the case was something which did
not appear on the pleadings, but of which everyone
" in the know " was fully aware. The United Irishmen's oath had been administered to a soldier—
whether it was Orr or another who administered the
oath was merely incidental. Strict law might boggle
over trifles of that kind. What the Authorities were

after was a verdict that would strike terror into every United Irishman who had ever administered that oath or was ever likely to administer it.

Accordingly, though his execution was three times postponed, William Orr was hanged at Carrickfergus in January, 1798, surrounded by an extra-strong military guard. The inhabitants of Carrickfergus, to show their horror, deserted the town at daybreak on the day of the execution and did not return until all its traces had been cleared away.

Curran's Indictment of the Government

One reason for remembering the case of William Orr is that it led to a speech by JOHN PHILPOT CURRAN which is among the most remarkable of his many remarkable speeches.

Its occasion was a charge of libel against the *Press* newspaper, the journal founded by ARTHUR O'CONNOR to replace the *Northern Star*. The *Press* had published an open letter to the Viceroy commenting scathingly on his refusal to show clemency to Orr. Curran's line of defence was a counter-attack—an indictment of the Government, root and branch :

> " You [the jury] are called upon to say, on your oaths, that the Government is wise and merciful— the people prosperous and happy ; that military law ought to be continued ; that the constitution could not with safety be restored to Ireland ; and that the statements of a contrary import by your advocates, in either country, are libellous and false.

> " I tell you that these are the questions. And I ask you if you can have the front to give the expected answer in face of a community which knows the country as well as you do.

> " Let me ask you how you could reconcile with such a verdict the gaols, the gibbets, the tenders,

the conflagrations, the murders, the proclamations we hear of every day in the streets and see every day in the country? What are the prosecutions of the learned counsel himself [the Attorney General] circuit after circuit? Merciful God! What is the state of Ireland, and where shall you find the wretched inhabitant of this land?

"You may find him perhaps in a gaol; the only place of security—I had almost said, of ordinary habitation! If you do not find him there you may find him flying with his family from the flames of his own dwelling—lighted to his dungeon by the conflagration of his own hovel! Or you may find his bones bleaching on the green fields of his country! Or you may find him tossing on the surface of the ocean, mingling his groans with the tempests, less savage than his persecutors, that drive him to a returnless distance from his family and his home—without charge, or trial, or sentence!

"Is this a foul misrepresentation? Or can you, with these facts ringing in your ears and staring in your faces, say upon your oaths they do not exist? You are called upon in defiance of shame, of honour, of truth, to deny the sufferings under which you groan, and to flatter the persecution which tramples you under foot."

It was in these circumstances that the struggle between the Irish Nation, as represented by the United Irishmen, and its enemies, as represented by the Irish Administration and its supporters, entered upon its final phase.

Moving to a Crisis

In the light of after-events it is easy to see that the turning-point in the fortunes of the United Irishmen's movement came when the French failed to grasp the

golden opportunity presented to them by the Nava
Mutinies of 1797.

Till a French fleet was actually tossing on the wave
of Bantry Bay the real possibility of a French landin
had been believed in only by a few " Jacobin " enthus
iasts in the United Irish ranks and those ardent peasant
scattered through the countryside who still dreame
dreams of the coming again of the " wild geese " tha
had " flown to France".

All this was changed after the end of 1796. That
landing had not been achieved was, of course, ba
luck. But all doubts as to the willingness of the Frencl
to invade, and of their ability to make a landing, wer
dissipated when once the attempt had been made, an
had missed success only by the narrowest of margins
Expectation became tensed to its highest pitch, and a
the year 1797 slipped away, month by month, the strai
grew unendurable. Weaklings began to despair again
The fiery spirits began to chafe and ask each other
Why wait for the French before starting? Won't the
come anyway when they know we're *up*? The quicke
we start, the quicker they'll be here !

In this way the further the year 1797 advanced, the
more critical became the silent struggle between the
leaders on each side, the one to provoke, the other to
prevent a *premature* insurrection—" premature " in
each case meaning *before* the French had effected a
landing in force.

There was, of course, plenty to do to keep the ardent
spirits from fretting too much. There was recruiting,
organising, and drilling. Arms had to be got, and
distributed ; trees to be cut down and sawn up for pike-
staves ; pike-heads to be forged. And all the time a
look-out kept against surprise by the yeomanry or
the military. Now and then there were collisions—
a detected informer, tied heels to neck, thrown over a
bridge with weights in his pockets, to take his informa-

tion to the devil who begot him; a party of yeomanry to beat off; arms to be concealed in the bog. Or a party to organise to give help, mowing, reaping, stacking, carting, or potato-lifting for the friends fallen into the hands of the enemy. All the same, men began to weary—losing hope or growing angrily impatient.

Under the impact of martial law, primitive instincts—greeds, jealousies, and fears—rose nearer the surface. The Catholic gentry, equally with their Protestant neighbours, saw every day a rift widening between them and their tenantry. One by one these gentry drifted over to the Government camp. The Catholic Hierarchy, genuinely fearful of the worst, exhausted itself in appeals for " submission " to the " powers that be, ordained of God". The parish priests, as in duty bound, passed the injunction on. But their words were frozen on their lips as the tales spread of the Catholic chapels burnt and of other infamies perpetrated by the yeomanry on the Catholics of the North.

The Government, too, did not neglect the arts of propaganda. To the Catholic gentry and well-to-do they told tales of the horrors and the confiscations of the " atheistic " Jacobins of France. To the Protestant gentry they told tales of the Catholic " massacres " in the rising of 1641 and of the grave danger that a repetition was being planned. To the comfortable middle-class they told both tales—adding, for Catholics, reminders of what the " Republican " Cromwellians had done in 1649–50. To all they told the tale that maps had been prepared and were circulating which indicated where each historic clan had once been located, and suggested what lands should be confiscated and by whom. They spared no effort to ensure that the rising, when it did come, would find all the men of property, regardless of sect, in one camp, and ready to inflict condign punishment upon the mutinous *Jacquerie.*

For their part the United Irish chiefs diligently
circulated the information among the " faithful " that
an expedition was being prepared which would definitely
be despatched to Ireland not later than at the beginning
of May, 1798. It would consist of only 10,000 men
but there would be arms for plenty more. The United
men were enjoined to be ready to strike immediately
the landing had been made. The weary ones were
reinvigorated ; the impatient ones were calmed down.
Every prospect seemed bright when two blows fell
in quick succession.

The sudden death, at the end of 1797, of Lazar Hoche
had helped to clear the road for the rise to power of
NAPOLEON BUONAPARTE. All Ireland (in common with
all England) had heard of the army, designated as " of
England", which had been assembling in the North of
France since the end of 1797. Tone was attached to
this army ; and this, with other confidential information,
had led the United Irish chiefs to count confidently
on this Army's being despatched to Ireland. Suddenly
a rumour began to spread, which daily grew more
circumstantial—that this camp was being broken up,
and the army marched elsewhere.

Was Buonaparte going to break his pledged word ?

The United chiefs did not credit the slander : it must
be one of those brilliant manœuvres for which this
young general was already world-famous. They went
on with their work. An ominous calm " broken only
by constant accounts of attempts to murder magistrates
and informers, of attacks upon sentries, and of nightly
raids for arms" fell upon the country. It was felt to
be specially suspicious that the peasantry had suddenly
changed their habits. Drunkenness and faction-fighting
at fairs and markets disappeared entirely.

Then definite news came that Buonaparte had—all
pledges to the contrary notwithstanding—decided to
use the " army of England " *elsewhere* ! Tone got to

know of the bare fact and nearly died of chagrin and indignation. We know, now, what he did not till later, that what Tone (who never wholly trusted Buonaparte) had said in jest had turned out to be only too true. Buonaparte was " trying to reach London by way of Calcutta starting from Egypt ! " Years later, an exile at St. Helena, Buonaparte had leisure in which to realise how little he had gained—and how much he had lost— when he decided to " double-cross " the Irish.

This blow had barely had time to land before the second blow fell. The inner conflict in the United ranks between the " wait-for-the-French " and the " strike-by-ourselves " schools had been suspended by the definite promise of French aid by a particular date. With that promise rendered null and void, the disruptive conflict was bound to break out again in greater violence than ever. A special meeting of the Leinster Directory of the society—which included the members of the National Directory—was summoned on March 12th to devise means of coping with the crisis. This entire Directory—with the exceptions only of ARTHUR O'CONNOR imprisoned in England and Lord EDWARD FITZGERALD who was on his way to the meeting but had not reached it—was captured in a surprise raid by a military magistrate with a strong force.

In the nick of time the Government had found just the informer they needed.

Enemies to Ireland, and to the popular cause in all lands, have sought to spread the story that the Government knew all the secrets of the United Irishmen all along. It is an obvious falsehood, which expresses not the truth but what sycophants and reactionaries always wish to be true. The Government in 1798 knew of course that something was brewing. So much was self-evident without the use of a single spy. That there were professional informers in plenty in Ireland was also true. The Penal Code had been designed to

turn the whole nation into informers—it was bound to
have succeeded to some extent. And, for the matter
of that, there were swarms of informers in *England* at
that date—professionals, in the pay of Pitt, and amateurs
who did it out of pure malevolence. But the fact
remains that, when the Government wished to convict
the prisoners captured in this raid of March 12th, the
only witness they had was this one informer, Thomas
Reynolds, a landed proprietor and retired silk merchant.
His price was £5,000 down and a pension. His excuse
was that he feared the confiscation of his property
whichever side won. Whatever his motive, his information gave the counter-revolution its victory. In
regard to informers we note here that the most useful
secret information Pitt obtained about Ireland was
got from ex-aristocrats employed in the French Government service. And, we may say here, categorically, that
the only Irish informers who did serious damage to
the United Irishmen's cause were all of them drawn
from the well-to-do and educated classes—as was
Thomas Reynolds.

Counter-Revolutionary Terror

From the moment of the swoop of March 12th the
civil war of 1798 began, for all practical purposes.
The Government, for its part, announced to an appro-
priately "horrified" House of Commons that a "dia-
bolical conspiracy" to bring in the French and "plunge
the country into the horrors of civil war" had been
unearthed. But, in cold fact, when the Attorney
General had done with expressing astonishment, horror,
indignation, and his loyal resolution to die, heroically,
with his back to the last wall, all that needed to be done,
really, was to send to England for more troops and to
extend to all Ireland the Insurrection Act passed early
in 1796.

This, however, was quite enough to reconcile the

two schools of thought which had contended in the Government councils. Those who thought an insurrection ought to be prevented by firm measures, and those who thought it ought to be provoked in order that it might be crushed with force and arms, were equally satisfied with a measure which treated all Ireland as if it were in actual insurrection though no rising had been formally declared.

The proclamation of March 17th, 1798, says Lecky, one of the most cautious and have-it-both-ways of historians, " opened a scene of horrors hardly surpassed in modern Europe". And, we may add, even the Hitlerite thugs of our own day have been able to go beyond its horrors only in the greater extent of their operations.

Pending the arrival of troops from England—which, when they arrived, included, as well as dragoons and infantrymen, a number of conscript-serfs of the Grand Dukes of Hesse and of Brunswick, hired to the English Government at so much per head—the troops in Ireland were ordered to " repress disturbances " especially in Kildare, Tipperary, Limerick, Cork, Kilkenny, King's County, and Queen's County. They were authorised to " crush rebellion " in every shape and form, and forcibly to disarm all rebels. Officers were ordered to quarter their troops *without payment* upon anybody they thought fit; to requisition horses, carriages, and carts; to demand forage and provisions; to hold courts-martial; and to issue proclamations.

All that had happened in Ulster was now repeated all through the Midlands and the South, but on a more wholesale scale and with even greater ferocity. As was to be expected, the Yeomanry and their rivals, the Ancient Britons, were well to the fore in every barbarity, and they were soon joined by worthy rivals in the Hompesch Dragoons, some of the Hessian troops before-mentioned, who were, as it chanced, actually on board a troopship

bound for the West Indies when the need arose for
diverting them to Ireland.

The consequences to the people may be imagined.
Homes were burned wholesale; stores of provisions
were looted; hundreds were murdered; thousands
were arrested. Tortures of incredible barbarity—flogging especially, carried to the point of actual death
under the lash—were inflicted systematically upon a
scale that would seem incredible if the evidence permitted any doubt. Even the relatively good-humoured
horse-play of the military, militia, and yeomanry—
their snatching, tearing, or cutting from women any
green garments they wore ("searching" them for green
petticoats or green garters was deemed a great joke)—
even when this did not prelude fouler outrage, all
indicated to the Irish common people that they were
to be regarded, at best, as conquered slaves, and at
worst as wild beasts to be hunted without mercy.

Even when military discipline somewhat abated the
grosser forms of physical outrage, the economic inflic-
tions imposed by military decree all worked to the same
end. The imposition of "free quarters" was in itself
sufficient to ensure ruin and starvation to any region in
which it was imposed. And to cap all, and reveal the
class motive behind the whole system of barbarity,
military proclamations warned the victims that the
troops would remain at free quarters, not only until all
arms had been surrendered, but also until "*all rents,
taxes, and tithes had been completely paid up*".

And, be it noted, all these things were done *before*
the rising of 1798 formally began.

Lord Edward Fitzgerald and the Rising

At the time of the swoop of March 12th, the Secret Directory of the United Irish conspiracy—its military command—consisted of three men, THOMAS ADDIS EMMET,
ARTHUR O'CONNOR, and LORD EDWARD FITZGERALD.

Emmet was, as we have noted, a friend of Tone, who held him in higher esteem than almost any man he knew. Like Tone, Emmet came of Protestant Cromwellian stock. He was a barrister, famous for his dramatic act of subscribing the United Irishman's oath in open court in the course of a speech in defence of a prisoner charged with the "crime" of administering that oath.

ARTHUR O'CONNOR, a nephew of Lord Longueville, was a landed proprietor in County Cork. He had been a member of Parliament, and had distinguished himself by his championship of the Catholic claims—losing his seat in consequence through the withdrawal of his uncle's patronage. He was an ardent champion of agrarian reform, and rather prided himself upon the possession of military capacity. He did, in fact, in after years, serve with distinction under Napoleon and retired with the rank of General. He has a special interest for English readers as *the uncle of Feargus O'Connor the Chartist leader*, whom he actually outlived by a few months, being 97 when he died.

LORD EDWARD FITZGERALD occupied a commanding position in Irish eyes as a younger brother of the Duke of Leinster, and therefore one of the senior line of the Geraldine family, the premier family in the Norman-Irish aristocracy. He had served with distinction as an officer in the English army; but his political sympathy with republican France went beyond that of his cousin Charles James Fox.* He had repudiated his courtesy title, and preferred to be addressed as *Citizen* Fitzgerald. But to the Irish, and especially the peasantry, he was always known affectionately as "Lord Edward". There is evidence of an indirect kind that he had more than once devoted his time to teaching the Defenders to drill, and how to handle their weapons.

On the eve of the swoop of March 12th, this Secret

---

* The mothers of Fox and Fitzgerald were sisters—grandchildren of King Charles II.

Directory—who between them, it is interesting to note
combined the three main " racial " strands in the Irish
nation : the old Gaelic, the Norman-Irish, and the
planted English-Irish—realising that action could no
for long be delayed, had sent Arthur O'Connor to make
contact with the French and represent the imperative
necessity of keeping to the promise of an expedition
the earliest possible moment. Arthur O'Connor with
others was arrested while attempting to get a boat for
France at Margate. Acquitted on an English charge b
an English jury, O'Connor was detained at the instance
of the Irish Administration. He was on his way back
to Ireland in custody when, in the swoop of March 12th
his fellow-director, Tom Emmet, also fell into the hand
of the enemy.

This left the Directorate solely in the hands of
" Citizen " Fitzgerald who, realising that no further
delay was possible, at once set to work to arrange
rising. He gathered a new Directory consisting of
himself, two gentlemen-barristers from Co. Cork, the
brothers JOHN and HENRY SHEARES, and WILLIAM
LAWLESS, a son of the newly-ennobled merchant-peer
Lord Cloncurry. Together they fixed upon the night
of May 22nd–23rd as zero-hour, and issued a call
accordingly.

Lord Edward himself and the others—with SAMUEL
NEILSON acting as Lord Edward's shadow—spread the
word as well as they could, with the military and the
yeomanry smashing connections in all directions. A
proclamation had been issued offering £1,000 reward
for Lord Edward's arrest, but he contrived to evade
capture. All seemed reasonably hopeful until, on May
19th, Lord Edward was surprised in a house in Dublin
and arrested. He resisted arrest so strenuously that
he killed one of his would-be captors and wounded
three others ; but was himself in a dying condition
when he was carried to gaol.

The brothers John and Henry Sheares were arrested on May 22nd, a few hours only before the zero-hour. The remaining director, William Lawless, warned in the very nick of time, just contrived to slip on board a ship as it sailed from the North Wall quay, Dublin. To complete the destruction, Samuel Neilson, the ablest of the United chiefs left at liberty, was captured while rounding up a party to storm the prison and liberate the captives.

Thus zero-hour arrived, with the whole central direction of the rising destroyed by " enemy action".

The result was what it was bound to be. Dublin was too well-watched for a move to be made ; and anyway there was no one left there to give the signal. In more than a score of places in the Midlands the peasants rallied to the appointed rendezvous, and scored local successes of greater or less moment. But, all central direction and plan being lacking, each local rising was as isolated as if it had been the only rising in the country. The rebels in every case fought bravely, in some cases conspicuously so and with temporary success. But one by one each party was overpowered and forced either to surrender, to disperse, or to take refuge in the hills and bogs.

The temper with which the rising was met could have been inferred from the terror which had preceded it. In nearly every case the troops gave no quarter. They pursued the flying rebels into the houses in which they took shelter ; and after they had despatched them, burned down the cottages. A general who allowed the rebels to disperse, unmolested, after they had given up their arms, was denounced in the Irish Parliament as a " traitor " for his " criminal clemency". By the end of a week, the rebellion had all but burned itself out in the Midlands ; but, to the general surprise, it was just then that it flamed out, where it was least expected, in Wicklow and in Wexford.

The Boys of Wexford

Much speculation has been wasted over the alleged fact that Wexford, " the County least organised into the United Irish system", was the one in which the nearest approach to success was attained. The speculation is wasted because the " fact " is mythical. The Government did not capture details of the Wexford organisation at the swoop of March 12th—not because there was no organisation, but solely because the Wexford delegates had not arrived when the swoop was made.

Wexford was, in fact, well organised; but mostly by the Whiteboy-Defender branch of the organisation; and it is of special interest as manifesting the response which the malignants in the Government camp had tried earlier to provoke from Ulster.

Since the March 17th proclamation Wexford and the adjoining counties had been dragooned by militia and yeomanry, led by local magistrates, with a savagery that stood out all the more sharply because of the complete absence of disturbances in the area since the excitements attending the militia-conscription of 1793.

The whole East-Munster and South-Leinster area was ravaged by the North Cork militia, of evil notoriety,—a corps whose officers and sergeants were all rabid Orangemen, who instituted new Orange Lodges in every place where they were quartered, and whose rank and file was composed mostly of debased " Castle Catholics." The magistrates of County Wexford were conspicuous for their Orange arrogance; and for the alacrity with which they instituted systematic flogging to extort confessions of concealed arms, and also the practice of burning down every cabin from which the inhabitants had fled in terror on hearing of their approach.

One of these magistrates paraded his district at the head of a corps of yeomanry escorting a cart on which a flogging-triangle, a cat-o'-nine-tails, and a hangman's

alter *all decorated with orange ribbons* were prominently
displayed.

So great was the terror excited by the nightly visita-
tions of the magisterial parties, that whole villages were
habitually deserted every nightfall. The villagers took
refuge in the woods; preferring to risk the destruction
of their homes rather than face torture by flogging and
other barbarities. At least one case is known of an
elderly man who dropped dead from fear on hearing
that a magistrates' party was near at hand.

Even the Protestant gentry were not safe, unless they
had purchased immunity by joining an Orange Lodge.
Several landowners, including BEAUCHAMP BAGENAL
HARVEY—who owned a considerable estate in the
barony of Bargy in the extreme south of the county—
were imprisoned as suspects because of their United
Irish leanings. ANTHONY PERRY, a son of a Co. Wicklow
proprietor, was submitted by the North Cork to a
refinement upon the pitch-cap torture. Gunpowder
was rubbed into his scalp and the hair set on fire to
" give him a real rebelly crop! " *

From the official point of view the rising in Wexford
began when the magistrates of its Northern Baronies
met in Gorey on April 25th and, declaring the county
in a state of insurrection, ordered all arms to be given
up on pain of severe reprisals. There had been arrests
and domiciliary raids even before that; but it was then
that repression began in earnest.

The rebellion, as such, began on the night of May
25th, when signal fires were lit on the hills of Corrigua
and Boulavogue in answer to similar fires lit on the
Wicklow Hills. The Wicklow men had risen out on

---

* *Crop, Croppy* : As had been the case in England in 1640, a visible distinction
between the idle rich and the working population was preserved by the fashion
of the gentry for wearing their hair *en queue*, while workers and peasants wore
theirs close-cropped. A " croppy " became the cant name for a rebel peasant
and by extension for any United Irishman ; as " roundhead " had been a similar
cant name in 1640–60.

L

the night of May 22nd–23rd; but had found, as the
approached Dublin, that something had gone wron
with the plans. They had, accordingly, retreated t
the hills, where they defied every effort to dislodg
them. Now they signalled to let the surroundin
counties know they were still holding out. The me
of Boulavogue, infuriated by the militia-persecution
had resolved to respond to the call. They waited in
body on their parish priest, Father John Murphy, an
called upon him to lead them. He had agreed, and
was at his command that the fire had been lit on Boula
vogue. The morning following, acting under his com
mand, they successfully ambushed a party of yeoman
ry; and then marched to capture the seat of Lord Moun
Norris at Camolin Park. Here they found a grea
prize—all the pikes and muskets that had been surrende
ed since March 17th were stored here; and with them
were some sixty carbines, and as many sabres, intende
for the use of the Camolin Yeomanry.

The news of this success spread far and wide, an
brought recruits swarming to every hill-top in th
county. Any hesitation was dispelled when, the da
following, Father John's men routed and nearly exter
minated a party of the North Cork militia; and it wa
in this fight that it was discovered what a terribl
weapon the ten-foot pike can be when used with energy
under the direction of a resolute commander.

The North Cork, despising the ill-armed peasantry
had pursued some outlying parties whom they met on
the skirts of the hill, and followed them up to the hill-top
without troubling about formation. The fleeing
peasants were, however, acting under orders—retreating
to where, concealed behind a ridge, the main body o
the rebels lay in waiting. At the proper moment thi
main body leapt from concealment and charged. The
straggling line of infantrymen, most of whom had no
time to load, could do nothing against the shock-assaul

f the pikemen. Only five of the North Cork, out of
10, managed to escape alive.

After this success the rising became virtually universal
hroughout Wexford; and parties from all the nearby
ounties made their way to join in the fight. An
pproximate estimate of the rebel strength puts their
umber at 130,000 men. Their great handicap was
ack of firearms, and still more lack of the powder
equired for even such firearms as they had. Their
nly cannon were such as they contrived to capture;
et for a week or two they held virtually the whole of
County Wexford and made desperate efforts to advance
eyond its borders.

The feature which most distinguishes the Wexford
ising—one which has provided a pretext for gross
nisrepresentation—is the number of priests and curates
vho figured as leaders in the fighting. In the case of
'ather JOHN MURPHY the excuse has been advanced
hat he only joined the rising because his chapel had
een burned down by the yeomanry. This fails as an
xcuse, since the chapel and priest's house were burned
with 140 other houses in Boulavogue) *after* the rising
ad begun. Moreover, all excuse is needless. To
xplain the "croppy" priests of Wexford it is only
ecessary to know that they all came from the same
indred, the same birthplace, and the same *class* as the
easants whom they went out to lead. JOHN MURPHY,
MICHAEL MURPHY, FRANCIS KAVANAGH, MOSES KEARNS,
MICHAEL REDMOND, and PHILIP ROCHE—all these
riests had been educated originally by "hedge-
choolmasters," and all had been, in the only way such
thing was possible under the Penal Code, "scholarship
upils" in the seminaries in which they qualified for
oly orders. That is to say, the expenses of their
ourneys abroad, and of their maintenance in their
eminaries had been made up, wholly or in part, by
oluntary contributions from the peasantry in the

parishes of their origin. That they were priests w:
incidental—and made only the difference that if the
had survived, they would have incurred the seve:
ecclesiastical censure they risked when they took up arm
They went out and fought not because they were pries
but because they were themselves *Irishmen* in revo
along with their kinsmen and their lifelong neighbour

That the touts of the Ascendancy faction shoul
represent the Wexford rising as a *Catholic war* waged t
exterminate Protestants, was to be expected. They ha
been predicting something of the kind as a staple o
their scare-propaganda. But that Catholic Nationalis
should fall into the trap and apologise for the Wexfor
rising as they have done is less easy to understanc
When it is remembered that the Wexford peasantr
were faced with what amounted to a *Protestant* war o
extermination waged, primarily, against men ninety-pe
cent. of whom were Catholic, it should be self-evider
that any rising in self-defence was bound to take th
form it did. The peasantry did, it is true, burn most o
the houses of Protestants in Co. Wexford. But as te
times as many homes of Catholics had been burne
previously either by these very "Protestants" acting a
magistrates, or by their political associates, the theor
that Catholic "religious fanaticism" caused the risin
is not merely gratuitous but dishonest. A much mo:
reliable clue is provided by the fact that while th
yeomanry and militia burned every *thatched cottage* the
came across, being confident that its occupant wa
bound to be a Catholic, and a rebel or a sympathis
with the rebellion, the rebels, in retaliation, burned a
the *slated houses* on the corresponding theory that the
occupants were either "Orangemen" or sympathise
with their deeds. It was in short a *class war*—in fact ju
what Tone feared would follow from the "prid
arrogance, and cruelty" of the "gentry" of Irelanc

Another and more fatal weakness of the rebellio

arose from its very universality and spontaneousness. They sadly lacked competent leaders, and their effort to obtain *Protestant* leaders, if they could, was pathetic in its very naïvety.

BAGENAL HARVEY, who had figured with distinction in the Dublin Society of United Irishmen before it was driven "underground" was, when Wexford Town was captured, and the prisoners were released, morally forced to agree to take the post of leader of the rebel army. His plans for the attack upon New Ross were quite well designed; and, with a better-disciplined army, success would have been assured.

But the rebel army was not an organised force: it was an agglomeration of groups, each of which fought under its own standard, usually that of its parish or barony.* It resembled very closely an army of clans of the prehistoric period, in that its one conception of strategy was to hurl itself upon the enemy in a mass and decide the issue by personal valour in a series of personal combats.

At New Ross all Harvey's plans for a converging series of attacks from different points—feints followed by real assaults—came to naught when the enemy, in a dastardly manner, shot down the bearer of a flag of truce who was carrying Harvey's ultimatum to the opposing commander. Seeing their comrade shot down, the rebels rose up as one man and hurled themselves upon the enemy. Exhaustion, failure of supplies of ammunition, over-indulgence in looted whiskey and, more than all, the skilled dispositions of the opposing officers, compelled the rebels to retreat; but not until the battle had raged for a full ten hours.

Similar displays of reckless personal bravery, combined

* *Flags*: One of these flags occasioned an item of Protestant mythology worth preserving for its crass stupidity. The flags were of any colour that came handy (except orange). One black flag bore the letters M.W.S. signifying "Marksmen: Wexford and Shelmaliere". "No Popery" mythology interpreted this as meaning "Murder Without Sin". The murder of this mythologist would probably fall under this category.

with a total lack of collective discipline, characterised each of the fights in the Wexford rising. Against the yeomanry cavalry they were invariably successful. The daring fox-hunter squires, who would take any hedge, dyke, or stone wall at full gallop when nothing more lethal than a running fox was to be met with on the far side, found it another sort of proposition when in the field beyond a bristle of pikes in determined hands waited to hurl them back. The rebels were successful, too, in reviving an ancient war device in the shape of a drove of bullocks goaded into a maddened rush upon the enemy ranks and followed smartly by a charge of pikemen. But they could do little against disciplined infantry, well-supplied with ammunition, and operating under skilled commanders. And against artillery even the most fabulous courage merely multiplied the extent of the slaughter.

At one point, if they could have known it, they had as good as won the campaign. From dawn until dark they attacked Arklow, on the coast road through Wicklow to Dublin. The enemy, his own ammunition exhausted, and his troops wearied-out, and cowed, by the reckless persistence of the Irish attacks, had begun the evacuation of the town. Only a covering party was left which would have been withdrawn in the night. If the rebel army had merely camped for the night on the battlefield, they would have found in the morning the way clear before them; and no serious obstacle between them and Dublin itself. As it was, they did not know; instead of camping they retreated, and the chance never came again.

They won at least half a dozen distinct successes against yeomanry, militia, and English infantry; they fought heroically in at least as many hard-fought defeats; but they were overpowered in the end by the combined operations of a dozen English generals, including the famous Sir JOHN MOORE himself.

Apart from the party holding out in the Bog of Allen, the rising was over when the rebel headquarters at Vinegar Hill, near Enniscorthy, were stormed on June 21st.

The Rising in Antrim and Down

While the Wexford rising was in progress, a rising broke out in Antrim and Down. On June 7th—a fortnight after the zero-hour fixed by Lord Edward Fitzgerald—the Antrim Republicans took the field under the command of HENRY JOY MACCRACKEN. The numbers who rallied were fewer than Tone would have hoped for; but more than might have been expected after the dragooning of Ulster. The Defenders in Antrim turned out almost to a man; in fact, in general, the lower orders responded to the call, while the well-to-do, who should have occupied the posts of colonels and generals, were nearly all missing. At Ballymena, Kells, and other places the rebels were able to take possession of the town; but, as no one came to lead them, they dispersed to their homes.

MacCracken led his forces gallantly to the capture of Antrim town, and had secured possession of the town-centre when a false alarm caused the rebels to retreat. The Government forces rallied, and were reinforced. At their second attempt the rebels were beaten off. Thereafter the rebel force disintegrated; and after a day or two MacCracken dismissed the few that remained. Captured while trying to make his way into Down, MacCracken was court-martialled and hanged.

In Down 7,000 men assembled. Ably led by a Lisburn linen-draper, HENRY MUNRO, the rebels scored inconclusive successes in two hard-fought engagements. But despite their courage and determination they were defeated and scattered on June 14th at Ballynahinch. All the leaders were hanged; Munro before his own shop-door.

Vengeance on the Vanquished

When it was clear that the rebellion had missed its
mark, Ascendancy circles, whom its outbreak had thrown
into a literal panic, took vengeance for their fright in
a frenzy of blood-lust. As a rule no prisoners were taken ;
or were spared on the field of battle only to be executed
later. All the Wexford leaders were hanged, Bagenal
Harvey one of the first, as were the leaders in Antrim
and Down.

Any commander in the field suspected of giving
quarter was denounced for " treasonable clemency ".
Horribly as the yeomanry and militia had behaved
before the rising, they were incited by Ascendanc
clamours to out-do all their previous efforts and pursue
to extermination everyone who had taken to arms and
everyone who gave them help or harbourage.

"The minds of people," said Lord Cornwallis,
Viceroy and Commander-in-Chief, speaking of the
Viceregal circle, " are in such a state that nothing
but blood will satisfy them . . . Their conversation
and conduct point to no other mode of concluding
this unhappy business but that of extirpation."

It was more than suspected that the poorer quarters of
Dublin harboured thousands of sworn United men and
quantities of concealed arms. To extort confessions,
suspects were rounded up and systematically flogged
without mercy one after the other. This went on for
days under the personal supervision of the chief sine-
curist and corruption-fund-manager to the Government,
JOHN CLAUDIUS BERESFORD.

The hunting for rebels, the courts-martial, hangings,
floggings, and house-burnings went on for weeks.

In their blood-frenzy the Ascendancy gang made
determined efforts, with the aid of transparently vile
informers, to secure the conviction and hanging of both
GRATTAN and CURRAN. To such a length did this
frenzy go that the Viceroy himself and even the savage

arl of Clare and the merciless Viscount Castlereagh
hen Chief Secretary) were accused of showing " criminal
mpathy with traitors " when they insisted that officers
militia and yeomanry must keep their men under
sciplined restraint.

The English Generals, each as he arrived and saw
e state of things, were horrified. They insisted flatly
at clemency must be conceded to the men who surren-
ered. And it was their clemency, and the good
ehaviour of the English and Scottish regular troops
wards the civilian population and the prisoners,
hich did most to restore quiet in the countryside.
he contrast between the private soldiers who insisted
pon paying for everything they obtained (the Scottish
roops having an especially good repute for this) and
at of the gentleman-officers of the yeomanry and
ilitia was so great that it was preserved in fireside
gend for years afterwards.

And Sir John Moore himself, writing a fierce protest
t the conduct of the yeomanry, and of some of the
nglish militia regiments whom they had corrupted,
eclared emphatically that " if I were an Irishman I
vould be a rebel ".

The English Government, stirred up by its generals,
oined them in pressing the Irish Administration for an
Amnesty Act, under which all not proved guilty of murder
hould be allowed to depart unmolested. This Amnesty
Act was passed by the Irish Parliament on the 20th July.

It excluded from pardon two categories : (1) the State
risoners arrested before May 23rd and (2) those guilty
of murder. This second category gave the yeomanry
and Orange magistracy a pretext for maintaining their
terror for years. The pretence of searching for suspected
" murderers " was nearly as satisfactory to them as had
been that of searching for arms. Men were still being
hanged in 1802 for crimes they were alleged to have
committed in 1798.

Barbarities had been committed by the rebels in tl
course of the rising in Wexford. A slave-revolt is, f
obvious reasons, always likely to reflect in barbarou
deeds the barbarities which have provoked it. But tl
"horrors" of the Wexford rising have been so muc
the stock-in-trade of reactionaries that we are absolve
from the necessity of saying more than that—they wer
inexcusable; but they were, in every case, matche
with equal and greater barbarities inflicted befor
during, and after the rising by the other side.

As soon as the Wexford rising had been crushed, th
Government turned its attention to the State Prisoner:
Lord Edward had died of his wounds, so the first to b
disposed of were JOHN and HENRY SHEARES. Both wer
hanged. Then the Government turned its attention t
the prisoners captured on March 12th. They soon mad
it clear that, with the aid of the informer Reynolds
they proposed to work through the whole list one b
one. The prisoners through their representatives—
THOMAS ADDIS EMMET, ARTHUR O'CONNOR, and
WILLIAM JAMES MACNEVIN—asked for a parley; and
offered, in return for permission to go voluntarily into
exile, to give the Government all the information in
their power—except such as would incriminate individuals. The offer was, in the end, accepted; but two of
the leading United Irishmen had been hanged before
the negotiations concluded—a barbarity which Emmet
and his fellow-negotiators thought a plain breach of an
honourable undertaking, but which they were power-
less to resist. (Another breach was that the prisoners,
though released from gaol, were detained in internment
at Fort George in Scotland where they were kept until
the peace with France of 1802.)

But then, just as this negotiation was concluded,
the French came after all.

he French Expeditions of 1798

When the news of the rising of May 23rd reached
ıris, Tone and his fellow-exiles besieged the French
overnment with frantic demands that aid should be
nt to Ireland, at once. The Government eventually
;reed to try a plan Tone had suggested in 1796—that
: a " staggered " expedition.

Incompetence and the absence of the French Fleet
ı Egypt combined with downright sabotage to cause
eart-breaking delays. The first expedition did not
ave until August 7th, and then it left without proper
ıthorisation. This expedition, led by GENERAL
 [UMBERT, made a landing at Ballina, Co. Mayo, and
ıflicted a defeat upon a force of militia led by General
ake.

But Humbert's force was too small, and it came too
ıte. It was forced to surrender to a superior force of
ınglish regular soldiers at Ballynamuck, Co. Longford.
he French were given the treatment proper for prisoners
f war; the Irish peasants who had joined them were
ursued and exterminated without mercy. Two Irish
efugees who were officers in the French service—
ᴜᴋᴇ TEELING'S son, BARTHOLOMEW, and TONE'S
ounger brother MATTHEW—were taken to Dublin and
ıanged.

A few days after Humbert's surrender a single French
hip, with a few refugees on board, headed by NAPPER
ᴛANDY, and carrying a large cargo of arms and ammuni-
ion, reached Rutland Island, off the Coast of Donegal.
.earning that Humbert had surrendered, these invaders
leparted.

Three weeks later, a larger French force making for
.ough Swilly was intercepted near Tory Island by a
;reatly superior English force. After fighting against
our English vessels for four hours, the French flagship,
he *Hoche*, of 74 guns, was reduced to a wreck and
orced to surrender in a sinking condition. Among the

prisoners taken off her was THEOBALD. WOLFE TON
who, during the action, had "fought like a demon

Sent, chained, to Dublin, he was tried by court-marti
and sentenced to be hanged. He claimed, as a soldie
and an officer in the French service, the right to l
executed in the military manner. His claim being denie
he took an opportunity, on the night before the da
fixed for his execution, to cut his own throat. So
defiant to the last, died the first man to dream of
United Irish Republic.

He died on November 19th, 1798, and was burie
by his father in the churchyard in Bodenstown, Co
Kildare.

CHAPTER ELEVEN

THE UNION: ROBERT EMMET: SUMMARY

As soon as it was clear that the Rebellion was crushed, and that the French, in consequence of the crippling of their Fleet by Nelson at the Nile (August 2nd, 1798), had ceased to be immediately dangerous, PITT and the English Government proceeded to exact their price for saving the Ascendancy Administration from the mess into which it had landed itself. That price was the Act which, from January 1st, 1801, UNITED THE PARLIAMENTS of Great Britain and Ireland.

The attempt at insurrection by ROBERT EMMET, in Dublin, July 23rd, 1803, was, in part, a response to the Union; more basically it was the last flare-up of the fire lit by the UNITED IRISHMEN, and a transition to new conditions of struggle.

The Act of Union

Pitt had always regarded the independent Irish Parliament as (from his *imperialist* point of view) an anomaly and a danger. The rising gave him his chance to get rid of it.

There was no denying the fact that with every initial advantage in their hands the Ascendancy Oligarchy had only been saved from annihilation by the prompt intervention of British troops in large numbers and by the constant vigilance of the British Navy.

Everything the corrupt, bigoted, oligarchical, and tyrannical Ascendancy Administration and its "managed" Parliament had done counted in the indictment against it. The aborting of Grattan's Revolution—the arrest of its progress at the half-way stage which enhanced the power of the oligarchy while adding little to the power of the people; its refusal to unite the Irish Nation by making the Parliament truly representative; its proved inability to keep a divided nation under control; its resort to the counter-revolutionary barbarities of Orangeism and the ORANGE YEOMANRY; all these things proved the dangerous incapacity of the oligarchical Irish Administration.

The insurrection had, therefore, barely been crushed before Pitt was pressing proposals for a Union of the two Parliaments and, thereby, of the two "Kingdoms" of Ireland and Great Britain.

Passed independently by each Parliament, the ACT OF UNION came into force on January 1st, 1801. Thereafter Ireland became, politically, *part of Great Britain*, and the Irish people *in theory* became "British". The history of Ireland since that date is a demonstration of the absurdity of the theory and the growing contradiction between its assumption and concrete actuality.

In the "Repeal" and "Home Rule" agitations of the 19th century Irish Parliamentarians made much and overmuch of the methods whereby "Bloody" CASTLE-REAGH smoothed the path of the Act of Union through the Irish Parliament; and too little of the respects in which the Union under a pretence of making two nations into one greatly intensified the actuality of their separation—by adding considerably to the power of the English Government and ruling class to hold the Irish people in permanent subjection and to divert Ireland's economic development into channels profitable to the English ruling class.

So far as the Union was *real*, it was a union of two branches of one and the same *oligarchy*—of land-owning aristocrats with their financier allies. The "Irish" branch parted with a precarious semi-independence, and gained, in return, the security of fusion with its English counterpart. That the Irish aristocracy and gentry only consented to the change on receipt of a handsome compensation in cash, or titles, or both, speaks highly for their ability to drive a bargain. They allowed themselves to be "bribed" into doing what, after all, was *directly in line with their class interests*— something which, if Pitt had not been in a hurry, he would have found nearly every man of them willing to do for no bribe at all. The ability of the Irish gentry to " grab a guinea so tight that King George squealed for mercy " was never better demonstrated.

The Anglo-Irish landed aristocracy was, in 1798-1801, what it had been since 1690—England's garrison in Ireland. Even where they were "Old Irish " by descent they held lands and titles by tenures which English conquest had created and imposed, and which were secured against encroachment and destruction at the hands of an insurgent Irish Nation by English political and military might. A *connection* with England was, therefore, indispensable in one form or another to the landed oligarchy which monopolised Parliamentary power in Ireland. While England preferred to rule Ireland, indirectly, through this " garrison ", there were, of course, incidental emoluments, jobs, and pickings to be gained by the instruments. The much-talked-of " *bribery* " which secured the passage of the Act of Union was from this angle no more than the customary compensation paid to a hireling whose services were no longer required.

" Would you *sell* your country ? " asked an indignant patriot of a noble lord. " I would *that*," was the reply, " and thankful I'll be that I've got a country to sell ! "

The point will be seen most clearly if we look at it through the eyes of the English branch of the ruling oligarchy.

By the Act of Union the English ruling class got rid of *three great menaces* : (1) of Revolutionary Republicanism, militant in Ireland, but also potential in England ; (2) of a French invasion and occupation of Ireland ;

and (3) of Ireland's potential economic rivalry with England. In exchange it accepted a new *danger*—whose dimensions at that early date were, however, negligible—namely, that whereas till then the first impact of Irish discontent had fallen upon the *Irish* Administration, in the form of struggles by this or that *class* for relief of one kind and another, from the Union onwards these impacts fell directly upon the English Government and increasingly assumed the form of *Nationalist* struggles to recover *Freedom for the Irish Nation* as such.

This risk, however, had a set-off which at the time more than out-weighed its force. The 102 members added to the English Parliament—nearly to a man nominees of the landed interest—were an invaluable reinforcement to the oligarchy in its political resistance to the rising clamours of the *English* trading and manufacturing bourgeoisie for *Parliamentary Reform*. Growing out of this was yet another gain. Ireland supplied an unanswerable pretext for maintaining the standing army at a far higher level than Whig theory regarded, normally, as either desirable or safe. Thus, once again, Ireland filled the rôle of a reservoir from which the counter-revolutionary rulers could draw the force necessary to crush revolution in England.

In these various ways the Union revealed the agreement and solidarity of the landed oligarchs, English and Irish, and their radical opposition to the *classes* they exploited. Also, under a pretence of "uniting" the two countries, it revealed their *national* differences ; and made these differences acute by perpetuating the "colonial" subordination of Ireland's economy to that of England. In that negative sense the Union proved a powerful factor in the development of Irish nationality and Nationalism.

The Catholics and the Union

The Orange Order was, at first, hostile to the proposed

Union.   Its special interest being bound up with the
existence of an Irish Administration, which it could
blackmail in the name of " Protestant Ascendancy ",
the Orange Order saw in the relegation of that Administration to a very minor rôle a direct attack upon its
own immediate interest. It took strong political pressure,
and a promise of favours to come—with assurances
that " Ascendancy " was safe—to induce the Orange
Order to relapse into a sulky acquiescence with the
Union.

The Catholic Hierarchy, on the other hand, favoured
the proposal and brought over to its support a majority
of the well-to-do Catholics.   From its relation to the
Papacy as a temporal power the Hierarchy is invariably
biased in general in favour of the Established Order in
every country. The Irish Hierarchy, with its eyes on a
possible reconversion to Catholicism of wealthy England,
has always tended to regard Ireland, primarily, as a
jumping-off point for that desirable end. It has always
been eager, wherever possible, to *oblige* the rulers of
England.

During the Rising of '98, the Hierarchy led the way
in expressing its " detestation " of the rebellion, and
its " unswerving loyalty " to the Crown. It ordered the
parish priests to check the spread of rebellion, and to
secure the surrender of arms. There were many instances
where rebels were refused the sacraments until they
had proved their " repentance " by turning informers.

As the Rebellion developed into a " war of the poor
against the rich " the Hierarchy, members of the most
wealthy land-owning corporation in the world, sided
(as it always does in such emergencies) with the *owners
of property* against their enemies. They, too, desired the
Union as a safeguard against revolution. The same
motive made Catholic property-owners range themselves
on the Government's side against the rebels. Catholic
peers raised yeomanry corps which were active in

M

suppressing the rising. Catholic merchants and lawyers
especially, were zealous recruits to the yeomanry
showing as much bitterness against the poor " Croppies
as did any Orangeman. There was thus a powerfu
Catholic support ready-made for the Union.

The influence of the work of the Catholic Committe
was not, however, wholly lost ; and it needed a temptin
bribe offered—through Castlereagh—by Pitt to wi
the majority of Catholics over to an uneasy acqui
escence in the Union. Pitt, through Castlereagh, let it b
believed that, in return for the Act of Union, he woul
secure the admission of Catholics to Parliament, and t
the higher grades of the Law and the Services. He als
mooted the suggestion that the Catholic clergy migh
be subsidised by the State.

The proposal was particularly tempting to the Catholi
merchants, manufacturers, and town-dwellers generally
in that the admission of Catholics to Parliament woul
have broken the monopoly of the Irish Protestan
landed-aristocracy, and would have allowed the Catholi
urban bourgeoisie to wrest the representation of th
rural areas from the territorial lords. Fear of the con
sequences of such a happening caused the mor
reactionary section of the territorial oligarchy in Englan
to intrigue against Pitt's proposal through the Cour
cliques. Once again George III's religious mania prove
a trump card, and the Irish Catholic bourgeoisie foun
itself double-crossed.

Emmet's Conspiracy

Another aftermath of the rising of '98 was th
conspiracy organised in 1803 by ROBERT, the younges
brother of Thomas Addis EMMET—who, released wit
the other State Prisoners after the Peace of Amiens i
1802, had made his way to Paris and entered the Frenc
State service.

ROBERT EMMET—who had visited his brother in Paris

and been given an interview by Buonaparte, then First Consul of the French Republic—had returned to Ireland convinced that the French would soon invade England. This, he thought, would give Ireland her opportunity; and he planned accordingly. His calculations were based broadly upon two main considerations : (1) that the mass of the people in Ireland were disgusted and humili- ated by the Act of Union which had reduced to a nullity such small power as they had possessed of influencing the decisions of Parliament; and (2) that the United Irishmen of Dublin, with those of Wicklow and parts of Kildare, had suffered least from the savage repressions following the Rising.

His plan was essentially *Blanquist*—just such a plan as Auguste Blanqui himself would have loved. It built wholly upon a belief that the people would respond instantly, and in mass, if only the signal for revolt was given by a well-planned *coup*. He planned therefore to capture Dublin Castle, and thereafter Dublin city, by a surprise assault. And, on paper, his plan was excellent. He secured the co-operation of all the really trustworthy old United men he could find; and he had the support of the Wicklow men led by MILES BYRNE and MICHAEL DWYER and a body from Co. Kildare.

The plan broke down, as Blanquist *coups* are bound to do—since the secrecy which conceals the design from the authorities also conceals it from the masses. Consequently, the more completely the Government is surprised, the more the masses are bewildered and made suspicious. The more a Blanquist *coup* succeeds, at the outset, the more certain it is to fail in the end.

Robert Emmet's plans worked satisfactorily right up to the point where, in the dusk of Saturday, July 23rd, 1803, he sallied out from his headquarters with a small company and advanced to the capture of Dublin Castle. The Wicklow men were all hidden safely in working- class homes, stables, and warehouses along the lower

quays, awaiting the prearranged rocket signal. The
Kildare men were on the look-out for the second rocket
which would be their summons. But the condition
precedent for both signals—the capture of Dublin Castle
—was never attained.

Emmet's followers, wild with excitement, went chasing
after the first red-coats they saw. The Saturday night
crowds in the streets only joined in so far as they thought
it was a common riot against the soldiers and the police.
In a few minutes Emmet found himself a leader without
a following: a fine Saturday-night street-row was in
progress, but the insurrection as such had completely
evaporated. Worse still, one party of his followers,
chasing red-coats, had come upon a judge, riding in his
coach, whom they mistook for the " hanging-judge ",
Lord Norbury.* Him they piked to death on the spot.
He was, in fact, Lord Kilwarden, one of the few honourable and humane judges left on the Bench. Thoroughly
horrified, Emmet abandoned the enterprise. The signals
to the Wicklow and Kildare men were never given.

The rioters held possession of a street or two for a
couple of hours ; but the rising as such was all over in
a few minutes.

Emmet might have got away to France as easily as
Miles Byrne did. As is well known, he lingered in the
neighbourhood through inability to tear himself away
from his sweetheart, Curran's daughter, Sarah.

He was sold by an informer, and hanged, as were a
score of his followers. The romantic circumstances of
his end—his passion for Sarah Curran ; the fact that
Curran, normally generous and always dauntless, for
the first and last time in his life refused to defend a
United Irishman, he being infuriated at his daughter's
clandestine affair and not a little angry at being himself

* His character is indicated by an anecdote told of him and Curran at a Bar
dinner. " Is that *hung* beef you have before you, Mr. Curran ? " " Not until
your Lordship *tries* it, Lord Norbury."

put again in personal peril thereby ; the fact that the counsel who did defend Emmet, Leonard MacNally, was proved, years later, to have been the informer who had sold him—these things, with his youth and his gallantry, have thrown an imperishable halo of romance over the name and memory of ROBERT EMMET.

Deepening the tragedy was the fact that it brought death also to Tone's friend, THOMAS RUSSELL. With the other State prisoners he had been released in 1802 ; but, meeting Robert Emmet in Paris, he had been fired by his hopes, and had returned with him to try to rouse the North simultaneously with Dublin. To their dismay and sorrow he and JAMIE HOPE (the Antrim weaver who had fought under MacCracken and now joined Robert Emmet as his first recruit after Miles Byrne) found that not a man in the North would move. Russell, sheltered in the homes of Dublin labourers, despite three rewards of £500 each offered for his capture, was spotted in the street by a military magistrate who knew him personally. He was overpowered, carried to trial, convicted, and hanged.

Emmet died on September 20th, 1803 ; Russell died on October 21st in the same year. With them the Society of United Irishmen passed from the world of fact and practice into the realm of immortal memory.

What the United Irishmen Accomplished

To " write-off " the United Irishmen's movement as a complete failure simply because they did not attain the object they set themselves would be a complete error. After the movement was all over and done with, the fact that it *had been* remained operative in the transformed Irish national consciousness with which the English conquerors thenceforward had to deal.

How greatly the United Irishmen affected their period can best be estimated from the systematic deception which has conspired with romantic misconception to

throw a sevenfold veil of falsification over the whole
struggle from 1791 to 1798—a process in which Irish
romantics have done, if anything, more mischief than
English imperialists.

The favourite contention of reactionaries has been
that, in attempting to draw Catholics, Dissenters, and
Protestants into a common, united, *national* movement,
they were attempting the unattainable—since the
insurrection " proved " the absolute impossibility of
uniting Catholics and Protestants.

We have set out in broad outline the proof of the
falsity of this assertion. We have shown how practical,
economic, political, and social forces had been at work
which had evolved historically an Irish nation as a fact,
and one which found its expression in the Society of
United Irishmen. Far from the United men attempting
the impossible, they fought primarily to bring to life
a general awareness of something which history had in
fact already established. And the frenzied malice of the
Orange Order—founded expressly for the purpose of
dissipating the success the United Irishmen had attained
—is proof that the reaction was at its wits' end how to
stave off that general recognition. But for their frenzied
intervention, Irish National *unity* would have been
inevitable—as indeed it has proved and will prove to
be in the long run.

The utter falsity of the charge that the rising of '98
proved, in practice, to be nothing but a war of extermination waged by the Catholics against the Protestants,
we have already demonstrated. The *form* of the rising,
in Wexford in particular, was dictated as we have shown
by the counter-revolutionaries, who had been at work
in the Government's interest for years before '98, and
who, in all their activity, manifested a savage readiness
to exterminate Catholics in general and *rebel* Catholics
in particular. So far as the Rising of '98 did take the
form of a war of sect against sect, this must be attributed,

firstly, to the historical process which had made the line of division between the sects coincide broadly with the line dividing the rich and the poor ; secondly, to the sectarian savagery of the Government itself and its Orange agents ; and, thirdly, to the unbridled falsifications the Government agents put out on purpose to inflame anti-Catholic prejudices in England.

The often-repeated allegation that it was the Rising's turning out to be nothing but a "great Catholic conspiracy" which caused the falling away from the United Irishmen of the Protestant North shows, as to the first part, a total ignorance of the actual state of the Catholic question between 1782 and 1798 ; and, as to the second part, shows a total ignorance of the historical determinants of the rise and decline of the United Irishmen's movement in the North.

The central fact this allegation ignores is that (except in one respect) there was less need, in 1791-8, for the Catholics to conspire *as Catholics* than there had been for a century previously. The worst and most insulting provisions of the Penal Code had been repealed, especially those which imposed restraints on the clergy and the Hierarchy. And, by the subsidies paid by the Administration for the building and maintenance of the Catholic seminary of Maynooth, the Catholic religion was actually more favoured then than it had been at any time since the Reformation. To make the "conspiracy" theory good its propounders are forced back upon the desperate expedient of contending that Grattan and the Volunteers, and Tone and the United Irishmen, were all (along with the Whiteboys and the Defenders) the purchased tools of "Popish" intrigue—something difficult to believe, even in Portadown ; but easy to credit, it would seem, in English newspaper offices.

The exception we have noted proved the rule : the only reason Catholics *as such* had for conspiring in 1798 was to protect themselves against the sectarian barbarity of *the Orange Yeomanry and Militia*. This, as we have sufficiently indicated, was a frantic endeavour by the worst and most degenerate reactionaries in the Protestant camp, to destroy the unity the *revolutionary Protestants* had achieved, and to re-establish in practice the social and political subjection of the Catholics which had been abolished in law.

To the evidence we have already cited may be added here the testimony of a Quakeress, MARY LEADBEATER, who lived throughout the rising in Co. Carlow. She testifies categorically (according to Lecky) that, while the rebels had the upper hand,—

> " Nothing in the least resembling a desire to massacre the Protestant population came within her observations. ' Women and children ', she says, ' were spared and Quakers in general escaped ; but *woe betide the oppressor of the poor*, the hard landlord, the severe master, or him who was looked upon as an enemy ' "

This direct testimony of the *class* character of the Rising gives a clue to the ferocious character of the repression which, more than once, evidenced a desire to exterminate the rebels wholesale as slaves who had mutinied and broken their chains. The extent of the slaughter and the cold-blooded deliberation with which the " Croppies " were butchered while unarmed and helpless—and often when entirely innocent of participation in the rising— are glossed over in the official and " loyalist " records but cannot wholly be concealed even there. Mary Leadbeater notes a grim fact :

> " For several months there was no sale for bacon cured in Ireland from a well-founded fear of the hogs having fed on the flesh of men."

The special savagery of the yeomanry and the militia officers is more than accounted for by the fact that they were mostly drawn from the ranks of the most arrogant and brutal class that ever existed in Ireland—the rack-renting, middlemen, squireen class. The circumstances in which this class had evolved made it regard the peasantry, in general, as at best a cheap variety of beasts of burden, and at worst as vermin to be hunted to complete extermination. ARTHUR YOUNG, who toured Ireland on the eve of Grattan's revolution, recorded his disgust and detestation of this class and of the abject servility they demanded from their tenantry and labourers. EDWARD WAKEFIELD, who made a minute study of Ireland just after the Union, concurs with Young's opinion at every point.

Even without their testimony we would be forced to the same conclusion by the opinion this class entertained of its own character. This opinion has been embalmed in a couple of songs which have survived in consequence of the spirited Irish airs to which they were set—namely, the *Rakes of Mallow* and *Garryowen* respectively. A few lines from each are all we need to quote :

> Beauing, belleing, dancing, drinking,
> Breaking windows, damning, sinking,
> Ever raking, never thinking,
>   Live the rakes of Mallow.
> Racking tenants, stewards teasing,
> Swiftly spending, slowly raising,
> Wishing to spend all their days in
>   Raking as at Mallow !

Mallow, it may be explained, was at this period in Ireland what Bath was in England. Garryowen was then a fashionable quarter of Limerick City. Its anthem echoes the Mallow theme :

> We are the boys that take delight in
> Smashing the Limerick lamps when lighting,
> Through the streets like sporters fighting,
>   Tearing all before us.

> We'll beat the bailiffs out of fun,
> We'll make the Mayor and Sheriffs run,
> We are the boys no man dares dun,
>   If he regards a whole skin.

It needs little imagination to picture how such a class would react to a general revolt of their tenantry. Nor is it hard to understand that yeomanry corps raised, purged, and commanded by such men would become, as the Commander-in-Chief, Lord Abercromby, said: " a licentious and brutal banditti, terrible to everybody except the enemy". To cover up their deeds and the retaliation they provoked under the pretence that it was all a regrettable display of " religious bigotry " is a feat of hypocrisy so colossal that one stands in awe before its matchless impudence.

The falling-away of the North

But why was it that the North, once the stronghold of the United movement, fell away so sadly?

In part, of course, this is accounted for by the dragooning of Ulster; but historical causes were operating to produce a decline in the revolutionary tempo of the North even before this dragooning began.

The North was roused in the first place by the enthusiasm engendered by the French Revolution. While that revolution was passing through its ascendant phases, rising from triumph to triumph, the revolutionary democratic and humanitarian enthusiasm of Belfast and the North knew no bounds. When, in due course, the Revolution passed its zenith and entered upon its phase of increasing conservatism and decline, the revolutionary enthusiasm of Ulster underwent a corresponding change.

In 1792 it was the newly-born French Republic which was isolated and forced to fight in desperation against a coalition of aristocratic enemy states. In 1798—

and still more in 1803—it was Britain which was isolated; while France, at the head of a European coalition, was developing rapidly into an imperialist rival of Britain.

If Tone and the United Irishmen could have seen into the future they would have perceived that the possibility of a revolutionary war of universal liberation began to fade from the moment when in July, 1794, Robespierre was overthrown and he and all the members of the Commune Council of Paris were executed in a single batch. While Carnot remained the Commissar for War, and Jacobin Generals such as Hoche remained to head the armies, a measure of the Jacobin impulse survived. But when Hoche died of consumption in 1797 and, in the same year, Carnot was driven into exile, the hope of Ireland's liberation by a revolutionary French army shrank rapidly towards extinction.

The more sharp-sighted and sensitive Ulster Jacobins perceived this process intuitively. As the revolutionary tempo slackened in France, and the revolution entered ever more plainly into its conservative phase, these Ulster Jacobins felt their willingness to run risks in the cause of world-revolution suffer a killing frost. In addition their own circumstances had undergone a change. Many merchants and manufacturers in Antrim and Down participated in the new enterprises begotten by the industrial revolution and grew rich correspondingly. When the testing hour came their riches determined their choice between preserving the *status quo* and risking all in a general overturn.

That is how it came to be that, in the end, it was, as Patrick Pearse said, " *the great, faithful, splendid common people* " who rose in '98.

PART III

FROM O'CONNELL TO YOUNG IRELAND

CHAPTER TWELVE

AFTER THE UNION

THE theory that the Union made one country of England and Ireland is contradicted by the fact that, between 1820 and 1850, Ireland was the field for two great constitutional agitations, one agrarian " war " and one attempted insurrection ; from all of which England was free.

The economic causation from which these movements arose is examined in this chapter.

Ireland's Place in England's Economy

In England, between 1801 and 1850, the industrial revolution rose to its peak and on its basis England attained a hegemony of the world-market. Ireland's manufacturers were prevented from sharing in this advance (1) by the loss of Parliamentary power to protect their home market ; (2) by the lack of adequate coal and iron deposits ; (3) from lack of capital : all the revenue extracted from Ireland by the landlords being drained away for consumption and investment in England. Thus Ireland's manufacturers were, with few exceptions, left further and further behind while England became, conversely, a better and better market for Irish agricultural products.

What the Commercial Restraints and Navigation Acts were needed to bring about in the seventeenth and eighteenth centuries, economic competition did unaided in the Age of Steam.

Inexorably Ireland was forced back upon the rôle of feeder to England's economic superiority; supplying it with cheap foodstuffs, with raw materials, and cheap labour as well as investment capital wrung from the Irish people in the form of rent and tithes.

Landlordism in Ireland

These causes produced a progressive increase in the numbers and proportion of the population engaged upon the land. At the same time this increase brought no improvement of methods or conditions in agricultural production. In each case the poverty of the people and the indifference of their exploiters was an absolute bar to advance.

EDWARD WAKEFIELD, a careful observer, notes one fact as universally observable in the period immediately after the Union. The Irish landlord was not a partner in production, investing capital in fencing, draining, farm-buildings, and cottages, and bound thereby to the cultivator by social and economic ties. He was simply the receiver of a rent charge. When the labour of the cultivator multiplied the produce of the soil the rent-charge was raised ruthlessly until the whole increase was swept into the landlord's maw. Irish landlords, says Wakefield, were not to be compared to English squires so much as to the " feudal " lords who owned the land upon which London stands.

The absence of any alternative to land-work (short of emigration) gave rise to an intensified demand for land, especially in small plots ; and this, as in the earlier period, gave scope for the operations of the middleman. On good land competition led to excessive division and subdivision—or, alternatively, to the replacement of tillage by pasture farming. On poor land the landlord saved himself trouble by letting land to whole villages collectively. In these " rundale " villages relics of the clan system survived in the custom of allocating strips or portions of the common fields by lot, annually. A rundale village usually indicated an easy-going landlord who renewed leases as a matter of course.

Thus, whether landlords were " easy " or " hard ", agricultural technique had no chance to progress. A " good " landlord was merely one who did not use to the full his power to crush the tenants utterly.

Labour paid by an allocation of potato patch and cow's grass continued in this period. Wakefield records that labour was valued at from 4d. to 8d. per day; 220 working-days in the year were fairly often the price of a cottage, potato-patch, and cow's grass.

An observer giving evidence in 1825 cited examples of rent which exceeded the total yield of the land. The cottager had to supplement the gains from his holding by earnings from domestic industry or from harvest work in England or Scotland before he could pay his rent.

> " There are parts of Connacht where a man plants his potatoes at the proper season and shuts up his cabin and goes to England and labours; and perhaps his wife and children beg on the roads; and when he comes back to dig his potatoes, with the wages of his English labour in his pocket, he is able to pay a larger sum in rent than he could have extracted from the soil."—Lewis: *H. of L. Select Committee* (1825).

Despite the general poverty, house-rents in towns were often high in consequence of landlord monopoly. " Houses are dearer in some of the remote corners of Ireland," says Wakefield, " than in the best parts of London. . . . The whole town of Belfast belongs to one proprietor who has it in his power to exact whatever rents he thinks proper."

Poverty in Ireland: its extent

Some indication of the numbers included in the various categories of the population may be gained from the returns for the hearth-tax. The figures for 1791 show 701,102 dwellings in Ireland. Of these 112,556 were exempt from the 2s. tax as " inhabited by paupers ". One-hearth dwellings numbered 483,990. Add these

N

two together and 85 per cent. of the total houses are shown as of the poorest class.

This category was increased after the Catholic Relief Act of 1793 which gave the vote to " freeholds " of an annual value of 40s. Landlords, agents, and middlemen multiplied these tenancies without stint to enhance their political importance (and the bribes they could command). The vote was expected to be " *paid as part of the rent* ".

Excessive subdivision, and the poverty of the tenants, ensured a progressive deterioration of the soil which intensified the poverty. The tenant either could not manure or feared to do so lest his rent be raised. It was common practice as a lease drew to its termination for the tenant to destroy his improvements (fences, drains, outbuildings, even chimneys) as otherwise their value would be included in the " fine " exacted for a renewal of the lease. Alternatively, if left intact they might induce greedy " land grabbers " to overbid the occupier ruinously when the lease was put up for public " cant " (auction).

In Ulster a custom had become established which gave the tenant a property in his improvements. The absence of such a custom elsewhere in Ireland had a fearful effect in depressing the condition of the culti-vators. In 1791 quite a number of the dwellers in one-hearth habitations held 40 acres or more. It was positively dangerous for them to indulge in the luxury of an improved dwelling. The census of 1841 revealed nearly 500,000 families as still living in one-room mud-cabins.

An additional infliction would be unbelievable if it were not well attested :

> " I have frequently seen the cattle of the occupying tenant driven to the pound and . . . sold, when he had paid his rent to the middleman who had failed to pay it to the head landlord. The numerous

instances of such distress, which everyone who has resided some time in Ireland must have witnessed, are truly deplorable, and I believe them to be one of the causes of the frequent risings of the people which . . . have been attended with atrocities shocking to humanity and disgraceful to the Empire."—WAKEFIELD : *Survey of Ireland*, vol. i. p. 244.

There was acute distress in England all through this period. The handicraft workers and the peasant cultivators were being crushed, ruthlessly, out of existence. They, with their wives and children, were being drawn into the vortex of the new " factory hells ", and cheap food was required to keep their labour " cheap".

The Irish manufacturer or handicraft worker, unless he was willing to emigrate, was flung back upon the land—and the mercies of the middleman, agent, landlord, and title-proctor. The cheap food wrung from the Irish peasant ruined the English peasant and drew him into the factory, where the product of his sweated labour ruined more Irish handicraftsmen and drove them to the land—to put up the rents and increase the cheap food supply that kept the vicious circle spinning.

There was famine in Ireland in the late '40's ; they were the " Hungry Forties " in England, too. The difference was that in England the toilers were exploited as a *class* ; the Irish producers were, in addition, exploited as a subject *nation*. That is why, when agitation in England took the form of working-men's CHARTISM, in Ireland it took the form of a *National* agitation for a REPEAL OF THE UNION and even for the setting-up of an IRISH REPUBLIC.

CHAPTER THIRTEEN

O'CONNELL AND CATHOLIC EMANCIPATION

FROM such a crushing defeat as that experienced by the Irish masses in 1798, recovery was necessarily slow. It was made through tentative approaches, much more limited in their aims than the earlier demand for an outright national independence.

The first recovery was made under the leadership of DANIEL O'CONNELL (1785–1847), a master-agitator, who dominates his period as few agitators have ever been able to do. His victorious struggle for CATHOLIC EMANCIPATION (1829) is the theme of this chapter.

Daniel O'Connell

Born in Kerry, in humble circumstances, but the nephew of a landed proprietor who made him his heir, Daniel O'Connell, whose ancestry was Gaelic-Irish without admixture, was educated originally for the priesthood. The Jacobin revolution (1792–4) broke up the French seminary in which he was a student ; and he returned to Ireland and studied for the law. The foundation for his great national popularity was laid by his outstanding success as an advocate.

A big man physically, full of abounding vitality, he showed distinctively Gaelic qualities at a score of points. Innumerable tales are told of his wit, his dexterity as a cross-examiner, his athletic feats, his amours, his eloquence, and above all his wonderful voice which could attain an astonishing range without losing any of its extreme beauty of tone.

He made his way to the front in the debates of the Catholic Committee, from whose leadership he eventually ousted old JOHN KEOGH. In 1823 the Catholic Committee having dissolved, O'Connell made a new departure by founding the CATHOLIC ASSOCIATION.

Its key-idea was a " rent " paid voluntarily by every Catholic. This " rent " was collected at the Chapel doors, and was forwarded through the priests who were made *ex officio* members of the Committee of the Association. The " rent " was fixed at a minimum of a shilling a year; or, as O'Connell was fond of saying, " a penny a month, a farthing a week—and four weeks thrown in for nothing". In this way O'Connell (1) secured the finances of the Association; (2) gained the support of the priests; (3) stilled the doubts of the Hierarchy; and (4) ensured his own leadership, since it was his personal popularity which made the scheme workable.

Orangeism, the Tories, and the Whigs

O'Connell chose his time for launching the Association very astutely.

The social transformation and unsettlement produced by the Industrial Revolution in England and by the reverberations of the French Revolution, which still echoed on the Continent and in America, were making it evident that the aristocratic oligarchy which had ruled England since 1688 would have to concede reform at some point or become itself reformed out of existence.

Growing conflict between such commercial and industrial interests as were represented indirectly in the House of Commons, and the landlord interest represented largely in the Commons but to the exclusion of all rivals in the House of Lords, was leading to constant quarrels between the Houses.

A coalition of moderate Whigs and progressive Tories held office, precariously; steering its way tortuously between Reformers and Radicals to the Left and reactionary Tories to the Right.

To such a Government an Association acceptable to the mass of the Irish, whose leadership and control was in responsible and moderate hands, was doubly welcome as a stabilising force which would canalise explosive discontents into safe channels; and, at the same time, act as a counterpoise against the reactionary Orange Order which was giving considerable trouble.

Extended to the Army and Navy by the officers, English and Irish, who had served in Ireland in '98, the Orange Order, with the Duke of Cumberland (brother of George IV and William IV) as its nominal head, had fused with extreme anti-Jacobin Toryism to become an all-but-open conspiracy aiming at a counter-revolutionary *coup* which would repress with violence the " Jacobin democracy " and discontent with which the lower orders were seething; or ferments which the factory owners were encouraging by their clamour for Parliamentary Reform.

At a later date the Orange Order actually reached the point of conspiracy to exclude the Princess Victoria, the heir-apparent, from succession to the throne—on the ground that a young girl, notoriously under Whig influence, would be unable to cope with the rising tide of Radicalism. This danger was averted; and the succession of the Duke of Cumberland to the Throne of Hanover* took the leaders of the conspiracy out of the country. But it is cardinal to remember that in the period from 1820 to 1837 the Government of England was more than once in greater peril of a counter-revolutionary *coup* from the Right than of any armed insurrection from the Left.

An indication of the Orange danger was evoked when a Whig Viceroy, Lord Wellesley, wishing to placate the Catholics, forbade the customary parade and decoration of William III's statue on College Green on November 4th, 1822. The Viceroy was

---

* Owing to the operation in Hanover of the Salic Law, Victoria, while succeeding her uncle Wm. IV. on the throne of Britain, was debarred from succeeding him on the throne of Hanover. This left Cumberland as the next heir.

assailed with insults in the theatre, and porter-bottles were thrown from the gallery at his head. An Orange jury refused to convict those notoriously guilty. And while the Irish public in general condemned the outrage without stint, the English House of Lords found it a good excuse for rejecting a *Catholic Relief Bill* which had passed the Commons by a majority of one.

It was at this point that O'Connell launched the Catholic Association which met with an immediate success—and, at first, with cordial approval from the Whigs.

The Association established a series of reading-rooms and discussion societies which were immensely popular. And under O'Connell's inspiration the Association set up, with the voluntary aid of sympathetic lawyers and magistrates, a machinery for arbitrating disputes between neighbours and between landlords and tenants. This went a long way towards preventing any recurrence of " outrages " by those " Whiteboy " secret societies which O'Connell held in profound abhorrence.

His very success was turned into a weapon against him. Alarmed Reactionaries in the English Parliament, egged on by Orange intriguers, asked what would become of *property* and of the *Constitution* if the lower orders in England were to copy O'Connell's example and set up a similar Association to serve their " pre-datory " *class* ends.

Under pressure the Government introduced a Bill suppressing both the Catholic Association and the " Brunswick Club", the open association set up by the Orange Society as a cover for its secret organisation. The Bill passed; but proved a nullity. The Tory magistrates would not act against the Brunswick Clubs; and O'Connell merely changed the name of his Association. For the next year or two comic-relief was introduced into Irish public life by a diverting catch-as-catch-can game played between O'Connell and the Attorney-

General for Ireland—O'Connell inventing new names and rules for his Association, and the Attorney-General thinking-up legal pretexts for suppressing anew what he had already "suppressed", in theory, a score of times before.

The Revolt of the 40s. Freeholders

During the General Election of 1826 an incident occurred which changed the situation radically.

The Beresford family, which had monopolised the representation of Co. Waterford for seventy years, found themselves, to their astonishment, opposed, in the Whig interest, by another county landowner, Villiers-Stuart. To make matters worse, Villiers-Stuart appointed, as his election agent, Daniel O'Connell; and there descended upon the county a swarm of canvassers from the Catholic Association. Even then the Beresfords were not seriously alarmed. They had the goodwill of the other county landlords; they had created a number of new 40s. freehold* votes; and they had spent a considerable sum in direct and indirect bribery.

At the nomination, O'Connell himself was proposed (by collusion). He spoke for two hours in declining nomination, devoting most of the time to giving a history of the Beresford family before, during, and since '98. At the poll itself, to the horror of the Beresfords and the delighted amazement of Catholic Ireland, the 40s. Freeholders—once so docile—revolted almost to a man. After the first day the issue was never in doubt; on the fifth day the Beresfords abandoned the struggle.

The perfect order and discipline shown by the peasantry amazed beholders. They marched to the hustings in military formation, each man behind the

---

* 40s. *Freeholders* : These were really *leaseholders* for life, or the lives of three people named in the lease.

banner of his barony, and returned in the same order.
A vow to touch no whiskey, while the poll was open,
was universally taken and scrupulously kept.

Similar revolts on a less spectacular scale took place
at the elections for Westmeath, Monaghan, Armagh,
and Louth.

In revenge the landlords distrained upon or evicted
every freeholder with his rent in arrears—which meant
not less than 90 per cent.

O'Connell replied by announcing a Campaign for
Catholic Emancipation.

The Clare Election and Emancipation

O'Connell's chance came with the advent of a new
Ministry in 1829. He arranged meetings to petition
for Emancipation in every Catholic parish in Ireland—
all of them timed for the same hour on a single day.
At least a million and a half attended, and voted for the
petition. Both Houses of Parliament began to show
signs of giving way.

A by-election was due for Co. Clare. The Government candidate was a man with a good record, personally,
but the Government was not pledged to emancipation.
It was decided to oppose him, and O'Connell himself
was nominated against him.

A certain liveliness was introduced into the contest
by two of O'Connell's agents, both famous duellists,
who offered to give " satisfaction " to any gentleman
aggrieved at having his tenants canvassed against his
wishes. There were no takers. In fact, the election
was an exact replica of the Waterford election. On
the sixth day, his opponent having retired, O'Connell
was declared elected.

Catholic Ireland went delirious with joy ; and even
the English soldiers sent to keep order in Ennis joined
in the cheering.

The Orange faction threatened to " kick the Crown

into the Boyne" if there was any "weakening" of resistance to the Catholic claims, but the Government recognised that further resistance would only produce serious trouble.

Accordingly, the Government, in 1829, introduced and carried three Acts:

> (1) An Act admitting Catholics to Parliament, to Commissions in the Services, and to the Inner Bar;
>
> (2) An Act disfranchising the 40s. Freeholders; and
>
> (3) An Act suppressing the Catholic Association positively for the last time.

It was proposed that, in imitation of the grant to Henry Grattan, a similar sum should be raised and presented to Daniel O'Connell. On consideration, this was changed to an annual "tribute", collected at the Chapel doors, on an appointed Sunday in each year. Until the Famine it was collected without fail every year.

CHAPTER FOURTEEN

THE TITHE WAR

WITH O'Connell at Westminster absorbed in the
struggle for the Reform Bill (1832), it was expected that
Ireland would remain tranquil.

Instead, it flamed into a fury of agitation against
Tithes. In this chapter the story of the TITHE WAR
is told.

The Tithe System in Ireland

When there was only one church in England, and its
priest or parson was a public official whose services
all made use of, to pay him every tenth sheaf, and so
on, constituted no special grievance for the tillers.
In Ireland the tithe was claimed for a church which
nineteen-twentieths of the rural population did not use,
and never had used.* Moreover, the tithe had been
racked up by lay impropriators, and in other ways,
until it often reached nearer to a quarter of the produce
than one-tenth. Cases were known where the tithe
actually exceeded the rent.

In theory an appeal could be made to the courts;
and in Ulster, where half the tillers were Protestants
or Dissenters, the owner of the crop could count on
a sympathetic hearing. The Church complained that,
in Ulster, assessors' courts were all conspiracies to rob
the Church. In the rest of Ireland it was a proverb
that appealing against a tithe-assessment was " going to
law with the devil, and the court in hell ! "

There were special exasperations. Landlords had
secured exemption from tithe for all grazing farms.

* One parish in Armagh, with only 4 resident Protestants, yielded the rector
£216 a year in 1832.

The poverty of the peasantry made it hard for them to
support even their own Catholic clergy. To have to bear
the *whole* support of the Protestant parsons as well was
felt by the Catholic peasantry as a first-class grievance.

In addition, Catholics had to pay a rate for the upkeep of the Church building ; and, as a final stroke, the
proctor who assessed the amount due for tithe *charged
a commission* for doing it.

The Tithe War : First Phase

Emancipation made no practical difference to the
mass of the tillers ; but the fact that it had been won
stimulated the peasantry into a readiness for mass-
resistance. This was made manifest in March, 1831,
when the curate in charge of the parish of Graigue, Co.
Carlow—with less than 70 Protestant parishioners to
over 5,000 Catholics—broke a customary law and
claimed tithes from the Catholic priest.

This would have been resented anyway ; but this
particular parson united in himself every possible cause
of unpopularity. He was young, conceited, and quarrel-
some. He was English. He knew nothing whatever
about Ireland or its people ; and he thought there was
nothing to know. He was a fervent Evangelical,
rancorously anti-Catholic, zealous for a " new Reformation", and had already caused trouble by his proselytis-
ing efforts. To cap all, he insisted upon acting as his
own tithe-proctor ; and, to show he was not to be
trifled with, he impounded the priest's horse.

There was an instant response from the Catholics
of the parish ; to a man they refused to pay tithes at all.

The parson, nonplussed for once, appealed to the
resident magistrate, who appealed to the parish priest.
He replied that " things had got quite beyond his
control". They had. The " White Boys " had come
to life again, and had passed the word for a fight to
a finish. " All Ireland was watching Graigue."

Called upon to enforce the law, the R.M.,* with 600 soldiers and police, spent a couple of months dodging and chasing cattle round the county. He gave up in despair with less than a third of the tithe collected.

The strike against tithe spread from county to county. Collisions between police and people grew into serious affrays. One occurred at *Newtownbarry*, between Wexford and Carlow, in June, 1831. Cattle rescued by the peasants were recaptured by the police. The yeomanry opened fire; the peasants, armed only with farm implements, charged the yeomanry repeatedly, in the face of sustained fire and a free use of the bayonet. The peasants dispersed with the loss of 12 killed and many wounded, 12 of them mortally. Similar conflicts, attended with bloodshed, occurred at Thurles, at Castlepollard, and in Kilkenny Town.

The most serious conflict occurred at *Carrickshock*, Co. Kilkenny. A notable fact here was that the peasants had offered to pay if granted an abatement—the previous rector had claimed only £350, the present one demanded £1,700. Refused redress, the peasants organised under the leadership of a hedge-schoolmaster, an old *United* man. Attempts to serve writs wholesale led to fights between the peasants and the police escort. Trapped in a sunken lane between high stone walls, the police, attacked front and rear, were nearly exterminated. Eleven were killed and 17 wounded. The peasants also suffered severely.

After this a truce was granted. O'Connell had asked for one, in vain, after the fight at Newtownbarry.

The Tithe War : Second Phase

In general, the clergy ceased to press for tithes. Pending legislation, they were granted a Government loan of £60,000; and in June and August, 1832, Acts

* *Resident Magistrate* (" R. M. ") : Stipendiaries appointed by the Government to keep the squireen Justices of the Peace within some sort of legal constraint.

were passed converting the Tithe into a fixed annual
payment. The arrears due, however, had to be paid
up in full. Meanwhile, the truce had been broken.

In April, 1832, the parish of Doon, Co. Limerick,
witnessed a spectacle. A cow, seized from the parish
priest, was brought to the auction ground by an escort
composed of: (1) a strong body of police; (2) one
troop of Lancers; (3) five companies, Gordon Highlanders; and (4) two pieces of artillery. Amid deafening
uproar, the cow was sold to the priest's brother—a
constable, acting under orders—for £12. The
military then retired. The soldiers were barely out
of sight when the crowd attacked the police and drove
them, some out of the town, the rest into their barracks.
The Lancers, brought back at the gallop, charged the
crowd in the teeth of volleys of stones. But not until
the Highlanders returned and opened fire did the
crowd disperse.

A similar sale under military protection was attempted
in May at Rathcormack, Co. Cork; but here the throng
and the uproar were so great that the sale was abandoned.
An impromptu mass meeting of the peasants adopted
three resolutions:

(1) It is *requested* that no auctioneer will lend
himself to the sale of cows distrained for
tithe.
(2) It is *requested* that no person will purchase
cows distrained for tithes.
(3) It is RESOLVED that the citizens will have no
intercourse or dealings with any person
who aids in the sale of cows either as
auctioneer or as purchaser.

This was the start of a nation-wide movement of
" exclusive dealing " directed against all who paid
tithes, or aided the sale of distrained cattle. Anti-
tithe meetings were held everywhere; a directing

committee sat in Dublin; and when Parliament gave its sanction to the forcible collection of arrears the resistance became universal.

Wealthy landowners—Protestants as well as Catholics —were forced into line by the refusal of farm-workers and domestic servants to work for anybody who did not take the Anti-Tithe Pledge. The movement culminated in a huge assembly near the battlefield of Carrickshock. 100,000 farmers and cottagers marched to the meeting—5,000 on horseback—all in military order, behind the banners of their baronies, and obeying promptly the orders of their chosen leaders. A Protestant magistrate presided, and resolutions calling for the abolition of tithe were carried unanimously. The meeting dispersed in perfect order, as it had assembled.

For presiding at this meeting, its chairman was dismissed from the magistracy, and Dublin Castle ordered magistrates to "prevent any meeting likely to lead to a breach of the peace".

This in effect forbade all meetings and, expecting disobedience, the Castle rushed troops over from England.

The peasantry defeated the Castle by attempting no meetings at all. None were needed. The "underground" organisation was sufficient. The peasants were solid against tithes.

The Tithe War : Third Phase

War was renewed in September, 1832, when government agents, protected by police and soldiers, set about valuing farms for the purpose of the Tithe Composition Act.

At Wallscourt, Co. Tipperary—a parish of over 3,000 inhabitants, only *one* of whom was a Protestant—the valuers, headed by the rector, and protected by police and Highlanders, were held up at a farm, in which the tenant insisted there were growing crops, which trespass would damage. He was backed by a strong party of peasants.

The police fired; the peasants charged, scattered the police, and were only halted by the Highlanders drawn up in square. A battle developed in which four peasants were killed and many were wounded. The valuation was carried out; and the Ascendancy Press was jubilant.

Dublin Castle, despite O'Connell's protest that the trespass was illegal, announced that it had 12,000 attachments for arrears of tithe (now due to the Crown) ready for service; and it intended to collect every penny, if necessary, at the point of the bayonet.

In October, 1832, the police engaged in posting notices about tithe arrears in Co. Cork came into conflict with the peasants. The police officer said a young girl, Catherine Foley, headed a rush upon the police. The peasants alleged that the police fired without warning, and then charged with the bayonet. The arrival of soldiers stopped the fight; the peasants had 12 killed (including the girl named) and a considerable number wounded. A coroner's jury of responsible citizens brought in a verdict of wilful murder against the police officer. He was arrested, but released soon after without being charged. The Protestant rector was forced to quit the parish permanently.

This incident roused the whole countryside. The secret societies became active; the land-war reopened. Landlords, agents, and tithe-proctors were shot at; several were killed. Raids for arms on the houses of the gentry recommenced. Parties of police were attacked in open day. The General Election of 1832 was held in the midst of turmoil, and 82 members were returned from Ireland, all pledged to *Abolish Tithes*; 45 of them were also pledged to the *Repeal of the Union*. The Government's answer was a Coercion Act.

In May, 1833, a party of military entered the village of Kilmurray, Co. Waterford, broke into the houses, seized cattle, and carried men off as debtors to the Crown. In June a fight at Carrigtwohill, Co. Cork, was broken off when one of the soldiers was shot, accidentally, by the police. In June also 70 soldiers and police were routed at Mullinahone, Tipperary, by an "immense" body of peasants. A few days later the *Gazette* announced that the collection of tithe arrears would be suspended.

The valuation, however, went on. In August, 1833, the valuing party beat off an attack near Tipperary. In September, at Thomastown, Tipperary, the valuers were routed and their tapes, instruments, etc., were destroyed. Meanwhile, in various parts cattle were hocked, landlords shot at, and tithe-proctors horse-whipped. *Exclusive dealing* was universal. Police were prevented from posting notices at Pallaskenry, Co. Limerick, in February, 1834. The peasants were defeated, with 3 killed and 20 wounded, at Newcastle West, in April, 1834.

The last blood was shed at Rathcormack, in Co. Cork, in May, 1834. The collection of 40s. arrears of tithe from a widow was only effected after 12 peasants had been killed, 7 mortally wounded, and 35 wounded less seriously. A considerable number of the soldiers engaged were wounded.

The Rathcormack "Massacre" raised such a storm that the Tories were forced to abandon resistance to the TITHE COMMUTATION ACT, in principle. They still obstructed, however, in detail, and thereby delayed its passage until 1837.

This Act (a) reduced the amount due for tithe under the valuation then in progress by 25 per cent.; (b) converted the remainder into a rent-charge payable directly by the landlord, but recoverable by him in the rent.

On the surface, the gain to the peasantry was small. Actually it was greater than it seemed. Intimidated by the peasants' solidarity, the landlords in many cases did not attempt to pass on the tithe-charge; others only passed on a portion. The evil of extortionate assessment was done away with, and particularly the evil resulting from the tithe-proctor's unseasonable demand for ready cash from people who only handled money in any quantity at special times of the year. The proctor had, in fact, acted as pace-maker for his jackal, the *gombeen-man*—the small-loan money-lender who was the curse of the countryside.

Thus, despite its shortcomings, the Act registered a real victory for the peasantry and their solidarity.

Thomas Drummond

A chapter on the Tithe War would not be complete without a mention of the man who really brought the war to an end. This was THOMAS DRUMMOND, Chief Secretary to the Viceroy, 1835–9. He brought the war to an end by refusing to use the troops or police for the collection of tithe arrears, except where a breach of the peace had actually occurred.

To circumvent him, the landlords, an Orange peer at their head, revived the medieval procedure of obtaining "writs of rebellion" which empowered the person named in the writ to call upon magistrates to supply a force for the "arrest of the rebel". Drummond ordered all magistrates to refuse to obey. Tested in Court, Drummond's action was upheld. The Orange Order memorialised both Houses for Drummond's removal; but Melbourne, the Prime Minister, stood by him and the attack failed.

Drummond counter-attacked by issuing strict instructions to the police to put a stop to all faction-fighting between Orangemen and Catholics. When a magistrate, high in the Orange Order, presided at a banquet to commemorate the "Battle of the Diamond", Drummond dismissed him from the magistracy with a scathing public rebuke.

He followed this by dismissing from the police force everyone, officer or constable, proved to belong to the Orange Order. When, in April, 1838, the Tipperary magistrates asked the Viceroy for " the strongest force the laws permit " to put down agrarian crime, Drummond retorted that evictions in Tipperary had been double in 1837 what they were in 1833. He suggested that the landlords themselves were the cause of their own troubles :

> " Property has its duties as well as its rights. To the neglect of these duties in times past is mainly to be ascribed that diseased state of society in which crimes take their rise."

The fury with which these home-truths were received gives a measure of the mind of the landlord-class and of their political tools, the Orange-Tory party.

Drummond's early death in 1839 was a great loss to the Irish peasantry. He is the only English administrator ever honoured by a statue in the Dublin City Hall.

CHAPTER FIFTEEN

THE TRANSITION TO REPEAL AGITATION

O'CONNELL is best known in England from his leadership of the agitation for the REPEAL of the Act of Union. This, however, did not begin in earnest until 1843. The causes of the delay between 1829 and 1843, when examined, help to fix O'Connell's real position as a National leader.

O'Connell's Political Standpoint

First and last, DANIEL O'CONNELL has been the object of so much extravagant abuse, and so much equally extravagant laudation, that it is difficult to recover an objective view of the real man.

That he was sincerely set upon Catholic Emancipation, even his worst detractors would not attempt to deny. They question, at most, his sincerity in his agitation for Repeal—arguing, as they do, that he merely agitated the question, demagogically, as a means of maintaining his popularity and preserving his political ascendancy among the Irish people. The contemporary jibe, " The Big Beggar-Man", has no other meaning.

An examination of O'Connell's career gives the lie direct to this foolish theory. It proves two things : (1) That O'Connell spent more years and more energy in keeping Ireland *quiet* than he did in stirring it into agitation ; (2) that in the years between 1829 and 1843 he was all the time seeking to gain a Repeal of the Union by a dexterous succession of political combinations— first with one English party, then with another.

Repeal, the logical consequence of Catholic Emancipation, was the goal O'Connell set himself to achieve. His limitations were that he desired to preserve, along with Repeal, the *connection* with England, and further, that he was inveterately opposed to anything in the nature of insurrection or revolution.

O'Connell, in fact, emerges as a tragic figure of colossal proportions—a man born with every qualification for a revolutionary leader of the very first rank, save only the essential qualification of the *will to revolution*. Instead, his horror of these things, acquired in his youthful experience in France in 1792–3, and in Ireland in 1798, constantly made him stultify himself just when the road seemed clear before him. He, more than any man who ever lived, could have called all Ireland to arms with a single word. Yet he was the one Irishman who ever lived who would never, in any circumstances, utter that word.

In 1829 he caught the rulers of England napping. They thought then that he was ready for revolution; and they knew that in England *at that time*, he would find a large mass of powerful allies. In later years they knew him better; but there was always the fear that the agitation he conducted might grow beyond even his magisterial control. His attitude towards the *Tithe War*—which he not only refused to lead, but did everything he could to divert into safe constitutional channels—and his attitude towards *Chartism*—which he patronised while it was weak, and fought unsparingly when it grew strong—gives an accurate measure of O'Connell's place as a National leader.

O'Connell and the Chartists

O'Connell's attitude to the Chartists is especially decisive because he was in general sympathy with all of the points of the People's Charter, and because the Chartists for their part were always staunch supporters of Ireland's claims, even to making *Repeal of the Union* one of the demands in their Second National Petition, in 1842. O'Connell, from his first entry into the House

of Commons, had helped the Reformers in their fight
for the Reform Bill; in fact, it was by the votes of
O'Connell and his supporters that the Bill was carried
in 1832. He classed then as a Radical, and the Chartists
counted upon his aid. His later lukewarmness and his
eventual opposition seemed to them a base desertion.

It is, however, explicable quite otherwise. O'Connell's attitude to the Chartists was embittered by personal
hostility between him and the Chartist leaders JAMES
BRONTERRE O'BRIEN and FEARGUS O'CONNOR; but
this hostility itself arose from a fundamental political
antagonism. Both O'Brien and O'Connor were agrarian
revolutionaries who wished to make an end of landlordism altogether. O'Connell, himself a landlord, who
envisaged Utopia as a place where landlords did their
duty indulgently, hated on instinct everything that
O'Brien and O'Connor fought for. O'Brien applauded
every stage of the Tithe War, and blamed O'Connell
for spoiling it by his interference. O'Connor applauded
the " glorious deeds of the Whiteboys "—whom O'Connell thought " miscreants " who ought to be exterminated. And O'Connor, inordinately proud to be
the nephew of a leading UNITED IRISHMAN (Arthur
O'Connor) always thought and spoke in terms of just
such a revolution as the United Irishmen had envisaged.
O'Connell's fanatical hatred of revolution in general
and the French Revolution in particular extended
without abatement to the " Jacobin " United Irishmen.
Thus, at every point O'Connell's outlook was radically
incompatible with those of all the Chartist leaders—
except, possibly, the " moral force " Chartists. For
these reasons he used his every endeavour to keep the
Chartist movement out of Ireland, and he was careful
on principle never to embarrass the Government with
Irish agitation when they had anything to fear from
the Chartists.

It was with genuine pride that he boasted in Parliament

July, 1840) that, when England had been faced with Chartist rising, in November, 1839, Ireland remained erfectly tranquil :

"He was Counsel for Ireland and he was there to plead her cause. England was discontented and disaffected—Ireland was tranquil. England was distracted by lawless bands of physical force Chartists. Ireland did not seek to attain her ends by violence, by resistence to the law, by destruction of property. In England rebel bands were led against the armed soldiery ; but these soldiers knew their duty and performed it. What were they ? *Irishmen !* In England the lives of the gentry were threatened. . . . Had the Irish in England joined the Chartists ? Had they evinced a desire to link themselves with these assassins ? With a few insignificant exceptions they had not. Had the Irish in Ireland taken any part with the Chartists ? . . . No ! Ireland had become tranquil. . . . Her military force was diminished. And why ? Because the troops which were necessary to struggle against rebellion, sedition, and treason in England were not required to maintain the good order which prevailed in Ireland."—M. F. CUSACK : *Speeches and Public Letters of the Liberator*, Vol. 2, p. 21.

This would seem strange reading—so soon after the Tithe War—if we did not know that it expressed what O'Connell wished for, rather than what he believed o be the literal truth.

A fresh flare-up of Chartism in 1842 found O'Connell usy in office as Lord Mayor of Dublin. But he found ime to use all his influence to keep Ireland quiet even hough the Chartists had declared for the Repeal of the Union.

Before his term of office as Lord Mayor expired, an event occurred destined to be of far-reaching import-

ance. A weekly journal, the *Nation*, appeared for th
first time in October, 1842.

"What is the tone of the new journal?." asked on
High Court Judge of another.

"*Wolfe* Tone!" was the sufficient answer.

The 'Nation' and Its Writers

Three young men, the oldest under thirty—CHARLE
GAVAN DUFFY born in Monaghan, JOHN BLAKE DILLO
born in Mayo, and THOMAS OSBORNE DAVIS born i
Mallow, Co. Cork—were the founders of the *Nation*
Duffy and Dillon were Catholics; Davis, a Protestant
and the son of an Englishman, an army surgeon. Davi
and Dillon were barristers, Duffy a journalist. All ha
literary talent, and all three were ardent members of th
Repeal Association which O'Connell had founded i
1841.

They declared the object of the *Nation* to be "t
foster a public opinion in Ireland and make it racy o
the soil"; and they sought to reach this end by makin;
the journal informative without being dull, and inspirin;
without being hysterical. They were staunchly loyal t
O'Connell, and ardent for Repeal, but they sough
always to give a *reasoned* case in support of their objects
and, therefore, paid particular attention to cultivating
that pride in self-reliant nationhood which they conceived would be the best means of re-creating a *Unite*
Ireland. From the first they took their stand upon the
claim that the Irish people was, in fact, a NATION, and
should insist upon being treated as such.

A feature of the *Nation*, which was immensely popular
from the start, was its original ballad-poetry; usually
upon historical themes in which Davis and Duffy both
excelled. They became a source of inspiration to a host
of other young writers, whose work bore comparison
with that of their inspirers. Written to be sung to
well-known airs, these ballads were martial and inspira-

ting.   In their leading articles, and their prose generally, the writers of the NATION kept loyally within the programme marked out by O'Connell; but in their poetry they transcended these limits, and sang of the Rising of the Clans, of Owen Roe O'Neill, of the Irish Brigade at Fontenoy, of Clare's Dragoons, of the Volunteers of '82, of the Men of '98, and of Wolfe Tone.

The *Nation* writers were in the main a group of middle-class intellectuals; but some very fine verse, and some sound prose, was contributed by plain wage-workers and working-farmers.   Acute observers detected the resemblance between the work the *Nation* group was trying to do in Ireland and the work Heine and others had done in the " Young Germany " movement of the 'thirties and the work Mazzini was doing with the " Young Italy " movement.   Not inaptly they dubbed the *Nation* group " Young Ireland ".   It has been well said that whereas O'Connell's demand was, in effect— " Good Government or else—*Repeal !* "   Young Ireland's demand, implicit at first, but becoming explicit later, was " Repeal or else—*Separation !* "

Thomas Davis

Of the many writers in the *Nation*, the one whose influence was most vital, was Davis.   His teaching was the clearest and most searching, and he summed up its total significance himself in the phrase " *Ireland's aspiration is for Unbounded Nationality* ".   O'Connell, in banking everything upon persuading an English party that it would be safe, as well as expedient, to grant Repeal, was apt at times to whine, and, at others, to bluster. Davis did neither.   His teaching was always manly, and always charged with the self-respect which is a necessary condition for developing a respect for others.   Says Patrick Pearse :

" There was a deep humanism in Tone ; and there was deep humanism in Davis.   The sorrows of the people affected Davis like a personal sorrow . . . he was a democrat in this truest sense that he loved the people, and his love of the people was an essential part of the man and of his Nationalism."

Davis showed his sound democratic instinct when he persisted quietly in spite of O'Connell in urging a change of attitude towards the English Chartists. Duffy reports that :

> " Davis, who recognised in the English democracy a growing power, with no interest hostile to ours, and which *might become our ally*, recommended the Repealers to come to a good understanding with them, making no more account of O'Connell's personal quarrel where a national object was in view than he would have made in such a case of any personal feeling or interest of his own."

And, although Davis's advice was not taken soon enough, it was this spirit which caused the influence of the *Nation* to spread from the first with the speed of a flame running through dry grass.

An immediate increase resulted in the membership of the Repeal Association. The movement came suddenly to life. O'Connell, prompt to scent every change in public sentiment, especially among his followers, realised at once that unless he acted promptly, and on a big scale, the young men of the *Nation*, without intending it, would take the leadership of the movement quite out of his hands.

Accordingly at the beginning of 1843 O'Connell announced that a new agitation would be launched; and that " this year " would be, definitely, the *Repeal Year*.

CHAPTER SIXTEEN

THE CRISIS OF THE REPEAL AGITATION

THROUGHOUT 1843 O'Connell developed an AGITATION such as, till then, the world had never known. How the agitation ran its course; how it was met by the English Government; and what followed in consequence, is told in this chapter.

The Monster Meetings

In his REPEAL AGITATION O'Connell stirred Ireland to its roots; and aroused the excited interest of the whole world. His method was simple. Local meetings in every parish led up to meetings in large towns and counties. These again led up to *Monster Meetings* in which the people of areas equal to provinces were assembled in immense masses. The whole was designed to culminate in a mighty meeting which would declare the Nation's will.

As in the Waterford and Clare elections, and in the Anti-Tithe demonstrations, the order, sobriety, and method of the meetings were as remarkable as were their phenomenal proportions. In the preparations for these meetings—the appointment of wardens and marshals, the planning of routes, and stations, and for the provisioning of the people on their way to and from (as well as in the discussions before and after) and the reading in the Repeal Reading-rooms of press-reports, and of the correspondence the meetings evoked—the whole people became *organised* and *nation-conscious*.

No man ever did so much to rouse a people from abjectness as O'Connell did by his Repeal agitation of 1843. But it is only fair to add that his work was made much easier by the propaganda of the *Nation*. Needless to say, all the meetings of any size were addressed by O'Connell, who was indefatigable in supervising, planning, and inspiring the whole effort.

How big, exactly, these Monster Meetings were will never be known. Duffy, a stickler for accuracy, puts that at Mallow at half a million. He will not allow more for the meetings at Mullaghmast and at Tara, though he concedes that others put the one at three-quarters of a million and the other at a whole million. He notes that at Tara not one of the objects of antiquarian interest excited so much notice as the " grave of the men who fell at Tara in '98". He notes how the grave was decorated by the people spontaneously ; how they waited patiently for their turn to kneel and say a prayer for the dead at the graveside.

Even a voice as marvellous as O'Connell's could reach only a fraction of a throng so immense. Duffy notes that from no point was it possible to see the whole meeting in one view. " People covered the plain as far as the eye could reach."

While O'Connell, in all his speeches, was careful to say that the Repealers would never rely upon physical force to gain their ends, the immensity and fervour of the gatherings imparted a note of militancy to his oratory which somewhat overstepped his politic bounds. Replying to an Orange demand that his Agitation should be put down by force, he delivered at Mallow a famous " Defiance " :

> " Are we to be trampled underfoot ? Oh, they shall never trample *me*, at least ! [Shouts of ' No ! No ! '] I say, they *may* trample me ; but it will be my dead body they will trample on and not the living man ! "   [Loud cheering prolonged for several minutes.]

In spite of himself, O'Connell was driven by his own success to the very brink of insurrection.

Reactions to the agitation

Every democratic, republican, and revolutionary movement in the world was excited by O'Connell's agitation. Radicals on the Continent joined Irish exiles in sending encouragement and offers of help. American politicians hinted that " if England made war upon Ireland, she would lose Canada". English Chartists, despite O'Connell's disparagements of them and their leaders, declared that, if Ireland were attacked, " the English aristocracy would have two nations to crush instead of one".

Even Orangemen began to be infected and to join the Repeal Association—on the understanding that they were free to advocate a *Federal* connection with England as a substitute for the Union. A Committee of Whigs was set up to devise a Federal plan.

The Ascendancy faction, almost beside themselves with fright, warned the landlords that O'Connell was talking now of " fixity of tenure " for the peasants. Those who had refused tithes could equally well refuse *rents*. Where was it all to end ?

English manufacturers took the alarm. If Repeal were conceded to agitation, what an example that would be to the Chartists !—to the factory hands clamouring for the Ten Hour Bill !—to the Trade Unions ! Even the Liberal Whigs, who favoured Repeal, feared the consequences of conceding it to *agitation*.

Early in the agitation Dublin Castle, under Orange influence, had struck its first blow by removing from the lists of magistrates those who supported the Repeal Association. This had brought an ominous reply. Scores of distinguished Protestant magistrates resigned, in protest, and joined the Association. Soon they were presiding over arbitration courts all over the country, which left the official courts nothing to try but casual drunks and common thieves.

As the agitation grew, this defection from the magis-

tracy grew more alarming. The Government, thoroughly
scared, began to move troops into Ireland; and
re-enacted the Arms Act of 1793.

The Crisis at Clontarf *

It had been planned that the series of monster meetings
should culminate in a final, stupendous, All-Ireland rally
on the historic battlefield of Clontarf.   As the day
fixed (Sunday, October 5th) drew near, every resource
was employed to ensure that the gathering would be the
greatest ever.

The Authorities prepared no less strenuously. More
and more troops arrived. Police barracks were loopholed
for musketry, and prepared to stand a siege. Forts and
martello towers were prepared for defence. But how
far this was show, and how far an indication of real
resolution, nobody knew.

The Tory Government was in a dilemma. Half, at
least, of the Protestant Community in Ireland had either
gone wholly over to Repeal or were working feverishly
with the Whigs to discover some means of conciliation.
The Chartists had been crushed in 1842, but they were
reviving.   The Whigs and Radicals were agitating
against the Corn Laws and looked more than half
inclined to use the Irish as a stick to beat the Tory dog
with. It was a moot point; but, on a balance, Wellington
and Peel decided that to concede anything to agitation
then, meant conceding everything.   They decided,
therefore, that O'Connell's " bluff " must be " called ".

On the afternoon of Saturday, October 4th, Dublin
Castle issued a proclamation forbidding the Clontarf
meeting.

Boatloads of excursionists had arrived from Belfast,
Glasgow, Liverpool, and Holyhead; and more were
arriving with every tide. Contingents were on their way

*Clontarf: Here Brian Boru inflicted a decisive and final defeat on the
" Danish " invaders in 1014.

com all parts of Ireland. More would set out through he afternoon and night. Only a tiny fraction of this nultitude could ever learn of this proclamation before eaching the meeting-ground which they would find occupied by the military. What would happen?

O'Connell, for his part, had no doubts. Whether the people submitted or resisted, the result would be equally disastrous for his leadership. If they gave way to the proclamation, the Government would know they commanded more authority than he. If the people did not give way, whether they were massacred—as he hought, or said, they would be—or whether they overpowered the troops by sheer weight of numbers, it would be equally impossible for him to keep them any longer under control. It was possible, even, that, while he troops were all occupied at Clontarf, a determined band might seize Dublin Castle, proclaim a Republic, nd distribute arms to the people. The reaction to a massacre would be as it had been in the Tithe War; but on an immensely higher scale. To go on was to be committed to insurrection and revolution—the final disaster for his " moral force " policy and his leadership.

O'Connell therefore met the situation promptly. A counter-proclamation was issued by the Repeal Council *ancelling the meeting.* Messengers, on fast horses, galloped lown all the roads leading out of Dublin to meet and urn back the marching myriads. Workmen removed he gigantic platform erected at Clontarf. Crowds rrived, of course, but only as sight-seers to view the oldiers in possession of the ground.

For O'Connell the situation was saved. But a veteran of '98 passed a different judgment: " Ireland was won t Clontarf; and at Clontarf it was lost again."

The Trial of " O'Connell and others "

Swift on the heels of the surrender came the pursuit. A State prosecution was launched against O'Connell

and eight others—including the editor of the *Nation*
Gavan Duffy.

The indictment as presented when the trial opened
on January 16th, 1844, was a scroll, one hundred yards
long :

> " In this huge document forty-seven overt acts
> were set out, sixteen of which consisted merely
> of attending monster meetings. It was charged
> against the editors [of the *Nation*, the *Pilot*, and the
> *Freeman's Journal*] that they had reported speeches
> at these meetings. Fifteen other overt acts consisted
> in attending meetings of the Repeal Association
> where speeches by O'Connell, alleged to be seditious,
> were delivered, the plan of the Arbitration Court
> was adopted, and (as respects the journalists) in
> ' unlawfully, maliciously, and seditiously ' reporting
> these transactions in their newspapers. Another
> overt act was the ' endeavour to collect a meeting '
> at Clontarf. Ten of the eleven remaining overt acts
> were charged against the newspapers. Six were
> publications in the *Nation*. Of these, four were
> leading articles, one a poem [' *Who fears to speak of
> Ninety-Eight ?* '] and one a letter proposing that
> modern names of places in Ireland should be
> abandoned and the old Gaelic names revived."
> —DUFFY :   *Young Ireland*, pp. 396-7.

There was never much doubt about the verdict—the
jury list had been too well " cooked " for that—or
about the judgment—though one of the judges dissented.
The trial, in fact, after its opening excitements, grew
unutterably wearisome from lack of any doubt about
the result. It was a relief from boredom when the jury
returned their expected verdict and the judges sentenced
all the prisoners (save one who had died) to six months
imprisonment and a fine apiece.

Brought before the House of Lords, on a Writ of
Error, the verdict and sentence were quashed—three

months later—on the grounds that the jury list was defective, the indictment bad, and the judge's direction faulty.

The prisoners (who had been *incarcerated* in the private apartments of the prison Governor, with access to his grounds) received an immense ovation on their release.

O'Connell changes his front

O'Connell, who was a past-master in political finesse, tried to pretend that at Clontarf the people had defeated the Government (by obeying his cancellation order); and that the House of Lords verdict had restored the position to what it had been before Clontarf. Actually he, like everybody else, knew that Clontarf had been a nodal point at which the whole quality of the agitation became transformed.

That part of the movement which had been merely drawn into it by the impetus of its success became detached again, and began to disintegrate from the moment when it was no longer possible to believe that O'Connell had only to command and the Government must obey. That part of the movement which was more *Catholic* than Nationalist—which venerated O'Connell as virtually a lay Primate of all Ireland—remained docile to his leadership as before. But, as O'Connell knew, passive docility counts only negatively in a political struggle. The part of the movement which was most virile, most to be relied upon in action, and most intensely Nationalist—the part which had followed O'Connell as a National leader primarily because he was going *their* way—began, from the moment of the Clontarf surrender, to look for ways and means of *going on without him*. This break-away tendency was sub-conscious; but it was none the less real. DAVIS, though he remained loyal to O'Connell's leadership to the end, expressed this tendency instinctly in a poem written immediately after Clontarf:

P

> " Earth is not deep enough to hide
> The coward slave who shrinks aside ;
> Hell is not hot enough to scathe
> The ruffian wretch who breaks his faith.
> But—calm, my soul !—we promised true
> Her destined work our land shall do ;
> Thought, courage, patience will prevail !
> *We shall not fail !—we shall not fail !* "

On the eve of his trial O'Connell was perturbed about the leadership of the Association during his (expected) imprisonment. The machine had been run, under his direction, by his son John and his friend Rae, both of whom were included in the indictment, along with the two editors (of the *Pilot* and the *Freeman's Journal*) whom he controlled. The man he most feared—DAVIS, whom he appraised more justly than Davis, in his modesty, appraised himself—would be left free to take the place of command that was his by natural right.

O'Connell was, therefore, more delighted than anybody when the State Prosecution brought the Repeal Association a new recruit in the person of WILLIAM SMITH O'BRIEN, son of Lord Inchiquin and lineal descendant of *Brian Boroimhe*. O'Brien, as M.P. for Limerick, had always taken a boldly Nationalist line ; but he had, till then, held aloof from O'Connell and his " demagogue " methods. With O'Connell's delighted approval, Smith O'Brien was popularly acclaimed *Tanist* of the Repeal Association.

To his intense chagrin he found that Davis and " Young Ireland " took to O'Brien and he to them, by instinct. If O'Brien had been anything of a soldier they would have constituted a Lord Edward-Tone combination all over again. As it was, Davis and O'Brien set to work upon the patient, ideological, and educational consolidation they saw to be imperative ; and in this work the *Nation* was invaluable. It and it alone saved the Repeal movement from collapse in the moral revulsion after Clontarf.

Once released, O'Connell soon showed signs of a complete change of front. There was no renewal of agitation; but neither was there any encouragement for that policy of systematic education of the rank and file which Davis had initiated, with O'Brien's support, through the Repeal Reading-rooms. There were displays of impatience with the " young oracles " of the *Nation;* and a hint of real anger when Young Ireland displayed scornful merriment at the suggestion that the decision of the House of Lords was the result of a direct intervention of Providence in answer to the prayers of the faithful. Along with this went a steady drift towards O'Connell's old policy of co-operation with the Whigs.

In later years Young Ireland writers attributed this to O'Connell's jealousy, to the break-down of his *morale* in " prison ", to the onset of the mental break-down of his last days. A truer and more obvious explanation is that the Young Ireland group and the *Nation* were, by revivifying the Repeal Movement, welding it into a real *force*, and so were re-creating for O'Connell the dilemma from which the Government had rescued him by banning the Clontarf meeting.

It was significant that his first open quarrel with Davis and the *Nation* was contrived in a way which made him appear as the champion of Catholic faith against insidious " godlessness ". Davis had welcomed the proposal to establish undenominational University Colleges in Belfast, Galway, and Cork. He welcomed the co-education of Catholics and Protestants as a means towards breaking down sectarianism; and till then O'Connell had advocated that line, too. Now, without warning, he repudiated the line taken by Davis and the *Nation* as " not a *Catholic* view ". Davis defended himself, and for his pains was grossly insulted by a notorious blackguard—the O'Connells, father and son, applauding the insulter loudly. A disgraceful scene was ended by the personal intervention of Henry Grattan, junior, and Smith O'Brien, who extorted a grudging apology from O'Connell.

The deed, however, had been done. O'Connell had contraposed " Old " Ireland to " Young " Ireland and made the division identical with that between Catholic zeal and " godlessness ". It was tragically significant that it was O'Connell who thus contraposed Catholicism to Separatist Nationalism as mutually exclusive opposites ; and the incident derives additional force from the fact that the Orange-Tory zealots also denounced the colleges as " godless ".

The immediate effect of the incident was to undo at a stroke all the work the *Nation* had accomplished in binding " Orange " and " Green " together in a *United National Movement*. Davis in particular had been especially successful in convincing liberal Protestants that Repeal would not mean *Catholic Ascendancy*. In effect O'Connell had now declared, *ex cathedra*, that it would.

Before the mischief could be repaired the *Nation* suffered a fearful blow. On September 15th, 1845, Thomas Davis died after only a few days' illness. " It seemed," says Duffy, " as if the sun had gone out of the heavens." " The loss of this rare and noble Irishman," said Mitchel, " has never been repaired, neither to his country, nor to his friends."

CHAPTER SEVENTEEN

FAMINE : AND 'FORTY-EIGHT

A NEW endeavour to revive the United Irishmen's movement culminated in an abortive attempt at revolution in July, 1848,—viz, SMITH O'BRIEN'S REBELLION.

The events which led up to this—especially the GREAT FAMINE of '46-7—are examined in this chapter.

The Great Starvation

Underlying and conditioning the political events of 1845-50 was the great calamity which the English called the Irish Famine but which the Irish called THE GREAT STARVATION.

The bedrock facts are these : (1) Failure of the potato crop (a consequence of the concurrence of several sorts of epidemic disease) was partial in Ireland in 1845, general in 1846, and absolute in 1847. (2) In consequence, in each of the years next following the ones indicated there were deaths from hunger, hunger-typhus, and cholera, upon such a scale that the numbers have never been ascertained. Deaths and emigration reduced the population of Ireland by one-third in ten years ; which means that the rural population was reduced to little more than one-half. (3) The failure of the potato-crop, from the causes named, was general throughout Europe ; but only in Ireland was there famine, because—(4) only in Ireland was the peasant population totally or mainly dependent upon the potato-crop.

A second set of facts must be set in comparison with the foregoing : (1) In the " famine " years Ireland produced foodstuffs (grain, cattle, dairy-produce, etc.) in abundance ; (2) No disease (except that of the tillers)

afflicted either the corn harvest, which was super-
abundant, or the cattle ; (3) The landlord and the tax
collector not merely took their tribute as usual but
also took the occasion to squeeze out arrears due ;
(4) The amount of corn, cattle, etc., exported from Ireland
in these years would have fed all those who hungered
twice over. (5) Therefore, the Irish are quite right when
they say : " God sent the blight ; but the English
landlords sent the *Famine !* "

Further facts reinforce this deduction.   English
philanthropists, as well as American and Continental,
were much moved at the distress, and raised large sums for
famine relief. Parliament voted as much as would have
kept the late war going for half a day. But " political
economy " prescribed that these sums must not be
given to the Irish lest they become " demoralised ".
(If any Irishman objected to " demoralising " landlords
by *giving* them corn and cattle he was liable to transportation as a felon.) The Irish were made to *earn* their
relief by labour—building bridges over dry brooks,
making roads to nowhere, etc.—work which qualified
for a ration of maize meal, etc. But before they were
qualified for relief *they had to part with all the land they
held in excess of one quarter-acre*. In conditions in which
families holding as much as twenty acres died of starvation—or of cold when all the blankets and sheets had
been sold from their beds and the clothes from their
backs to buy food—the value of this *quarter-acre clause*
to landlords desiring to " consolidate " their estates,
and to statesmen anxious to get rid of the " discontented
Irish " cannot be over-estimated.

An English remedy, applied in 1846, was to REPEAL
THE CORN LAWS and so make grain cheap enough for
the Irish peasants to buy. But making grain cheap meant
that it took *more* Irish-grown grain to make up the
landlord's rent. The man who had contrived till then
to save a little grain for his family, had now to part with

it all and starve. Or, alternatively, to be evicted! Thus
the English remedy brought thousands more beneath
the famine line ; and made evictions easier than ever.
Moreover, cheap food is as much beyond the reach of a
man with *nothing* as dear food is. What the blight spared,
the landlord took. What the landlord spared, " political
economy " and " legitimate enterprise " gobbled up
between them. Irish grain bought in England was
shipped by relief committees to Ireland and resold there
at half its cost. The starving peasants had no money ;
so it was bought up by speculators, who reshipped it
to England, where the relief committee bought it a
second time, to send it round the circle again and
again.

Before the peasants were too exhausted by hunger,
there were (one is glad to note) outbreaks of agrarian
" crime ". Barns were looted ; flour mills stormed ;
landlords and their agents were shot ; and their houses
were plundered and set fire to. These things were,
however, comparatively rare. Meanwhile, a Royal Duke
in England was saying :

> " I understand that rotten potatoes and seaweed—
> or even grass—properly mixed, afford a very whole-
> some and nutritious food. We all know that
> Irishmen can live upon anything, and there is plenty
> of grass in the fields even if the potatoes should
> fail."

A sovereign English remedy was EMIGRATION. Philan-
thropic agencies subsidised emigrant ships to carry away
gratis the victims of famine and the eviction bailiff.
The ships were over-crowded, sanitation was bad, the
emigrants were insufficiently supplied with money, food
or clothing. They were rich only in the germs of typhus
and cholera they carried. Soon the worst horrors of the
famine were being reproduced in the emigrant ships on
the high seas.

The End of O'Connell

The full dimensions of the Famine disaster were not apparent until the autumn of 1846. Between the death of Davis and this date O'Connell achieved his last political victory—that of driving Young Ireland out of the Repeal Association.

His pretext (a transparent hypocrisy) was that the Young Ireland group "believed in physical force". So they did, in principle; but for immediate practice he might as well have accused them of designing to steal the Dome of St. Paul's. It was a trap into which Young Ireland fell—MEAGHER worst of all, since in his ardour he was tricked into delivering an oration in praise of The Sword, which earned him his by-name of " Meagher of the Sword " but none the less gave John O'Connell his chance to make the breach absolute.

O'Connell's position was that he saw as clearly as any man that the only alternatives before Ireland—and the victims of the threatening famine—were, *either* (1) an insurrection which would retain the harvest in Ireland (which in the circumstances would have to be a *social* revolution as well as a political one). *Or*, (2) a complete dependence upon the grace and favour of the ruling-class in England. From his standpoint this gave no choice at all. A social revolution, to him, was unthinkable. He was forced to come to an agreement with the Whigs; and to make sure of driving the best possible political bargain with them he had first to get absolute control of the Repeal Association, so that he could turn it into a machine for the repression of agitation and the suppression of " sedition ".

So well had O'Connell done his work in the " Repeal Year " that the new policy of coalition with the Whigs had to be broken to the rank and file very gently. He knew that the *Nation*—and especially JOHN MITCHEL, who had taken Davis's place as its leading writer— would oppose his coalition policy root and branch.

He knew that the *Nation* had so strong a hold on the rank-and-file Repealers that the *Nation's* opposition might swing them against him and defeat his plans. Therefore it was, politically, a life-and-death necessity for him to drive Young Ireland out of the Association and the *Nation* out of the Repeal Reading-rooms.

Once this had been done, as it was, O'Connell prepared to leave Ireland for the last time—being completely broken down in mind and body. He was struggling vainly to reach Rome, and a Papal benediction, when he died at Genoa on May 15, 1847—of brain-softening and senile decay.

His inept, ill-natured, and dishonest son John promulgated the lie that the Young Irelanders had " broken the Liberator's heart". The truth was that the O'Connells, between them, had broken the hopes of Ireland.

The Irish Confederation

Until O'Connell retired (Dec., 1846) from the leadership of the Repeal Association the Young Irelanders made no attempt to set up a rival organisation. His retirement released the bonds of personal affection and habit, which had kept thousands loyal to O'Connell, while dissenting sharply from his policy. Left to stand or fall on his own merits, JOHN O'CONNELL found himself deserted by hundreds daily. The formation of a new organisation was forced upon Young Irelanders by the visible disintegration of the Association and its degeneration into nonentity

THE IRISH CONFEDERATION was founded at a meeting in Dublin (Jan. 13, 1847), attended by 1,500 people. Its object was defined as :

> " protecting our national interests and obtaining the Legislative Independence of Ireland by the force of opinion, by the combination of all classes of Irishmen, and by the exercise of all the political, social, and moral influences within our reach."

It was decided also that the Confederation was to remain absolutely independent of all English parties, and that any member accepting office from an English government would be automatically excluded from membership. Discussions upon religious questions were forbidden.

So far the Confederation was little other than an attempt to re-establish the Repeal Association as it had been before Clontarf. But there were forces at work which were bound to drive them much further. The work done by the *Nation*—particularly the vigour with which it had stressed the danger of delay in coping with the famine situation—had created an outlook which far transcended that of simple Repeal ; and this was shown especially in the writings of the man, JOHN MITCHEL, whom Duffy had brought on to the *Nation* to help fill the gap created by the death of Davis.

John Mitchel : Duffy : The Chartists

JOHN MITCHEL (1815-1875) was born at Dungiven, Co. Derry, the son of a Unitarian Minister—who had been himself a United Irishman. He was a more powerful prose writer than Davis and a much better speaker. He lacked both the breadth and depth of Davis ; but he made up for this by the greater directness and intensity of his *personal* hatred of English rule, and of everybody connected therewith.

He is a difficult man to classify since, although he was ready to co-operate with anybody—including Chartists, Jacobins, Red Republicans, and Socialists—who would help him fight the British Empire, and, moreover, hated the landlord class, and despised the tinsel trumpery of Royalism, he was not, basically, a *democrat* in the sense that Davis was. He astonished and saddened his admirers in later years by siding with the Southern Confederacy in the Civil War in the U.S.A.—partly because their claim of a Right to Secede seemed on all fours with Ireland's claim for separation (wherein he was profoundly in error), but chiefly because the " Yankees ", as manufacturers and traders, seemed to him too like the English to be *right about anything*.

Probably the truest classification of Mitchel would place him as an *oligarchical-republican* in the true revolutionary-Presbyterian tradition. He showed the outstanding qualities of the *Ulsterman*—the qualities which the Orange Order has perverted to base, anti-national ends ; but qualities which are, none the less, invaluable, and indispensable ingredients in the sum total of Irish Nationality.

All through 1846 and 1847 Mitchel developed those talents—which Davis discovered in him before he was aware of possessing them himself. By the middle of 1847 he had reached the conviction that something more swift and forcible was required than the patient brick-by-brick building-up of an all-class Association which was Davis's first thought after the surrender at Clontarf.

CHARLES GAVAN DUFFY, proprietor and editor of the *Nation*, had none of Mitchel's ingrained impulse towards physical-force insurrection. He had a talent for practical politics, and his Nationalism—which only momentarily became downright separatism—found expression in the conception of an independent Nationalist Party which would force Repeal by a Parliamentary policy which would make the English parties see in Repeal a welcome way out of an intolerable situation. Parnell, years later, credited Duffy with the invention of what came to be known as " Parnellism ". Davis, no doubt, could have induced Mitchel and Duffy to work as a team under his leadership. Left to themselves they were bound to drift apart.

On its organisational side, the Confederation developed by the formation of a series of political clubs in all the towns and larger villages of Ireland. Their names— Sarsfield Club, Emmet Club, Wolfe Tone Club, etc.—

testified to the inevitable trend of the teaching of the *Nation*.

On the ideological side the Confederation was stimulated by the letters and articles of JAMES FINTAN LALOR, one of a family of farmers in Laoighis (Queen's County) who had figured prominently in the Tithe war.

Lalor's idea was that of MORAL INSURRECTION; that the farmers should be taught and encouraged to *refuse all rents and taxes* until the needs of their families had been satisfied. This " insurrection "—in which we see clearly the influence of the Tithe war—should be organised, he proposed, by a TENANT LEAGUE for the country, a TRADES COUNCIL for each town, and a GENERAL COUNCIL set up by both to co-ordinate the struggle and prepare for a NATIONAL CONVENTION.

Lalor's standpoint is openly separatist; and it is clear from the reception his work received that the Young Irelanders (Mitchel at their head) had already reached virtually the same conclusion. If Lalor had not been physically disqualified from rallying the farmers to his plan—he was a consumptive cripple, and nearly blind—much more might have been heard of him and his plan. As it was, the debates on Lalor's plan brought out the growing divergence between the tendencies of Duffy and O'Brien on one side, and of Mitchel and his friends on the other.

This divergence led Mitchel, eventually, to sever his connection with the *Nation* (December, 1847). The occasion was the introduction of a new coercion Act introduced by the Whig Government. Mitchel explains his position thus :

" I had watched the progress of the Famine-policy of the Government and . . . had come to the conclusion that the whole system ought to be met with resistance at every point, and the means for this would be extremely simple : namely, a combination among the people to obstruct and render impossible

the transport and shipment of Irish provisions ;
to refuse all aid in its removal ; to destroy the
highways ; to prevent everyone by intimidation
from daring to bid for grain or cattle if brought to
auction under distress . . . in short, to offer a passive
resistance universally, but occasionally when opportunity served, to try the steel."*

—JOHN MITCHEL : *Last Conquest*, Chap. XVII.

Neither Duffy nor O'Brien was prepared for desperate
courses at that stage. They were acutely conscious of
the negative aspects of Mitchel's plan—its excessive
reliance upon spontaneity ; its alienation of the landlords ;
its exposure of the *Nation* to attack and suppression—
and on the other hand they lacked Mitchel's faith in the
readiness of the farming community for a revolutionary
struggle. They still had hopes of achieving results
constitutionally ; or, alternatively, they feared to alienate
the middle class by an " unprovoked " resort to violent
courses. A majority of the Confederation sided with
O'Brien and Duffy.

There is this much excuse for Duffy's and O'Brien's
desire to wait before rushing headlong into insurrection,
that a strong agitation had arisen in England against
the Coercion Bill, and a strong demand was arising,
led by the Chartists—whose agitation was booming
again—for JUSTICE TO IRELAND. Confederate Clubs
formed in England by Irish exiles were joining in the
Chartist movement ; and the prospect of a joint agitation
seemed to be, and was, very bright.

In Parliament, FEARGUS O'CONNOR (elected for Nottingham in 1847) had taken the leadership of the Repeal
Party out of the hands of John O'Connell, had moved

---

* *Mitchel and Lalor* : The dispute whether Mitchel did or did not " borrow "
his plan from Lalor without acknowledgment is idle. Both owed the basis
of their conception to the experiences of the Tithe war. Lalor's plan, as first
formulated, was Utopian in the sense of trying to achieve a revolutionary
result by pacifist methods. Mitchel on the other hand wished to get an
insurrection started ; trusting to improvisation for the outcome.

for a Committee of Inquiry into the condition of Ireland, and had resisted the Coercion Act so effectively that it was only carried by a majority of 14. These were facts which, rightly, weighed heavily with Duffy and O'Brien.

Mitchel, meanwhile, was, with THOMAS DEVIN REILLY, visiting the Confederate Clubs and urging them to refuse to surrender their arms ; or if they had none to surrender, to get armed as quickly as they could even if only with pikes. Fearing the consequences of this course O'Brien introduced a motion on the Council to stop Mitchel and Reilly from advocating their unauthorised policy. This being carried, Mitchel and Reilly, with others, left the Confederation (Feb. 5th, 1848).

A week later Mitchel brought out the first number of the *United Irishman* which took as its motto Tone's tribute to the " men of no property ". From the first issue onwards Mitchel gave each week lessons in the art of street-fighting.

The Rising of 'Forty-Eight

Mitchel's *United Irishman* created a sensation in England as well as in Ireland. He frankly appealed for Chartist aid—which, according to their ability, the Chartists readily gave—and his friends in the Confederate Clubs began to set up Charter Associations in the chief towns in Ireland. In England the Chartists sold Mitchel's Journal as one of their own. Chartism in England became a " danger " again, while the Confederate Chiefs in Ireland discovered that the mass of their supporters were becoming Mitchel-ites almost to a man.

The British Government, the Catholic Hierarchy, and the rump of the Repeal Association all took alarm together—the latter being tearfully indignant at Mitchel's scornful references to Daniel O'Connell. Their alarm was intensified, before the third issue of the *United Irishman* had appeared, by the overthrow of the Monarchy in France, and the setting up of a Republic, and by the enthusiasm with which this was greeted by Irish Confederates, English Chartists, and Radicals in both countries. Rumblings of revolution began to be heard from every country on the Continent : in fact the Year of Revolutions had begun.

The French Revolution transformed the situation in Ireland in a flash. Mitchel and Reilly walked back into the Confederation without ceremony, to be welcomed there with open arms. The *Nation* began to vie with the *United Irishman* in its incitements to prepare for revolt. The Clubs began to drill and to arm. A deputation— composed of O'Brien, Meagher, and a Dublin craftsman, Hollywood—was sent with fraternal greetings to the French Republic. It got a flowery speech from Acting- President ALPHONSE DE LAMARTINE ; but nothing tangible beyond an IRISH TRICOLOUR of Green, White, and Orange (modelled on the French Flag), made to Meagher's design by the daughters of '98 exiles and women descendants of the Wild Geese. It was exhibited first at Waterford, and at a public meeting in Dublin, where it was received with terrific enthusiasm.

Alarmed at the fraternisation of Confederates and Chartists—and by the inflammatory condition of Europe at large—the English Government designed a new Act and rushed it through all its stages in a single day. This Act facilitated the procedure in cases of " sedition " and " treason ", and made the offence of " treason " a " felony " instead of a " misdemeanour ". In the case of SEDITION the Act did away with the distinction between " political " and " ordinary " criminals. In the case of *treason-felony* it substituted a term of trans- portation for the customary death penalty. The idea was to rob possible Emmets of their glory by giving them broad arrows instead of a martyr's crown.

Before the Act had passed, prosecutions had been launched against O'Brien and Meagher for their speeches ; and (two) against Mitchel for his articles in the *United Irishman*. Juries refused to convict O'Brien and Meagher, so the prosecutions against Mitchel were abandoned—new ones, under the new Act, being substituted.

Meanwhile the Government had contrived to discredit the Chartist movement. A demonstration had been called for Kennington Common on April 10th, at which the Chartist Petition was to be formally handed over to O'Connor for presentation to the House of Commons. It had been proposed, originally, to carry it in procession to the House ; but, learning of the law (a relic of the Gordon Riots) which forbids any assembly within a mile of the House when in session, the proposal had been abandoned. The Government affected to believe however that an attempt would be made in defiance of the law ; and it made preparations that would have been ample if London had been faced with a Napoleonic invasion. When the Petition was sent off in a cab, and the meeting dispersed without disorder, the Press, taking their cue from the Government, pretended to believe that the Chartist movement had been cowed. The anti-Chartist derision of the London middle-class was in proportion to their panic terrors before April 10th was safely got over. Many of the less well-informed Chartists were carried away by this propaganda of derision.

The official press discreetly omitted all mention of the large body of *London-Irish Confederates* who marched to Kennington Common under a *green flag* and, in defiance of police regulations, *marched back again* as they had come. The police, who insisted that no Chartist body should repass the bridges in military formation, allowed the Confederates to pass.

Propaganda was also used in Ireland to scare the middle-class. Dublin was placarded with warnings against Irish " Jacobins " and " Communists whose only object was plunder ".

As a final precaution, quantities of arms were sent from Dublin Castle to " *reliable Orange Lodges.*"

The real test came on May 25th, 1848, when Mitchel was tried for " treason-felony". The verdict was never in doubt, once the Sheriff had contrived, as he did, to " pack " the jury. The veteran ROBERT HOLMES, a '98 man and a brother-in-law of Robert Emmet, made a dauntless speech ; and the judge inflicted a savage sentence—*fourteen years' transportation.* Mitchel, surrounded by mounted police with drawn sabres, was galloped away at full speed to a tender, waiting at the North Wall Quay, which carried him at once to a warship, lying in Dublin Bay, with its anchor " up and down " ready to set sail as soon as the prisoner was on board.

The crucial fact was that the authorities feared a rescue ; and Mitchel's whole strategy had been based upon the conviction that a rescue should be, and would be, attempted.* Actually, the men of the Dublin Clubs—particularly the working-men—were eager to make the attempt, and Meagher had promised to lead them. O'Brien, Duffy, and others, however, thought such an attempt would be suicidal. They contrived to persuade Meagher and Reilly to go round the Clubs, and countermand all preparations.

There is little doubt that an attempt to rescue Mitchel would have been a bloody affair ; but there is a good deal of reason to believe that it might have proved by far the wisest course. There is quite a possibility that it would have succeeded ; not only in effecting the rescue, but also in precipitating a general rising. Earlier, when Meagher had been arrested in Waterford, the Confederates there had barricaded the long bridge over the river which the police had to pass to carry him to

* *Mitchel and Rescue:* Mitchel nowhere admits that this had been his strategy ; but it is a fair inference from his conduct in general, and from his observations on the fact that nothing of the kind was attempted.

Q

prison. Meagher himself ordered the Confederates to demolish the barricade and let the police pass. He was carrying out the policy of the Confederate Council which had decided (*a*) upon an insurrection *in the Autumn* when the crops had been gathered in ; (*b*) upon simultaneous revolts in *the rural districts ;* and (*c*) upon a strict preservation of the peace until the Government struck the first blow. A pedantically-formal adherence to the strict letter of this plan ruined the Rising before it could start.

The Government showed no such stickling over formalities. It suspended the *Habeas Corpus Act* and began arrests right and left.

Within a fortnight of the suppression of the *United Irishman,* DALTON WILLIAMS had founded the *Irish Tribune.* It was suppressed a fortnight later, just as its successor appeared—the *Irish Felon,* edited by Mitchel's life-long friend JOHN MARTIN, with whom was associated JAMES FINTAN LALOR. It contrived to reach its fourth number before it was suppressed.

Seeing that it was only a choice between letting themselves be arrested one by one, or taking the field at once, the Confederate Council decided to issue the call for a Rising immediately. Before Duffy could get the call circulated the police raided the *Nation.* They broke the formes before a copy had been printed— *before the official note-taker could see what it was that Duffy was about to print.* Because of this ill-directed (or possibly collusive?) excess of zeal, the prosecution against Duffy failed, as did that against Williams. John Martin got fourteen years' transportation like his friend. Lalor was in such a state of health that the authorities thought he could not live long enough to be tried. He was released, without being charged, to linger for more than twelve months before he died.

Meanwhile the leaders of the Confederation had dispersed to various parts to find out what readiness existed for revolt. In the country-districts in general they found none. The famine had broken men's spirits. Now that it was abating, the tiller's one thought was of his crop. In the towns there was readiness, here and there, but there were no arms, and O'Brien (who had gone to Tipperary) would not sanction any confiscation of arms *until the enemy had struck the first blow*.

Some hundreds gathered in Tipperary at O'Brien's call. They had few arms, and no provisions. There was no commissariat. O'Brien gave them what money he could; but he would sanction no looting of the houses of the gentry. He would not allow a barricade to be erected until the owner's permission had been obtained for his trees to be cut down for the purpose. In the end the insurrection fizzled out ingloriously in an attempt to persuade the police imprisoned in a farm-house to surrender their arms. When two of his men had been killed, O'Brien ordered the rest to disperse.

O'Brien had many fine qualities, but those of a leader of revolt were not included among them. Like the majority of the Council he feared the consequence of a revolt of the working-men of the towns nearly as much as the Government did.

For their share in this Rising—in which hardly a blow was struck on the rebel side—O'Brien, Meagher, and others (including those already named) all received long terms of TRANSPORTATION.

PART IV

THE TENANTS' RIGHT LEAGUE TO THE FENIAN BROTHERHOOD

CHAPTER EIGHTEEN

ECONOMIC CONSEQUENCES OF THE FAMINE

In this Part IV we trace the process of *Nationalist* revival in Ireland from the disastrous calamities of the Famine and 'Forty-Eight, through (1) the Constitutional agitation led by GAVAN DUFFY and the TENANTS' RIGHT LEAGUE, and (2) the classic revolutionary conspiracy of the FENIANS; culminating in their attempts at insurrection in 1865 and 1867.

In this first chapter of Part IV we examine the economic impulsions underlying these movements.

Free Trade in Land

Until 1832 the English landed-oligarchy controlled the English government absolutely. From then until 1846 they retained preponderance through an alliance with that section of the manufacturers which had a direct interest in maintaining in Ireland an *industrial reserve army* which they could draw upon for supplies of cheap labour. From 1846 onwards the manufacturing capitalists gained increasingly a preponderance, until in the 1870's they yielded place to the imperialist finance-capitalists. The fall in world prices for agricultural products implied that, if possible, agricultural productivity should be increased to cover the fall in monetary returns. Hence arose that drive towards the " consolidation " of farms which was facilitated drastically by the calamity of the Famine.

Two things resulted (*a*) the elimination of the middleman, and (*b*) the getting rid of large numbers of smallholders. The middlemen disappeared as a category either by selling-out to the more prosperous farmers (which occurred largely between 1822 and 1840), or by themselves becoming ground-landlords (as a result of the Encumbered Estates Act).

The getting rid of the small-holders was a necessary precondition for the establishment of capitalist farming on any considerable scale, and this was necessary to meet (and supplement) the growing yields from the wheat fields of America. Cheap labour was required for this type of farming, and a supply of cheap labour was created by the " consolidation " which " cleared " estates of their " superfluous " small tenants.

In 1841 there were 135,314 holdings of less than one acre. In 1851, their numbers had shrunk to 37,728. Holdings between one and five acres numbered 310,436 in 1841 ; in 1851 there were 88,083. Farms between five and fifteen acres were 252,799 in 1841 ; in 1851 there were 191,854. There was a corresponding *increase* of farms from fifteen to thirty acres, and a much greater increase of those above thirty acres.

Evictions from 1845 to 1847 numbered 3,000 ; from 1847–49 there were 25,700 ; from 1849–1852 there were 58,423 (affecting 306,120 individuals). The significance of this development was multiplied by the sentimental attachment felt by the Irish peasantry for their localities of origin—itself a fruitful source of calamity in the Famine years :

> " The class of poor and destitute occupiers, who are debarred by law [from poor law relief] unless they give up their land, struggle, notwithstanding their great privations, to retain it ; and endeavour by every effort to pass through the season of difficulty by which they see a prospect of their former mode of subsistence returning, provided they continue in the possession of their land. The use for a long time of inferior food has in such cases sometimes induced disease fatal to the occupier himself, or one or more members of his family."
> *Report, Poor Law Commission,* 1847.

The report of the Census of 1851 is more frank. It admits that those who died in this desperate struggle to save their holdings ran into " *thousands*". The quarter-acre clause was universally regarded as " eviction made easy", and the survivors felt a bitter hatred at the callousness with which it was enforced.

It is, of course, not true to say that either the resident landlords (many of whom ruined themselves in their efforts to aid the suffering) or the English people *en masse* regarded the calamity callously. The point is that Government policy was fettered by theories of " political economy " which had as brutal an effect as the most complete callousness would have produced. That the Government applied these theories equally to the English poor saves their credit for impartiality, but only at the expense of their credit for humanity and good sense.

The Manchester school had one universal panacea— Free Trade—the application to the relations of landlord and tenant of the principle of unrestricted competition. The application of this principle to Irish land tenures underlies the whole of Irish unrest from 1850 to 1870.

The Encumbered Estates Act

The first step was the *Encumbered Estates Act* (July 1849). Before then entailed estates could be sold only through the slow and expensive procedure of the Court of Chancery. Under this Act owners or creditors could appeal to a special court which disposed of the matter expeditiously—the creditors' claims being liquidated from the proceeds of the judicial sale. The purchaser was compelled to take over leases already granted, and could not vary their terms ; but the old lax days when a favoured tenant paid what he thought he could afford, or when a year or two of arrears was thought nothing of were swept away. Particularly there was swept away the personal knowledge possessed by the old landlord of the improvements made by the more diligent and enterprising tenants. These things were now treated as part of the property bought and paid for. The tenants' right was a thing undreamed of.

More than 3,000 estates were sold, and of their 80,000 purchasers 90 per cent. were Irishmen. The purchase price amounted in gross to £25,000,000, nearly all of which went to creditors. Estates sold for a half or a third of their estimated value. The loss of the estate-owners was not less than £15,000,000.

As an endeavour to induce English and Scottish farmers to settle in Ireland the scheme was a failure. The estates passed to speculators who were concerned only to rack the last penny of rent possible out of the soil of which they became absolute owners. All customary and traditional protection for the tenant was swept away. Leases tended constantly to be replaced by yearly tenancies, or simple tenancies-at-will. Virtually the entire agricultural population, who were not occupying owners, became evictable, and liable to increases of rent inflicted as punishments for any improvements they were rash enough to make.

In such conditions Whiteboyism, under its new name of "Ribbonism", was bound to reappear. Capitalist landlordism was a thing till then unknown to the Irish tenant. He paid rent as a tribute which secured him the right to occupy a plot of land in perpetuity. Its *acceptance* was an acknowledgment of the *tenant's* right; not his *paying* it an acknowledgment of the *land-lord's* right. If he erected fences, made drains, cleared, manured and worked up the soil, the tenant felt he had a right to dispose of these *improvements* at will; to sell his right in them if he wished to leave; to bequeath them to his children; or, at the least, to occupy his holding without interference so long as he paid the quit-rent custom decreed. The "right" of the owner to raise the rent on him, or to eject him at will, still more to confiscate his improvements—these commonplaces of " Free Trade in Land " were to the Irish tenants abominations which negated all right.

Against the landlord's robber-claims he set up his claim to the " three F's "—*fixity* of tenure, at a *fair* rent, with *freedom* of sale for his own improvements— and whether he fought for them by the methods of the Whiteboy, or through parliamentary agitation, these were the central objects of agrarian struggle in this period.

Emigration and its Consequences

Excessive subdivision of holdings was an evil ; but its prevention produced the alternative evil of emigration.

Emigration to America from Ireland began early in the 18th century ; but a radical difference distinguishes the earlier from the later emigration. The earlier emigrants had been the more successful farmers, or their children, who had amassed sufficient working capital to justify a belief they could prosper on a bigger scale in a freer land. The later emigrants, particularly those of the Famine and post-Famine years, were driven to emigrate not by success but by failure. They went as *proletarians* seeking wage-labour, and never lost the sense of grievance at having been driven into exile by the rack-renter and the evictor.

The Famine, the evictions, the rack-rents, the worsening of conditions, the enforced emigration—these were the root causes of the upheaval of revolutionary republicanism known to Irish history as FENIANISM.

CHAPTER NINETEEN

DUFFY'S TENANTS' RIGHT LEAGUE

CHARLES GAVAN DUFFY, the only Young Ireland leader left at liberty in Ireland after the turmoils of '48, attempted to organise a constitutional agitation to secure the "three F's". His TENANTS' RIGHT LEAGUE met with considerable success in 1852, but was brought to nothing by the sabotage and desertion of a group known derisively as the POPE'S BRASS BAND.

The Persistence of Agrarian Terrorism

A persistent fact in Irish history from 1760 onwards, to 1922, is the fact of *agrarian crime*—terroristic attacks upon landlords, agents, tithe-proctors, and above all " land-grabbers " (those who bid for farms from which other men had been, or were to be, evicted). At its most brutal level this crime took the form of cattle-maiming and murder, and the notable fact is that this type of outbreak dwindled to nothing when a promising political movement was on foot, only to recur again when that movement ended in failure, or lapsed into quiescence.

Reactionary English writers have inferred from this a guilty connection between the organisers of the political movement and the local organisers of outrage. But the analysis made by Karl Marx of the situation of the French peasantry and its political affiliations suggests a much profounder explanation :

" The small peasants form a vast mass, the members of which live in similar conditions, but without entering into manifold relations with one another. Their mode of production isolates them . . . the isolation is increased by bad means of communica-

tion and poverty. . . . The smallholding admits of no
division of labour, no applications of science, and
therefore no multiplicity of developments. . . .
In so far as millions of families live under economic
conditions of existence which separate their mode of
life, their interests and their culture from those of
other classes, and put them in hostile contrast to
these others, they form a class. In so far as there is
merely a local interconnection among these small
peasants and the identity of their interests begets
no unity, no national union, and no political
organisation, they do not form a class. They are
consequently incapable of enforcing their class
interests in their own name, whether through a
parliament, or through a convention. They cannot
represent themselves, they must be represented."
—MARX : *Eighteenth Brumaire*, p. 109.

Applied to Ireland this means that, left helpless, save
for such purely local combinations as he could contrive,
the peasant's first thought in extremity has been—the
despairing resort to terrorism.

If it is remembered how much of the English conquest
of Ireland has turned upon confiscating the land, and
imposing alien conditions of tenure upon the tillers,
it will be clear why the tradition of resistance to the
alien—in the person of the landlord or his agent—forms
a permanent ground-theme in the history of Irish
struggle. It will also become clear why the peasants,
although intensely *national*, never themselves set on foot
a *nationalist* agitation. At the same time they were
constantly ready to respond *en masse* to the call of each
national agitation as it arose.

An analogous consideration applies to religious
conflict. A North of Ireland Protestant clergyman
wrote (1870) :

" All that is really important in the history [of
Ireland] for the last three centuries is the fighting

of the two nations for the possession of the soil.
The Reformation was in reality nothing but a
special form of the land war.   The oath of supremacy was simply a lever for evicting the owners of
the land.   The process was simple.   The king
demanded spiritual allegiance ; refusal was high
treason ; the punishment of high treason was
forfeiture of estates, with death or banishment to
the recusants.   Any other law they might have
obeyed and retained their inheritance.   This law
fixed its iron grapples in the conscience and made
obedience impossible without a degree of baseness
that rendered life intolerable.   Hence Protestantism
was detested, not as a religion so much as an
instrument of spoliation."—REV. JAMES GODKIN :
Land War in Ireland.

It must also be remembered, as we have had occasion
to observe earlier, that in the various localities the Whiteboy or Ribbon lodge functioned as a defence-organisation analogous to a trade-union :

" Rockism and Whiteboyism are the determination
of a people who have nothing that can be called
theirs, but a daily meal of the lowest description
of food, not to submit to being deprived of that
for other people's convenience."—JOHN STUART
MILL : *Political Economy.*

Or, as an English Radical M.P. wrote to a Prime
Minister :

" But for the salutary dread of the Whiteboy
Association ejectment would desolate Ireland, and
decimate her population, casting forth thousands
of families . . . to perish in roadside ditches.
Yes, the Whiteboy system is the only check on
the ejectment system ; and weighing one against
the other, horror against horror, and crime against

crime. it is perhaps the lesser evil of the two."
—CHARLES POULETT SCROPE: *Letter to Lord Melbourne* (1834).

The Tenants' Right League

When Gavan Duffy restarted the *Nation* in 1850, he had to record, along with a wide-spread outbreak of "Ribbon" outrages, the progress of two distinct agitations for legislation to abate the rapacity of that new type of landlord which was emerging daily from the Encumbered Estates Courts. In the North the agitation, led by Protestant and Presbyterian ministers, arose from a well-based fear that the new speculator-landlords would destroy (as under the new Act they could) the "*Ulster custom*" which gave tenants a property right in their improvements. Concurrently, in the South, a group of public-spirited young priests were agitating for the adoption there of the (imperilled) Ulster custom, as a *reform*.

Under the influence of the *Nation*, these distinct "Tenants' Protection Associations" came together and formed a *Tenants' Right League*. It had the support of the surviving "Repealers" in Parliament; and of a number of English Radicals, such as SHARMAN CRAWFURD and POULETT SCROPE. It was agreed, all round, that a Land Act embodying the three F's would be a real gain. A call was issued urging voters everywhere to support only such candidates as would pledge themselves to give support to TENANTS' RIGHT PRINCIPLES, which were defined thus:

"Rent must be *fixed by valuation* of the land; the power of raising rents at will, or of recovering a higher rent than one so established must be taken from the landlord.

"The tenant must have a *fixed tenure*; he must not be liable to disturbance, so long as he paid the rent established by valuation. If he chose to quit, or could not pay he must have the right to the market value of his tenancy.

"Nothing shall be included in the valuation, or be paid under it to the landlord, on account of improvements made by the tenant in possession, or those under whom he claims, unless these have been paid for by the landlord in reduced rent, or in some other way."

A campaign in support of these principles was carried all through Ireland ; and, to the delight of the campaigners, and the astonishment of all, North and South joined hands with enthusiasm. The *Fermanagh Mail*, strictly Protestant in its principles, and circulating in a deep Orange area, acclaimed the movement without reserve. "All! All are uniting," it said, "in harmonious concert to struggle for this dear old land!"

The lyric enthusiasm of the *Mail* was forgivable. A movement in which Catholics, including *priests*, were welcomed at public meetings in the North, while Protestants, including *Orangemen*, were similarly welcomed in the South—one which promoted meetings at which resolutions were proposed by Grand Masters of the Orange Order, and seconded by Catholic priests; which brought a delegation of Presbyterian ministers South to receive an enthusiastic welcome in Wexford, and in Kilkenny—such a movement deserved all the enthusiastic approval the *Fermanagh Mail* had to bestow.

As the general election of 1852 approached, the League busied itself successfully in extorting from candidates pledges to support the principles of the League. Few candidates were more emphatic in giving this pledge than WILLIAM KEOGH and his fellow members of the Catholic Defence Association.

The Pope's Brass Band

Keogh, in 1851, was already a member of parliament, and the Catholic Defence Association, of which he was the head, had newly sprung into being in response to a casual circumstance which opportunist politicians of all colours had fastened upon as an excuse for bogus displays of zeal.

The Pope of the period, newly returned from the exile into which he had been driven by the revolution of 1848, celebrated his return by appointing a Catholic Hierarchy for England. The Whig Prime Minister, Lord John Russell, urged on by " No Popery " zealots, at once brought in a Bill to make it an offence for Catholic prelates to adopt territorial designations in the British Islands.

Protestant landlords, and ultra-Orange zealots, saw here a first-class chance to side-track the Tenants' Right League and the unity it was promoting. Through the Grand Lodge of the Orange Order they issued a call to Protestants to stand firm by their " menaced institutions". Protestant landlords, meeting in Dublin, beat the No Popery drum until the echoes rang.

As it chanced, the head of the Catholic Hierarchy in Ireland (Dr. Cullen) was both newly-appointed and an ultramontane of the most pronounced type. He reacted semi-automatically to the " No Popery " challenge by forming a *Catholic Defence Association* at whose head he placed WILLIAM KEOGH (barrister and M.P.) and JOHN SADLEIR, the founder of a Tipperary Bank (which in intimate financial circles was suspected of shady practices).

As Russell's *Ecclesiastical Titles Bill* made its progress through the Commons—in the teeth of opposition from the Tories, led by GLADSTONE, and from the Radicals led by COBDEN—both Keogh and Sadleir out-rivalled everybody in the ferocity of their opposition. Hence it became easy for Keogh and Sadleir, with a team of followers, to enter the General Election of 1852 as the ecclesiastically-approved Champions of the Catholic Church in Ireland.

R

Keogh, who (one contemporary said) " could whistle the birds off the bushes " and who (Duffy says) " rarely gave an honest vote, or uttered an honest sentiment", never appeared in public without bishops to back him. So flamboyant were he and Sadleir and their followers in their protestations of zeal for the Faith, and in defence of the Pope that they acquired the nick-name of *the Pope's Brass Band*.

Duffy and the Tenants' Right League resisted the sectarian diversion initiated by the Band so successfully that its members all pledged themselves (" So help me, God ! " swore Willie Keogh) to fight unswervingly for Tenants' Right and keep the Party pledge.

The general election in the autumn of 1852 resulted in the return of nearly fifty members pledged to Tenants' Right ; Duffy himself being elected for New Ross. A conference of these Tenants' Right members (attended by Keogh and Sadleir) agreed unanimously to support no ministry that would not support a Tenants' Right Bill.

When Parliament assembled the Whig Government found itself in a precarious position. Whigs and Tories were nearly equal ; the Irish Party held the balance. The Government, accordingly, temporised ; and allowed *two* Tenants' Right Bills, one promoted by Sharman Crawfurd, the other by the League, to pass their second reading and go to a select committee. Shortly afterwards the Whig Government was replaced by a Coalition Administration.

Success seemed certain for the Tenants' Right League —but, of course, on condition that its party members in Parliament honoured their pledges and maintained their independence, and with it the power of overthrowing the Government.

The Great Betrayal

To the consternation and disgust of the Tenants' Right Party the new ministerial appointments when

announced included John Sadleir as a Junior Lord of
the Treasury, and William Keogh as Solicitor-General
for Ireland. Nineteen of their " Catholic Defence "
followers went over with them to the Government
benches. All, in due course, received material rewards.

This defection at once placed the new Government in
a position to disregard the Irish vote. Both Tenants'
Right Bills were allowed to die in Committee.

At the by-elections necessitated by their acceptance
of office, Sadleir and Keogh were assailed fiercely by
the Tenants' Right League. They were defended by
both the Protestant landlords *and* the Catholic Hierarchy.
The latter body affirmed that Sadleir and Keogh had
obtained a pledge that the Ecclesiastical Titles Act
would be allowed to fall into disuse. Russell denied
this flatly, but that was in fact what happened. Meanwhile the Hierarchy took the view that preserving the
right of bishops to their titles was work of far greater
importance than preserving the Tenants' Right to their
improvements in the soil. Hence they defended Messrs.
Sadleir and Keogh with all their strength and authority.

The League succeeded in defeating Sadleir by a margin
of six votes only. They failed to defeat Keogh, who,
says Duffy, " came on to the platform to return thanks,
just like Richard III, hanging on the arms of two bishops".

How far the result was achieved by actual collusion,
or how far it was begotten by a fortuitous conjunction
of interests cannot be known ; the fact remains, however,
that the Catholic Cardinal Cullen, the Orange Grand
Master, the landlords, the Whigs, and the Tories, were
all of one mind. The aims of the Tenants' Right League
were, they said, " *Communistic*", and they had to be
thwarted accordingly.

Within a few weeks of the Great Betrayal, the young
Catholic curates who had done the donkey-work of
agitating and organising were each and all ordered by
their respective bishops—set on by Cardinal Cullen—

not to set foot outside their parishes, and to confine themselves, strictly, to their *spiritual functions.*

In desperation, the Catholic laymen in the League sent a delegation to Rome to beg for a Papal reversal of the Cardinal's inhibition. The delegates were received politely, and were assured that the matter would " receive consideration". For all anyone knows it is receiving it still.

Duffy, completely disheartened, gave up the struggle. There was, he said, " no more hope for Ireland than for a corpse on a dissecting table". He resigned his seat; and, in 1855, emigrated to Australia, where he had a distinguished career.

It capped the story of the Great Betrayal when, a few years later, the Tipperary Bank failed, ruining thousands of small depositors. Sadleir, to escape the penalty for a truly colossal series of forgeries and frauds, poisoned himself at midnight on Hampstead Heath. Two other prominent members of the " Band " fled the country to escape prosecution for complicity in fraud.

William Keogh, though suspected, was never charged. Instead he became Lord Chief Justice of Ireland, and in that capacity, as we shall see, inflicted savage sentences on most of the leading Fenians.

CHAPTER TWENTY

THE FENIAN BROTHERHOOD

DUFFY's emigration left the field of (constitutional) political action in Ireland free for political adventurers and crooks, of whom Keogh and Sadleir were classic examples. Apart from sporadic outbreaks of " Ribbonism", there was no alternative—until there arose the FENIAN BROTHERHOOD, which revealed its existence in the period of the Civil War in the U.S.A. (1861–65).

Fenianism—or the IRISH REPUBLICAN BROTHERHOOD—was, frankly, an endeavour to resume the work done by the *United Irishmen*. It constituted one of the most remarkable and enduring revolutionary secret-societies in history. In this chapter we recount the story of its rise and progress to the crisis of 1865.

The " Phoenix " Conspiracy

Left over from the Irish Confederation and the Repeal Association—which collapsed in 1848—were a number of isolated clubs and local debating-societies. These were most numerous in West Cork and Kerry ; and, under the influence of JEREMIAH O'DONOVAN of Skibbereen, the clubs of that region federated in 1856 into a secret society, known as the PHOENIX—so called because, like the fabled-bird, it intended to rise from the ashes of the burnt-out Young Ireland movement.

O'Donovan was better known then and later by his title " ROSSA", which denoted, alternatively, his flaming red head and his origin in the Ross-Carbery region of South-West Cork. He was famous for his size, and his fiery energy.

In 1857 the *Phoenix* was visited by JAMES STEPHENS, a Kilkenny man who had acted as *aide* to Smith O'Brien in 1848 ; and who, since then, had lived partly in Paris and partly in the U.S.A. Stephens brought news of a movement about to be launched in the U.S.A., which would be a valuable reservoir of aid to any revolutionary movement in Ireland. At Stephens' prompting, the Phoenix men began drilling, and preparing to collect arms.

Revolutionary Affiliations of Fenianism

The American movement, of which Stephens brought news, was, then, little more than an idea and a name. Three exiles from 1848—MICHAEL DOHENY, originally a schoolmaster, who had been connected with the *Nation*, JAMES STEPHENS himself, and JOHN O'MAHONEY, an enthusiastic Gaelic scholar—had conceived the idea of an oath-bound military conspiracy, which in allusion to the legendary following of FINN MACCUMHALL, they called the FIANNA or FENIANS.

Their stay in Paris had brought these three into contact with the Red Republican Clubs and Communist secret societies of the period ; particularly those led by AUGUST BLANQUI. And it was from Blanqui's notion of a pledge-bound, hand-picked, disciplined *élite*—which would act at command as the shock-troops of Revolution —that they derived their conception of a revived and improved version of the United Irishmen's conspiracy.

Neither of the original three ever declared himself, openly, a Socialist or a Communist ; but all three, at different times, showed close sympathy with Socialist and Communist aspirations. O'MAHONEY—so O'Leary tells us—was " an advanced democrat or even a social-ist", STEPHENS, at one time " planned to write a history of socialist theories". DOHENY was strongly in sympathy with the agrarian " communism " of Fintan Lalor. All hinted more or less plainly at an agrarian revolution as a necessary consequence of the establishment of an Irish Republic ; and there is evidence, of a kind, that both

O'Mahoney and Stephens were individual members of the International Working Men's Association. It helps considerably to elucidate the obscurities of Stephens' conduct if we suppose him constantly waiting and hoping for a grand-scale resumption of the Continental Red-Republican and " Communist " upheavals of the 1848 period.

In 1856 (or thereabouts) the triumvirate moved to New York. Doheny, the oldest, engaged in journalistic work. O'Mahoney and Stephens, working among the Irish exiles, gathered a nucleus which they thought sufficient to begin with. They called their open organisation the " Fenian Brotherhood "; but this was primarily a cover (as well as a recruiting ground) for the " underground " I.R.B.—which initials, O'Leary says, could be translated as Irish *Republican* Brotherhood, or Irish *Revolutionary* Brotherhood according to taste.

O'Mahoney stopped in the U.S.A. to organise the supply of funds, arms, and trained *officers*. Stephens went to Ireland to recruit the army. He had returned to America to report the progress made with the Phoenix men when, in 1858, the police made a swoop and captured all the Phoenix leaders. In this connection a new aspect of the affair arose.

" *Felon Setting*"

After Duffy's departure, the *Nation* had been continued by various successors without a break. Its editor and proprietor in 1858 was Alexander M. Sullivan, a Bantry man, whose policy was nearer to that of O'Connell than to that of Davis. He was not only a Catholic but an ardent clericalist, and he had fossilized O'Connell's hostility to insurrection into an absolute dogma. Never, under any circumstances, might Irishmen resort to arms without mortal sin—unless, of course, the Church called them to arms.

Early in 1858 Sullivan was urged by the Catholic

Bishop of Kerry to warn the people against "foolish courses", such as dabbling in "privy conspiracy and rebellion". Sullivan consulted Smith O'Brien, then newly returned from exile; and he, honestly enough, wrote for the *Nation* an Open Letter advising against insurrectionary conspiracies on general grounds.

Nobody found fault with O'Brien; everybody knew he would never favour a revolution not led by the gentry and the educated class. What infuriated the revolutionaries was that Sullivan added a leading article, in his own, best, sentimental-picturesque style, pleading with *the young men of Kerry and West Cork in particular* to take O'Brien's advice, and to heed the injunctions of their clergy. Shortly afterwards the police arrested all the leaders of the Phoenix Society in *Kerry and West Cork*. There was little the police could urge against them, and, by arrangement, they all pleaded guilty and were bound over.

Stephens never forgave Sullivan, whom he accused of playing the part of a setter-dog who points out the game to the huntsman. "Felon-setter" was his name for Sullivan, and "felon-setting" his description of "moral force" propaganda. This feud between Stephens and Sullivan continued to provide a running commentary of acrimony through the whole course of the Fenian agitation. Indignant at Stephens' "unfairness", Sullivan became every day more hysterically and sentimentally Pacifist, Papalist and clerical.

Garibaldi and the Pope

In 1859–60, for example, when NAPOLEON III, for opportunist reasons, joined VICTOR EMMANUEL, King of Sardinia, in expelling the Austrians from North Italy, European Radicals and Republicans were disgusted to see the long-desired unification of Italy advanced a stage by the interested manœuvres of a King and an "Emperor". That Napoleon III got Nice and Savoy as his share of the loot, made it a thoroughly bad business from the Radical point of view. The disgust of the Radicals reassured Sullivan, who seized the opportunity to organise a " stunt "—the presentation of a Sword of Honour to the French Marshal *MacMahon* on the ground that his name and descent were Irish.

That the traceable ancestors of the Marshal, in Ireland, had always fought on the anti-popular side ; that MacMahon himself was an adventurer like Louis Napoleon, and had helped him to bring off the *coup d'état* which destroyed the Second Republic and replaced it with the Second Empire ; that MacMahon, earlier, had assisted in butchering the Parisian workmen in the Days of June, 1848—as he was later to butcher the Communards of 1871—these things weighed nothing with Sullivan. MacMahon was an ardent clericalist ; therefore he could be boosted as " Irish", and presented with a sword of honour by the very men who were " horrified " to learn that Irish lads were drilling by moonlight.

A few months later a rising occurred at Palermo in Sicily, and the Republican leader, JOSEPH GARIBALDI, made his famous raid with a thousand volunteers, which led the rising which drove the Neapolitan troops out of Sicily. Crossing to the mainland, Garibaldi then drove the King of Naples from his throne.

Even Sullivan could not defend King " Bomba "— the best-hated king in Europe—but he could, and did, take alarm at the prospect of a Garibaldian-Republican revolution in the Central Italian States, ruled by the Pope as a temporal prince.

Amid the applause of the *Ultramontanes*, headed by Cardinal Cullen, Sullivan raised a whoop about the " Pope in Danger", and the Irish lads who might not drill by moonlight to learn to fight for Ireland were invited to volunteer to form an Irish Brigade for the defence of the Pope.

Here again it was nothing to Sullivan that the administration of the Papal States was a by-word for
incompetence and corruption—as was proved when
at least half of the Irish brigade never so much as got
arms in their hands.   Nor did it bother Sullivan much
that the Pope made a deal with Victor Emmanuel—which
squeezed Garibaldi out.   Nor that the Pope thought
so little of his Irish helpers that Sullivan had to raise
more money to save them from starving and bring them
home again.   These things did not bother Sullivan and
his friends.   They had pulled off a " stunt " and found
a slogan.   When Fenians said " *Felon-setter* " Sullivan-
ites replied " *Garibaldian* "—which meant an enemy of
the Pope in all things.   " Garibaldi or the Pope ? " was
the opening challenge in many a faction fight for years
thereafter.

The MacManus Funeral

An event which considerably aided the Fenian movement was the funeral of TERENCE BELLEW MACMANUS,
a popular Liverpool Confederate who in 1848 crossed
to join in the rising and who, after his escape from
Tasmania, had lived and, for a time, prospered in San
Francisco.

When MacManus died, in the last days of 1860, his
friends in the Irish Colony in San Francisco thought so
highly of him that they decided to send his body
(embalmed) home for burial in Ireland.   A refinement
upon the original project—one of which the organisers
of the Fenian Brotherhood made full use—was to send
the body to Boston *overland*, in those days a perilous
adventure in itself.   At each resting place upon the
journey memorial meetings were held ; and each memorial meeting became a recruiting-rally for the Fenian
Brotherhood and the *Clan na Gael* (the American equivalent of the I.R.B.).   So many towns in America with
Irish colonies put in demands that the funeral should be

routed to include them, that it was not till September, 1861, that the body at last left America for Ireland.

In Ireland arrangements had been made for continuing the work. Cardinal Cullen, however, instructed the Church to refuse its countenance; none the less, virtually the entire population of Cork took part in the ceremony. It was noted that a considerable number of private soldiers and non-commissioned officers in uniform joined in the procession.

The final procession in Dublin on November 10th, 1861, saw a number variously estimated at from 50,000 to 100,000 marching in military formation, while an equal number lined the streets. A halt was made at every spot sacred in the revolutionary-republican history of Ireland—the house where Lord Edward was mortally wounded; the house where Wolfe Tone's body lay before burial; the Church before which Emmet was hanged; and so on. Night had fallen before the body was at last laid to rest in Glasnevin.

The Civil War in the U.S.A. and Fenianism

The MacManus funeral had proved the existence of a solid core of intense Nationalist feeling among the Irish, both in the U.S.A. and in Ireland. The outbreak of Civil War in the U.S.A. between the pro-slavery South and the anti-slavery North gave the American-Irish a chance to learn the use of arms under actual war conditions. Both sides raised IRISH BRIGADES; but that on the Northern Side, led by THOMAS FRANCIS MEAGHER, was by far the more popular with the Irish-American masses.

Mitchel's pro-Southern propaganda—based, as it was, mainly on the expectation that the English government would at once support the North—was concretely refuted by the strong pro-Southern sympathies shown by the English ruling-class—who would have recognised the South, and gone to war in its aid, if they had not been stopped by the mass-opposition of the English workers, and a section of the middle-class.

"It was not the wisdom of the rulers but the heroic resistance of the working-classes of England which saved the West of Europe from plunging headlong into an infamous crusade for the perpetuation and propagation of slavery on the other side of the Atlantic".

—MARX : *Inaugural Address I.W.M.A.* (1864).

Stephens and O'Mahoney took the much more plausible line of arguing that as hostility between England and the U.S.A. was bound to result in war either before or after the ending of the Civil War—which they thought the North was bound to win—all Irishmen of military age should join either the Federal Army or, if they preferred it, *the English Army*, in order to become trained in readiness for the crisis.

It is significant that Irish Emigration to America noticeably increased during the Civil War years of 1861-5. When the North began definitely to gain the upper hand by the victories of Vicksburg and Gettysburg (both on July 4th, 1863) Stephens decided to open a political offensive in Ireland by publishing a revolutionary journal.

The " Irish People "

The Fenian journal, the *Irish People*, was first published in Dublin on November 29th, 1863. Its editors, THOMAS CLARKE LUBY and JOHN O'LEARY, had both been " out " in '48 ; and both were close friends of Fintan Lalor. CHARLES JOSEPH KICKHAM, who was associated with them, was an older man who had contributed to the *Nation*. All were men of education. Luby came of a scholastic family ; O'Leary was a man of independent means who had studied for the medical profession.

The business-manager of the journal, upon whom much of the work of building its circulation fell, was JEREMIAH O'DONOVAN-ROSSA.

The founding of the *Irish People* marked a turning point in the history of Fenianism. The work of building a circulation ; the contacts gained ; the correspondence published ; and the struggles against rival constitutionalist journals backed by the priests—all were means of aiding that development of the " underground " organisation at which Stephens and Luby laboured diligently. The open hostility of the priests, and of employers set on by priests—who discharged employees freely for having any connection with the *Irish People*—made the journal itself the best organiser of the Fenian movement.

CHAPTER TWENTY-ONE

THE CRISIS OF FENIANISM

Civil War ended in the U.S.A. in April, 1865. This released for action in Ireland something near to 200,000 men who had been sworn in as Fenians in the course of the struggle. It was a natural inference that something would be attempted in Ireland soon. Actually the English Authorities made the first move by raiding the *Irish People* and arresting the leaders. A daring escape effected by STEPHENS excited hopes (and fears) ; but the other prisoners were left to be convicted and carried off to penal servitude with nothing done. Fenianism had already suffered a heavy moral set-back when an attempt at INSURRECTION made in 1867 ended in complete failure. The MANCHESTER RESCUE and the CLERKENWELL EXPLOSION were the closing episodes in the Fenian Movement in its classic period.

The Arrests of 'Sixty-Five

JAMES STEPHENS, Chief Organiser of the Irish Republic " now virtually established "—so ran the I.R.B. membership pledge—was placed squarely before the need for action by the cessation of the Civil War in the U.S.A. He had boasted of the numbers of Fenians in the American armies, and of those enrolled likewise in the ranks of the English army. Would he give " the word " ? Or would he wait ?

He chose to wait. Many guesses were made as to the reason. The most probable guess is that he had no real plan at all ; but was waiting, opportunistically, upon events. The English Authorities thought it wisdom to get their blow in first ; and, accordingly, they raided the *Irish People*, and the homes of the Fenian leaders, on the night of September 15th, 1865. LUBY, O'LEARY, ROSSA, and a number of minor chiefs were arrested.

Stephens evaded arrest for a time, and in anticipation of the expected insurrection great military precautions were taken by the Authorities in all the main centres of Ireland. Nothing happened ; and a month later (November 15th) STEPHENS and KICKHAM were arrested at a private house in the suburbs of Dublin. Brought before a magistrate Stephens refused to plead ; and, being committed for trial, vanished from his cell in Richmond Prison, Dublin, on the night of November 25th. Not until long after did the Authorities learn that his escape had been contrived by two (Fenian) prison warders, acting in concert with JOHN DEVOY, who was the chief organiser of Fenian circles in the English Army.

At the time of Stephens' escape everybody expected that insurrection would follow immediately. And, as we know now, JOHN DEVOY urged it strongly. Nothing, however, happened. The English Government was left free to fill the press with propaganda worked up from the documents produced at the preliminary hearings of the cases against the prisoners. By an unscrupulous use of the correspondence files of the *Irish People*— especially of letters deemed unsuitable for publication which had not been destroyed—the Ascendancy and Constitutionalist press were able to represent the Fenians as contemplating every conceivable barbarity, including (of course) the " extermination " of landlords.

There is weighty reason for believing that if JOHN DEVOY's advice had been taken, the result would have been to secure for Ireland as much as was secured by the Treaty of 1921-2, *without Partition*. On the other hand, it is fair to say that American military experts strongly supported Stephens in insisting upon delay.

The Trials of Luby, O'Leary, Kickham and Rossa

All decent feeling in Ireland was outraged when the

Judge appointed to try the Fenian leaders proved to be none other than Chief Justice *William Keogh*—the " solo-trombone in the Pope's Brass Band ". He was set off in some measure by the appearance, as chief counsel for the defence, of ISAAC BUTT, the leader of the Dublin Conservatives, who in 1843 had defended the Union in debate against O'Connell himself. Butt defended all the prisoners (except Rossa, who insisted upon conducting his own defence) with great courage, persistence, and skill. And, in fact, he was so impressed by the character of the prisoners, and by the logical force of their stand-point, that he began from that moment to move over to the Nationalist camp.

The case against the prisoners was that they had said, repeatedly and plainly, that they desired to see Ireland an independent republic, and that no means were available for attaining this end except an armed uprising. The evidence connecting them with the actual prepara-tions for an armed uprising was, at most, indirect, and consisted entirely of documents found at Stephens' domicile. The verdict however was a foregone conclusion ; but the sentences shocked even Englishmen. Luby, O'Leary, and Kickham were sentenced to *twenty years' penal servitude*. Rossa, who fought Keogh with defiance and insult for over eight hours, was sentenced to *penal servitude for life*.

The Rising of 'Sixty-Seven

The failure of '65 precipitated a violent internal upheavel in Fenian circles. In America, O'Mahoney was " deposed " ; a split ensued ; and the majority faction, drifting into questionable hands, wasted its force in futile attempts to invade Canada.

Stephens remained in Ireland, despite the £1,000 reward offered by the Authorities for information leading to his capture, until his protector, John Devoy fell into the hands of the enemy. Stephens then left for

America (in March, 1866) where he contrived a temporary healing of the split by promising, categorically, that the year 1866 " would not pass without a blow struck in Ireland ". When that year ended with nothing done the movement split again. In desperation Stephens ordered preparation for a rising early in 1867. But the movements in Ireland and in America each agreed spontaneously to depose Stephens definitely and finally. Not the least enigma attending an enigmatical character is that Stephens accepted his deposition without protest; and never, thereafter, attempted to emerge from the obscurity of private life.

The Irish-American Colonel KELLEY, now Head-Centre of the I.R.B. in Ireland, issued the word for a rising on February 11th, 1867. This date was later changed to March 5th.

Two places failed to receive notice of the change of date—Kerry and the North of England.

In Kerry the Fenians turned out in considerable numbers, and captured a coast-guard station and a police barracks. They also captured the despatch from Fenian headquarters (which the police had intercepted) fixing a new date for the rising. The Fenian commander, at once, ordered his men to disperse to their homes.

In the North of England, the Fenian leader, JOHN McCAFFERTY—a competent commander, and a most desperate character—had devised an ingenious plan to capture the stock of arms stored in Chester Castle. But for a last-minute warning given to the authorities by an informer the surprise would have been complete. As it was the raid proved abortive, and the authorities were put on the alert against any repetition.

The rising on March 5th was foredoomed to failure. The authorities were well on the alert ; and, in addition, a blizzard of exceptional force set in that night which raged without abatement for a full week. Thousands of young men turned out—most of them mechanics and shop assistants—but being unprovided with the means

s

of facing such weather, they could do nothing but return home, to be arrested in many cases as they made their way back.

The Fenian General MASSEY arrived on time at Limerick Junction ; but only to find it in the hands, not of Fenians, but of the military. Realising that the plans had been betrayed, he, too, gave the authorities all the information he had. This made the failure absolute.

The Manchester Rescue

Col. Kelley, the Head-Centre, having occasion to visit Manchester, fell into the hands of the police with a companion, DEASY, on September 11th. Identified by detectives from Dublin as Fenian leaders, they were committed for trial on September 18th. The Black Maria conveying them to prison was held up by local Fenians, armed with revolvers, who drove off the police escort, broke open the van and got the prisoners away safely. Unfortunately in blowing open the locked door of the van, a police sergeant was killed. Some of the rescue-party sacrificed themselves to hold back pursuit, four of them being captured. These were, later, charged with the " murder " of the police-sergeant. A panic raid on the Irish quarter produced a number of other prisoners, and one of them was selected to be charged along with the first four. He proved to be a " loyal " private in the Marines, home on furlough, who had no sort of knowledge of the affair.

He and the other four, WILLIAM PHILLIP ALLEN, MICHAEL LARKIN, MICHAEL O'BRIEN, and EDWARD O'MARA CONDON were all, despite the efforts of their counsel, *Ernest Jones*, the Chartist leader, found guilty and sentenced to death.

The journalists present protested unanimously their conviction of the innocence of the Marine, and he was ' pardoned '. Condon, as an American citizen, was respited and after a term of imprisonment was released.

The other three were hanged on November 23rd, 1867, despite the fact that not one of them had fired the fatal shot, and that, at worst, the death was accidental.

The executions produced a revulsion of horror all over Ireland. Great funeral processions were organised to follow coffins piled high with wreaths and marked with the names of the " Manchester Martyrs". Men who had been bitterly hostile to Fenianism were prosecuted for their share in these demonstrations, *John Martin*, the '48 man, and *A. M. Sullivan* among them.

TIMOTHY D. SULLIVAN, brother of A. M., took the cry of the prisoners in the dock—" *God Save Ireland !* "— and wrote a poem which was at once adopted as the " National Anthem " of Ireland—an esteem which it retained until it was superseded, after Easter Week, 1916, by the *Soldier's Song*.

The Clerkenwell Explosion

An incident of a different order marked the close of the year. An important Fenian organiser being detained in the House of Detention, Clerkenwell, a group of Fenian sympathisers, acting on their own responsibility, sought to rescue him on the afternoon of December 13th, 1867, by exploding a barrel of gunpowder against the wall surrounding the prison yard.

The force of the explosion drove forty tons of masonry out of the wall clean across the prison yard. In the opposite direction it completely wrecked the row of tall, tenement houses which was separated from the prison wall only by the width of a narrow lane. Four people were killed outright, three died of their injuries, and 120 others were injured more or less permanently.

This was not the work of the Fenian organisation, whose leaders all condemned it as a barbarous folly. But it indicated that a degeneration had set in, in which Fenian discipline had evaporated, to leave only irrational hate and an irresponsible readiness for violent deeds.

CHAPTER TWENTY-TWO

THE OUTCOME OF THE FENIAN MOVEMENT

As a military conspiracy the Fenian movement failed completely; none the less it produced permanent results. For one thing it reincarnated for Irishmen the ideal of WOLFE TONE and the UNITED IRISHMEN, and re-established it as the *norm* of Irish National struggle. It revealed to Englishmen, and the world, the actuality and extent of the Irish aspiration for unfettered Nationality. At the least it proved that as a means of welding two nations into one, the Act of Union was the completest failure ever. Largely under the inspiration of KARL MARX and the *International Working Men's Association* the English Radical and working-class movement returned to the Chartist standpoint and demanded "Justice for Ireland". Gladstone's reply was to DISESTABLISH THE (PROTESTANT) CHURCH OF IRELAND (1869).

The International and the Fenians

The period of Fenian agitation in Ireland was also a period of Radical and working-class revival in England.

The INTERNATIONAL WORKING MEN'S ASSOCIATION was founded in 1864; the National Reform League, largely inspired by the International, commenced its agitation for an extension of the Franchise in 1865. In 1866, the Reform League demonstration being debarred access to Hyde Park tore up half-a-mile of railings and forced an entry. When the events of 1867 forced the Fenians and the Irish Question to the front, the International led the way in demanding consideration for Ireland's claims, and mooted a possibility of agitating for the Repeal of the Union.

KARL MARX, the theoretical and political leader of the International, was foremost in guiding it along this line. He and his friend ENGELS had been interested in Ireland since the days when, as supporters of the Chartists, they had supported the demand for Repeal. One of Marx's earliest contributions to the New York *Tribune* had been (June '53) a closely reasoned argument in favour of Tenants' Right. In November 1867—just after the Manchester executions—Marx wrote to Engels describing the debates on the General Council of the I.W.M.A. in which the trial and execution were roundly condemned. He suggested to Engels that while he (Marx) and the I.W.M.A. could not agitate legally for more than Repeal, Engels, who was in close touch with leading Fenians, should urge them to adopt a programme embodying these points: (1) Self-government and Independence ; (2) Agrarian Revolution ; (3) Protective Tariffs against English competition.

This letter crossed one, no less notable, from Engels to Marx, written on the morning after the executions :

" All the Fenians lacked was martyrs. These they have been presented with . . . Through the execution of these men, the liberation of Kelley and Deasy has been made an act of heroism which will now be sung over the cradle of every Irish child . . . The Irish women will take care of that. The only instance of an execution for any similar act is . . . that of John Brown after Harper's Ferry. The Fenians could not wish for a better precedent . . .

" Louis Napoleon . . . at the head of his band of adventurers at Boulogne (1840) shot the officer on duty . . . For this the English government have hanged Allen ; but the English queen kissed Louis Napoleon's face, while the English aristocracy and bourgeoisie kissed his backside."

Marx did not succeed in getting the I.W.M.A. to launch an agitation for Repeal—his efforts were cut

across by Gladstone's accession to power, and his
decision to at once introduce the Disestablishment Bill
(1869). But Marx and Engels worked strenuously
through the I.W.M.A. in support of the Amnesty
Movement which secured the release of most of the
leading Fenian prisoners on January 1st, 1871.

Gladstone's Disestablishment Act

The Protestant Church in Ireland was undoubtedly
an anomaly. Set up on a scale amply sufficient to serve
the entire population, it was the Church of a fractional
minority only. Of five millions and three-quarters, four
and a half were Catholics, three-quarters of a million
were Dissenters, and only half-a-million at most were
even nominally Episcopalians. Out of 1,478 parishes,
only 181 possessed a resident " church " population of
over 1,000. In 201 parishes, they numbered less than 40
all told. 91 parishes had less than a score apiece ; and
among these were a number with not a single Church
adherent. The Church had been for centuries merely a
device to supply salaries to non-resident parsons nominated by aristocratic patrons.

The best of the resident clergy in the Established
Church welcomed Disestablishment ; and even the
Orange Order could find little to complain of except
Gladstone's admission that it was the activity of the
Fenians which had brought the Irish Church question
" within the range of practical politics ". Once the
infliction of tithes was removed the resident Protestant
Clergy had usually been popular, and were commonly
on the best of terms with the parish priests. The best
feature of the Act was that by abolishing redundant
bishoprics and other ecclesiastical offices it created a
fund from which a number of underpaid curates and
rectors received welcome additions of salary.

As it removed only superficial grievances, Church
Disestablishment made no real difference to the situation

in Ireland, except that it destroyed the basis for the easiest form of " Catholic " demagogy.

The Fenian Tradition

The most abiding result of the Fenian agitation was that it established firmly in the minds of Irishmen, in Ireland and in exile, *a tradition of fidelity and steadfastness* in the cause of National Freedom which has never since been wholly overlaid. While it was in being Fenianism absorbed into itself and its discipline the whole member-ship of the Ribbon conspiracy. After its failure, the recrudescence of agrarian outrage which followed was condemned, even in the countryside, as a falling away from the *disciplined manliness* of the Fenian ideal. The concept of an *Irish Republic " now virtually established "* might be treated as folly and romanticism by self-seeking worldings ; it remained operative, none the less, as an abiding element in the Irish tradition of Nationality.

The political content of the Fenian doctrine was, consciously and purposefully, in line with the teaching of TONE, and DAVIS, with an infusion of MITCHEL and of LALOR. It was categorically *democratic*, as well as *republican*, and it was *socialistic*, or even *communistic*, in its agrarian-revolutionary outlook (at any rate in the negative sense of advocating the expropriation of the landlords as a class). Still more was Fenianism categori-cally hostile to sectarianism and clericalism. A few passages (mainly from the extracts from the *Irish People* included in the indictments of the Fenian leaders in '65) will illustrate these points.

Their democratic faith is thus attested :

" Twenty years ago Thomas Davis appealed to the aristocracy to save the people with their own hands. We make no appeal to the aristocracy . . . They are the willing tools of the alien government whose policy it is to slay the people, or drive them like noxious vermin from the soil. The *people must save themselves.*"

" The overthrow of tyranny has always been the work of *the people*. It is by their combined and determined efforts that rulers are made and unmade. America and France have furnished us glorious examples of this."

" By force of arms Ireland was wrested from her rightful owners, *the Irish people*. By no other means will she ever be restored."

Their agrarian ideal was not less specific :

" Something more even than a successful insurrection is demanded. And What is that ? *An entire revolution which will restore the country to its rightful owners.* And who are these ? *The People.*"

" Every man has one simple object to accomplish. It is to rid the land of *robbers*, and render every cultivator of the soil his own landlord, the proprietor in fee-simple of the house and land of his fathers, which will be an inheritance worth a free man's while to bequeath to his children, and worth the children's while to enjoy in a nation which bows to no power under heaven."

In regard to clericalism, Charles J Kickham, himself an ardent Catholic, wrote :

"Nothing would please us better than to keep clear of the vexed question of priests in politics . . . But the question was forced upon us. We saw that the people must be taught to distinguish between the priest as a minister of religion and the priest as a politician before they could advance óne step on the road to emancipation . . . Our only hope is in revolution, but most bishops and many of the clergy are opposed to revolution . . . When priests turn the altar into a platform ; when it is pronounced a ' mortal sin ' to read the *Irish People*, a ' mortal sin ' to even *wish* that Ireland should be free ; when priests call upon the people to turn informers . . . When, in a word, bishops and priests are doing the work of the enemy, we believe it is our duty to tell the people that bishops and priests may be bad politicians and worse Irishmen."*

Luby wrote to similar effect :

" Emancipation was a measure calculated almost exclusively to benefit the upper and middle-classes of the Catholics . . . Emancipation separated from the cause of Independence has turned out to be simply a means . . . of bribing or corrupting wealthy or educated Catholics—of seducing them from the National ranks."

O'Leary summed up the first year of the *Irish People* thus :

" In one part of the old *Nation's* policy . . . we could do no more than follow in its footsteps, and by so doing we have incurred the same reward— the hatred of bigots. And here it may not be out of place to use the words of Davis on a similar occasion : ' We look upon the Protestants' fear of the Catholics, and the Catholics' fear of the Protestants as rank nonsense. Their mutual dislike is something worse. And yet this trash and this crime have ruined the country.' Alas that it should be almost as necessary to write this to-day as when Davis wrote, and our pseudo-national papers are the main cause that this is the case."

That all these passages (save the last one) should have been included in the Government's indictment against the Fenian chiefs testifies to the effectiveness of the Fenian teaching.

Finally it is worth noting, as James Connolly does, that Fenianism, though unquestionably a *national* move-

---

* *Kickham* suspected the theological orthodoxy of O'Leary and Devoy. Learning that they, on their release from penal servitude, were spending a holiday in France, studying architectural monuments, he remarked " If *that one* [O'Leary] goes on looking at Cathedrals much longer, the Grace of God may strike him yet ! "

ment and not a class movement, appealed most successfully to the *wage-worker class* especially among the exile communities in England, Scotland, the U.S.A. and Australia. In Ireland the *Irish People* barely held its own in competition with the constitutionalist journals backed by the power of the Church. Where the field was more free, and the power of clerical intimidation was correspondingly less, as it was among the exiles, the *Irish People* swept its rivals completely out of the field.

That is to say : The I.R.B. *represented* the peasantry and received their general support ; but its main strength and source of inspiration was in the towns and among the proletarian exiles. Working men, very often of the labourer-class, formed overwhelmingly the backbone of the army of those who sang :

> " Side by side for the Cause, have our forefathers battled,
> When our hills never echoed the tread of a slave ;
> On many green fields where the leaden hail rattled,
> Through the red gap of glory they marched to their grave.
> And we who inherit their name and their spirit
> Will march 'neath the banners of Liberty, then—
> All who love Saxon law, native or *Sassenach*,
> Must out and make way for the *Fenian Men*."
>
> —J. BOYLE O'REILLY.

PART V

FROM PARNELL TO EASTER WEEK AND AFTER

CHAPTER TWENTY-THREE

ECONOMIC DEVELOPMENTS, 1870-1916

In Part V we treat of the process of revival after the failure of the Fenians. It is an epoch which had as its peak phenomena Parnell and his PARLIAMENTARY STRUGGLE : the concurrent LAND STRUGGLE ; and, then, the REVOLUTIONARY STRUGGLE, opened by Connolly and Pearse in Easter Week 1916, which issued in the TREATY of 1921 and the PARTITION of 1925.

In this chapter we deal with the economic roots from which the struggle was fed and grew.

Agricultural Development in Ireland

Before the Famine of '46-8, political economists attributed Ireland's difficulties to its " surplus population ". This was removed *with a vengeance* in those years of calamity ; consequently " progress ", thereafter, was able to take a course *normal* to the conditions then existing. The nature of the conditions can be inferred from the figures set out in the following comparison of the area under crops in the years 1849 and 1914 respectively :

Crop	1849	1914
Wheat	697,646 acres	26,916 acres
Oats	2,061,185 ,,	1,028,645 ,,
Barley	290,690 ,,	179,824 ,,
Potatoes	718,608 ,,	583,609 ,,
Turnips	260,069 ,,	276,872 ,,
Hay	1,141,371 ,,	2,487,513* ,,

*For 1914 these were the figures for Meadow and Hay

Every item in this list bears witness to the steady shift over from arable to pasture-farming ; and, therefore, to a constant economic squeeze of the classes dependent directly upon tillage. Potatoes, for example, declined by one-fifth approximately—a decline which corresponds to the decline of population. The decline of wheat to one-eighteenth of the 1849 acreage is decisive, since this followed a previous decline from the level of 1800. The decline in oats—the staple crop—by one-half, and of barley by over one-third—declines in each case much *greater* than the fall in the population but much *less* than the decline in wheat—testify the one to the influence of cattle-rearing, the other to that of brewing and distilling as partial checks upon the general abandonment of tillage farming. This steady lessening of the demand for labour constantly threw the lowest strata of the agrarian population back upon the alternatives of subsistence-cultivation on small-holdings, or—*emigration*. A census of livestock for the corresponding years gives a conforming picture :

	1849	1914
Horses	525,924	619,028
Cattle	2,771,139	5,051,645
Sheep	1,777,111	3,600,581
Pigs	795,463	1,305,638
Poultry	6,328,001	26,918,749

These figures also tell their own tale. Ireland in these years concentrated increasingly upon *producing and exporting livestock and poultry* for the English market. Comparative statistics are not available, but we can infer likewise an increase in the export, but in a different proportion, of eggs, butter and bacon.

This development, to be appreciated, must be envisaged as one pole in a relation. As Ireland's farm-production developed, while its manufactures declined, so correspondingly England's manufacture developed out of all proportion to its agriculture. And—since England's demand for bread-stuffs must have grown with its population—the decline in Irish (as well as English) tillage-farming implies the growth of an alternative, and cheaper, source of supply. Similarly the importance of live-stock exports must be viewed against England's demand for (*a*) prime " home-killed " meat and poultry for luxury consumption ; and (*b*) cheap frozen or chilled carcasses, and tinned meats, for mass-consumption. The result emerges that, in fact and practice, Ireland was in this period relegated to the position of a *feeder* for the English market almost exclusively ; and was, in that market, subjected to an ever-intensifying competition from overseas wheat and grain production—especially that of North America—the meat production of Australia, New Zealand and South America, etc., and the State-fostered dairy-farming and bacon-manufacture of Denmark, etc.

Ireland, in short, had to face the full impact of expanding and intensifying world-competition, with, as its consequence, the progressive fall in prices for agricultural produce. At the same time Ireland was denied all possibility of gaining any countervailing advantage from the growing demand for manufactured articles ; and had no power of protecting even its own agriculture. Ireland's power of accumulating capital was reduced to a minimum by the rigorous exaction of the landlord's tribute—much of which went to swell the capital accumulation of England. Necessarily, the intensifying pressure of world-competition ensured a progressive worsening of living-standards for rural Ireland, taken as a whole.

This worsening is denied by those who look only to the very lowest sub-stratum of the population, and judge this stratum from its worst periods. It should be remembered that from 1845 onwards Famine and emigration constantly drained away a proportion of the population equivalent to the number who would have been otherwise submerged and relegated to pauperism. The persisting poverty of the agricultural classes in Ireland is not a *static* phenomenon; it is a poverty which was as constantly *recreated* as it was " cured " by emigration.

That, in essence, is the fact that finds expression in constant agitation, on the one hand, and perpetual Coercion on the other.

The Case of Belfast

Belfast, with its surrounding region, provides, in this period, an outstanding contrast to the state of rural Ireland. And it has been a favourite device of anti-Nationalist politicians to point to Belfast and ask the Nationalists : " If Belfast can prosper, why cannot you prosper also ? "

The facts, correctly related, expose the hypocrisy—as well as the ignorance—shown in this question.

In rural Ireland, in the period under examination, the English rulers insisted upon applying the principle of *laissez faire*, of " Free Trade in Land ". Belfast rose to prosperity because, in its own case, at every critical period, the principle of *laissez faire* was abandoned, and special *protective measures* were applied.

In 1856 the Belfast Harbour Board were granted special powers by Parliament and a money-donation by the government to enable them to convert a harbour, accessible only at high-tide, into one usable at any time. This was done, deliberately, to supplement the ship-repairing (and, later, ship-building) resources of the Mersey and the Clyde. And it was done, too, to provide the capitalists concerned with an escape from the " rapacity " of the Trade Unions in those areas. The " prosperity " of the region around Belfast is primarily the product of its ship-building and repairing industry, which in turn owes its existence (1) to the English Parliament, (2) the English Government, and (3) to the English capitalist class which fostered the rise of Belfast (with capital largely drained from the rest of Ireland) because it suited their economic and their class interests —as it had suited their interest in the 17th and 18th centuries to protect and foster Belfast's second stand-by, the Linen industry.

In rural Ulster generally, the establishment of the Ulster custom (explained earlier) was another negation of the principle of *laissez faire*.

In short, Belfast and Ulster supply a crushing condemnation of the English economic policy enforced in the rest of Ireland.

The Struggle for the Land, 1870-1909

The point just made was exemplified in the condemnation by the Tories of Gladstone's *Land Act of 1870*— the first of a long series of such Acts—as a " gross interference with the rights of property "—with the right of the landlord to " do what he likes with his own ".

Gladstone's Act was, in fact, an attempt to extend the Ulster custom to the rest of Ireland. It failed; partly because it contained restrictions which prevented tenants taking advantage of it ; but chiefly because its operation was sabotaged by the landlords.

The growth of a world market for agricultural products, and the progressive fall of prices in that market, made the tenants increasingly unable to pay their rents. The landlords sought a remedy by " consolidating " their estates—clearing them of the holders of small-scale farms, to make room for farming on a large scale. Concurrently, the landlords increased their rents ; partly to facilitate clearance, partly as its consequence. When the land-hungry, driven from one place, competed all the more intensely for those small plots which were

T

still available elsewhere, rents, in general, rose. Simultaneously, prices for agricultural products fell—one consequence of this policy of freezing out the " little man ".

This policy produced its results ; first the *Land League* organised by MICHAEL DAVITT, and supported by PARNELL and the PARLIAMENTARY PARTY ; then the *Land Act of* 1881, which introduced the principle of "dual ownership". This proved satisfactory only in so far as it facilitated, though not greatly, the purchase of their holdings by the tenants.

Unrest and agitation, continuing, led to (*a*) Gladstone's first *Home Rule Bill* (1885) which was defeated, and (*b*) to the *Land Act of* 1885 which increased the facilities for tenant-purchase. This Act was amended in 1887, 1888 (twice), 1889, and 1891 without giving satisfaction either to tenant or to landlord.

Gladstone's Second *Home Rule Bill* (1893) was designed, primarily, to shift the responsibility for settling the Land Question on to the shoulders of an Irish local " parliament ". Passed by the Commons, it was thrown out by the Lords.

The Land Acts were further amended in 1894, 1896, and 1901. Then in 1903, the Tory Chief Secretary, GEORGE WYNDHAM, introduced a measure providing a Government subsidy to induce the landlords to sell holdings to their occupiers on hire-purchase terms. The Act was modified by the Liberals in 1909, and so, in its turn, was a prelude to the *Third Home Rule Bill* (1910). After a protracted and embittered Parliamentary struggle, this became law in 1914. Its operation was held up by the Carsonite " revolt ", and by the outbreak of European War.

The *Rising of Easter Week* transformed the situation completely.

It will be seen from this summary that the period from 1870 to 1916 was one in which an agrarian struggle gave impetus to a parliamentary struggle, which after reinforcing the agrarian struggle was itself in turn superseded by an armed uprising.   That the national struggle as a whole arose from the economic consequences of the English conquest is self-evident.

Ireland was, in practice, forced to restrict itself in the main to agriculture, for whose products no market but that of England was available.   In the English market Irish producers had to sell at prices fixed by *world competition*, while Irish agriculture, in general, could not advance because it was crippled by the burden of a *parasitic landlordism*.

Lalor : and the Theory of Agrarian Struggle

The theory of agrarian struggle as leading up to a political policy was first formulated by JAMES FINTAN LALOR in the Young Ireland period.   At that time, however, his work was noted only for its immediate significance, as one among many modes of effecting an insurrection.   He acted as a stimulant to the Young Ireland movement generally, and he exercised a personal influence upon Luby and O'Leary, the Fenian leaders. But it was through the influence of MICHAEL DAVITT, the leader of the Land League, that LALOR first became recognised in Ireland as the propounder of a distinct political philosophy.

Lalor wrote little, and only for a short time ; but his importance warrants a few quotations from his writings :

" To any plain understanding the right of private property is very simple.   It is the right of man to possess, enjoy, and transfer the substance and use of whatever *he has himself created*.   This title is good against the world ; and it is the sole and only title by which a valid right of absolute private property can possibly rest.   But no man can plead any such title to a right of property in the substance of the soil."

" I hold and maintain that the entire soil of a country belongs of right to the entire people of that country and is the rightful property, not of any one class, but of the nation at large, in full effective possession, to let to whom they will on whatever tenures, etc. they will ; one condition, however, being unavoidable and essential . . . full, true, and undivided allegiance to the nation, and the laws of the nation whose land he holds."

" I hold further that the enjoyment by the people of this right of first ownership is essential to the vigour and vitality of all other rights ; to their validity, efficacy and value ; to their secure possession and safe exercise."

" I trouble myself as little as anyone does about the ' conquest,' taken abstractly—as an affair that took place ages ago. But that ' conquest ' is still in existence, with all its rights, claims, laws, relations and results. The landlord holds his lands by right and title of conquest, and uses his powers as only a conqueror may."

" Mark the words of this prophecy—the principle I propose goes to the foundations of Europe, and sooner or later will cause Europe to uprise. Mankind will yet be masters of the earth. The right of the people to make the laws—this produced the first great modern earthquake whose latest shocks even now are heaving in the heart of the world. The right of the people to own the land— this will produce the next. Train your hands, and your sons' hands, gentlemen of the earth, for you and they will yet have to use them."

These are sufficient to show the essence of Lalor's doctrine. That it should have fermented in the mind of Michael Davitt, brooding in his cell in Portland Gaol, until after his release it bore fruit in the LAND LEAGUE, is not surprising. Nor is it surprising that one of the first pamphlets produced by *James Connolly* was a reprint of Lalor's *Faith of a Felon* ; or that in the proclamation of the Republic in Easter Week, 1916, we should find these words :

> " We declare the right of the people of Ireland to the ownership of Ireland, and to the unfettered control of Irish destinies to be sovereign and indefeasible."

Whether drawn directly or indirectly from Lalor, or discovered afresh by each successive leader for himself, this principle finds perennial expression in the Irish National struggle ; and that the more clearly the further we proceed.

CHAPTER TWENTY-FOUR

HOME RULE : THE RISE OF PARNELL

THE agitation for HOME RULE FOR IRELAND, and the Parliamentary nationalist Party it threw up—which Party came to dominate English politics to the exclusion of everything else—was founded in 1870; largely as a result of the agitation for an AMNESTY FOR THE FENIAN PRISONERS of '65 and '67.

In this chapter we trace the movement from its start until the rise of CHARLES STEWART PARNELL in 1877.

The Home Rule Movement Begins

The Home Rule Party differed from its predecessors in so far as it was thrown up by a popular movement whose inspiration was very largely Fenian. Any renewal of armed struggle between 1870 and 1877 was impossible to think of. But to secure any following in Ireland at all the Home Rule Party, which arose in those years, had to be, or seem to be, an attempt to reach the Fenian end by other means.

The passionate sympathy the Fenian struggle had engendered found expression, first of all, in the demand for AMNESTY. Gladstone had admitted that the grievances of Ireland were real. It was obviously barbarous to submit men who, however unwisely, had sought to remedy those grievances to treatment worse than that inflicted on the most sub-human of malefactors.

That the Dublin-Castle-inspired police attacked the first Amnesty meetings savagely only multiplied the passion of indignation.

Led by KARL MARX and the *International Working Men's Association*, the English workers were roused in support of the Amnesty demand ; and a union in struggle

of the English workers and the Irish National movement
was what every English statesman, from William Pitt
onwards, had feared as the final calamity. Timing his
" duck-and-get-away " perfectly, Gladstone averted this,
in 1870, by concessions to Ireland which included
amnesty for a hundred or thereabouts of the Fenians
first convicted. The release of the rest followed at
intervals.

Gladstone's decision was prompted by the election
of O'DONOVAN ROSSA for Tipperary in 1869. Rossa was
declared ineligible as a " convicted felon " still in
gaol; and this checked a move to nominate LUBY for
Co. Longford. The " advanced " men accepted JOHN
MARTIN (of the *Irish Felon* of '48) as a compromise;
but the local clergy were committed to support the son
of the local landlord (Greville-Nugent)—whose eleva-
tion to the peerage had caused the vacancy.

The election battle was fought with extreme bitterness—the pious, papalist, anti-Fenian A. M. SULLIVAN,
for example, found himself assailed, much to his surprise,
as a " Garibaldian", a " priest-killer " and a " Fenian "
for supporting Martin. The priests won, but at the
cost of rousing a demand for a mass political movement
which would break the power of the landlord-clerical
alliance. Only a national movement could do this—
one infused with a strong measure of the Fenian spirit
tempered with Fenian discipline.

Some brutal " clearances " underlined the need. In
Tipperary, a landlord who attempted to serve notices to
quit was three times beaten off—with his police escort—
by a rally of neighbours led by a Fenian. An attempt
to take another tenant by surprise was defeated by
" Fenians " with revolvers and shot-guns. A bailiff
and one constable were killed on the spot. The landlord and several of his party were severely wounded;
two died of their wounds.

This incident is credited with having " passed the

Land Act of 1870". It did more than that. It induced a party of notables of all shades of Nationalism to meet in Dublin in May, 1870, and constitute the "*Home Government Association for Ireland*". The leader of the movement was ISAAC BUTT, Q.C., once the leader of Dublin Conservatives, later counsel for the Fenian chiefs ; and his lieutenant was *A. M. Sullivan*.

The new movement scored an immediate success when JOHN MARTIN won Co. Meath against strong clericalist opposition. But its great test came in the Kerry election of 1872.

Kerry was regarded as the property of the local landlord, Lord Kenmare ; and a vacancy being created by the succession of the sitting-member (Viscount Castlerosse) to the peerage, on the death of his father, the new Lord Kenmare thought he could nominate his successor as a matter of course. To his dismay his nominee was opposed by a Home Rule candidate, who was elected with a comfortable majority. It was the " Clare election " of Home Rule. It was also the last open-voting election in Ireland. Believing the result had been secured by " intimidation", Parliament at once passed the BALLOT ACT of 1872.

A few weeks later a conference formally established the IRISH HOME RULE LEAGUE and pledged its members, if elected, *to act and vote together as an independent party*.

In the surprise General Election of 1874, the League met with success far beyond its hopes. Only two of its candidates were defeated ; one by only *three* votes. Sixty Home Rulers were elected, a gain of fifty seats. All but seven were won from the Liberals. Gladstone's education on the Irish question was advanced by a long stride.

The Home Rule Party in Parliament

By founding a Party pledged to permanent opposition to *every* Government which would not make Home

Rule a Cabinet issue, and to disciplined independence even of a Government that would, the Home Rule League opened a new page in Parliamentary History. To have realised the concept of a *Third* Party; and to have built it out of Catholics and Protestants, Liberals, Conservatives, '48 men, and Fenians, was in itself a notable feat. The English parties, Liberals and Tories, showed its worth by uniting to vote down every *Irish* proposal made by the new party. This in itself was a gain. It helped materially to enhance the solidarity, and the National consciousness, of the Party; and it had a still more profound effect upon the mass of the electors in Ireland. Before 1874 they had either been indifferent to Parliament and its concerns, or actively hostile to it—as diverting men's minds from " direct action " and insurrection. Now they began to see that there were possibilities in Parliamentary action after all.

As an instrument for achieving concrete results directly, the Parliamentary Party was a poor enough tool, then as later. But as a means of rousing, mobilising, educating and intensifying the *mass-consciousness of Nationality* in Ireland, the Party was—or at any rate could become—of a very high value indeed; of much higher value, in fact, than any but a few of its members realised.

One of the few, and the one to realise it most fully, was a young Wicklow man, a Protestant and a landlord—who came from a family which had earned distinction in Grattan's Parliament. This was CHARLES STEWART PARNELL (1846-1891) who was elected, for Co. Meath, in the spring of 1875, to fill a vacancy caused by the death of John Martin.

Scientific Obstruction : Biggar and Parnell

Obstruction—" the art of parliamentary procrastination "—had always been recognised as a legitimate weapon for the opposition to use in emergencies. Parnell arrived in the House in time to witness some of the earlier efforts of a group of Home Rule members who had come to adopt the practice, not consistently, but as an occasional irritation tactic.

Its real initiator was a Belfast man, JOSEPH GILLIS BIGGAR, a wholesale pork merchant, Member for Cavan. Unknown to most of his colleagues, Biggar was a member of the Supreme Council of the I.R.B. when he first scandalised the House by "espying strangers" just as the Prince of Wales had taken his seat in the gallery to listen to a debate on improving the breed of horses. "Espying strangers" involved clearing everybody—the Prince of Wales along with the reporters—out of the galleries. As the rules of the House then stood, Mr. Speaker had no option but to order "strangers" to withdraw.

Members of all parties, including his own, joined in denouncing the Member for Cavan for his "ungentle-manly" conduct. As "Joe" Biggar never pretended to be a gentleman, these eloquent denunciations were entirely wasted. So were such press comments as this, from the *World* of March 5th, 1875 :

"Mr. Biggar brings the manner of his store into this illustrious assembly, and his manner, even for a Belfast store, is very bad. When he rises to address the House . . . a whiff of salt-pork seems to float upon the gale, and the air is heavy with the odour of the kippered herring. One unacquainted with the condition of affairs might be forgiven if he thought the House of Commons was a meeting of creditors and the right hon. gentlemen sitting on the Treasury Bench were members of the defaulting firm, who having confessed to their inability to pay ninepence in the pound, were suitable and safe subjects for the abuse of an ungenerous creditor."

The gentlemanly correspondent of the gentlemanly *World* was quite oblivious of the fact that it was precisely in the light of fraudulent debtors, who, having showed no mercy themselves, were entitled to expect none, that Joe Biggar—who saw nothing discreditable in salt-pork or kippers—regarded the Treasury Bench.

On the evening upon which Parnell took his seat, Biggar " entertained " the House by speaking for four hours on the subject of swine fever. Butt had asked him to spin out the time, to prevent the next item on the agenda from being reached—a common obstructive device. Biggar came equipped with a pile of blue-books; all of which he insisted upon reading to the House, with a running commentary of assent, dissent, or illustrative anecdote. He gave in at last, because his voice had deserted him. As a parliamentary performance it was so extremely scandalous that it went beyond condemnation to reach the audaciously sublime.

Parnell watched the performance with undisturbed gravity. It had given him an idea, which he and Biggar thereafter worked out between them. It was very simple really. There was nowhere near time enough for the work Parliament had to get through. If every member insisted upon inquiring into and " taking the sense of the House upon " every detail of the routine business the Government had to get through, sessions would have to be four times as long and there would be no time at all for private members—or for measures of reform. Parnell and Biggar, with the followers they gathered round them, began therefore to take their duties conscientiously. They were helped by the archaic and complex procedure the House had evolved through centuries—a procedure which left a wealth of openings to any man who would trouble to master its rules. Certain business could not be taken after a certain hour if it were opposed. Other business could not be taken after a given hour at all. It was a simple matter to say "I object" in the one case, and in the other to develop critical doubts requiring elaborate explanations on the subject preceding it on the order paper.

No contrast could possibly be greater in the externals of speech, physique, and manner than that between Biggar and Parnell. The one squat, deformed, and homely, with a voice and accent as harsh as a corn-crake; the other tall, slender, aristocratic, and speaking with an accent that, except for a slight trace of America, marked him as a Cambridge man.

The House could have forgiven them if they had merely wasted time. What it could not forgive was their unconcealed contempt for the "illustrious assembly"; and the pains they took to prevent, if possible, any business being done at all.

Neither was, at first, a fluent speaker. Each was a master of plain statement. Biggar derived a never-ending joy from addressing Mr. Speaker in the manner and vocabulary of one Belfast crony addressing another. Parnell, one of an extremely rare type, not only meant what he said, but said what he meant to say and not a word more or less.

Parnell's complete freedom from rhetoric caused him to be regarded as "frigid". Men were to learn that his conventional correctness of bearing, and his abhorrence of decorated speech, were expressions of a ruthlessly imposed self-discipline, which masked an intensity of political passion which, when it did show itself, made the stage "thunders" of the professional rhetoricians dwindle into insignificance. Orators like Charles James Fox have scorched the Government benches with the fire of their eloquence. Parnell *froze* them solid with the intensity of his contempt.

It must be recorded to the credit of Parnell and Biggar that, when a chance arose to force a reform upon the Government, they seized it instantly, and made the most of it. In the session of 1877—in which a crisis was precipitated—they worked over in detail two Prison Bills, a Navy and an Army Mutiny Bill, and a South African Government Bill, and even their enemies admitted that they secured valuable amendments— some their own, others those of Radicals—which would never even have been considered but for their efforts. Most notable was the (partial) abolition of flogging in the Army and Navy. Radicals had advocated this for years without forcing a discussion. The tenacity and skill of Parnell and Biggar forced it to the stage of debate for the first time. As soon as the true facts were made public the Government had to give way.

The Crisis in the Home Rule Party

It is surprising, but true, that it took the House quite a time to realise that Parnell and Biggar were something different from the mere cranks and bores which they were at first supposed to be. When it was realised at last that they were trying, deliberately, to make it impossible for the Government of England to be carried on, so long as the House insisted upon legislating for Ireland, Tory fury knew no bounds.

A characteristic episode arose when Parnell, opposing the South Africa Bill, explained that, as an Irishman, who knew at first hand what England's treatment of subject races was like, he would have great satisfaction " in preventing and thwarting the intentions of Government in regard to the Bill ". When the storm had abated sufficiently for Parnell's suspension to be moved, it dawned upon the saner section of the House that " thwarting the intentions of the Government " is the normal function of an opposition. The suspension motion was accordingly withdrawn. The incident is typical as showing the state of hysteria into which Parnell and Biggar contrived to throw the House merely by rising to speak—a condition which Biggar took an unholy delight in exacerbating to the limit.

On the South Africa Bill they proceeded to frank obstruction. They had been accused of it when they moved amendments admittedly " framed with considerable skill ", and which seldom found fewer than fifty English supporters in the division lobby. Now that it was an issue on which the Irish stood alone they obstructed without scruple.

When members tried to drown Parnell's voice by coughing, groaning, whistling and loud conversation, Biggar suggested, in a voice which rasped through the uproar like a rusty saw, that, if the hon. gentlemen were not prepared to listen, the debate had better be adjourned; and he moved accordingly. This reprisal of moving the adjournment whenever the House refused to listen to an Irish speaker grew into a regular game. After the House had been kept sitting until four in the morning for a number of nights in succession, an English member thought of appealing to Isaac Butt the (nominal) leader of the Irish Party.

Before Parnell and Biggar began their campaign it had been deemed improper for Irish members to intervene on English questions. Butt's generation had accepted that view as a matter of course. Couldn't he do something about these fellows who were turning " the best club in the world " into a bear-garden ?

Butt, a kindly soul—as well as, in his prime, a man of great courage and capacity—was always susceptible on this side. He was a gentleman—an Irish gentleman of the old school—one who would either pay his cabman a sovereign for a shilling ride or borrow half-a-crown from him !—Yes ! Butt could do something, and would. He went into the House and treated Parnell and Biggar to a lecture on " How to Behave in an August Assembly".

He delighted the Liberals and Tories immensely, and

the old man retired hugely satisfied.   But the only difference he made was that from that night he ceased in fact to be leader of the Irish Party.   He retained the position nominally until his death in 1879, but from that night the real leader of the Party was Parnell.

The Parting of the Ways

The issue at stake lay far deeper than Butt or any of his school could perceive.   It was a fight between Parliamentarians who merely happened to be Irish, and Irish revolutionaries who merely happened to be in Parliament—who were in Parliament only because there the revolutionary work of the moment was to be done.

From Butt's point of view, obtaining the good opinion of the House was essential.   From Parnell's, it was a matter of indifference—except in so far as it was a positive disadvantage.   Butt was genuinely eager for Home Rule, but only as a reform in the controlling machinery of the *British Empire*.

For Parnell the British Empire was something his ancestors had fought with all their strength.   On his mother's side he was descended from men who had broken off the major part of the British Empire to found the U.S.A.   His mother's father had been the " Nelson " of the American Navy in the War of 1812.   His paternal great-grandfather had been the colonel of a regiment of Volunteers in '82—the " colours " of the regiment hung over the great mantel-piece in the hall of the Parnell family mansion.   That great-grandfather, with his son, had been among the incorruptibles who stood by Grattan in his last struggle to stave off the Union. Parnell was not—as his detractors took care to let the world know—deeply read in Irish history.   But from his earliest years he had seen those flags and been familiar with their story.   And familiar, too, with the tale of Grattan's dramatic reappearance in the House—like a

corpse rearisen from the grave—to pour scorn and denunciation upon Castlereagh and the rest of those—
> " Slaves who sold their land for gold
> As Judas sold his God."

He had heard, too, from the lips of the peasant-greybeards on his father's estate first-hand tales of '98—of Michael Dwyer and his men, of the yeomanry and their deeds. He could, when he pleased, repeat stories of the barbarous floggings inflicted by the yeomanry, word for word as he had heard them from the lips of the sons of victims and survivors.

Parnell, in short, had no need to ransack libraries to discover reasons for " thwarting the intentions of the Government ". They were born in him as an ancestral heritage.

There was another consideration to which Butt was oblivious, but which was self-evident to Parnell. The consideration given to an Irish member by the House did not depend upon his eloquence, or upon his social or personal qualities, at all. It depended bluntly upon the amount of trouble he could cause if he really put himself to it. Parnell was concerned to rouse the Irish people. For that end the hatred and reviling of the House was a hundred times more to be desired than its affection and its flattery. He knew that the more the *English* members united against him the more the *Irish People* would unite on his side. He soon had proof. In August, 1877, a crowded assembly in the Rotunda, Dublin, gave him and Biggar an ovation. In November, 1877, the *Home Rule Confederation* in England—an exiles' organisation—elected him President in place of Butt.

When old-man Isaac Butt died quietly of heart disease in May, 1879, he cleared the last barrier from the road ahead for Parnell. Otherwise the event was—sad to say—of negligible significance.

CHAPTER TWENTY-FIVE

DAVITT ; THE LAND LEAGUE ; AND PARNELL

THE Irish situation was altered beyond recognition between 1879 and 1882 by the *Land war*, waged by MICHAEL DAVITT and the LAND LEAGUE (with Parnell's powerful co-operation) and by the concurrent rise of Parnell to the leadership of the Parliamentary Party.

In this chapter the development is traced from the founding of the Land League (1879) to the KILMAINHAM COMPACT (1882).

The Famine of 1879

Between the end of 1877 and the General Election in 1880, Parnell's position was anomalous. In the Parliamentary Party itself he ranked as an ordinary member only—but one whose line the majority did not like but dared not reprove too openly because of its immense popularity with the mass of Irishmen, in Ireland as well as in England. Parnell added greatly to his personal popularity by taking his stand, at Davitt's invitation, at the head of the newly-formed LAND LEAGUE.

The rising tide of militancy the Land League expressed can be traced to the rapid general deterioration of the economic position of rural Ireland ; a deterioration intensified into a positive famine in the West of Ireland by a combination of causes, chief among which was the failure of the potato crop. This deterioration threw light on the working of the Land Act of 1870 ; and led in turn to the *Land Act of* 1881.

Basically the deterioration was due to a fall in world prices for agricultural produce ; and this again was due to large-scale agricultural developments, especially in

305

U

the U.S.A. It was aided also by the great expansion and speeding-up of Marine transport. Between 1870 and 1875 harvests and prices had both been good in Ireland. From 1875 to 1879 prices fell rapidly and harvests were bad.

This revealed the fatal weakness in the Land Act of 1870 which was designed to give the tenant a qualified property-right in his improvements. While prices remained high, the tenant could borrow on the security of these improvements ; when prices fell he was caught in a " squeeze " between the landlord and the usurer.

While prospects had been bright, and borrowing brisk, the banks had done good business. Favourable rates had induced such farmers as had no need to borrow to invest their savings in these local loan-banks. Banks and depositors alike were caught in the *squeeze* ; and along with them were caught the tradespeople who, being allowed long-term credits by the banks, had thought it safe to allow their customers credit likewise.

Under the Act of 1870, security of tenure was wholly dependent upon the punctual payment of rent. " Any arrears ; no security " was the rule. In addition, the tenant could sell his improvements for cash only *after* he had given notice to quit ; and had applied to a land-court for a valuation. This valuation, when made, the landlord could appeal against. Thus, in practice, the tenant could only realise his improvements in cash *after* he had been ejected, and *after* a legal procedure which took a wearisome time, and swallowed up most of the value in costs. Thus, in practice, the banks found they had made advances which could not be recovered. They failed, and ruined their depositors ; but not before these had ruined the tradespeople by calling in their credits, and forcing them in turn to ruin their customers or be ruined themselves.

The only ones who escaped were the landlords, and the *gombeen-men*—the small-loan money-lenders whose usual rate was a *shilling per pound per month.*

In the West suffering was intensified by the failure of the potato crop. The all-Ireland value of this crop in 1876 was £12,500,000; in 1877, £5,300,000; in 1878, £3,300,000. Other crops failed too; in the three years after 1878 the value of the total crop of all kinds fell by more than £26,000,000. In addition, in 1879, incessant rains prevented the drying of peat so that in many parts a fuel famine was added to the total of miseries. And, to cap all, a failure of the harvest in England cut off entirely the harvest wages upon which thousands depended for their rent-money.

Ejectment notices began to fall " like snow-flakes ". In 1877, 980 families were evicted (a total well above the average). In 1880, there were 2,110.

This was the soil from which sprang the *Land League* led by Davitt and Parnell.

Davitt, Devoy and the New Departure

Before launching the Land League, MICHAEL DAVITT was from 1870 to 1877 imprisoned as a Fenian convict in Portland Gaol. Released in the latter year—in response to an Amnesty Agitation which Parnell and his Party in Parliament supported vigorously—Davitt had paid a visit to America to test the feeling of the Fenian leaders.

Born (in 1846) in Mayo—from which his parents were driven by the Famine to seek work in Lancashire—Davitt, while quite a child, working in a cotton-mill, had his right arm caught in the machinery and mangled so badly that it had to be amputated. Despite this, he joined the Fenians in 1865—" if he couldn't shoulder a rifle he could use a revolver, or at least could carry ammunition "—and as the leader of his " circle ", took part in the " raid " on Chester Castle. He became the chief " Arms Organiser " for the Fenians in England, and held that post when he was captured and imprisoned in 1870. His standing in the movement was exceptionally high; and his first act on being released on ticket-of-leave was to make contact with the Fenian organisation. He was at once included in the Supreme Council.

While in prison he had occupied himself with reflections on the writings of Fintan Lalor and had come to definite conclusions as to the feasibility, as well as the desirability, of trying Lalor's methods in a modified form. Davitt's theory was, in general, that an organised resistance to eviction, and an organised demand for a reduction of rents, might lead, in time, to a situation from which a transition to armed struggle could be made with a maximum chance of success.

In America, Davitt found that the most reliable and respected of the Fenian leaders, JOHN DEVOY and JAMES BOYLE O'REILLY, were more than ready to agree with him; but on condition that the land-agitation was linked with, and operated through the machinery of, the Nationalist political agitation which had arisen in support of Parnell and Biggar. It was a ticklish business broaching to the Fenian Old Guard a policy which involved not only "peddling with reforms" but "compromise" with the hated parliamentarianism which it had been a cardinal Fenian principle to repudiate. John Devoy, however, was not easily frightened; and to his great satisfaction, and Davitt's, the "New Departure" of working through an open agitation (while keeping the "underground" organisation in being, ready for eventualities) met with a wide measure of acceptance. The non-Fenian Irish-Americans also rose readily to the slogan "Irish land for the Irish people".

Some of the Old Guard were more than dubious. JOHN O'LEARY, and CHARLES J. KICKHAM in Ireland would have nothing to do with this "New Departure"; but they agreed not to do anything that would prejudice its chance of a fair try-out in practice. O'DONOVAN ROSSA, the implacable, in America, would not only have nothing to do with it; he denounced it in fury, and quarrelled so fiercely with Devoy that they remained enemies till Rossa lay on his death-bed in 1915.

In the overwhelming majority of cases the Fenian rank and file welcomed the New Departure cordially; and an obstacle which might have proved fatal to Davitt's plan was thus surmounted.

Parnell, for his part, also welcomed the land agitation. There is no reason to doubt his knowledge of what the Fenians hoped would come from this policy, and, from his point of view, that was all to the good. He could not rouse all Ireland in support of his political policy if the Fenians remained hostile; and their active help was far better than a frigid-neutrality.

When therefore he was asked by Davitt to speak at a meeting at Westport, Co. Mayo, on June 7th, 1879, Parnell assented cordially.

The Westport meeting followed a successful meeting at Irishtown, Mayo, and it was intended to inaugurate a Land League for Mayo. It was successful beyond Davitt's highest expectation. On the eve of the meeting, it and its objects were denounced fiercely by the Catholic Archbishop of Tuam. Parnell refused to be intimidated; and, in his speech to a gathering of over 10,000, gave the movement a slogan :

"A fair rent is a rent the tenant can reasonably pay according to the times; but in bad times a tenant cannot be expected to pay as much as he did in good times three or four years ago. If such rents are insisted upon a repetition of the scenes of 1847 and 1848 will be witnessed. Now what must we do in order to induce the landlords to see the position? *You must show them that you intend to hold a firm grip of your homesteads and lands.* You must not allow yourselves to be dispossessed as your fathers were dispossessed in 1847. You must not allow your small-holdings to be consolidated. . . . . You must help yourselves, and the public opinion

of the world will stand by you and support you in
your struggle to defend your homesteads."

Parnell's presence at the meeting had ensured the
presence of press-reporters ; hence his slogan was carried
into every home in Ireland.   From that moment the
movement spread rapidly.

In September an *Irish National Land League* was
founded—with Parnell for President. He was requested
by the inaugural conference to proceed to America to
" obtain assistance ", but his journey was delayed by
an act of reprisal by the Government. Egged on by the
infuriated landlords the Government *cancelled Davitt's
ticket-of-leave*.

Parnell replied with a huge protest meeting in the
Rotunda, Dublin, at which he announced that a meeting
Davitt had arranged in Balla, Co. Mayo—to stop a
threatened eviction—would be held as arranged ; and
that he, with other leaders, would take Davitt's place.

The meeting was held. It was attended by 10,000 men
who, as instructed, came " provided with means of
self-defence against police attack".   Faced with this
assembly, the police abandoned the eviction.   The
Government changed front ; it restored Davitt's ticket-
of-leave, but included him in the list of those to be
prosecuted for their speeches at a meeting in Sligo.
When this case came up for its preliminary hearing, the
League contrived to turn the occasion into a week of
nightly demonstrations, all addressed by Parnell and
other leading speakers. The Press rounded upon the
Government, and denounced it for " advertising " the
League. In the end the trial was abandoned.

Parliament and the Land War

The famine of 1879 did not reproduce all the horrors
of '47. It was not so universal ; but the resident-landlords
as a class were much less sympathetic than in '47, when
scores of them had ruined themselves in their efforts to

alleviate distress. That the Land League averted the worst horrors by preventing, at source, the *creation of distress*, cannot be doubted. It raised a large relief fund, too, in America, at meetings addressed by Parnell in the early months of 1880.

Davitt finds no praise too high for Parnell's work at this period :

> "It was essential to encourage the country in the policy laid down at the Western meetings—no rent without abatements, no tame submission to evictions, and no land-grabbing to be permitted. . . . No revolutionist in the movement surpassed Parnell in the fearless assertion of this policy . . . [He] openly challenged the law to proceed against him."
> —DAVITT : *Fall of Feudalism*, p. 188.

Recalled from America by a surprise dissolution of Parliament, Parnell had to face the forlorn hope of conducting an election campaign, without a Party machine, with hardly any available candidates, and with no funds. If Davitt had not been willing (against the rules of the League, and at the risk of trouble with the American *ultras*) to lend a considerable sum from the League funds, Parnell's efforts would have been crippled. As it turned out the Irish vote, in England and Scotland, was cast solidly against Disraeli and the Tory ("landlords") Party. In Ireland, Parnell fought the "moderate" Home Rulers, as well as *both* Liberals and Tories.

He was helped by the anxiety of his enemies to defeat him. The landlords denounced him as a "communist" and a renegade from their ranks. The Catholic Archbishop of Dublin added his voice to the clamour of the landlords. The "moderate" Home Rulers echoed "Archbishop MacCabe's anxious concern for Faith and Morals based on rack-rents and evictions" (Davitt) and thereby promoted notably the process of their own elimination. On the other side, several bishops, and nearly all the priests in the disturbed areas, supported the League, and, so far, Parnell.

Parnell was so short of the candidates he wanted that he had to accept what support he could get. He himself stood for three places—Cork City, Co. Meath and Co. Mayo—in each of which he was elected. In the upshot sixty-eight Home Rule candidates were returned; but of these less than forty could be relied upon by Parnell for disciplined support, and of those again a number were hostile to the Land League. The set of the tide was shown, however, by the election of Parnell as " sessional Chairman " of the Party.

When the House assembled, with Gladstone commanding an absolute majority, Parnell introduced a Bill to give compensation to all tenants disturbed by eviction. Gladstone countered with a Bill of his own. In a fierce struggle the Parnellites forced a number of amendments. Sent to the House of Lords on July 26th, 1880, the Bill was ignominiously thrown out.

The news was received in Ireland with anger. There were riots at evictions, assaults upon land-grabbers, rick-burnings, and cattle-maiming. The Fenians captured a gun-boat in Cork Harbour and abstracted thence 40 cases of rifles. These things were all shocking enough in the eyes of the Authorities; but Parnell " outraged " the feelings of the ruling-class worse still by his speech at Ennis, on September 19th, 1880.

He had reached in his speech the point of what to do with a man who bids for a farm from which another had been evicted. There were loud cries of " Shoot him ! " which in turn were loudly applauded. Parnell, in his usual quiet manner, proceeded with his argument :

" I think I heard somebody say ' shoot him ' "— (loud cries of ' quite right too ' with renewed applause)— but I wish to point out to you a very much better way—a more Christian, and a more charitable, way—which will give the lost sinner an opportunity of repenting."

After a pause which secured a rapt silence, Parnell continued quietly and distinctly :

"When a man takes a farm from which another has been evicted, you must show him on the road-side when you meet him, you must show him in the streets of the town, you must show him at the shop-counter, you must show him in the fair and the market place, and even in the place of worship, *by leaving him severely alone*—putting him into a kind of moral coventry—isolating him from his kind like the leper of old—you must show him your detestation of the crime he has committed. And, you may depend upon it, that there is no man so full of avarice, so lost to shame, as to dare the public opinion of all right-thinking men, and to transgress your unwritten code of laws."

It was characteristic of Parnell's precise care in the choice of his words that when an excited auditor trans-lated his " you must *show* him " into an interjected " *shun him !* ", Parnell quietly but emphatically repeated " you must *show* him ". On reflection it will be perceived that " shun " was *not* (while " show " *was*) precisely the word Parnell needed.

The words did more than electrify the audience at Ennis. They fired all the land-tillers in Ireland ; and they roused, too, all the trade-unionists in England, who knew what it was to have to deal with blacklegs. Corres-pondingly they were received with screams of rage from the whole landlord class, who realised, as Parnell did, that this policy, if persisted in, would destroy entirely the effectiveness of their chief weapon—*eviction*.

Three days later their worst fears were realised in an event which gave this modern application of the old Greek *ostracism* a " local habitation and a name ".

The Case of Captain Boycott

CAPTAIN BOYCOTT, an estate-agent for Lord Erne, refused the " fair " rent offered by his tenants ; and issued ejectment notices. Mass-resistance prevented the service of the notices. The local branch of the League, with the parish priest at its head, proclaimed him under ban. All his domestics and farm-hands left him. Shop-keepers refused to serve him ; the laundress and the blacksmith would not accept his orders ; his letters and telegrams had to be delivered by the police.

He set out his woes in a letter to *The Times* ; and every drawing-room in England was shaken (while every proletarian was tickled) at the thought of Captain Boycott's ladies washing their own linen, cooking their own meals, and carrying their own coals.

To save his crop, the Captain asked for volunteers. Hundreds in Ulster volunteered. Still retaining some of his wits, the Captain said *fifty* Orangemen would suffice. They arrived after a ten-mile tramp from the nearest railway station—neither love nor money would procure vehicles—amid a terrific downpour, escorted by a large contingent of police and soldiers (with two field guns). His crops were " saved ". But what his saviours, and their escort, left of his shrubs, his kitchen garden, his poultry, and his pigs, wasn't worth " saving " further.

When the volunteers and their escort made their return journey, they marched through the village, in which every blind was drawn, and every shop closed and shuttered. Not a soul was in sight, save the parish priest—who marched at their head to " protect " them from affront.

In a few days Captain Boycott resigned his agency and retired with his ladies along the track of his saviours.

Gladstone tries Coercion

Seriously alarmed, the Government indicted Parnell and the leaders of the league for " *seditious conspiracy* ".

The trial opened in Dublin on January 5th, 1881, and lasted for twenty days. Such chance as there was of a conviction was reduced to a minimum by the device of citing as witnesses for the defence all the inmates of the workhouse at Castlebar, Mayo, who had suffered eviction. Paraded in the court-house yard, they made such an impression that the counts upon which their evidence would have been relevant were abandoned.

As it became clear that a conviction could not be obtained, the Government, though reluctantly, introduced a Coercion Bill. Next day the State Trial ended in a disagreement of the jury.

In opposition to the Coercion Bill, the Parnellite Party put out its full strength. The debate on the Address announcing the Bill lasted eleven sittings. The Bill's first reading was carried only by a *coup de main* after five more sittings.

On Monday, January 31st, the Government announced its intention to secure the first reading during that sitting. Parnell and his men settled down to work. Monday night passed into Tuesday, Tuesday night into Wednesday morning, and still the Irish Brigade fought on. Both sides adopted the relay system— some held the front while others slipped away for a wash, a meal, and a couple of hours in bed. Members " on duty " tried to snatch a few hours (or minutes) of sleep sitting in chairs in the library. Chairs were at a premium when the frugal Biggar grasped an opportunity to put four chairs together to make a bed on which he would have slept peacefully if the infuriated Liberals and Tories had not walloped the heaviest volumes within reach on the floor with a crash as often as he dozed off. Even so it was Biggar who was addressing the House at 9 a.m., on Wednesday when the Speaker entered, relieved the Chairman, and waved Biggar back to his seat.

The Speaker announced his decision (in which the

Liberal and Tory leaders concurred) to stop the debate; and put the question of the first reading. This being done, the House adjourned until twelve noon the same day. The Parnellites contrived to waste the rest of Wednesday; but meanwhile the Government had drafted new rules of procedure, which it put down for discussion on Thursday.

Overnight the Parnellites learned to their disgust that Michael Davitt, his ticket-of-leave cancelled, had been arrested and restored to Portland Gaol. Questioned at the opening of the sitting on Thursday (February 3rd) the Home Secretary baldly announced the fact. JOHN DILLON rose to extort further information, just as the Speaker called upon Gladstone to introduce his procedure resolution. Dillon tried to explain; the Speaker ordered him to sit down. Dillon persisted; was howled at; grew furious; refused to give way; was " named ", and duly suspended.

The House settled to listen to Gladstone, who had hardly uttered three words before Parnell rose and moved, coolly, " *that the right hon. gentleman be no longer heard*". Amid howls of rage, the Speaker declined to hear Parnell. He, too, persisted; was named, and suspended. During the division on Parnell's suspension the thirty-two Parnellites then present refused to take part in the division. They were named and suspended in a body. The few Parnellites who had missed the fun hurried into the House, moved that Gladstone " be no longer heard " and were suspended, each in his turn. The suspension only lasted for the sitting; so the Party was in action again next day ready to fight the Coercion Bill to the last.

The Coercion Act empowered the Authorities to arrest any person " reasonably suspected," and detain him for any period, up to September 30th, 1881. Hundreds of League officials were arrested; but each place was filled as soon as it was emptied.

The agitation, instead of abating, grew more intense than ever. In the background the Ribbon Lodges—which the League had superseded—took up their old work, and terrorism kept in step with arrests and evictions. The Government, to sweeten the pill of Coercion, introduced meanwhile the *Land Act of* 1881.

The Land Act of 1881

This Act was designed to concede, with reservations, the " Three F's " for which agrarian reformers had fought for years. It succeeded only in part; its most successful provision being one enabling tenants-at-will to obtain leases at " fair " rents fixed by a Government valuer. The value of the tenant's improvements was excluded when determining the " fair " rent.

The Parnellites did what they could to amend the Act; the landlords in the House of Lords did what they could to wreck it. A conflict between the Houses was averted by a compromise, and the Act became law in August, 1881.

The tenants viewed the fixing of " judicial " rents by a Government valuer with the deepest suspicion. There was an obvious danger at this point, and the League decided to put the matter to a test before passing a final judgment. A number of cases were selected for this test; meanwhile the tenants were recommended to abstain from applying for valuations.

This, however, the Government interpreted as a flagrant sabotage of their Act. League meetings were " proclaimed ". League speakers began to crowd Kilmainham Gaol, where Parnell was sent to join them on October 12th. The news of his arrest, divulged to the magnates of the City of London at a Guildhall banquet, roused them to frenzied demonstrations of joy.

The League responded with a Manifesto calling for a general withholding of rent. The Chief Secretary, FORSTER, retorted with more coercion, and armed

support for the eviction squads.   Relief for the victims
was organised by the *Ladies' Land League* which Davitt
had prepared for such an emergency.   Its American
branch was especially helpful.   Meanwhile, as Parnell
had predicted, in the rural areas " Captain Moonlight "*
took charge.

The Kilmainham Compact

Realising that things were going from bad to worse,
the Government decided to open " confidential " negotiations with Parnell, for a compromise settlement.
Parnell was approached by one of his nominal followers
—Captain O'Shea—who acted, so he said, on behalf
of the Radical leader, JOSEPH CHAMBERLAIN.   Parnell
was asked, in effect, to state upon what terms he would
agree to an armistice in the Land War, which would
give the Government a chance to try the effect of
legislation.

Parnell, for his part, knew that without a central
organisation to guide it the agrarian struggle would
degenerate rapidly into a multitude of local struggles,
which would culminate in anarchistic-terrorism, surrender, or both.   Most of the tenants who could pay
had already paid their rents and secured judicial abate-
ments.   Those who could not pay were threatened
with inevitable eviction, sooner or later.   It was clear
that a tactical retreat was necessary, to secure a basis
for any new advance.

Parnell therefore accepted the suggestion and (after
consulting Justin MacCarthy and other leading Party
members) offered the following terms : (1) Cessation of
Coercion ; release of all State prisoners, especially Davitt.
(2) State Aid to wipe off arrears which prevented tenants
taking advantage of the Act of 1881.   If these were
granted, then (3) the authority and machinery of the

Captain Moonlight : The Pseudonym customarily appended to the terroristic
notices issued, at this time, by the Ribbon Lodges.

League would be used to repress agrarian crime; and
(4) the Home Rule Party would co-operate in the
promotion of legislation in line with " liberal principles".

These terms were accepted; and, under this KILMAIN-
HAM COMPACT, Parnell, Davitt, and their followers
were released in May, 1882, while the " Coercion "
Viceroy, EARL COWPER, and Chief Secretary FORSTER,
resigned in disgust.

The Phœnix Park Murders

Parnell had clearly won a great victory, and had opened
a road to still further gains. But the whole situation
was transformed, when, on May 6th, 1882, the new
Viceroy (LORD FREDERICK CAVENDISH) and his permanent under-secretary BURKE were set upon and
murdered in the Phœnix Park by assassins armed with
long, amputating knives.

CHAPTER TWENTY-SIX

PARNELL, THE " UNCROWNED KING "

FROM the embitterment resulting from the Phœnix Park murders (May, 1882) and the furious political strife in which it found expression, there emerged the succession of notable events we survey in this chapter : The rise of the HOME RULE PARTY to its maximum (1880-1885); Gladstone's first HOME RULE BILL (1885), with the LIBERAL-UNIONIST SPLIT (1885); the Balfour PERPETUAL COERCION ACT (1887); *The Times'* attack upon Parnell and his Party (1886–9), and the SPECIAL COMMISSION thereupon (1888–90) which completely vindicated Parnell and left him virtually the " Uncrowned King " of Ireland, and, also, immensely popular with the English masses.

Left-Wing Terrorism and the National Struggle

The Phœnix Park assassinations killed the Kilmainham Compact. They made it impossible for GLADSTONE to carry out his share of the bargain and end Coercion ; and this in turn made it impossible for PARNELL to operate the compact from his end. Neither Gladstone nor Parnell was able openly to admit that a compact had been made ; Gladstone from fear of his Right Wing, Parnell from fear of his " Left ". This turned what had been a strategic withdrawal to a new front, into a retreat in disorder to a base from which no advance could be made, until the Party had been rebuilt from the bottom upwards.

Like the DYNAMITE WAR proclaimed from America by ROSSA and his associates, the murders were the work of a "break-away" from the Fenian body—self-styled the " Invincibles ". Each was closely analogous to the terrorist-anarchist manifestations which evidenced the break-up and degeneration of the Bakuninist sections of the First International, after the fall of the Commune in 1871—which manifestations supplied these quasi-"Fenian" degenerations with their initial inspiration.

Terrorist phenomena are liable to occur at two periods in a revolutionary struggle—in its immaturity ; and in its degeneration. They are to be distinguished carefully from the disciplined employment of mass-terror which a revolutionary struggle may use as legitimately as does the Government which it seeks to overthrow. The point of distinction is that in the one case (as in an insurrection) the resort to violence *does*, while in the other (as e.g. Clerkenwell Prison) it does *not* promote the integration and growth of the revolutionary mass-struggle. Rossa's attempt to "beat England to her knees" by dynamiting public buildings, railway stations etc., was folly, and worse, from the start. The men who carried out the operations did, it is true, take great care to avoid the sacrifice of human life. But more than one of them lost his own life and nearly all the rest suffered the indignity and torture of long periods of penal servitude, resulting in more than one case in the loss of reason. The dynamite "war" did not terrify the Government ; it did anger and alienate the common people. And it created exceptional difficulties for the better-disciplined regular movement, whose efforts at recruiting and organising were, more than once, brought to a nullity by such senseless displays of brutality as the murders in Phœnix Park*—displays which manifest not the strength, but the weakness of the revolutionary movement ; and which accelerate the disintegration and demoralisation from which they arise.

* *Phœnix Park murders :* Few people have done so much disservice to the Irish National struggle as the egregious exhibitionist P. J. Tynan, who tried to palm himself off upon the world as the " Number One " of the Invincibles' conspiracy (which he most certainly was not) and who in a huge volume sought to glorify the deed as a masterly and heroic feat of war.

V

" Left "-ism was very prevalent among Irish-Americans at this period. The bitterness left over from the Famine, from the Fenian defeat, and from the repression which followed combined with isolation from the practical realities of struggle in Ireland to make temperamental patriots ready to applaud everything which manifested hostility to England sharply and without reserve. This temper laid Irish-Americans open to the wiles of political bosses (of real or assumed Irish descent) who found that Irish antipathy to English rule could be manipulated to the profit of " spread-eagle " American Jingoism. And some of these dupes succumbed in consequence all the more readily to the propaganda of sincere fanatics who preached " dynamite war " upon England.

The organised hard-core of American Fenianism was saved from the political racketeers to the Right, and the dynamiters to the Left by the personal influence of MICHAEL DAVITT, JOHN DEVOY and BOYLE O'REILLY. All were more *revolutionary* (in the sense of being ready to advocate and take part in armed insurrection) than Parnell was ; but they all saw the paramount need for a realist procedure in Ireland.

Davitt, in particular, deserves special praise for his loyalty to Parnell at this crisis.

Davitt's loyalty was severely tried when Parnell insisted upon dissolving the Ladies' Land League, and damping down agrarian agitation. But it was becoming clear even to Davitt that the possibility which JOHN O'LEARY and other old-timers had feared—that exclusive preoccupation with the struggle, each man for his own separate holding of land, would tend to eclipse the struggle for the *National* objective—was fast becoming an actual danger. Once the landlords' monopoly had been broken, as it had been by the Act of 1881, the attack upon the Irish landlords ceased to be an attack upon the central citadel of English rule. Agrarian struggle tended to degenerate into *Reformism*.

Now that the State had intervened to create—and in a measure, to regularise—dual ownership in the land, the direct political struggle against the central government took on a new significance. Therefore a new mass organisation was required, one oriented upon the *political* struggle ; and this was achieved in 1882, in the IRISH NATIONAL LEAGUE, which was both the Land League *revived* and the Land League *transformed* into a mass political party.

Gladstone's Conversion to Home Rule

To the surprise of its promoters and opponents alike the effect of the Land Act of 1881 was to *lower* the gross revenue of the Irish landlords by a full twenty per cent. In part this was due to an error in drafting the Act ; but in the main it was due to the continuing fall in agricultural prices. This carried with it a decline in the political importance of Irish landlords for English capitalism as a whole. Dual-ownership gave the tenant the initiative in developing the productive resources of the land ; but only so far as he could borrow the capital with which to operate. This urge towards borrowing helped to shift the political centre of gravity away from the Irish landlords over to the English loan-banks and financiers.

The two amendments to the Land Act passed in 1883 both illustrate this. One made a State grant to assist tenants to pay off their arrears and so qualify for a judicial rent. The other made it compulsory for landlords to provide cottages for agricultural labourers (each with half-an-acre of land) at a nominal rent. The enforcement of the Act was entrusted to elected boards of guardians. Amended and extended in latter years, this Act (which Davitt inspired) proved ultimately a great boon to the labourers ; but it was immediately profitable to the money-lending agencies.

These Acts illustrate the way the political game was played. The Irish Party introduced Bills which Liberals and Tories united to denounce as alike predatory and ruinous. Faced with Irish agitation, Liberals and Tories rivalled each other in the strife for power to coerce the agitation with one hand while conceding some of its demands with the other. The Liberal " Codlin " and the Tory " Short " jostled each other in their eagerness to pose as friends of reform in Ireland—and draw the cash rewards of this " virtue ".

The Land Acts of 1883 were accompanied with a ferocious Crimes Act which the Parnellites fought to the point of getting suspended in a body. This did not prevent the Liberal Gladstone, the Radical Chamberlain, the Tory-Democrat Randolph Churchill, and the Tory Lord Carnarvon each making an independent (but *secret*) approach to Parnell with proposals for political collaboration.

Parnell's response to these approaches was masterly. He would reject no concession, however small, so long as it left him free to fight for the legislative independence of Ireland ; he would accept no concession, however great, which did not leave him that freedom. He supported Gladstone's Franchise Reform since, in widening the electorate in Ireland, it widened the basis for his own party ; and because also (as Davitt urged upon him strongly) it made available for Ireland a valuable ally in the English and Scottish democracy. At the same time he took a much more realistic view of Gladstone than did any of his contemporaries.

Gladstone, he saw, was adjusting his policy to the fact that power was passing from the aristocratic-landlord wing of the landlord-capitalist alliance to rest more securely upon its industrial and finance-capitalist wing. This would, Gladstone saw, unless it was counteracted, make for a re-oriented Tory-imperialist alliance. He therefore sought a counterpoise in the great middle-class which was traditionally Liberal, and hostile to Tory protectionism.

Gladstone saw also another potential danger (which might alternatively provide a new ally) in the growing political consciousness of the wage-worker class. The more capitalism developed the more the working-class became consolidated and conditioned for offering a concerted resistance to capitalist encroachments. To persist in the traditional Whig-Tory attitude towards the working-class was to ensure the formation of an *independent workers' party* which, in alliance with the Irish, could more than nullify any backing he got from the middle-class. Ahead of any of his contemporaries, Gladstone saw that an *independent* working-class party would destroy the Liberal party—by driving its moderate supporters over to the Tories—while, simultaneously, it attracted the genuine Radicals over to the proletarian and socialist standpoint.

To save the situation it was necessary to do two things : (1) to retain the allegiance of the workers to the Great Liberal Party ; and (2) either to get rid of the Irish Party altogether, or to sap its independence, and win it also for a permanent alliance to the Liberal Party. The history of the period is the history of how Gladstone, with masterly adroitness, set about achieving this double objective. Franchise Reform, and Municipal and Local-Government reforms were his first moves. About the Irish he was doubtful ; but long before 1885 he had decided something must be done about Ireland. The need for a pronouncement was delayed by a prolonged struggle with the House of Lords—over the Franchise Act which, at one time, looked like giving him a winning election-slogan in " Down with the House of Lords ". The peers, however, gave way, and for the election of 1885—the first fought under the new franchise—Gladstone had to find a new slogan.

Parnell, weighing up the Party leaders, soon saw that no dependence could be based on JOSEPH CHAMBERLAIN. " He will make the running for Gladstone, " Parnell said, " but he will stop short of Home Rule." RANDOLPH CHURCHILL had possibilities, but Lord CARNARVON offered the best prospects since he stood high in the Tory party, and was himself almost a Home Ruler. It was, Parnell foresaw, merely a question of time before Gladstone came over to Home Rule ; and that meant that there was always a chance that the Tories would jump in first to " dish the Whigs ". A Tory Home Rule Bill would have the advantage that it would not be opposed on Party grounds by the House of Lords.

Parnell was therefore " sitting pretty " when, in May, 1885, Gladstone gave him his chance by announcing (under pressure from his Right Wing) that the Government intended to renew the expiring *Crimes Act*. Parnell retorted by leading the Irish Party into the Opposition lobby in the division on the Budget, and thereby securing the defeat of the Government. A Tory Government took office wholly dependent upon combined Irish and Radical support. In the few months which elapsed before the inevitable General Election, Parnell secured the lapsing of the Crimes Act, and the passing of an Act which earmarked £5,000,000 to enable Irish tenants to purchase their holdings.

Gladstone's slogan for the 1885 election was an appeal for a majority big enough to make him independent of a Tory-Irish combination. Parnell retorted with " Vote solid against Gladstone and Coercion ". The result was ideal ; the Liberals outnumbered the Tories by 86, which was exactly the number of the Irish Party. Parnell possessed, absolutely, the balance of power.

In Ireland, the result was the harvest of years of work ; and it proved the efficacy of the Irish National League. In Ulster, a majority of 17 seats to 16 went to the Nationalists ; in the rest of Ireland, two Tories returned for Dublin University alone broke the completeness of

Nationalist triumph. Whigs, Tories, Liberals and non-party Home Rulers—all had been swept away, to leave Ireland represented by 18 Tories, and 85 Nationalists. One Nationalist (T. P. O'Connor) returned for a division of Liverpool made the total 86.

Within a few days, Gladstone returned to office; and he at once announced his intention of introducing, *immediately*, a HOME RULE BILL FOR IRELAND.

"Judas" Chamberlain

Gladstone's Home Rule Bill (April, 1885) approximated to a proposal to restore Grattan's Parliament. It went beyond this *norm* in proposing a Ministry responsible to the Irish Parliament; it fell below it in that the Irish Parliament was deprived of all power over Customs duties. It had other grave defects from the Irish standpoint. Its one outstanding merit was that it conceded the *principle* of Ireland's national right to self-government.

The Bill was foredoomed to defeat from the start. Quite apart from the dead-weight of anti-Irish prejudice which Gladstone himself had helped to create, the Whigs in his camp were filled with great fear. They chafed under a Liberal-Irish alliance; but if the Irish were packed off to Dublin there was every reason to fear that Gladstone would continue his policy of "surrender" by making large concessions to the working-men Radicals in his Left Wing. The defection of the Right-Wing Whigs Gladstone had foreseen and might have got over. It could have been set-off by gains from the Liberal-Conservatives. But nothing could compensate for the desertion, along with the Whigs, of Chamberlain and his following, which included many of the Radicals of the Left. The Home Rule Bill failed to pass its Second Reading.

Chamberlain's opposition to Gladstone was quite unprincipled, and opportunist. He shared the Whigs' dislike for Gladstone's " socialistic "* leaning—not realising as clearly as Gladstone did how urgent the need was to delay the formation of an *independent* working-class party. At the same time, he was himself fond of posing demagogically as the friend of the poor and enemy of the rich. Tory cartoonists of the period loved to depict him as " Jack Cade ". His basic motive was derived from a cold-blooded calculation that Gladstone (who was then over 70) was bound to die, or retire, soon. Thinking himself the legitimate heir to the leadership of the Liberal Party, Chamberlain deliberately sabotaged Gladstone's Home Rule Bill to *create an opening for a Home Rule Bill of his own*. Many of the Radicals whom he led against the Home Rule Bill, opposed it because it did not " go far enough".

A second possibility, which Chamberlain banked upon as a " saver ", was that the Tories, being very badly off for a leader in the Commons, might accept him (with his following) in that capacity ; and so open an alternative route to the coveted Premiership which he desired with a miser's passion.

As things turned out he lost on both gambles. Gladstone did not retire till after Chamberlain had settled down into a Parliamentary maid-of-all-work to the Tories ; and, for their part, the Tories never trusted the man who could throw over his leader as shamelessly as Chamberlain had double-crossed Gladstone. There is little doubt that his final decision to sabotage Gladstone's Bill proceeded from a calculated desire to retain the Irish at Westminster—his jackal O'Shea having led him to believe that Parnell with his Party could easily be manipulated for his own opportunist ends.

Gladstone at once appealed to the country on the

* *Gladstone's " socialism "* : This, of course, was nothing in the least resembling genuine Socialism. In so far as it was not a figment of Tory imagination, it was an anticipation of the Lloyd-George tactic of obstructing real Socialist advance by dexterous concessions to the lower middle-class and the conservative upper-strata of the proletariat.

Home Rule issue and suffered a heavy defeat. Parnell, in Ireland, retained his following intact.

The Plan of Campaign

On actual votes Gladstone's defeat in the 1886 election was a narrow one ; a turnover of 100,000 out of the 4,000,000 votes would have given him a majority. On seats the Tory-cum-Liberal-Unionist alliance had a majority over both Liberals and Irish combined ; and the new premier, LORD SALISBURY, soon let the Irish know that they had nothing to hope for from him. He compared them to " Hottentots, and other races incapable of self-government ". He said he would sooner spend public money to secure the emigration of a million Irishmen than in buying-out a single landlord ; and that all Ireland wanted was " twenty years of resolute Government ". He let it be known, in short, that concurrently with Chamberlain's desertion of Gladstone there had gone on a corresponding shift in the balance of class-power on the Tory side. The new " Unionists " were still aristocratic ; but they were FINANCIAL and IMPERIALIST oligarchs rather than predominantly land-owners ; and, as such, they intended to *consolidate* the Empire, and stand no nonsense from the Irish, the Colonial Nationalists, or from the Socialists either.

But for the reluctance of English capitalists to venture into such a risky field as Irish agriculture, the Tory policy would have been a return to " Elizabethan " *clearance and plantation*. Alternatively there was—plain Coercion.

Parnell's health at this date was such that he was compelled to leave the guidance of the Party almost entirely to his subordinates ; and they—or one of them, WILLIAM O'BRIEN, the editor of the Party journal *United Ireland*—evolved the *Plan of Campaign*.

This Plan started from the fact that the continued fall of agricultural prices—and the intensified competition from standardised and state-aided dairy-farming in Denmark, America, Australia and New Zealand—automatically converted what had been " fair " rents in 1882 into *rack* rents in 1886-7. The Plan was that : (*a*) in each district the land would be revalued by an agent appointed by the local branch of the League ; (*b*) the " fair " rent thus ascertained would be paid by the tenants *to the League* ; which would offer it to the landlords in full settlement of their claims ; (*c*) if the offer was refused the money would be used to pay legal expenses and compensate evicted tenants.

Whatever faults the Plan had, or virtues, the Tories never troubled to enquire. They treated it as a general mutiny ; and in March, 1887, replied with a *Perpetual Coercion Bill.*

Under this Act the League was suppressed, its papers were seized, and its meetings prohibited. No charge was too fantastic. A lad of ten was convicted of " intimidating " a constable (by whistling *Harvey Duff*) ; an Italian organ-grinder who had trained his monkey to draw and fire a toy-pistol was fined under the Arms Act and the pistol was confiscated.

There was, too, more serious work. At MITCHELS-TOWN, Co. Cork, 8,000 people packed the market place for a political meeting so tightly that the official note-taker could not get through. The police tried to clear a path with their batons ; they were beaten off to their barracks, whence they fired from the windows upon the crowd, and killed three men. The intervention of priests, and a few soldiers off-duty, alone saved the police from extermination. The District Inspector had telegraphed that morning *Don't Hesitate to Shoot !* That and *Remember Mitchelstown !* became slogans in the embittered struggle that followed.

It was, the Tories found, impossible to rely solely upon Coercion. Reform was also necessary. Hence arose the Land Act of 1887 which (shamelessly plagiarising the Parnellites) enabled *lease-holders*, to the number of 150,000, to take advantage of the Act of 1881. It also conceded the basic claim of the Plan by enabling the land-courts to *reduce judicially-fixed rents* on their own initiative. The reductions thus secured averaged 28 per cent.

Concurrently the Tories intrigued with the Pope for aid. English Catholics, wire-pulling at the Vatican, had secured, in 1883, a Papal condemnation of the *National Tribute to Parnell*. The result was that the Tribute *trebled* in a few days to reach a total of £38,000. Now they wire-pulled again, and secured a Papal condemnation of boycotting, and the Plan of Campaign. A few bishops took notice ; the bulk of the clergy and the whole of the Irish laity ignored the ban.

Tory Anti-Parnellite Propaganda

For English consumption, the Tories relied chiefly upon propaganda, which sought to fasten upon Parnell and his Party direct responsibility for " outrage "— especially for the Phœnix Park murders.

A series of articles in *The Times*, under the general heading of *Parnellism and Crime*, was commenced in 1886—to influence the elections—and was continued thereafter to justify Coercion. The basic method of the series was to connect a given speech with some " outrage " occurring in, or near, the neighbourhood where it was delivered. Most of the " outrages " were things—such as boycotting and resistance to eviction— which no reasonable Englishman ever condemned. And much was made of the (never-concealed) fact that Davitt and other leaders had once been Fenians. Naturally, the more rabid utterances of the " Left "-Fenians in America were meat-and-drink to the " atrocity "- mongers of *The Times*. The crowning point of the series was a letter reproduced in *facsimile*, condoning the Phœnix Park murders, which ostensibly had been written by Parnell himself. It appeared on the morning of *the day* (April, 1887) *fixed for the second reading of Balfour's Perpetual Coercion Act.*

The Tory Government at that date rested upon a somewhat precarious alliance of old-fashioned Tories with ex-Gladstonians, who disliked Home Rule, but also disliked Coercion. The *pseudo-*" Parnell " letter was calculated to reassure the waverers and, at the same time, to discredit not only PARNELL but his temporary ally, GLADSTONE, also. In a word it did the sort of things that JOSEPH CHAMBERLAIN, more than anybody, stood to gain from.

Parnell at once denounced the letter as a self-evident forgery ; and indeed it was quite incredible that Parnell, or any man in his position, should have written expressing sentiments he was well known not to hold. *The Times*, however, behaved as if no denial had been uttered.

The Parnellite Party demanded a Parliamentary inquiry. The Government refused ; and suggested a libel action. This was adding insult to injury, since a judge, in a civil action, has no power to compel the production of evidence, and a jury of City men would have been glad to find a verdict against Parnell, whatever the evidence. The Party was therefore compelled to let the matter rest for the time ; confident that " murder will out ".

To the general surprise, an ex-member of the Parnellite Party—F. HUGH O'DONNELL (who had resigned from the Party in scorn of the " out-of-works of humble professions " whom Parnell was choosing as his lieutenants, and who, at this time, had *attached himself to Joseph Chamberlain*)—sued *The Times* for libel, on the ground that he was incriminated, as a member of the Party, during some portion of the period covered.

The charge was fantastic. Libel actions were costly ; O'Donnell was, at most, a foreign correspondent to a Tory newspaper. Yet the action was proceeded with. When the action was heard, plaintiff's counsel produced no evidence beyond the copies of *The Times* complained of. In any ordinary action, the defending counsel would have asked at once for the judge's direction that no case had been made out. This, in the end, counsel for *The Times* did; but not until he had used *three full sittings* of the court to recite all the evidence he would have produced, if it had been necessary—including a large bundle of what purported to be original letters (from Parnell and others) never till then made public, and all highly damaging.

The Times of course got its verdict, and made much of it. O'Donnell (*born* MacDonald, *became* "Mac Donnell" and then "O'Donnell") dropped out of the picture. He had done what was wanted. He had created the situation which made it possible for the Government to offer (and impossible for Parnell to refuse) a *Special Commission* of inquiry into the allegations against "certain members of Parliament, *and others*".

"*The Times*" Special Commission

The point of a SPECIAL COMMISSION is that the Judges, to whom the work of inquiry is committed, have power to call for and *compel* the production of whatever evidence they feel is necessary to the performance of their task. In form the subject of inquiry was the conduct of *The Times*: in fact the Commission was a *trial* of the whole Parnellite Party. The fact that the Attorney-General and Solicitor-General were (in their "private" capacity) leading counsel for *The Times*, made this apparent to the dullest.

The crux of the inquiry was of course the authenticity of the *facsimile* letter (with the other "originals" produced at the O'Donnell action); but *The Times* counsel showed a great disinclination to come to the point. Instead, they roamed at large over the whole history of agrarian crime in Ireland, and produced all sorts of unsavoury witnesses to "prove"—what was never in

dispute—that " outrages " had been committed.
At length, after many days, and several long adjournments, the question was reached ; and counsel began to
tell a lurid tale of how the agent of *The Times* had bought
the letters (for spot cash) in a hotel-room in Paris from
one, RICHARD PIGOTT, who acted as broker for certain
(imperfectly identified) " Fenians "—who, in turn, had
found the letters, in a black-bag, in a hotel-room, where
they had been left by Somebody Else—who, like the
" Fenians," had absconded !

It was hardly necessary to put Pigott through the
torture of a two-days' cross-examination by SIR CHARLES
RUSSELL. His Dublin reputation—as proprietor of
" fake " Fenian newspapers, trickster, black-mailer,
pornographer, begging-letter-writer and stooge—had
caused him to be suspected from the start. Good staff-
work by DAVITT had nailed PIGOTT down with a *subpœna*
early in the proceedings ; and had compelled *The Times*
to put him in the witness box. By the end of the
second day's cross-examination PIGOTT was reduced to
such a condition that the very judges laughed him to
scorn. A Sunday intervened. On the Monday he
failed to answer his name : he had absconded, leaving
a full confession of his forgery in the hands of the
journalists (Labouchere and Sala) who had extorted it.
Pursued to Madrid, with an extradition warrant, Pigott
blew out his own brains rather than face arrest.

Counsel for *The Times* had, ruefully, to withdraw so
much of their case as rested upon the forged letters,
which was, in practice, all there was in the business so
far as the general public was concerned.

It should not be supposed that PIGOTT was the only
blot upon *The Times* case—and their counsel. They
were able to do—what no counsel, ordinarily, can do—
draw upon the resources of Scotland Yard, and of the
Secret Service at will.   They paraded as their witnesses
convicts from prison, and professional informers. And

among their witnesses was Captain O'SHEA, called, apparently, for no other purpose than to express his belief in the authenticity of the forged letters. Under cross examination he admitted to associating with a gang of notorious *agents provocateurs*—several of them implicated in bogus " dynamite outrages". (We know, now, that it was this gang of crooks who concocted the testimonial to O'Shea's sterling patriotism which induced Joseph Chamberlain to give him countenance, and to ask Parnell, as a personal favour, to secure O'Shea a seat in the House.) An offshoot of the same gang, domiciled in Paris, specialised in concocting " secret information " of Fenian doings, for sale to the more credulous newspaper editors in England and abroad. That *The Times* should have fallen for such a gang proves the length to which their anti-Parnell and anti-Irish prejudice had gone.

The Commission lingered on, with adjournments, for seven months more. Then the judges took three months to draw up their findings. But for all practical purposes the trial ended when Pigott absconded. Thereafter it was *The Times*, and the Government, which were on the defensive ; struggling to salve what relics of credit they could.

The English Masses and the Irish Party

The English common-people gave their verdict at the close of Pigott's cross examination. Parnell and his colleagues could barely make their way through the throngs which cheered them enthusiastically. For days their appearance, anywhere, was a signal for renewed enthusiasm. When Parnell entered the House, on the night after the news of Pigott's confession, flight and suicide, he was given an ovation. The entire Liberal party—with Gladstone conspicuous at their head—the Irish party, and many of the Tories, rose to their feet and cheered continuously until Parnell had taken his seat. For months the Parnellites were the most popular men in England.

The truth is that—apart from the things implied in the forged letters—everything charged against the Irish Party exalted them in the eyes of the English masses. That the Land League had been (as the Commission decided it was) virtually a conspiracy to drive the land-lords out of Ireland, was, in the eyes of English working-class Radicals and Socialists, very greatly to its credit. Boycotting, and " intimidating " land-grabbers, were too much in line with English Trade-Union tradition for the English masses to do other than applaud them. That Irish peasants, infuriated by ill-treatment, had inflicted fierce physical vengeance on their oppressors was, English working-men thought, only to be expected. In short, the whole endeavour of the Tory-cum-Liberal-Unionist conspiracy to blacken Parnell, and his party, recoiled upon the heads of the conspirators. The English masses, therefore, applauded the Parnellite Party ; and felt nothing but contempt for its enemies.

And to show the sincerity of their admiration these English masses began to clamour for a working-man's party designed in imitation of the Irish Party. Talk of a *United Land and Labour League* began to be heard in all sorts of places. The beginnings of a revival of active, independent, political organisation among the English masses date from the time of these excitements.

The Tory-Liberal Unionist conspirators, however, still had a shot in the locker.

The Commission concluded its sittings in November, 1889. It reported in February, 1890. In December, 1889, a petition for divorce was filed (in the first instance by the solicitors who had acted for *The Times*) in the name of Captain O'SHEA, citing PARNELL as co-respondent. The conspirators were (in Winston Churchill's words) out " to recover in the Divorce Court the credit they had lost before the Special Commission".

CHAPTER TWENTY-SEVEN

THE BETRAYAL AND DEATH OF PARNELL

ON November 17th, 1890, a verdict was given for the petitioner in the case of *O'Shea* v. *O'Shea and Parnell*. Mrs. O'Shea was represented, but offered no defence; Parnell was not represented.

From this verdict developed a political crisis which has no parallel in Irish history—either for the swiftness with which it arose, the bitterness with which it was fought, or the completeness of the tragedy resulting.

The O'Shea-Parnell Triangle

Parnell and Katherine O'Shea met first, on her initiative, in 1880. They were soon drawn into relations which resulted in February, 1882, in the birth of a child, which lived only a few weeks. Thereafter, from May, 1882, Parnell and Katherine O'Shea lived in unregularised marital-relations, which were not concealed from anyone connected with, or visiting, the household. Two more children were born; in 1883, and 1884, respectively.

During the latter part of this period, and afterwards, Parnell's health was very seriously impaired. His illnesses, followed by spells of recovery, continued until, in 1890, Parnell's health seemed to be restored completely. Apart from any other consideration, Katherine O'Shea made herself indispensable to Parnell, as a nurse and household manager. There is little doubt, that, but for her care, Parnell would have died years before he did.

Before passing judgment, it is material to remember that Captain and Mrs. O'Shea were living apart—had virtually separated by agreement—some time *before*

W

Parnell and she first met. It is also material that
although O'Shea had been a *nominal* Home Ruler, he
had never, even formally, submitted to the discipline
of Parnell's party.

O'SHEA, ex-captain of hussars, was essentially a
financially-embarrassed " squireen "-aristocrat. The
son of a wealthy solicitor-middleman (who had acquired
an estate through the Encumbered Estates Act), he
inherited the estate and squandered it in the traditional
manner. Bluntly, Captain O'Shea, in 1890, was substantially in the position of (Thackeray's) *Rawdon
Crawley*, except that he was not so good at billiards, and
looked to political place-hunting rather than to cards
as the source of his revenue. Also, Mrs. O'Shea had
a rich, and aged, aunt who was sufficiently fond of her
and her companionship, to pay her and the " Captain "
each a separate allowance.

The " Rawdon Crawley " analogy holds further to the
extent that O'Shea had been, before 1880, quite willing
for Katherine—who was well-connected, cultured, not
unintellectual, and personally attractive—to play *Becky
Sharp* to any man of wealth or position from whom
" dividend " could be extracted, for his (O'Shea's)
benefit. With this end in view, he encouraged the
growth of friendship between her and Parnell. He was
even willing (he said later) that the friendship should go
the length of an " *amourette* " ! But, Parnell was no
Lord Steyne, and Katherine was only able to play *Becky
Sharp* up to a point.

O'Shea, distinctly chagrined, consoled himself with
what was, to all intents and purposes, *blackmail*.
Parnell had chosen to defend the divorce action, his
cheque-book alone would have destroyed all O'Shea's
pretences. And, for her part, if Katherine O'Shea had
decided to persist in her counter-charges, she could
have produced proofs supported by " some seventeen
co-respondents in person.

The action was not defended. The essence of the tragedy, on its personal side, was, that Parnell was so set upon regularising his relation with Katherine, that he was willing, temporarily, to incur the stigma thrown upon him in the Divorce Court. The essence of the treachery, with which Parnell was hounded to death, lies in the fact that the hounding was done by men who knew, and *had known for years*, that the facts of the case were exactly as we have stated them.

Every Irish Nationalist in Parliament knew—and had known, for years, before O'Shea filed his petition—what were the relations between Parnell and Katherine O'Shea. Every member of Gladstone's Cabinet had known it, as early as May, 1882. Every Liberal and every Tory M.P., every journalist about the House knew it; and every leading journalist in the provinces. And everyone in the gossip circle fed by each of them knew it—and had known it for so long that it had lost all value as a spicy tit-bit of scandal.

Finally, the evidence, led in court—which represented Parnell as furtively intriguing with the wife of an unsuspecting husband—was, in part, a legal smoke-screen, invented to cover O'Shea's notorious connivance. In part it was wilful perjury, suborned, deliberately, to damage Parnell.

This brings us to the sinister *timing* of the divorce petition. Before the middle of 1889, O'Shea—having "expectations" under the will of Katherine's aunt—had everything to lose and nothing to gain from a divorce-petition. Even at the end of 1889 his position was not enviable—in view of the reprisals it was in the power of Katherine and Parnell to make. There is definite evidence that he could have been bought off with £20,000 in cash. Unfortunately for Katherine and Parnell, her aunt's will was contested; and this sum was beyond their compass. Even then, there is evidence that O'Shea took proceedings only with extreme reluctance—as one forced by pressure against his will.

Who was there who could, and would, exert such pressure successfully?

O'Shea at this time was calling himself a "Liberal Unionist". There is evidence that when the disputed-will case was settled, and O'Shea was left seriously disappointed (as he had feared)—directly as a result of his divorce action—that he complained bitterly to JOSEPH CHAMBERLAIN "about everybody and everything"; that he tried to persuade Chamberlain to find him a borough seat in Parliament as a *Liberal-Unionist*. Then, abruptly, Chamberlain severed relations with O'Shea, who, very unusually for him, lapsed uncomplainingly into silence and obscurity. In view of the fact that, after this breach, Chamberlain was left in possession of every document by means of which O'Shea might have proved an association between them, it is not difficult to formulate a theory to account for O'Shea's silence. He had done his "work". One infers that he drew his "wages".

The Nonconformist Conscience

The first reaction of the Nationalist Party and the Irish people to the Divorce Court verdict was a yell of defiance. Popular instinct judged intuitively and correctly that it was a follow-up of the malevolence which, having missed its mark in *The Times* Commission, now sought to reach its end by hitting "below the belt".

Mass meetings in Dublin, in England, and in America, proclaimed unabated confidence in Parnell. Meeting, at the House of Commons, on November 25th, 1890, the Nationalist Party unanimously re-elected Parnell their chairman.

The very next day an "emergency" meeting of the same Party assembled, and Parnell was requested, by a section, to resign. What had happened in the interval?

Gladstone had issued an ultimatum, virtually threatening to abandon the struggle for Home Rule unless Parnell retired, or was retired, from the leadership of the Nationalist Party.

He hinted that this was a necessary sacrifice to the clamour of the Nonconformist Conscience ; and, indeed, the self-appointed spokesmen of that " conscience " were very vocal. But Gladstone knew that those clamours themselves were not to be taken at their face value ; that they expressed, really—what he himself felt—an intense irritation at the continued Parliamentary dependence of the Liberal Party upon the support of Parnell and the Nationalists.

While Parnell occupied the position of Leader of the Irish nation Irish Nationalism, united behind him, constituted a force it was dangerous either to resist, or to give way to. Gladstone had offered Home Rule to quieten the Irish clamour ; but Chamberlain had proved that a large body of English politicians and voters feared that conceding Home Rule would only quicken the Irish National demand for separation. Parnell had never declared for separation ; but then he had never declared against it either. And it was not to be denied that under his leadership the Irish had become a political force more to be feared than they had been since the time of Daniel O'Connell ; if not greater than ever before. With Parnell deposed, the leaderless Irish would sink perforce into a tail of the Great Liberal Party. And, moreover, Chamberlain (himself a Nonconformist) would at once lose his power of undermining Nonconformist-Liberal allegiance by sneers at the " enslavement " of the Liberals to " papists " and " rebels". In a word, Parnell was *dangerous*—to the British Empire, to English capitalism, to Gladstone himself, and to Gladstone's political jackals. Therefore Parnell had to go—the Divorce Court and the Nonconformist Conscience merely provided a timely excuse.

Why did members of Parnell's own party fall into this political snare? In part they were hypnotised by the personality of Gladstone, who certainly was a master of the Parliamentary game. Partly they were scared because they did not realise how big a " bluff" this " Nonconformist Conscience " was. But the chief reason was that many of them were like Gladstone ; at bottom they *feared* Parnell, and feared him *because he had the common people united at his back.* A majority of the Parnellite Party were as afraid of *Separatism* as Gladstone was. That is why they made haste to do Gladstone's bidding.

The Party Split

From November 15th to December 6th, save for adjournments of varying length, a battle raged in Committee Room 15 in the House of Commons.

Formally the question under discussion was a proposal, by one of Parnell's supporters, that the question of the Party leadership should stand over, until the members had consulted their constituents ; and should then be decided at a meeting in Dublin.

The Anti-Parnellite faction opposed this violently. From the contemporary reports of the debate it is clear that Parnell's enemies were quite as convinced as his friends were that, if this course was followed, the masses in Ireland, and especially in Dublin, would declare for Parnell unhesitatingly. The hysterical, and abusive, fury with which TIMOTHY HEALY opposed the proposal, bears no other interpretation. Both sides kept the telegraph wires and cables throbbing with appeals and counter-appeals. Parnell, with masterly skill, took advantage of every technicality to keep the debate alive. He refused to accept a motion for his deposition. " It was not you who called me to this position," he said " but the Irish people. They alone shall depose me."

On December 3rd the balance was swayed heavily against Parnell by a manifesto from the Catholic Hierarchy of Ireland. It condemned Parnell on " moral " grounds ; but it gave, also, a political excuse—" the inevitability of a split, if Parnell were retained". Clearly the intrigue initiated by Gladstone had deep roots.

Three days later, the debate reached a point where the shrieking blackguardism of Healy so provoked Parnell (and several of his supporters) that, Healy swears—though his word is not to be trusted—Parnell would have drawn his revolver, if he had not been forcibly restrained. Healy certainly did his best to produce such a result ; but, at that point, JUSTIN MacCARTHY, for the Anti-Parnellite majority, led his supporters from the room. Forty-five went with MacCarthy. Twenty-six remained with Parnell.

The Parnellites resolved to appeal to the Irish people directly. As Parnell took his place in the Holyhead train, a large crowd of London-Irishmen thronged round to give him an ovation. TIMOTHY HARRINGTON, one of a delegation touring America at the time of the split, tells a moving story. As he departed from his New York Hotel on his way back to support Parnell, all the Irish hotel attendants gathered to see him off ; and all begged him, some of them with tears : " *You'll* not desert him, will you, Mr. Harrington ? "

Broadly that was the case in Ireland, in England, and in America. The youth, the wage-workers, the labourers, and the poorer tenants were all for Parnell ; the upper and middle-classes, in town and country, followed the call of the Hierarchy and the lure of the politicians.

There were several by-elections pending. Parnell fought them all, and lost them one after the other. Healy transferred to Ireland the blackguardism he had developed in the committee room, while press and platform reeked with verbal and pictorial filth emitted in the name of " religion " and " morality".

Parnell never lost heart. He knew it would be an uphill fight; but he was confident that, if he and his followers could only stick it out for five years, he would win the battle.

The Death of Parnell

As the year 1891 drew to its end, and with the fight growing more and more savage as the weather worsened, Parnell began to show signs of strain. He was seriously ill, when, in September, he travelled to Creggs, Co. Galway, where he spoke in the pouring rain. When he reached Dublin on his way back, the doctor told him it was dangerous for him to travel. He insisted he must go home. " But I'll be back next Saturday week." He was true to his word; but it was in his coffin that he came back.

He died at Steyning, near Brighton, on the morning of October 6th, 1891. At every point in the journey where the coffin had to be transferred, crowds of Irishmen were there to do the work. In Dublin he lay in state in the City Hall, and then again rested at the base of O'Connell's statue while scores of thousands filed past. Arthur Balfour, then Chief Secretary, said, years later, that the only crowd of which he was ever afraid was the crowd of 150,000 grim-faced Irishmen who marched in formation past the coffin of their dead chief; and then bore him by torchlight to his resting place in Glasnevin.

With him, for a full generation, were buried the Hopes of Ireland.

CHAPTER TWENTY-EIGHT

THE YEARS BETWEEN

FROM the death of Parnell, and the Second (1893)
Home Rule Bill which followed, a period of comparative
calm prevailed in Ireland. Then from 1910 the THIRD
HOME RULE BILL and its attendant excitements led to
the crisis of 1912-14.

In this period circumstances and parties all underwent
a complete change. Salient points are (1) the Tory
policy of *Killing Home Rule with kindness*; (2) the
degeneration of the Parliamentary Nationalist Party;
(3) the rise of a succession of *popular movements* in
opposition to the Party (the *Gaelic League*; *Sinn Fein* and
the Connolly-Larkin *Socialist* and *Trade-Union* agitations).

Killing Home Rule with Kindness

Returned to power in 1892 by an election which left
the Liberals dependent upon the (divided) Irish Party,
Gladstone announced his intention at once to proceed
with his SECOND HOME RULE BILL. Passed by the
Commons, the Bill was (1893) at once thrown out by
the Lords. Gladstone retired; and the Liberals, finding dependence upon the Irish irksome, sought relief
in an election (1895), from which the Tories
returned triumphant, to retain power until the end of
1905.

In their ten-year spell of office the Tories tried their
hardest to break-up the Irish national movement by
cutting its roots. The peasants were placated by
facilities for the purchase of their holdings; the landlords were subsidised to make them agreeable. The
urban and rural middle-class were pacified by extensions
of local government, and also by a judicious distribution

of government appointments, and a network of ameliorative institutions was spread over the country.

This policy the Liberals continued from 1906 to 1910.
Then a combination of causes compelled the introduction of the THIRD HOME RULE BILL. The principle
of the policy is seen most clearly in the series of Land
Acts, which culminated in the Acts of 1903 (Tory),
and 1909 (Liberal), whose general effect was to enable
the peasantry to buy their holdings on hire-purchase
terms.

The Land Acts, 1870-1909

The "Wyndham" Act of 1903 (amended only in
detail in 1909) shows the tendency of the whole English
land legislation. Its primary presupposition was *a
permanently falling market* for land products, and, therefore, for land itself. It secured the landlord who sold
his estate a much higher price than he could have got
in a competitive market. It secured immediate relief
to the tenant, by lowering the amount of his annual
payments (which counted as purchase-instalments),
and bridged the gap between the sale-price and the
purchase-price of the land with a cash donation from
the State to the landlords. The tenant, on the average,
paid double its market-value for his holding; but,
even so, his burden was less than the rent had been.

Between 1870 and 1910, over 10,000 estates, comprising over 13 million acres, were acquired by under
half-a-million tenants, at a gross purchase price of £120
million; of which the tenants paid £2 million cash
down, and the rest in instalments. The cost to the
State (without counting administration costs) was £25
million.

An incidental effect of the Wyndham Act was that
the landlord found he could *buy his own demesne land*
(land not let to tenants) with State aid and in such a way
as to get rid of mortgage encumbrances. He sold to

the State; and the State paid off the mortgage (on which he paid 8 to 10 per cent). He bought back from the State at a premium of three and a half per cent. on the cost—thus saving the difference. This alone, once it was discovered, killed opposition to the Act.

The gain to the tenant was set off by the extent to which the tenant merely escaped the landlord to fall into the clutches of the money-lender. And the Acts did nothing to check the fall of the world-price for agricultural produce. Their advantage to the small-holder of uneconomic plots was barely perceptible.*

Something was done (from 1891) for the " uneco-nomic " holders by the CONGESTED DISTRICTS BOARD—a subsidiary of the State Agricultural Department. Its best work—that of buying out landlords whose tenants held plots smaller than the minimum contem-plated by the Land Acts—and other landlords whose estates were untenanted—and redistributing the tenants upon farms of economic size—was at first outside the scope of its legal powers: the members of the Board took the risk of being repudiated and surcharged. More was done for the small and middling farmers by the IRISH AGRICULTURAL ORGANISATION SOCIETY, launched (1893) by Sir Horace Plunket, which sought to improve methods of farming and of marketing—especially in dairy-farming—by instruction and co-operative effort. The advance of the I.A.O.S. was made in the teeth of bitter political prejudice, worked up by the Irish " kulak " class—the gombeen-men and the " ranchers "—but its success, and the benefits it secured, were evident in the number of co-operative creameries which dotted the countryside (to be burned in most cases by the " Black-and-Tans " in 1920-21).

Much of the gain resulting from the work of the

* Land Purchase : It should be noted by apologists for English rule in Ireland that enabling the substantial tenant to purchase his holding perpetuated the final outcome of centuries of English conquest and exploitation.

C.D.B. and of the I.A.O.S. was lost again to the exploiting transport agencies—the Irish Railways and the Shipping Companies—in each of which English capital predominated. In fact the net result, after all efforts at reform, public and private, was stated by a continental expert-observer in 1906:

> "Were the Irishman not capable of reducing his standard of living to the lowest possible point, the continued existence of many farmsteads in the country would be inconceivable."—MORITZ J. BONN: *Modern Ireland and her Agrarian Problem.*

A further point arises here. The process of substituting grass-farming for tillage had been fostered by English capitalism to serve its ends—cheap food as a precondition for cheap labour, and cheap wool for English textile manufacture. The development of alternative sources of supply (the U.S.A., Canada, Argentine, Australia) plus the pressure of the shipping interests slackened off considerably the need for English capitalism to continue the process in Ireland. It continued, none the less, since the tenants, when they became proprietors, had to specialise on supplying the English market either with meat for luxury consumption (on the hoof or in carcass) or with dairy-produce. Thus the Acts did little or nothing for the landless labourers, or to abate such land-hunger as resulted from the normal increase of the population.

Such benefits as the Land Acts really conferred were, therefore, all conditioned upon the continued activity of the *emigrant ship*. Once that ceased to operate the problem reappeared.

The extension to Ireland of the English system of local-government was a similar "reform" which aided English rule—rather than the Irish people—by creating a vested interest in maintaining the connection with England—to secure a share of Government patronage for the, newly-promoted, dominant class. The dictatorship of the landlords through the County Grand Juries was broken. But to replace the landlord by the *gombeenman*, the parson by the priest, and the Protestant lawyer by a Castle-Catholic place-hunter was an ambiguous gain; especially as the Castle, by assuming what had been the landlord's obligation to provide half the local rate raised, secured thereby a virtually complete veto on all local spending.*

To complete the picture it must be remembered that all Ireland outside of Dublin was policed by a semi-military force, the Royal Irish Constabulary, directly controlled by the Castle; which also controlled the (unarmed) Dublin Metropolitan Police.

By anticipation, THOMAS DAVIS had given, in 1844, a prediction of the inevitable failure of this attempt to check the growth of Irish nationalism by piecemeal instalments of " reform " :

> " And now, Englishmen, listen to us ! Though you were to give us, tomorrow, the best tenures on earth ;—though you were to equalise Catholic, Presbyterian and Episcopalian ;—though you were to give us the amplest representation in your Senate ;—though you were to restore our absentees, disencumber us of your debt, and redress every one of our fiscal wrongs ;—and though, in addition to all this, you plundered the treasuries of the world to lay gold at our feet, and exhausted the resources of your genius to do us worship and honour ;— still we tell you . . . we would spurn your gifts if Ireland were to remain a province. We tell you, and all whom it may concern, come what may, bribery or deceit, justice, policy or war—we tell you, in the name of Ireland, that *Ireland shall be a Nation.*"

---

* The perpetuation of this system, after the Treaty, explains the otherwise inexplicable indifference of the Irish to local governing bodies.

The Degeneration of the Parliamentary Party

The division of the Party into warring Parnellite and Anti-Parnellite factions was ended in 1900 by the establishment of a UNITED IRISH PARTY with JOHN REDMOND (Parnellite) as its nominal leader. The numerical strength of the Party in the period of division never fell below an aggregate of 80. Morally, and politically, however, it never regained the impetus it had squandered. The factional opportunism which inspired the split was duplicated in every locality; and the hysterical black-guardism with which Parnell was hounded to death set the tone for the *gombeen-men* as they fought, each in his locality, for control of the Party machine. Soon there was, beneath a surface show of size and " unity ", nothing left of the disciplined *army* Parnell had led but *the machine* for whose control rival opportunists squabbled and intrigued incessantly.

The degeneration of the Party was seen in its abandonment of Parnell's endeavour to use constitutional struggle as a mode of approach to a revolutionary end. Parnell's position had been stated, frankly, at Cork, in 1885:

> " We cannot under the British Constitution ask for more than the restoration of Grattan's Parliament, but *no man has a right to fix the boundary of the march of a nation.* No man has a right to say ' thus far shalt thou go and no further '. We have never attempted to fix the *ne plus ultra* to the progress of Ireland's nationhood, and we never shall."

After Parnell, the Party drifted rapidly to the point at which Nationhood became a figure of speech used demagogically to enhance the Party's bargaining-power in a Parliamentary racket—whose object was a division of the spoils plundered from the British Empire at large! To the " racketeers "-in-chief in England the Irish vote in Parliament was a valuable asset to be paid for in jobs and offices allocated to the nominees of the Irish members of Parliament.

Another grave cause of degeneration in the Party was its relapse into the religious-sectarianism, which Tone, Davis, the Fenians and Parnell had all laboured to overcome, and which was the primary cause of O'Connell's failure. Parnell had proved more than a counterpoise to the Vatican's political wire-pullers—which was one of the reasons why the Hierarchy was so prompt to oblige Gladstone, and use its authority to destroy Parnell. Once Parnell was gone, the Sullivan faction, led by the " foul-tongued " Healy, became again " more Catholic than the Pope ". Out of this arose, after 1900, the domination of the Party machine by the " BOARD OF ERIN "—a break-away from a (bona-fide) Irish-American friendly society, the Ancient Order of Hibernians.

Originally founded in Ulster, ostensibly to protect Catholic traders and work-people from the Orange racket, the " Board of Erin " (A.O.H.) degenerated into a Catholic " racket ", which reproduced, and outdid, the worst sectarianism of the Orange racket. The falling away of mass support from the Party created an opening for the racketeers to gain complete control of the Party machine.

Patrick Pearse said :
> " The narrowing down of Nationalism to the members of one creed is the most fateful thing that has occurred in Ireland since the days of the Pope's Brass Band."

Connolly called the Board of Erin
> " the foulest brood that ever came into Ireland."

Its domination of the Party was a prelude to the Party's destruction.

Elements of National Revival outside the Party

Shrunk in numbers, and involved in the set-back, general after the fall and death of Parnell, the (Fenian) I.R.B., which drew its recruits from the intellectuals and

men in the humbler walks of life, continued, notwithstanding, to exercise an influence out of all proportion to
its numerical strength.   It did nothing in its own name,
preferring to " sham dead " ; but any movement, making
in any way for Separatism, could be sure of getting
(without suspecting it) Fenian support :

> " When money was needed, at a pinch, for any
> of the organisations it regarded as key organisations,
> the I.R.B. found the money [getting it usually from
> sources controlled by John Devoy].   The *Gaelic
> Athletic Association*, the *Gaelic League*, the *Sinn Fein*,
> the *Fianna* [Gaelic Boy Scouts], the *Irish Volunteers*—
> strange and transient committees and societies were
> constantly cropping up, doing this and that specific
> national work.   The I.R.B. formed them ; the I.R.B.
> ran them ; the I.R.B. provided the money.   The
> I.R.B. dissolved them when their work was done."
>
> —P. S. O'HEGARTY, *Victory of Sinn Fein.*

There is a measure of exaggeration in O'Hegarty's claim;
but, this allowed for, what he says is substantially true.
Of the organisations he names, two—the GAELIC LEAGUE
and SINN FEIN—call for special comment.

Founded, in 1883, by men who had no interest in
partisan politics of any kind, the League set itself the
task of reviving the everyday use of the Gaelic language.
Only a small fringe of impoverished peasants on the
Western Coast and its islands still used Gaelic as their
normal speech.   The League set itself to bring education
imparted in Gaelic within the reach of that fringe ; and,
at the same time, to foster the teaching of Gaelic in the
schools and among the people of the rest of Ireland.

The League had a surprising and a continuous success.
Revival of interest in the language led to revival of
interest in Gaelic music, dancing, arts and crafts; and
it—most surprisingly and gratifyingly—united Protestant
parsons and Orangemen with Catholic priests and
laymen in a common enthusiasm for the language.

Fearless in their zeal, the pioneers of the language revival repelled every attempt of the Parliamentarians, on the one side, and of the theologians on the other, to impose conditions on its advance. When a parish priest objected to *mixed* study classes on the—

> " specious ground of public morals it asserted its right to control its own activities, and established once and for all, so far as it was concerned, that the sphere of the clergy's activities is not co-extensive with human life."
>
> —MITCHELL HENRY : *Evolution of Sinn Fein.*

The more recent (and mistaken) efforts to make it compulsory to teach all school subjects in Gaelic to children who normally speak English have obscured the revolutionary and liberating significance of the Gaelic revival. It is not because of any magic property in the *language* itself that its study, at *this* time, by *just these* Irishmen and Irishwomen produced revolutionary results. After all—all Ireland, outside the towns, spoke Gaelic in the penal days without producing a single revolutionary leader.   To *rediscover* the language was another matter. Having been arrested in its development at a comparatively early stage, Gaelic leads a student acquainted with the more developed modern languages to realise at once the evolutionary *fluidity* of language as distinct from its static character. The knowledge of Gaelic also made the place names of Ireland take on a rich meaning, and rescued them from the grotesqueness and absurdity of such English corruptions as, in the case of the " Phœnix " Park, confounded the Gaelic name for a clear spring (white-water) with that of a fabulous bird. Then the extant literature in Gaelic was not only of great antiquity, but also of immense intrinsic worth. The study of this literature, along with a surprisingly large body of folk-song and story, helped the youth of Ireland to rediscover concretely the Gaelic culture which the English conquest had destroyed.

x

They were helped thus to the revolutionary truth that, as English capitalism had a *beginning*, so most certainly it could be brought to an *end*.

Before the enthusiasm of the youth of Ireland, all the agencies of orthodoxy and conservatism had to bow. The Gaelic revival was such a success that it received the flattery of imitation from demagogic politicians and *synthetic* Gaels. A more healthy and enduring result was its influence in begetting a Gaelicisation of outlook in Irish literature and drama *in English*.

The SINN FEIN * movement which began to emerge between 1900 and 1903, had Fenian influences for its father and the Gaelic revival for its mother.

Fenian influences had begotten a series of Literary and Historical " Discussion Clubs " which combined to celebrate the *Centenary of '98*. Thereafter they formed a Republican federation which began to constitute an alternative to the Parliamentary Party. Armed insurrection, as an ideal, was never far from their thoughts ; but they evolved no practical programme capable of immediate application.

Such a programme was provided by ARTHUR GRIFFITH in his journal the *United Irishman*, whose foundation, in 1899, was a direct result of the centenary celebrations.

Griffith took an old doctrine (use only Irish manufactures) and elaborated it into a policy and a programme. His contention was that the adherents to the Gaelic League should, in addition to using Irish speech, and Irish recreations, insist upon buying only articles of Irish manufacture. This insistence would create a demand, which would beget a supply, and so promote the development of an Irish National *economy*. Then the Members of Parliament should be *withdrawn from Westminster* to form an Irish National Council, which, with the local governing bodies, would promote Irish

---

* *Sinn Fein* (pronounced approximately " Shin Fayn ") literally " ourselves alone ". Its implied meaning is SELF-HELP in the collective-national sense.

industrial development, and secure openings for *Irish trade abroad*! This "self-help" policy would promote the flow of capital to Ireland, arrest emigration, and enable Ireland, ultimately, to enforce the restoration of *Grattan's Parliament*.

Griffith's programme had two notable features: (1) It provided a practical alternative to Parliamentarianism, without committing anybody to Fenian "romanticism": (2) it shared with the Parliamentary Party the restriction of its objective to Grattan's Parliament; but it left its adherents free to aspire further if they wished. It should be noted however that the Griffith policy proceeded wholly upon bourgeois—capitalist assumptions.

Between 1903 and 1908 the movement was sufficiently powerful to launch a new political organisation, SINN FEIN, and to start a short-lived daily paper of the same name.

The Socialist Republicans

To these other agencies must be added the IRISH SOCIALIST REPUBLICAN PARTY, founded by JAMES CONNOLLY in 1896. Though it never gained a mass influence or much hold at all outside of Dublin and Cork, the personality of Connolly was sufficient to ensure that it left permanent traces. Its particular virtue was that it popularised the frank use of *The Republic* as the name for Ireland's objective.

This had a powerful effect upon the Young Republicans of the literary societies and led them to follow Connolly's example. His influence was exerted powerfully in support of the '98 *Centenary Celebrations*.

Connolly's influence was seen also in a reinvigoration of the Trade Union movement in Ireland; from which important results followed. His proposition that it is in a *Socialist-Labour-Movement* that the masses of Ireland can, and will, *transcend sectarian divisions*, has yet to be refuted. He himself scored successes on this line;

others, following in his footsteps, may yet carry it to triumph.

In England and Scotland Connolly had an influence that, at first, was greater than his influence in Ireland. Born in Monaghan, Connolly was carried by his parents to Scotland at an early age, and he had already acquired prominence in the Marxist-Socialist movement when he decided to return to Ireland to attempt to found a Socialist movement.

His theoretical proposition, that *Nationalism* and *Socialism*, in an oppressed country, were not *opposites*— as mechanical pseudo-" Marxism " supposed—but were complementary, each to the other, was treated as a " dangerous heresy " by the leaders of the I.L.P. and of the S.D.F. It was, however, accepted and applauded by a group of young men on the " left " of English and Scottish Marxism, and was finally vindicated by the teaching of Lenin and Stalin.

Connolly's popularity with the Left secured their backing when, at the International Socialist Conference in Paris, in 1900, he claimed separate voting rights for Ireland as a distinct nation. Referred to the English delegation for their opinion, Connolly's claim was, under Left influence, endorsed. It was therefore conceded by the Conference ; and the recognition of Ireland as a separate nation was thereby established as a permanent precedent in the International.

Economic stress drove Connolly to emigrate to the U.S.A. at the latter end of 1903. During his absence the I.S.R.P. went out of existence ; but a labour and Socialist revival led by JAMES LARKIN recalled him to Ireland in 1910.

By this time SINN FEIN had exhausted its impetus, and the Parliamentary Party was enjoying a revival in consequence of the introduction by the Liberals of the THIRD HOME RULE BILL.

CHAPTER TWENTY-NINE

THE HOME RULE CRISIS, 1912-14

TORY (and " Orange ") resistance to the Third HOME RULE BILL went to such lengths that Civil War seemed inevitable—until it was averted by the outbreak of EUROPEAN WAR in August, 1914. A contemporary event, unconnected with the crisis—a LABOUR WAR in Dublin, 1913—had consequences which materially affected the sequel.

In this chapter we trace the process, and examine the components, of this crisis.

The Parliament Act, 1911

A salient contributory-cause of the " *Home Rule* " *crisis* was the Parliament Act carried in 1911, which destroyed the absolute veto of the House of Lords. How that came to be must first be examined.

In January, 1906, the Liberals were returned to power with the greatest majority ever. Their majority was so enormous that they outnumbered by more than a hundred the Tories (133), the Labour Party (29) and the Irish Nationalists (83) all together.

This, however, concealed a danger. The Radical Left, led by LLOYD GEORGE, had been returned in such strength that a possibility was created that, in combination with Labour and the Irish, this Left might make the continued existence of the Government impossible. Lloyd George, in short, dominated the situation since he held a balance of power ; and he exploited the occasion by forcing the introduction of a succession of reforms all designed (*a*) to steal the Socialists' " thunder " while gratifying the reformists ; and (*b*) thereby to create obstacles to the introduction of real Socialism.

It is a cardinal clue with which to unravel the tangled events of this period to remember that *fear of the working class in general,* and, in particular, *fear of a combination of the English workers and the Irish Nationalists* were primary determinants of the policy of Tories, Liberals and Radicals alike, in every shift of political alignment.

Playing skilfully upon the weakness of the Tories, Lloyd George purposely pretended that his Liberal reforms were all much more " socialistic " than, in fact, they were. He deliberately intensified the alarm of the Tories in order to make them resist with their full strength, *in the House of Lords,* such Liberal measures as they could not prevent passing the Commons. This re-created the traditional *Lords v. Commons* situation, which Lloyd George exploited by including in the Budget of 1909 a *Land Tax,* which, negligible in itself, he palmed off upon the general public as well as the Tories as a first step in a programme of landlord-expropriation. The Lords fell into the trap and rejected the Budget.

This created the opening for the PARLIAMENT ACT which provided that an Act could become law, *without the concurrence of the Lords,* if it passed the Commons three times in one Parliament without alteration. Two more elections (January and December, 1910) were necessary before the Act could be passed—the accession of a new king (George V), and his scruples, making the second one necessary. But the end was achieved finally in 1911.

So long as the Tory-dominated House of Lords remained, with its powers undiminished, the Liberals could retain Home Rule in their programme without risk of frightening away the moderates and imperialists in their Right Wing. It pleased their Radical Left ; it saved the face of their Nationalist allies ; and, since the House of Lords could always be trusted to throw it out, it gained support on the Left without losing any on the Right. That is, the Liberals were in favour of *advocating* Home Rule, so long as it was *impossible to* carry it into effect.

The elections of 1910— fought by the Tories under slogans of fierce hostility to " Socialism ", " Spoliation", and " Irish Disloyalty ' —had reduced the Liberals to complete dependence upon the *Nationalists* (83) and the *Labour* Party (41). The price they had to pay for the Parliament Act—which their continued political existence depended upon—was a pledge to introduce a Home Rule Bill immediately the Parliament Act became law.

The Tory Opposition to Home Rule

The passage of the Parliament Act brought the ruling clique of Imperialist Finance-Capitalists face to face with the menace of an ascendant and militant proletariat. The combination of Lloyd-Georgian social-democracy, Labour-Socialism, and Irish Nationalism, might, if it were not checked, grow more menacing every hour. The House of Lords had ceased to be an impregnable defence of their privileges and property ; therefore they had to cast around for a new weapon. They found it in open conspiracy to thwart the will of the democracy by *force and arms.*

They were too astute to attempt this by a frontal assault upon the institution of Parliament itself (though there was talk of " ending the farce of democracy "). They chose the method of a flanking attack ; and, under cover of zeal for the " loyalty ", " liberty ", " religion " and " property " of a " persecuted minority ", organised their counter-revolutionary armed force in Ulster, in the disguise of a " volunteer " movement of collective self-protection in hostility to Home Rule.

It is cardinal to remember that what passed for a " spontaneous " resistance of " Ulster " to the " menace " of Home Rule was (*a*) not spontaneous but deliberately worked up, with not a little moral blackmail and economic coercion ; (*b*) did not originate in Ulster but in the inner-councils of the English Tory-plutocracy ; (*c*) was taken up with greater enthusiasm among the young counter-revolutionaries of the English aristocracy and the services than among the Ulster people ; (*d*) affected only a portion of Ulster and included only a minority of its population ; and (*e*) was aimed at no " menace " (since the Home Rule Bill contained none) but at preserving *the privileged position of a minority-caste* in Ireland, as part of the process of maintaining a *privileged minority-caste* as the real rulers of England, and exploiters of its Empire.

The progress of the opposition proves this. The agitation in Ulster was led by Sir EDWARD CARSON, a Dublin man, who had been Solicitor-General in the Tory Government from 1900-1906. In England it took the form of a demagogic " loyalist " and " Protestant " campaign against " unpatriotic " socialists, " papist " Nationalists, and their " little Englander " Radical allies. Resistance to Home Rule was palmed off as " defence of the Empire", " defence of property and personal rights", and " defence of the Protestant religion". Every drawing-room in good society became a recruiting office enrolling the young officer class in the conspiracy : and the organisers of the campaign did not scruple to allege that they had the sympathy (if not the support) of the " very highest in the land " for their revolt against the " *tyranny* " *of the House of Commons.*

The Opposition in Ulster

In Ulster the first move was to secure a mass of signatures to a COVENANT, pledging resistance to Home Rule. In the circumstances it was not difficult to obtain 500,000 signatures in a short time ; but nothing was left to chance. Employers let it be known that failure to sign the Covenant might have " consequences" for those who failed. Landlords passed the " List " to tenants ; customers did the same to tradespeople. Orange factionists saw to it, in the Belfast shipyards, that those who did not sign, promptly, were run off the job as " Papists ".

Then, at a critical stage, a body of Volunteers 80,000 strong was raised, in which force were included all the *hooligan elements* in Belfast, who were chosen deliberately for their ignorant anti-Catholic virulence. This force was officered and drilled almost entirely by officers holding commissions in the English Army and Navy. A proportion of the Volunteers were armed with rifles from the first—the majority being armed with revolvers. Arms were supplied by the " gentry " ; and arms were collected and stored in the Tory clubs in England, as well as in the Orange lodges in Ulster.

Finally, when the Act was introduced a third time, after being twice rejected by the Lords, Carson named a Provisional Government for the six counties of N.E. Ulster ; and announced that it would begin to function on the day set for the coming-into-force of the Home Rule Act. Steps were taken to procure rifles, machine guns, etc., for the whole Ulster " Volunteer " force.

The moderates in the conspiracy had hoped to bluff the Liberals out of using their powers under the Parliament Act. When this failed they became reconciled, perforce, to the militants' policy of counter-revolutionary revolt.

Classes in the Ulster Resistance

That there existed, ready-made for Tory use, the whole machinery of *Orangeism*—anti-democratic and counter-revolutionary from its first invention in 1795— goes without saying. That the Orange Order existed solely to preserve the political, social and economic *ascendancy* of a small oligarchical faction has been abundantly demonstrated already. · What calls for

comment is the fact that the proletarian masses of
Belfast and the industrial North-East were still blinded
by sectarianism sufficiently to react as desired to the
" No Popery " bogey, set up to terrify them by the
Orange agents of the Tory conspiracy.

The reason for this is found in the fact that, while
wages in Belfast averaged in general higher than the
average for the rest of Ireland, they were lower than for
corresponding occupations in England and Scotland.
Belfast's " prosperity " (for the employers) and, incidentally, its importance for British capitalism as a whole,
arose in its early stages from its *freedom from Trade
Unionism*. This in turn was a result of the sectarian
divisions, which the employers took great care to
foster. Once Catholic and Protestant workers had been
taught to hate each other like poison, it became a rule
for employers to engage just so many of each of the
hostile sects as would ensure that 100 per cent. solidarity
was all-but-impossible.

In a measure, the Orange Order became, in certain
of its lodges, an endeavour to counter this employers'
device ; and some, at any rate, of the attempts at driving
the Catholics out of the shipyards were, at bottom, crude
attempts at creating a basis for shop-solidarity. More
frequently the Orange Order functioned as a " scab-
herding " agency and as a " racket " to keep all appointments to the posts of foreman, charge-hand, etc., within
its privileged circle.

The A.O.H., as we have noted, was formed ostensibly
as a defence against these practices of Orangeism ; but
the A.O.H. made matters ten times worse, since under
clerical influences it was also predominantly *anti-Trade
Union*. More than one case of deliberate strike-breaking
caused the " Mollies " to be regarded with hatred in
proletarian quarters, Catholic as well as Protestant ;
and the net result of its activities was a revival of sectarian animosities in social-strata where they would

otherwise have lapsed entirely—along with all interest in dogmatic theology. As James Connolly said, at this period:

> "Were it not for the existence of the Board of Erin, the Orange Society would long since have ceased to exist. To Brother DEVLIN [Grand Master A.O.H.], and not Brother Carson is mainly due the progress of the Covenanting Movement in Ulster."

The Curragh Incident

Whether the Carsonite agitation was originally a "bluff" or not, it became clear that it ought to be checked. Rank-and-file pressure induced the Government, at last, to forbid the importation of arms and ammunition into Ireland (December 4th, 1913); and then to cause the officers at the Curragh Camp to be "warned" for duty in Ulster (March, 1914) to quell organised resistance to the lawful authorities.

Fifty-seven officers at once tendered their resignations; many more let it be known that they would take a similar course.

Faced with this virtual mutiny—which it was given to understand included potentially a majority of the officers in the Army and Navy Lists—the Government surrendered. It announced that it had no intention of "coercing" Ulster. The conspirators, now cocksure of victory, grew thereafter more arrogant hourly.

The causes of the Liberal hesitation were complex. REDMOND's biographers report that he had personally vetoed a suggestion that Carson should be prosecuted. He feared the consequences of letting loose civil war in Ireland. Carson, for his part, made no concealment of the fact that friends, in Court circles, had assured him of immunity from any penalty for his "treason". And the Liberals, for their part, saw reason to fear a civil war in England, which, if it did not end in a victory for

Tory counter-revolution, would risk creating the conditions for a *proletarian, socialist revolution.*

Two preceding events had induced this frame of mind: (1) THE " LARKIN " LABOUR WAR in Dublin, 1913 ; and (2) the formation in November, 1913, of the IRISH VOLUNTEERS.

The " Larkin " Labour War

Working on ground which Connolly had ploughed, JAMES LARKIN had built up, from 1907 onwards, a militant trade union of a new type—the *Irish Transport and General Workers' Union.* It catered primarily for the unskilled, and the, till then, unorganised workers ; and it relied more especially upon the weapon of the " lightning " strike, backed up by sympathetic action by workers in related jobs.

In 1913, W. M. MURPHY—the richest man in Dublin, Chairman of the Employers' Federation, virtual owner of the Dublin Tramways, and owner of the *Independent*— denounced in that journal some workers then on strike. Larkin called for a boycott of the *Independent* and Murphy replied by calling for an employers' boycott of the Union, purged all the members of the Transport Union from the Tramway Service, and locked out its members employed in Jacob's Biscuit Factory, which he controlled.

Transport Union members fought the scabs who ran the Tramways ; newsboys fought the scab sellers Murphy sent out with the *Independent.* Other workers joined in ; railwaymen, transport-drivers, dockers, and seamen all refused to handle Jacob's Biscuits or the goods of any of the firms who joined in Murphy's war on " Larkinism". Soon, half Dublin was on strike ; and all Dublin was in an uproar. Battles with the police were fought daily.

To follow the struggle in detail would require a volume. What is significant for our purposes is that the working masses of Dublin found themselves faced with an alliance of Dublin Castle (with its police), the Orange-Tory magistrates, the Nationalist employers, and the *Catholic Hierarchy*. To make the united front of reaction complete, ARTHUR GRIFFITH denounced Larkin, unsparingly, in the name of *Sinn Fein*.

Pressed for funds with which to wage the struggle, Larkin and Connolly turned to England and Scotland—from which they received a burst of enthusiastic solidarity such as had not been known since the great dockers' strike of 1888. Funds were granted by virtually every union, by the T.U.C., by the Labour Party, and by the Co-operative Union. Jacob's Biscuits were universally boycotted, and the Trade Unions and Socialist Societies combined to stock a food-ship which the C.W.S. supplied at cost-price, they chartering the ship as their share. English and Scottish Socialists volunteered by the hundred to find homes for the children of strikers "for the duration". A party of some three hundred children was actually on its way to the ship at the North Wall, when it was turned back by a frenzied band of hymn-singing women, headed by priests, who feared the consequences to the children's *souls* if they were fed for a month or so in the homes of "godless" English and Scottish Socialists. The middle-class women who had organised the affair, DORA MONTEFIORI and LOUISE RAND, were actually arrested on a charge of "attempted kidnapping".

In the end the strike wore itself out to an inconclusive finish. But it left behind as its permanent effects a great growth in militant class-consciousness among the Dublin workers, a great enhancement of the reputation of LARKIN and CONNOLLY as leaders, and the establishment of close relations between the young neo-Fenian intellectuals and the Labour movement.

Two incidental results were of decisive importance : (1) In England, a great wave of militant (" syndicalist ")

trade-unionism flared up to threaten the greatest
industrial conflict in history ; (2) in Ireland, the Transport Union's " Army ", formed of men armed with
hurley-bats who guarded the platform against police
assaults during strike-meetings, gave rise to the CITIZEN
ARMY, which, in turn, derived added importance from
the founding of the IRISH VOLUNTEERS.

The Irish Volunteers

In November, 1913, a group of well-known men,
not too prominently connected with the Nationalist
Party, and not connected at all, so far as was known,
with any more militant, or republican body, called a
meeting in the Rotunda, Dublin, to consider the formation of a *National Volunteer Force* to defend Home Rule
from Carsonite assault. Over 30,000 people attended
in the Rotunda and at the over-flow meetings in the
surrounding streets. Four thousand names were handed
in that night.

Ten days later (December 4th, 1913) a Government
proclamation forbade the import of arms or ammunition
into Ireland. The Government had watched Carson's
drilling and arming, for eleven months, without saying
a word. When Nationalist Ireland followed suit they
acted at once.

The conclusion is obvious : the Liberals were, on a
balance, less afraid of being beaten by the Tories than
of beating them, with the aid of *militant English proletarians*, and *armed Irish Nationalists*.

For a week or two Volunteer recruiting dragged.
Various bodies—branches of the United Irish League,
the American Hibernians, *Sinn Fein*, and the Citizen
Army—offered to join bodily. The Volunteer executive
insisted upon *individual* recruits, on a strictly territorial
basis. The I.R.B. men—who, working under cover,
were really in control—insisted upon this precaution,
as a means of keeping control in their hands ;   but,

naturally, they could not say so openly. The Citizen Army, affronted at refusal, set to work to equip and arm itself independently. For a few months there was keen hostility between the Citizen Army and the Volunteers.

The Curragh incident, in March, 1914, and the Ulster gun-running on the night of April 24th-25th—when the Ulster Volunteers seized the ports and customs houses at Larne and Donaghadee, and landed a large cargo of German Mauser rifles and ammunition— changed the situation completely; especially when it was seen that nothing whatever was done about this flagrant defiance of the law. It was clear, too, that there had been connivance; since the warships posted off the Ulster coast, expressly to prevent anything of the kind, could not be conceived to be so incompetent as the gun-running implied.

Accepting the implied threat as a challenge, Irish Nationalists flocked into the Volunteers by thousands every day; and a great demand arose that Redmond should " put his foot down", and insist upon the lifting of the ban on the importation of arms, which now operated exclusively to the advantage of Carson.

Redmond did, in the end, put his foot down; but not in the place expected. He demanded (June, 1914), that the Volunteer Executive, " to make the organisation representative", should admit to their number twenty-five men to represent the Party chosen by himself as Chairman. A majority complied, though with reluctance. Pearse and his Fenian colleagues protested, but submitted.

After this had been done, Redmond demanded (July) the lifting of the ban. He had privately protested before; now the bellicosity of the Ulster Volunteers was going beyond all bounds. They were talking, now, of a " march from Belfast to Cork". Their commander-in-chief, General Richardson—who held a high rank at the Horse Guards, despite his connection with partisan

politics—ordered all ranks (from July 1st onwards) to
"carry their arms openly and resist every effort to
disarm them". On July 25th, 5,000 Ulster Volunteers
paraded Belfast, fully armed, with four machine-guns.
Still Redmond received no answer to his demand.

On Sunday, July 26th, in Dublin, Assistant-Commissioner of Police, Harrell, received shocking news.
A private yacht, he learned, had landed eleven hundred
rifles, and a supply of ammunition, at Howth. They
had been met by a body of Irish Volunteers, who, even
then, were marching back to Dublin with their weapons.

Assistant-Commissioner Harrell realised at once
that the entire British Empire depended upon him alone.
He assembled all the police within reach, requisitioned
a company of Scottish Borderers, and sallied forth to do
deeds. He met the " enemy " at Clontarf.

Ammunition had not been served out, but some of
the men had revolvers, and Harrell's peremptory demand
for a surrender of arms was flatly refused. He ordered
the police to seize the arms ; a scuffle arose ; shots were
fired ; a few injuries were inflicted. The officer commanding the Borderers insisted upon a parley ; and the
incident fizzled out absurdly.

While the Volunteer officers were protesting—
arguing with the Assistant-Commissioner, and threatening to serve out ammunition and make a fight of it—the
Volunteers, beginning from the rear ranks, were dodging
through the houses at the sides of the road, and dis-
appearing over the garden walls in the fields beyond—
carrying their arms and the ammunition with them.
Assistant-Commissioner Harrell was still insisting,
indignantly, that the Volunteers were breaking the law,
when it dawned upon him that there was nobody before
him but a group of Volunteer officers and a few of the
rank and file—whose rifles had somehow disappeared.

Much injured in his dignity, Harrell gave the word
to return to the Castle. Unfortunately the news had

spread. The streets were thronged ; and as the police and soldiers neared the centre of the City, they were greeted with hoots and hisses, to which later was added stone-throwing.

The officer commanding the Borderers halted his company in Bachelor's Walk ; and ordered his men to prepare to fire. Some ranks, mistaking the order, opened fire at once ; others, thinking an order had been given, followed suit. In a few seconds three people had been killed, and some thirty wounded.

Anger had barely had time to blaze up in Ireland, when, radiating from Vienna in all directions, a wave of war spread to engulf the world. On August 4th, 1914, Britain entered the war ; and, for the time being, everything else was forgotten.

Y

CHAPTER THIRTY

THE ROAD TO EASTER WEEK

At the outbreak of war, in August, 1914, the general feeling in Nationalist Ireland was one of cordial sympathy with Britain and France, faced suddenly with the calamity of war. There was a tradition-based sympathy with France ; there was a newly-acquired sympathy with Britain, largely based on the belief that Home Rule had been conceded, and would come into force automatically as soon as the war ended.

The question posed in this chapter is : By what process was this cordiality turned into its opposite, so that *an attempt to establish an Irish Republic* was made in Easter Week, 1916 ?

Redmond, the Nationalist Party and the War

When the Prime Minister, Asquith, reviewed the situation, in the House of Commons, in the first days of the war, he was able to say that " Ireland is the one bright spot in the landscape". John Redmond, with a burst of spontaneous magnanimity, told the House they could take every English soldier out of Ireland, and trust its defence to the Volunteers, North and South.

Politically, this was a fatal error—one doomed to destroy Redmond and his party, utterly, and for ever. Yet the essence of the tragedy is—*it could have been made to come true* ; but only if the conspirators at the back of the " Ulster " ramp had been actuated by different motives. If the " Ulster " agitation had been *bona fide*, and open to conviction, Redmond's genuine eagerness to satisfy every complaint would have cleared the way for an amicable settlement.

Redmond's error was a strange one. It revealed him in a flash as an intensely reserved and sentimental Irish gentleman—of a type which survived only in himself—who had lost all touch with political actualities. He lived from choice (when he was not at Westminster) in a lonely dwelling, in an inaccessible part of Co. Wicklow, a part of Ireland more remote, in practice, than even the Western Isles. He loved the house because it had belonged to Parnell ; and his chief occupation, there, was to sit and brood—of his dead chief, and of days, still more remote, when his ancestors had been involved, fatally, on both sides, in '98. He was to learn in bitterness and sorrow how completely the world had passed him by.

What actually happened was tragically different from what, in his emotional excitement, Redmond had assumed would occur. The *Home Rule Bill* was given the Royal Assent ; but was then hung up for the " duration " on the understanding that an " amending " Bill would come into force at the same time, ex-cluding the Six Counties (temporarily ?) from its opera-tion.

Meanwhile, no English troops were withdrawn from Ireland ; and the flood of Irish recruits to the British army was treated, systematically, with supercilious and offensive lack of consideration. The extent to which the officer caste had been indoctrinated with the die-hard Tory ideology—*hostility in principle to the Irish* alike as democrats, Catholics, and Nationalists—was revealed in scores of ways.

A few examples will suffice. The proportion of recruits per thousand of population to the British Army was much higher in *Nationalist* Ireland than in " Ulster " ; but this fact was systematically concealed. The " Ulster " regiments were brigaded together ; had their own Ulster officers ; wore a distinctive badge ; and were given every publicity.

One Irish "division" was formed for the rest of Ireland; but it was officered, almost exclusively, by *English* officers, nearly every one of them being a Tory die-hard. It was refused its own distinctive Irish badge; and when a group of highly-connected Irish ladies worked a banner for the Division, permission to use it was peremptorily refused. Irish recruits were, in practice, refused permission to select their units; and were dispersed, as widely as possible, among *English* and *Scottish* regiments. When, by this diversion of recruits to fill the wastage of war, the Irish Division fell below its strength it was reorganised and lost its distinctively Irish character. Everything was done to prevent Irishmen developing any collective-National self-confidence, or any sort of *National pride*, based upon proved *Irish* valour on the battle-field.

When an English officer, with Home Rule sympathies, allowed these sympathies to appear in his recruiting speeches, *in an exclusively Nationalist area*, he was reprimanded; and *ordered to send in his papers*. When General RICHARDSON invited "Orangemen" to enlist, *as such*, so that they could "learn to drive Home Rule to Hell", no sort of notice was taken, other than commendatory.

Scornful Fenians told aggrieved Nationalists, who complained of these things, that it served them right for lending themselves to do *England's work*. It took time for the official policy to produce its natural effect of alienating the mass of Nationalist Ireland; but in time it was done, and done irreparably.

The Volunteer Split

The rebuffs and insults inflicted upon the Irish Nationalists by the young bloods and the old Blimps of the officer-caste—to whom a counter-revolutionary hostility to democracy and democratic-Nationalism was the "correct thing"—provided a practical criticism of the whole line of the Parliamentary Party since the throwing overboard of Parnell.

Parliamentary Nationalism had, in fact and practice, operated on these assumptions : (1) That Ireland's "Nationality" was a thing purely relative and conditional ; while the *connection* with England was a thing fixed and inescapable. (2) That England's *imperial* integrity was vital to Ireland's continued existence. (3) That Ireland's nationhood was, at most, a thing comparable to the provincial pride of an East Anglian or a Wessex man, or the county pride of a Yorkshireman. (4) In effect they denied any reality to Irish nationality—save as a relic from a past which they wished to be able to forget.

" Irish history is something which every Englishman should be encouraged to learn, and every Irishman encouraged to forget." So ran the comfortable paradox ; to which the die-hard Tories replied by deeds which proved that, to them at any rate, Irishmen were —what they had been to the Whigs of the Penal Code and the Tories of the days of the Union—" *aliens* in blood, in speech, and in religion".

The Orange point of view was as realistic as was that of the Fenians ; and was equally calculated to de-bunk all the sentimentality of the Redmondite recruiters. Said an Ulster journal :

" If the Redmondites will not support the war because it is just, they should not support it because they have got Home Rule. *They haven't got it.*"

That was the tragic awakening which was in store for Redmond and his Party.

Meanwhile they were loyal to their word ; and began to take note seriously of the anti-war attitude expressed by the three distinct trends of Republicanism, which began to make themselves manifest.

The Republicans of the *traditional school*, the old Fenians represented by TOM CLARKE, saw nothing in the war but "England's difficulty—Ireland's opportunity". As soon as war was declared, the Supreme Council of the I.R.B. met and decided, in principle, that a Rising must be attempted before the war ended. They followed tradition, too, in looking for aid from abroad. As was virtually inevitable they looked to America for money, and perhaps arms, and to Germany for military assistance. They had no illusions about Germany. They saw Germany as the die-hard Orangeman did, who protested at the depletion of the ranks of the Ulster Volunteers " only because of a European disturbance". "After all," he said, "*the Kaiser is a good Protestant.*" The traditionalist Fenians saw that clearly ; but thought that the virtue of being at war with England made up for every deficiency. And, anyway, as a business proposition, Germany, at war with England, might be glad to send arms and officers to Ireland.

The *Gaelic Republicans*, of whom PATRICK PEARSE was the best representative, were very sceptical of German help. They saw—what the traditionalists failed to see—that TONE appealed for military aid to France, in 1796, not merely, or even mainly, because it was at war with England, but because it stood, then, *at the head of the forces of World Liberation.* The FRENCH REPUBLIC to which Tone appealed was the embodiment and representative of the principles of Popular Freedom, and of the International Solidarity of a Liberated World. He appealed as a democratic-republican to his fellow republican-democrats. And nobody in 1914 could envisage the Kaiser or the Kaiser's Reich as anything of the kind. Pearse's doctrine, which, at times, he expressed in mystical terms which obscured its realistic essence, was that *Ireland must herself develop the force that achieves her freedom.* His doctrine of the magical efficacy of a "blood-sacrifice" boils down, in practice, to this elementary truth.

Distinct from Pearse were again JAMES CONNOLLY and the *Socialist Republicans.* Connolly had even less faith in German aid than Pearse had. " *We serve neither King nor Kaiser—but Ireland!* " This was his slogan from the first; but, with it, he had a passionate concern for the workers and peasants in all lands, who were being driven to slaughter each other in the interest of the predatory imperialism of their respective rulers. He looked everywhere, longingly, for a sign of what he wished to see—the general uprising of the masses against the rulers who had made the earth a shambles. And every day he grew more inclined to hope, and to believe, that a popular uprising in Ireland would serve as a signal for a popular uprising everywhere. A (false) rumour that the German Socialist leader, KARL LIEBKNECHT, had been shot for his anti-war propaganda, drew from Connolly a statement of his thoughts :

" The war of a subject nation for independence, for its right to live its life, in its own way, may and can be justified as holy and righteous. The war of a subject class to free itself from the debasing conditions of economic and political slavery should at all times choose its own weapons and esteem all as sacred instruments of righteousness. But the war of nation against nation in the interest of royal freebooters, and cosmopolitan thieves, is a thing accursed.

" All hail then to our Continental comrade who, in a world of imperial and financial brigands, and cowardly trimmers and compromisers, showed mankind that men still know how to die for the holiest of all causes—the sanctity of the human soul—the practical brotherhood of the human race."

Organisationally, the Traditional and the Gaelic Republicans were one; they were united in the I.R.B. and in the Volunteers. Connolly and the CITIZEN

ARMY—every member of which had to be a member of a trade union—were not merely distinct from the Republicans. There was a measure of hostility between them which was only partly bridged by those such as Madame MARKIEVICZ, who was a commandant in the Citizen Army and also a leader of the *Cumann na mBan* (the Women's Auxiliary Army of the Irish Volunteers). Pearse also, drawn by his democratic sympathies and his admiration for Connolly, began to function as an influence for unification.

At the same time each felt it was necessary to make a break with Redmondite Nationalism. Accordingly, in September, 1914, the Republican elements in the Volunteer Executive repudiated Redmond's pledge of support to the English Government, and expelled his nominees from the Committee. They issued a call for a *National Convention*, to elect a permanent executive and define the policy of the new organisation.

Redmond replied with a counter-repudiation ; and called upon all loyal Nationalist Party men to boycott the Convention and those responsible for calling it.

Thus, at a stroke, the Volunteer Movement was split between the Republicans—who kept the original name IRISH VOLUNTEERS—and the Redmondites who took the name of NATIONAL VOLUNTEERS. Of the 200,000 Volunteers enrolled at the time of the split, only 12,000 answered the call, and sent delegates to the Convention on November 25th, 1914. Redmond, in derision, called them the " *Sinn Fein Volunteers*", and the name stuck—to create endless confusion later.

The (Redmondite) National Volunteers, despite their majority, began to shrink from the moment of the split. By April, 1915, they had dwindled to a tenth of their original number. A year later, only a few companies survived. The Irish Volunteers, on the contrary, grew steadily until they reached a maximum of 18,000, a quarter of whom were drawn from

Dublin and its vicinity. The Dublin battalions were all fully equipped with arms and ammunition. Outside of Dublin only a few companies were fully equipped.

The *Citizen Army* had arms for 200 men ; if it could have got the arms, it could have paraded ten times that number. Many would-be Citizen Army men joined the Volunteers to get arms. Soon the Citizen Army and the Volunteers were holding joint parades and drills.

The Struggle with the Authorities

JAMES LARKIN left Ireland for America in October, 1914,—to evade arrest and deportation to England. JAMES CONNOLLY carried on as virtual chief of the Transport Union, Commander of the Citizen Army, and Editor of the *Irish Worker*. He wrote freely, also, for English Labour and Socialist journals ; urging, always, revolutionary proletarian solidarity in opposition to the " war of the kites and the crows".

In Ireland he combined that general propaganda with specific agitation of Ireland's national claims, and a repudiation in advance of Home Rule as any sort of satisfaction for those claims. He appealed constantly to the workers of Belfast and the Six Counties ; urging them not to be misled by the Ulster capitalist bosses, whose only interest in maintaining the connection with England was to secure the armed force with which to keep their workers in subjection.

Connolly's *Socialist-Republicanism*—preached fearlessly, with unremitting fervour, week by week—had a profound effect upon the young " Fenian " leaders— PEARSE, MACDONAGH and MACDERMOTT—the last-named being the editor of the I.R.B. journal, *Irish Freedom*.

They were all attacked as " pro-German " by the " loyal " Nationalist Press, and all were, ignorantly or maliciously, confounded with *Sinn Fein* with which none of them had any connection, and which, as a

Party, had dwindled to nothing. ARTHUR GRIFFITH still maintained his *United Irishman* and kept up his criticism of Redmond's war policy ; but he had severed his connection with both the I.R.B. and the Volunteers —disagreeing, totally, with the notion of forcing an insurrection " hot-house " fashion.

The Chief Secretary (AUGUSTINE BIRRELL) handled the situation with a *finesse* unusual in occupants of his office. As a Radical he disliked suppressing journals. As a party tactician he saw the unwisdom of " making martyrs". But the printers of Republican journals were told, quietly, one after the other, that if they continued to print matter objectionable to the Authorities, their plants *might be commandeered* " for war purposes". A point was reached where *Irish Freedom* had to be printed in Belfast, and the *Irish Worker* in Glasgow (on the press of the S.L.P., which Connolly had helped to found).

In Belfast, incidentally, the Irish and the Ulster Volunteers invariably saluted each other, ceremonially, when they passed each other in their marches. They had, at any rate, one point in common : they each hated (and were hated by) the Board of Erin, A.O.H.

As the fog of war descended, and all propaganda other than war propaganda was faced with increasing difficulty and danger, Connolly grew fiercely impatient for a chance to do something—or set something in motion—which would excite, by sympathetic suggestion, the universal revolt of the exploited and oppressed which he longed to see. He fretted impatiently to be up and doing, at the head of his gallant handful of Citizen Army men. He was confident that, once a start was made, the Fenians would not fail to join in.

CONNOLLY, in truth, became somewhat of a trial to the I.R.B. chiefs. They had learned his resolution, early in the war, when he with TOM CLARKE and SEAN MACDERMOTT had organised a party to seize the Mansion

House, Dublin, on the eve of a great recruiting-rally, at which both ASQUITH and REDMOND were booked to speak—intending to hold it, *with rifles*, against all comers. The plan broke down ; soldiers were already billeted in the Mansion House, and a surprise capture was impossible.

By February, 1916, Connolly had reached the limit of his patience. His writings in the *Workers' Republic* (which was printed then on his own press in LIBERTY HALL, under a guard of Citizen-Army men, with rifles loaded and bayonets fixed) began to grow reminiscent of JOHN MITCHEL in 1848. The I.R.B. chiefs grew scared lest the authorities should take the alarm. They kidnapped Connolly ; and, in a quiet spot, let him into the secret that their plans were laid for a Rising in Easter Week, 1916. Connolly agreed to come into the plan ; and from thence forward was a co-opted member of the War Directory, I.R.B.

Preparing for Revolt

The Plan of the Rising was known only to a dozen men, one of whom was the veteran of '65, JOHN DEVOY. Its general assumption was (*a*) that the mass of the Volunteers were Irish enough to respond, at call, to an invitation to attempt a revolutionary *coup d'état* ; and (*b*) that if the Rising could hold its own for a week, or a fortnight, the mass of Irishmen would be inspired by National instinct and tradition to join the revolt. Defeat might follow ; but the repression, with the fact that an attempt had been made, would reawaken and revivify the National aspiration for Republican Independence. On the concrete side, plans had been made to secure : (1) A supply of arms and ammunition from Germany ; (2) a body of officers and instructors with more arms, from the Fenians in the U.S.A. ; (3) possibly (though none too likely) an Irish Brigade recruited from war-prisoners in Germany.

The last of these points was ROGER CASEMENT'S pet scheme. He had cast himself for the rôle of Wolfe Tone in this " new '98", and played his part gallantly—though with little of the genius of his great exemplar.

The second point was one in which Clarke, Connolly and Devoy all placed great hopes. It came to nothing in the end, since the U.S.A. authorities, getting wind of the scheme, shifted the German liners—which it was proposed to seize and use for transporting men and materials to Ireland—away from their berths in the Hudson out to an anchorage beyond Sandy Hook. The first point all were agreed upon ; and this very nearly materialised.

The actual quantity of arms in their possession was not large. The cargo run at Howth had been supplemented by another, eight times as large, landed a few nights later on a quiet beach in Wicklow. Some of these arms had been lost in the Split ; but that business had been so contrived as to leave most of the arms in the " right " hands. Rifles and machine-guns were hard to get in war-time ; but with shot-guns, sporting-rifles, and rifles " looted " from the military (as well as revolvers and automatic pistols) they made out as well as they could. They had lost a number of active organisers, arrested by the authorities and deported to England ; but their places had been filled by enthusiastic volunteers. The movement at large knew nothing of the plan, as a concrete actuality ; but the atmosphere was electric with the spirit of revolt, and the expectation that something would soon be attempted.

The British authorities knew little more than the rank-and-file volunteers did. They learned, of course, of Casement's abortive effort to recruit an Irish Brigade among the war-prisoners ; but they learned little more from Germany—good as their espionage service was.

The German Government had little to tell. It knew only what Casement could tell them ; and that was very little. And in truth the Germans were very little interested in Nationalist Ireland. *They had banked on Carson's "rebellion"* tying the hands of the British sufficiently to keep them out of the war until France had been smashed. As Carson had failed them the Germans had no confidence in the rest of Ireland. They sent the shipload of arms—all paid for at top prices in spot cash—but they did that more to please their American Ambassador (who thought an Irish rebellion would keep America out of the war) than from any hope of military gain.

Unfortunately for the organisers of revolt, a message they sent, asking for the date of arrival of the arms-ship to be postponed for three days, never reached Germany. It was picked up in a raid, by the U.S.A. authorities, on the office the German military attaché used for " under cover " operations—*meticulously filed for reference !* —and it was immediately communicated to the British Government. Consequently British destroyers were off the coast nicely in time for the *altered* date.

As it chanced, that three days' difference might have saved the situation, but, unluckily, the party despatched with signalling apparatus to give the indication where to land the arms, racing full speed for the rendezvous, failed in the darkness to make a right-angle turn at a critical moment. The car, with its occupants, raced straight on—*over the edge of a quay into deep water.*

The arms-ship arrived on time at the first-fixed date, and waited the stipulated three days for the signal which never came. Instead, British destroyers arrived, and the arms-ship had to be scuttled to avoid capture. Its cargo would have made all the difference.

CASEMENT was landed on the coast of Kerry, from a submarine, with two companions, while the arms-ship was off the coast. He fell into the hands of the police almost immediately. He had returned, determined to call off the Rising as hopeless ; and to ensure that end, and save bloodshed, he had communicated the news that a Rising was planned to the authorities.

Meanwhile, the nominal chief of the Volunteers, Prof. EOIN MACNEILL, had received the shock of his life. Members of his executive—CLARKE, PEARSE and MACDERMOTT—had informed him, politely, that a Rising would take place on Easter Sunday.

Since their formation, route-marches and field-exercises had formed a prominent part of the Volunteers' training. The authorities had thought it best not to interfere ; and police and public had grown so accustomed to them, that they took no alarm—not even when the Citizen Army staged a realistic " storming " of Dublin Castle, which only stopped short of actually crossing the wall, against which their scaling ladders were reared. For the Easter week-end, manœuvres had been planned on a " holiday " scale. All ranks had been ordered to supply themselves with three-days' rations.

To his horror, MacNeill learned that, instead of a holiday " camp-out", what was contemplated was— *the real thing.*

Why was he told ? Partly out of politeness ; and in case he might be willing to come into the plan. Chiefly because the conspirators thought it was too late for him to do anything about it. He beat them, there. The Sunday morning newspapers all carried an advertisement, signed by MacNeill as Chief of Staff, cancelling all manœuvres for Easter Sunday. Telegrams and messages had already been sent to the same effect.

Dublin Castle—whose heart had leaped into its mouth at Casement's news that a Rising was planned—breathed a deep sigh of relief. When nothing happened on Easter Sunday, it relaxed to enjoy a welcome Bank Holiday.

Easter Monday, Dublin, 1916

Brilliant sunshine flooded broad O'Connell Street.

Bank holiday crowds thronged thick around the tram terminus at the Nelson Pillar.

Out of Abbey Street marched a small contingent of armed men in uniform—most in the dark-green and slouched hats of the Citizen Army; some in the grey-green of the Irish Volunteers. The contingent crossed to the far side and wheeled right to continue towards the Pillar and the G.P.O.

Nobody gave them more than a glance. " Connolly's lot from Liberty Hall," said the holiday-makers. " What a crew ! " muttered an English officer, watching through the window of the G.P.O.

Ranging level with the front of the G.P.O., the column suddenly halted ; faced to the front ; fixed bayonets ; and, at the word of command,—*charged into the building.*

In a few seconds the public were hustled out, as the glass was dashed from the window frames. Then, as the staff crowded from a back-door, a party of officers advanced from the main front door, their leader bearing a sheet of paper.

Over the pediment of the façade broke three flags— Republican tri-colours (Green, White and Orange) on either side, and, in the centre, a large green banner inscribed in golden letters " *Poblacht na hEireann*".* The officer with the paper, PATRICK PEARSE, President of the Provisional Government, began to read :

> " Irishmen and Irishwomen :—In the name of God, and of the dead generations through whom she receives her old tradition of nationhood, Ireland, through us, summons her children to her flag, and strikes for her freedom . . ."

He read on. Those, near enough to hear, who were not too dazed to comprehend, noted a striking clause :

* *Poblacht na hEireann :* Republic of Ireland.

" We declare the right of the people of Ireland to the ownership of Ireland, and to the unfettered control of Irish destinies, to be sovereign and indefeasible. . . ."

And, after more sentences with a trumpet-like cadence, the conclusion :

" Signed, on behalf of the Provisional Government, THOMAS J. CLARKE, SEAN MAC DIARMADA, THOMAS MAC DONAGH, P. H. PEARSE, EAMONN CEANNT, JAMES CONNOLLY, JOSEPH PLUNKETT."

As the reading concluded, with a general cry of *God Save Ireland*, a crackle of musketry from across the river told that the Irish Republic had been proclaimed in arms as well as in words.

Looking up at the flags gleaming in the sunshine, James Connolly, with tears of joy in his eyes, clasped the hand of the no-less delighted veteran Tom Clarke, saying : *" Thanks be to God, Tom, that we have lived to see this day ! "*

CHAPTER THIRTY-ONE

THE EASTER-WEEK RISING

THE Rising took the authorities completely by surprise ; but they were able to crush it after a week's hard fighting. Executions followed, and wholesale deportations. Superficially the Rising was a complete failure ; but, in the end, PEARSE and CONNOLLY were vindicated. The fact that an IRISH REPUBLIC had been proclaimed in arms changed completely the whole subsequent history of Ireland.

The Battle for the Republic

All things considered, the Rising, regarded merely as a military operation, quite justified itself. Decided upon *impromptu*, after MacNeill's countermand order had wrecked the original scheme, the rebels, at first, mustered no more than 750 men. Of these 200 were Citizen Army men—virtually its whole available strength —and 50 were an unexpected addition from the *Hibernian Rifles*—a corps of members of the (American) A.O.H. During the week the rebels' numbers increased to a maximum of near 2,000. Small parties, from Meath, Kildare, and Kilkenny, made their way to Dublin in time to take part. There were authentic cases of Irish soldiers in the British Army, home on leave from France, who joined in the fighting (in plain clothes) and, after the surrender, resumed their uniforms and returned to France undetected. Seventy women and girls took part as typists, cooks, and nurses—some of them taking a hand in the shooting. Madame herself was second in command on St. Stephen's Green. The social composition of the rebel force gave ample evidence of a deep-rooted popular readiness to join an insurrection even at a moment's notice.

z

The tactical plan—to hold a roughly circular area enclosing Dublin Castle—was sound enough; or would have been, if their numbers had been sufficient. Lack of numbers, and confusion, caused the two major faults of execution—the failure to immobilise the telephone exchange, and the failure to capture Dublin Castle by a surprise rush at the outset. Misjudgment—a belief that the authorities would shrink from using artillery in a crowded city—had caused the headquarters to be fixed in the G.P.O., where they were exposed to shell-fire from a gun-boat on the Liffey. (The shells were " lobbed " with great skill over the railway-bridge and the house-roofs intervening.)

By Friday night, JAMES CONNOLLY, who acted as military commander, was dangerously wounded in two places; and the G.P.O., fired by incendiary shells, was too well-alight to be tenable. Each of the strong-points in the circle had been surrounded. On Saturday afternoon PEARSE surrendered. During the Sunday, the Commandants at the other strong posts surrendered also. Isolated parties, and snipers, held out till the Thursday following.

In a few places in the provinces, also, risings took place. LIAM MELLOWS, in Galway, took Athenry; and was preparing an attack on Galway City when priests intervened and persuaded his men to disperse. In Co. Dublin one police party was ambushed, and the victors, led by THOMAS ASHE, captured another party at Ashbourne, in Meath. The Wexford men rose out, and were encamped strongly on Vinegar Hill, when the news of the surrender induced them to give up the struggle also.

Casualties were estimated at something over three thousand. Of these, fifty-six were Volunteers killed in action. The casualties on the British side included 130 killed, of whom *six were Redmond Volunteers.*

The Blood-Fury of the Reactionaries

The ugliest incident was the quite unauthorised
" execution " (while the Rising was still in progress)
of FRANCIS SHEEHY SKEFFINGTON, Ireland's leading
Socialist-pacifist. He and two editors (of the *Searchlight*
and the *Toiler* respectively) were shot, in the Portobello
barracks, at the order of an officer afterwards pronounced
insane. That it was " insane " to shoot a pacifist, and
two editors whose journals—the one a simple scandal-
sheet, the other an *anti*-Trade-Union rag*—were each
upholders of the Castle, is true. But the " insane "
Captain's attitude towards Irish rebels and Socialists—
the shoot-at-sight attitude—was exactly in line with the
customary thinking and talk of the Blimps and Die-hards
who had pulled the wires of the Carsonite conspiracy.
He was " insane " in the sense of being feeble-minded
enough to take this talk at its face-value, and act accordingly.

This was shown as soon as the rebellion was over.
English officers, being gentlemen, " wondered how
many marks Pearse had in his pocket when he surrendered ". The ignorant identification of the rebellion
with *Sinn Fein* enabled the authorities to make a great
show, and arrest everybody who had ever been prominent in that party. It had the advantage, too, of saving
the English authorities from having to confess that the
" Fenians "—whom Englishmen had supposed all dead
and buried years before—had come to life in sufficient
strength to put up the best fight for Ireland since '98.

Redmond, in the House, expressed " horror and
detestation " at the Rising. Redmondite County and
Town Councils followed suit. SIR JOHN MAXWELL,
governing Ireland under martial law, ordered a trench

* The *Toiler* was subsidised by the employers to injure Larkin and the Transport Union. One of its specialities was an endeavour to " prove " by faked
photos, etc. that Larkin was an illegitimate son of Carey, the " Invincible "
leader who turned informer.

to be dug *big enough for a hundred bodies;* and set his courts-martial to work.

On May 3rd, three of the Seven signatories to the proclamation were shot: THOMAS JAMES CLARKE, PATRICK PEARSE, and THOMAS MACDONAGH. One signatory—JOSEPH PLUNKETT—and four less-known men—EDWARD DALY, MICHAEL O'HANRAHAN, and WILLIAM PEARSE—were shot on May 4th. Next day only one was shot, Major JOHN MACBRIDE (who had fought for the Boers, and knew nothing of the rising until after it had started, when he joined at once). On May 8th, another signatory, EAMONN CEANNT and three others, MICHAEL MALLIN, CON COLBERT, and SEAN HEUSTON. Then next day, THOMAS KENT, a Corkman, who, with his brother, had resisted arrest and killed a policeman, after his brother had been killed, was shot in Cork.

It looked as if the killing in cold blood would go on interminably. It was rumoured that *ninety* prisoners whose sentences only awaited confirmation had been condemned to death. Irishmen, and others, did not fail to note that the War Cabinet which confirmed the sentences included EDWARD CARSON, and his Tory abettor, BONAR LAW.

The *Manchester Guardian* said bluntly: the executions are " becoming an atrocity ". BERNARD SHAW, prophesying that the men executed would take their place beside *Emmet* and the *Manchester Martyrs,* protested:

" I am bound to contradict any implication that I can regard as a traitor any Irishman taken in a fight for Irish Independence against the British Government, which was a fair fight in everything except the enormous odds my countrymen had to face."

LAURENCE GINNELL, M.P. for Westmeath, screamed " Murder " across the House, as Asquith read the list of the executed. JOHN DILLON who had been marooned in his Dublin home by the rising, rose, semi-hysterical, to add his protest. Asquith replied tartly, that the rank and file could be spared, but the instigators could expect no mercy. The words were ominous. Two of the seven remained, CONNOLLY and MACDERMOTT. They were duly executed on May 12th. Neither could walk to the execution post. MacDermott was crippled by rheumatoid-arthritis; Connolly had had a foot amputated, and was too weak from loss of blood to stand. He was shot seated in a chair. Reactions in Ireland had, at first, been sharply divided. The Redmondites, trained in the O'Connell doctrine of the sinfulness of armed insurrection, were, at first, loud in condemnation. Murphy's *Independent* was so bitter that he was accused of using a public occasion to gratify his private spite against Connolly and the Transport Union. He denied this; but another of his journals, the *Irish Catholic*, was even worse. Before any executions (April 29th), it said:

" The movement . . . was as *criminal* as insane."

After Pearse's execution, it said :

" Pearse was a man of ill-balanced mind, if not actually insane . . . selecting him as chief magistrate was enough to create serious doubt of the sanity of those who approved . . . crazy and insolent schoolmaster . . . extraordinary combination of rogues and fools . . ."

And after Connolly had been shot :

" What was attempted was an act of brigandage pure and simple . . . no reason to lament that its perpetrators have met the fate . . . *universally reserved for traitors*."

This was not the unanimous opinion among the Hierarchy. Dr. O'DWYER, Catholic Bishop of Limerick, was reputed to be pro-British. Possibly for this reason, Sir John Maxwell requested him to silence certain priests in his diocese who had shown sympathy for the

Rebellion. Dr. O'Dwyer (May 17th) refused flatly; and told Maxwell his conduct was " wantonly cruel and oppressive". He went on :

> " You took care that no plea for mercy should interpose on behalf of the poor young fellows who surrendered to you in Dublin. The first intimation we got of their fate was the announcement that they had been shot in cold blood. Personally I regard *your* action with horror ; and I believe that it has outraged the conscience of the country."

Dr. O'Dwyer was right ; the conscience of the country was outraged, and in England as well as Ireland. But nothing could save CASEMENT who was hanged in Pentonville, August 3rd. It added to the indecency that the Attorney-General who led for the prosecution was F. E. SMITH, who had been Carson's " Galloper," and was afterwards to become Lord Chancellor.

Judgments on the Rising

The English Labour Movement had been, and was, sympathetic to Home Rule. Its orthodox upper-strata was, then, co-operating cordially in the prosecution of the war. It easily took the view of the Redmondites— that the Rebellion had been totally unrepresentative of the main body of Irish opinion.

The anti-war Socialists, to the Left of the Labour Party, were, most of them, either bewildered or condemnatory. RAMSAY MACDONALD advanced the opinion that the Rising was as " militaristic " as the Government it thought to overthrow. The unofficial (Glasgow) Left-wing frankly could not understand how a *Socialist*, like Connolly, could have got mixed up in a *Nationalist* rising. Unable to pass the crux that " a man must be *either* a Nationalist, *or* an Internationalist", the editor of the Glasgow *Forward* had to confess—" it remains a mystery".

It was no mystery to the small group of militant

Marxists whom Connolly had helped to train. They had accepted Connolly's doctrine that Internationalism is not the *negation* of Nationalism ; and least of all when the Nationalism is that of a subject people. And they had—though none of them knew it—a mighty ally in—LENIN.

To those who sought to belittle the Easter Rising as a mere " push ", he replied that this was " monstrously pedantic " :

> " To imagine that a social revolution is conceivable without revolts of small nations in the Colonies and in Europe, without outbursts from a section of the petit-bourgeois, *with all its prejudices*—without the movement of the non-class-conscious proletarian and semi-proletarian masses against the oppression of the landlords, the church, the monarchy, the foreign yoke, etc.—to imagine that is tantamount to *repudiating social revolution*.

> " The misfortune of the Irish is that they rose prematurely, when the European revolt of the proletariat had not yet matured. Capitalism is not so harmoniously built that the various springs of rebellion can immediately merge into one, of their own accord, without reverses, and defeats."—
LENIN : *Selected Works*, Vol. V., pp. 301-306.

Connolly's vindication came when, nine months after his death, Tsardom fell ; and when, nine months after that, the Red Flag flew, triumphant, over the Kremlin.

CHAPTER THIRTY-TWO

THE TRANSITION TO A NEW CRISIS

AT the outbreak of war, in 1914, public opinion in Nationalist Ireland had been—on the surface—overwhelmingly on the side of the Redmondite Nationalist Party, and in sympathy with England in its war difficulty. How greatly that public opinion had been changed was revealed in the election which immediately followed the war, in December, 1918. In that election *the Nationalist Party was virtually wiped out.*

The process of that immense turn-over of public opinion is examined in this chapter.

The British Government and Ireland

It is often said that if the British Government had shown clemency to the leaders of the EASTER-WEEK RISING, subsequent events might (and would) have been radically different. To say this is to miss a great truth and, in addition, to make a false assumption.

The false assumption is that the Government in 1916 was still the Government which had forced the Home Rule Act to the stage of Royal Assent, over the heads of the House of Lords ; and had done so despite the threats of the Tory-Orange counter-revolutionary conspiracy. It was nothing of the kind. The counter-revolutionary conspirators had taken advantage of the war emergency to force their way into the Government on their own terms ; and, as events proved, LLOYD-GEORGE and his Radical followers had capitulated to them from (a) fear of socialism ; and (b) traditional Nonconformist dislike of " Papistry". Between them they had evolved the device which would enable them to pretend that they had " conceded " Home Rule, while in reality they were conceding nothing : the device of PARTITION.

But for the war-begotten need to conciliate the U.S.A., the repression after Easter Week would have been bloodier than it was, and Home Rule would never-more have been heard of. The sense of this radical reorientation of the English Government, coupled with a feeling that the Redmondite Party was either a con-senting-party to the re-orientation, or too stupid to notice it, went a long way towards effecting the revulsion of public opinion in Ireland. The treatment of the prisoners ; the war-time censorship ; and finally the attempt to impose Conscription in 1918 were all so many confirmations of the fact that the English Govern-ment had become essentially *counter-revolutionary*, and prepared for a fresh conquest of Ireland.

The Fenian Dead

The " great truth " that is missed in the view we are combating, is that the *normal* demand of the Irish Nation is, and has been since TONE and the UNITED IRISHMEN, the demand for complete INDEPENDENCE. Irishmen have not always been conscious of this ; and they have for long periods been willing to confine their demands within the limits of a constitutional demand for " Repeal " or " Home Rule". But, instinctively, the mass of Irishmen have valued these things because, and so far as, they saw in them means of approximating nearer towards the INDEPENDENCE they felt, intuitively, to be the only normal status for an IRISH NATION.

That is why the popular heroes of Ireland—especially among the young—have always been " the men who fought, and died for Ireland". PATRICK PEARSE expressed this truth in his speech over the grave of *O'Donovan Rossa* in the middle of 1915 :

"I hold it a Christian thing, as O'Donovan Rossa held it, to hate evil, to hate untruth, to hate oppression, and hating them, to strive to overthrow them. Our foes are strong, and wise, and wary ; but . . . they cannot undo the miracles of God who ripens in the heart of the young men the seeds sown by the young men of a former generation. And the seeds sown by the men of '65 and '67 are coming to their miraculous ripening to-day.

" Rulers and Defenders of the Realm had need to be wary if they would guard against such pro- cesses. Life springs from death and from the graves of patriot men and women spring nations.

" The Defenders of the Realm have worked well in secret and in the open. They think they have pacified Ireland. They think they have purchased half of us and intimidated the other half. They think they have foreseen everything, think they have provided against everything ; but—the fools! the fools ! *the fools!*

" *They have left us our Fenian dead, and while Ireland holds these graves, Ireland, unfree, shall never be at peace* ! "

And Pearse's true words gained added truth and additional point when his name, also, with that of his colleagues, was added to the list of the FENIAN DEAD.

The Emergence of a New Party

The English Authorities aided the elimination of the Parliamentary Party by the wholesale character of its arrests and deportations after the Rising. Whether they herded them as " convicted prisoners " in gaols, or as unconvicted prisoners in concentration camps, the result was the same. The inspiration of a bravely- fought battle nerved the prisoners to struggle un- flinchingly against every attempt to treat them with humiliation. Struggle begot solidarity, which found expression in organisation. The gaols and the concen- tration camps were so many training schools for a new party : and when the untried prisoners were released, at Christmas, 1916, they dispersed to their homes in every part of Ireland, *convinced Republicans*, eager to be at work building local organisations for a new uprising.

Six months later, in compliance with American opinion, which it was now imperative to placate, the convicted prisoners were released also—to be received with demonstrations of frantic enthusiasm by the people, who now realised that it was the MEN OF EASTER WEEK and not their Parliamentarian enemies who had truly represented the will and interest of Ireland.

The men first released at once set to work to build an organisation. A Prisoners' Aid Society was a good beginning : the Gaelic League branches were good rallying centres for a start. The Volunteers began to re-form, and *to parade in uniform*—but armed only with hurleys and sticks—in spite of proclamations and arrests. The convicted prisoners were in great demand, after their release, as speakers at meetings and demonstrations. Soon the English authorities were at work arresting speakers for " creating disaffection " and Volunteers for " illegal drilling".

The new mood of the Nation showed itself in the attitude of the arrested men. They refused to recognise the jurisdiction of the court ; and, in gaol, demanded the treatment of political prisoners, answering refusal with hunger-strike. The death of one of these prisoners, THOMAS ASHE (distinguished in Easter Week) evoked great indignation ; and brought an immense concourse to his funeral, which was made a military one.

Three volleys were fired over the grave. MICHAEL COLLINS (now the leader of the revived and powerful I.R.B.) said shortly :

> " Those volleys we have just heard are the only speech it is fitting to make above the grave of a dead Fenian."

Bowing to the inevitable, the authorities conceded
" political " status to the prisoners. Still the struggle
went on. Since the English insisted upon calling the
Republicans " *Sinn Feiners* " they accepted the hint and
revived the *Sinn Fein* party ; but with an entirely new
constitution and programme. DE VALERA, the only
surviving Commandant of Easter Week, was elected
its President at the Annual Convention in October,
1917, ARTHUR GRIFFITH accepting the position of
Vice-President. New ground was broken by (*a*) the
decision to maintain the Volunteers ; (*b*) by the tacit
adoption of a Republican standpoint, and (*c*) by the
tacit decision that the Volunteers would resist forcibly
any attempt to impose conscription. The hegemony
of the new *Sinn Fein* Executive, as virtually the Government of the Irish Nation, was recognised by the Gaelic
League, and by all the other Irish National organisations.

Lloyd George's Circus

All this time a " Convention", arranged by Lloyd
George (then the Premier) and composed of hand-
picked politicians and prelates, was meeting in Dublin
to attempt to reach an agreed modification of the Home
Rule Act which had been hung up " for the duration".
It was clear, from the start, that the Convention would
never be allowed to reach any conclusion but one—a
sharply restricted form of Home Rule, for the *twenty-six
counties only*. Redmond himself was repudiated by the
Parliamentary Party delegation when he proposed a
compromise which might have averted partition.

Worn down by illness, disappointment, and grief
at the loss of his son and his brother (both killed in
France), Redmond withdrew, cut to the heart—only
to die ten days later.

The Convention at last presented a " majority "
report qualified by no fewer than seven minority reports.

Lloyd George hailed the result with delight—since it " proved " to his satisfaction that " the Irish can't ever agree ! "

The Resistance to Conscription

Lloyd George discovered that the Irish could agree most notably, when, in the middle of 1918, he attempted to impose conscription in Ireland. Beaten in the House on this issue, the Parliamentary Party decided to " go Sinn Fein "—and left Westminster in a body.

A conference met at the Mansion House, Dublin, attended by representatives of Sinn Fein, Labour, the Nationalist Party, and the (Healy-O'Brien) " All for Ireland " Party, and the delegates adopted *unanimously* a pledge to join in common action against conscription. The Hierarchy, and the College of Maynooth, concurred with the decision.

Thus Lloyd George's design (which was to smash up the reviving Volunteers) did more than fail : it *united all sections of Nationalist Ireland in resistance.*

Lloyd George fell back upon the trick of " discovering " a German plot. All the leaders of Sinn Fein who could be picked up were hustled into gaol on a charge of " associating with the enemy". The warrant for the arrest of MICHAEL COLLINS could not be served. He had begun his " life on the run " which was to last till the Truce of 1921.

Labour showed its determination, and power, by calling a one-day General Strike, which was observed with scrupulous fidelity everywhere in Ireland outside the Six Counties. COLLINS set to work to build a GENERAL STAFF which would direct the resistance of the Volunteers to every attempt to conscript or disarm them. Whatever the reason, the attempt to impose conscription was delayed, on various pretexts, until the ending of the war made it unnecessary.

The General Election of 1918

A number of by-elections, since Easter Week, might have been taken as a warning of what was coming ; they were, however, treated as " wartime " elections which " prove nothing". COUNT PLUNKETT (a man of inchoate views, but the father of one of the Seven of Easter Week) was elected for North Roscommon in a three-cornered contest. JOE MACGUINNESS (then in gaol) was elected for Longford. A much sharper test was the election, for Clare, to fill the vacancy created by the death of W. E. REDMOND. DE VALERA (sentenced for life) was elected by a two-to-one majority. W. T. COSGRAVE (an Easter-Week man, then in gaol) was elected for Kilkenny. The Parliamentary Party went to the polls in December, 1918, tensed for the fight of its life.

Twenty-five seats were surrendered to the Republicans without a struggle : TIM HEALY and WILLIAM O'BRIEN being among those who surrendered. The rest went down like corn before the sickle. JOHN DILLON, the new Party leader, went down before a two-to-one majority in Mayo, his home county, which he had represented without a break since 1880. In the end, of the 83 seats they had held in 1914, the Party retained 7 ; and one of these was in England—and four of these seats, located in Ulster, they owed, in part, to an electoral agreement with *Sinn Fein.* In the twenty-six counties they won only Waterford, where John Redmond's son was elected to succeed his father. Two (new seats) were won by the Tories. The rest were unbroken *Sinn Fein* (that is, *Republican*).

It was noted that amid the yells of " Up the Rebels!" " Up *Sinn Fein!*" and " Up the Republic ! " that greeted the results, there were also cries of " *Remember Parnell!*"

English journalists, when Parliament met, noted with a pang that the benches below the gangway on the opposition side, which had been the " Irish Quarter ' since 1885, were now occupied by an overflow of the Tories unable to find room on the Government benches.

It was a *Nemesis* without equal in the whole history of parliamentary elections.

CHAPTER THIRTY-THREE

ANGLO-IRISH WAR AND THE TREATY

THE Republicans, elected in 1918, met in Dublin and constituted themselves the GOVERNING BODY of " *the Republic established in Easter Week*". From this gesture arose an ANGLO-IRISH WAR—fought with intense savagery from the English side, and stubborn bitterness from the Irish side. A TRUCE (July, 1921), followed by a TREATY (December, 1921), ended one war—but opened another between the acceptors and the rejectors of the Treaty.

In this Chapter we trace summarily the salient aspects of this struggle.*

Dáil Eireann

The completeness of the Republican victory at the polls was greater even than it seemed. Every endeavour had been made by the English authorities to prevent it. Election meetings were prohibited ; election agents and speakers were arrested ; election addresses were censored or suppressed ; election literature was confiscated. Warnings against electing *Sinn Fein* candidates were posted, and scattered from aeroplanes. Of the 73 Republicans elected, 36 were in gaol, and a score were either " on the run " or in the U.S.A. evading arrest. In these circumstances, to poll two-thirds of all the voters in Ireland for Republican candidates was doubly decisive.

Those of the elected who were at liberty decided to convoke an IRISH NATIONAL ASSEMBLY. Everyone

---

* In this work it is not possible to do more than summarise very broadly. The reader can find all the details, and all the relevant documents, set out clearly in DOROTHY MACARDLE's excellent work " *The Irish Republic* ".

elected in Ireland in 1918 was invited regardless of
Party. Only Republicans responded ; and the twenty-
seven of them who were available met in the Mansion
House, Dublin, on January 21st, 1919, and constituted
themselves DÀIL EIREANN (the " Assembly of Ireland ").
A declaration was adopted affirming : That Ireland is
" a sovereign and independent nation " ; that a Republic
(*Sáorstat Eireann*) had been established in Easter Week,
1916, of which the *Dáil* constituted itself the heir and
continuation. The *Dáil* adopted a " Democratic Programme", which showed profoundly the influence of
Connolly and Pearse, and which some members, later,
found " communistic".

An Acting President was appointed (CATHAL BRUGHA)
who had power to appoint ministers—it being understood that the post of President was left open for EAMON
DE VALERA, then in gaol. (His escape was being
contrived at that moment by MICHAEL COLLINS.) On
March 5th, all prisoners and internees were released.

The situation then was that there were two
" Government " Authorities in Ireland : one, *Dáil
Eireann*, backed by the moral authority of a majority
of the people, the other that of *the English Authorities*,
operating from Dublin Castle, who possessed the
physical force (police, constabulary, army and navy) to
impose their decrees. The struggle that ensued was,
therefore, in essence, an attempt by the English authorities, through their armed forces, to coerce the Irish
people into withdrawing the moral authority they had
given to *Dáil Eireann*. Subsequent electoral tests marked
the result of their efforts.

In municipal elections (January, 1920), out of 126
town and city councils, 72 went to Republicans, 26 to a
Republican-Nationalist coalition, and 29 only to the
" English " (Unionists). In elections (June, 1920) for
County and Rural District Councils, and Guardians,
28 counties out of 33, 182 Rural Districts out of 206,

and 138 Boards of Guardians out of 154 returned Republican majorities.

At a General Election in May, 1921, (of which mention will be made later), there were elected in the Twenty-Six Counties 124 Republicans and 4 Unionists; in the Six Counties, in this same election, there were elected 6 Republicans, 6 Nationalists, and 40 Unionists. This gave an All-Ireland total of 130 Republicans, 6 Nationalists, and 44 Unionists.

Tried by the electoral test, the Irish people gave their choice to the Republic persistently, and refused it to the English authorities. This was all the more emphatic because, from the middle of 1919 onwards to July, 1921, a ferocious war between the forces of the Crown and those of the Republic reduced all Ireland to a chaos.

The War with the Army

The first phase of this war was an attempt by the British to prevent the *Dáil* from establishing any machinery of Government. The *Dáil* itself, and all its subsidiaries—including a system of arbitration courts it was able to establish in nearly every county in Ireland —were proclaimed " illegal assemblies ". The Loan, called for by the *Dáil*, was treated as " seditious ". Newspapers which published advertisements of the Loan were suppressed ; it was an offence to possess or distribute any literature connected therewith ; and every endeavour was made to locate the places (and names) in which the (much-over-subscribed) Loan was banked. Virtually everybody, of any prominence in the Republican movement, lived, in this period, either " on the run " or in prison.

" Military " operations on the Republican side grew out of this constant harrying and pursuit of Republicans. To achieve their end the English authorities needed an elaborate apparatus of spies, informers, and " intelligence officers ". The backbone of this force was supplied by

the R.I.C., which, in the rural areas, knew everybody
and everything that was going on. In addition the
Authorities had their usual fringe of slum elements at
the bottom and English officers at the top.

To meet, check, and, finally, to defeat this force was
the work undertaken by MICHAEL COLLINS as Director
of Intelligence, operating with a force of specially-
selected Volunteers as a striking arm, and a network
of counter-espionage agents which grew to be as
numerous and as ramified as that of the English. The
" execution " of key men in the English espionage
service aroused intense fury among counter-
revolutionary English politicians, and their press. It
was justified by Collins on the ground that, while the
English could replace their soldiers almost interminably,
these key men, with their exceptional knowledge, and
their ability to identify particular individuals, could not
be replaced. In the end COLLINS succeeded in paralysing
the whole English intelligence service in Ireland.

Concurrently with the War of the contending Intelligence Services, the Volunteers developed a series of
raids for arms on isolated police-posts, stores, etc., out
of which developed a succession of fiercely-fought
battles. In this struggle it soon became apparent that
the Volunteers—who, from early in 1919, came to be
known as the " Army of the Irish Republic " ; or,
popularly, the I.R.A.—had the support of the people,
man, woman and child. The I.R.A., when hard-
pressed, could always rely upon assistance ; the R.I.C.,
and the military, could always expect obstruction. This
passive, social pressure produced the result of wholesale
resignations from the R.I.C. ; and this, in turn, produced
a corresponding diminution in the effectiveness of the
Crown forces. Troops from England, ignorant of the
country, and totally unacquainted with the people,
were no substitute for men who knew every path and
track, and every individual, for twenty miles around

As their sense of impotence grew, the troops degenerated into an undisciplined *banditti* of alien invaders ;
bent, perpetually, upon loot and reprisals.

The Black-and-Tans

This led (January, 1920) to the imposition of a
CURFEW ORDER in the towns, and the official adoption
of a policy of terrorism, operated (from March, 1920)
by the " BLACK-AND-TANS " and " AUXILIARIES ".

Those were both officially off-shoots of the R.I.C.
The first was a special grade of temporary constables,
recruited mostly in England, and chosen for preference
from the " tough " class. A criminal record was a
recommendation ;   men imprisoned for crimes of
violence had their sentences remitted if they volunteered
for service in the " specials ". They were paid 10s.
a day (with separation allowance) and all found.

The Auxiliaries were " Cadets " recruited from
ex-officers in the Army, Navy and Air Force. They
operated as a separate force of " shock troops ".   Indi-
vidually, they ranked as the equal of senior-sergeants
in the R.I.C. ;   their pay, rations and allowances were
double those of the specials—who came to be called
" Black-and-Tans " because of the haphazard mixture
of English khaki and R.I.C. black in their uniforms
and equipment.

The political significance of the institution of this
" *Black-and-Tan* " force—which term came to include,
in practice, the " Auxies " also, and which, it will be
noted, had exactly the same social composition as that
of the S.A. and the S.S. force of Nazi-terrorism, and
that of Mussolini's *fasci*—was that, for diplomatic
reasons, Lloyd George and his counter-revolutionary
backers found it imperative to pretend that nothing
was called for in Ireland beyond " police measures ".
To have agreed with the demand of the military commanders to proclaim MARTIAL LAW would have been

an admission that Ireland was in *general revolt* ; and that,
therefore, the real position of the English authorities
was that of an enemy invader in hostile occupation.
The BLACK-AND-TANS were, deliberately, a "fascist"
device—which Mussolini, Hitler and others copied—
to conceal the fact that, *morally, the English invaders were
back where they had been in* 1169.

The struggle that developed shocked the English
people profoundly, and revolted the whole world.
Murder, arson, torture of prisoners, rape, and the
systematic beating-up and looting of whole areas
developed into a routine of monotonous horror. The
I.R.A. fought back with increasing resolution ; and,
in the struggle, developed into a force which became
able to meet, and defeat, parties of Black-and-Tans and
Auxies on equal terms. The primary I.R.A. tactic was
that of *the ambush* ; to which the "Tans" replied by
beating-up, looting and destroying the habitations in
the area where the ambush occurred. This, in course,
drove more recruits to the I.R.A. ; and so the struggle
developed. The work done by LIAM MELLOWS, as
Director of Purchases, in supplying the I.R.A. with
arms—purchased abroad and smuggled into Ireland—
was an invaluable contribution to the Republican war-
effort.

As the R.I.C. dwindled, it retreated from the outlying
districts. In these areas, Republican Courts were
established, whose decisions were accepted by the
people. Order was maintained in these areas, and
punishments imposed by the Courts were enforced by
the *Republican police* (I.R.A. men detailed for this duty).
These proofs of the impotence of the English authorities,
and the popular acceptance of the authority of the *Dáil*,
reported in the press of the world, roused the counter-
revolutionaries to fury. Into those areas advanced
flying-squads of Black-and-Tans, in armoured cars,
resolved to loot, burn, smash, destroy, arrest and kill.

If they were resisted—or, more usually, were ambushed on their way back—more flying squads repeated the performance, with similar results.

The Black-and-Tans had all retreated to barracks in the bigger towns—from which they emerged only at the risk of attack and ambush in open day—and the gaols were crammed with prisoners arrested for conducting Republican Courts, or simply on suspicion, when (on July 11th, 1921) a TRUCE was agreed upon by LLOYD GEORGE and EAMON DE VALERA, as a preliminary to negotiations for a TREATY.

While the TAN-WAR raged, two events of great political significance occurred : (1) A *Government of Ireland Act* (December, 1920) ; and (2) *Organised pogroms in Belfast*.

The Government of Ireland Act (1920).

Faced with multiplying political difficulties on every side, LLOYD GEORGE, in 1920, made a gesture towards settling the *Irish Question* by introducing the long-deferred *amendment* of the Home Rule Act (1914). This GOVERNMENT OF IRELAND ACT (1920) represented a compromise which the " Ulster " representatives accepted with reluctance. It conceded a measure of Home Rule to the Twenty-Six Counties (called " Southern Ireland ") and imposed another measure of Home Rule on the Six Counties (called " Northern Ireland "). The die-hards who wanted no Home Rule at all accepted the compromise only because they calculated it would make Home Rule unworkable in the Twenty-Six Counties, by restricting their economic and fiscal resources to an almost exclusively agricultural region.

The Act included a provision that the two parliaments might, if they chose, set up an All-Ireland Council to which each might concede powers of common concern. In this way they could achieve a reunited Ireland. This was merely eye-wash for Americans, English

Labour Party men, and other political innocents, who did not know (as Lloyd George did) that the faction dominant in the Six Counties would never consent to any such reunion, since they had a vested interest in Ireland's *unsettlement.*

Dáil Eireann, as such, took no notice of the Act. But the *Sinn Fein* Party resolved to use the elections as a *demonstration of national unity.* The result was that the only non-Republican candidates elected were the four allotted to Trinity College. No contests took place. No one would accept nomination against a Republican.

The Belfast Pogroms

As a running-commentary upon the Tan-War and Lloyd George's manœuvres with the Government of Ireland Act, Belfast staged A SERIES OF POGROMS, aimed at driving the Catholics out of the industrial area completely. Their opening (July 21st, 1920) coincided with the introduction of the Black-and-Tan Terror; and they had been preceded by inflammatory propaganda meetings, in which it was suggested that the Catholics were " creeping-in", and " were taking away the jobs of Protestants". The beginning of the post-war unemployment crisis gave point to the oratory; and there is no reason to doubt that what followed was *organised,* as well as deliberately incited.

A corps similar to the " Black-and-Tans " had been recruited as " occasional special Constables " by the Six-County Government, and members of this corps, recruited from the hooligan *element in Belfast,* were in the front of the mobs which, carrying Union Jacks, attacked the Catholic quarter—looting and burning down the shops and houses of Catholics. Every Catholic was driven from the shipyards; every Catholic worker from the factories where " Protestants " predominated. Any attempt at self-defence was crushed with stones, bludgeons, and revolver or rifle-fire. Only after four days did the military interfere. Twenty-two civilians were killed, and 188 were known to be severely wounded.

The *pogrom* extended to Lisburn on August 23rd-24th ; forty Catholic houses and shops were destroyed. Then the *pogrom* was renewed in Belfast, August 28th-September 1st, and similar barbarities were enacted. Apart from scores of killed, and hundreds of wounded, 9,000 were driven from their employment, 30,000 were rendered destitute, and thousands were rendered homeless into the bargain.

Carson's cynical comment virtually admitted Orange-Tory complicity in the *pogrom*. He said that the Catholics " had only to take an oath of allegiance to the King, and pledge their loyalty to the Empire, and the trouble would cease instantly". Which means, if it means anything, that the Belfast Catholics were *to be used as hostages* in the war for the new English conquest of Ireland.

The resignation of 148 Irish magistrates ; mutinies in the police force, and of three hundred men of the Connaught Rangers in India—these were eloquent, practical comments on the policy pursued in Ireland.

The *pogroms* broke out again in Belfast in June, 1921, after the elections to the Northern Ireland Parliament ; in which, as an Ulster-Tory M.P. said, " too many *Sinn Fein* votes were cast". The riots were *almost entirely the work of Special Constables.* A score of Catholics were killed, and another 150 families were rendered homeless.

These atrocities, and the steadfast solidarity in the face of every barbarity of the Nationalist population of Ireland, had a profound effect upon democratic opinion in England as well as throughout the world.

The Truce and Negotiations

The TRUCE of July, 1921, and the protracted negotiations which followed, were forced upon both sides by material and moral circumstances. On the Irish side the chief difficulty was the economic chaos into which the country had been thrown by the ravages of the Black-and-Tans, and by the stubborn resistance of the Irish railwaymen and transport workers—who persistently refused to transport troops or war materials. A virtual cessation of railway traffic had resulted; and as, in the course of their defensive operations, the I.R.A. had blown up any number of bridges, and—by trenches and mines—had made the main roads impassable in large areas, the result was a chaos which could not possibly be endured for long.

In addition, the I.R.A. had, virtually, exhausted their supplies of ammunition. They had never been able to put more than 2,000 men in the field at any one time—though they had more than twenty times that number of men to draw upon. Now it was growing difficult to maintain in the field even so few as 2,000.

On the English side a rapidly-intensifying demand for a Truce and a Treaty arose from every democratic quarter, the Communist Party being most active. The Labour Party and Trade Union rank and file joined with the Communist Party and the exiles' organisation—the Irish Self-Determination League—to force the hands of their party chiefs; and they, in turn, brought pressure to bear upon the Government. In addition, a number of General officers, of high rank, had refused to lend themselves any longer to what was being done in Ireland.

General CROZIER, appointed to command the "Auxies", found to his disgust that his attempt to impose a decent, soldierly behaviour on the force was constantly thwarted from "higher up" (i.e. Dublin Castle). Prisoners were tortured and murdered in Dublin Castle itself. A Galway priest—who had been invited to America to give evidence of an attempt by the Auxies to make a raping assault upon a nunnery—

was murdered by the Auxies and his body was thrown
into a bog. A plot was on foot to murder the Catholic
Bishop of Killaloe. And all General Crozier's enquiries
into those responsible for those deeds were blocked by
the "men higher up". When he found that twenty-
five Cadets—whom he had dismissed the force for
looting—had *all been reinstated*, to "keep their mouths
shut", General CROZIER resigned and could not be
persuaded to retract his resignation. Then General
MACREADY, Commander-in-Chief in Ireland, reported,
in May, 1921, that nothing less than Martial Law over
the whole Twenty-Six Counties, with suppression of
Civil Courts and all newspapers, and the commandeering
of all transport would be effective. To do that would
require, he said, a new army and the replacement of
nearly the whole of the troops, commanders and staffs.

For the English Government this was an impossible
situation. Economic obligation compelled them to bow
to public opinion in the U.S.A. and in the Dominions,
and in each case this public opinion was largely swayed
by the Irish-exile element in the population. Political
insecurity compelled them to take notice of public
opinion in England, which—under pressure of world
chaos and the economic crisis—was rapidly polarising
into two great camps of revolution and counter-
revolution. An attempt to raise an army openly for a
military conquest of Ireland would have immediately
precipitated a crisis by ruining England's financial credit
in the U.S.A. and the Dominions.

Negotiations were, therefore, opened up with
DE VALERA and *Dáil Eireann*, and, later, with the pleni-
potentiaries of the Irish Republic, headed by ARTHUR
GRIFFITH and MICHAEL COLLINS (for whose arrest a
reward of £10,000 had been on offer for months).
Negotiations were prolonged until December 6th, 1921,
when a TREATY was signed by the representatives on
both sides.

The Treaty of 1921-22

What went on behind the scenes of the Treaty negotiations is not known. There are indications that, at first, LLOYD GEORGE and certain leading English Tories were ready to concede all Ireland a " Dominion " status from which the Six Counties, or some portion thereof, might exclude themselves if they wished. There are indications that this attitude was modified, under pressure from the counter-revolutionary faction in the Tory ranks—which represented the more aggressive elements of the Finance-Capitalist oligarchy which had taken alarm from the Bolshevik Revolution; and which was, even then, preparing to crush the forces of the organised workers in England. This faction (which later on brushed aside both LLOYD GEORGE, and the " moderate " BONAR LAW, to rule through STANLEY BALDWIN and NEVILLE CHAMBERLAIN) saw in open war in Ireland, and the raising of an army for that war, their best chance to pull off the *coup d'état* they were resolved upon. Consequently the Irish representatives were presented with an ultimatum of accepting the Treaty offered or—unlimited war *within three days*. The delegation reluctantly gave way.

The Treaty conceded virtually-complete self-government to the Twenty-Six Counties immediately ; with the handing over of Dublin Castle, and the withdrawal of all British troops, police and officials. It gave the Six Counties an option of coming into this arrangement, but did not insist upon their doing so. It did insist upon an Oath of Allegiance (to the King and Empire) to be taken by the Members of Parliament and officials of *Saorstát Eireann** and as a concession included a clause providing for the revision of the " boundary "

---

* *Saorstát Eireann :* This was the translation of the term " Irish Republic " preferred by the best Gaelic scholars. Lloyd George accepted its literal translation but not its original implication. It was suggested sardonically, at the time, that the new state should be called " The Royal Irish Republic ".

between " Northern Ireland " and the *Saorstát* (trans-
lated literally as " *Free State* ") " in accordance with the
wishes of the population".

There is not the slightest reason to question either
the honesty, the patriotism, or the courage of the Irish
delegates who signed the Treaty. The utmost that
can be said in their condemnation is that, not being
professional politicians, they were out-witted by such
past-masters in chicane as LLOYD GEORGE, BONAR LAW,
BIRKENHEAD (" Galloper " Smith), and AUSTEN
CHAMBERLAIN.

The protraction of the negotiations told all in favour
of the English politicians. The whole world was war-
weary; and the more men, in Ireland and out of it,
grew accustomed to the peace, the less they were
inclined for a resumption of war. Whoever was
responsible for such a resumption would start with a
heavy handicap of public condemnation. Therefore,
the English negotiators skilfully tricked the Irish
Delegates—and *Dáil Eireann*—into the position of
accepting or rejecting the Treaty on the purely formal
ground (as it appeared to all Englishmen) of the *Oath
of Allegiance*. The real objection, *Partition*, was evaded;
in part because " Northern Ireland " was already
an accomplished fact; and, in part, because it was
believed that the Boundary Clause, honestly worked,
would reduce the territory of Northern Ireland to
dimensions which would be economically and politically
incapable of separate existence.

Dáil Eireann after a prolonged debate accepted the
Treaty by a narrow majority.

Pro and Anti-Treaty Civil War

Debates on the Treaty generated intense bitterness;
and this found expression in a split which eventuated
in a CIVIL WAR between the forces of the " *Free State* "
and of the " *Republic*".

Formally, debate centred on the OATH—which casuists and ideologues held to be a violation of the Oath of Fidelity to the Republic already taken by the *Dáil* and the I.R.A. More concretely, it turned on the issue of PARTITION which, it was contended, the Treaty conceded in principle—leaving its rectification to problematical chances. A renewal of the *pogrom* in Belfast pointed the objection.

These grounds of ideological and political division were reinforced and developed into an absolute split by a sharp conflict of economic interests, centering upon the *Land Hunger*, which was a by-product of the stoppage of emigration to the U.S.A., the Dominions, and England— a result, first, of war-caused prohibitions, then of the post-war unemployment crisis.

As we noted earlier, the Land Purchase Acts pre-supposed for their ameliorative effect the constant functioning of the emigrant-ship. During the war its place was filled by recruiting. Some 500,000 men from the Twenty-Six Counties served in the British Forces during the war: their demobilisation, in face of the economic situation in England, and in the world generally, precipitated an intense crisis.

In 1919 a land-seizing movement had sprung up in the West of Ireland. The action of the *Dáil Eireann* land courts, and of the Republican police, in suppressing this movement created an intense resentment which helped to swell resistance to the Treaty, which, for its part, was supported strongly by the more bourgeois elements (including especially the much-hated " ranchers "). The line-up was between the actually or potentially *Land Hungry*, supported by Republican intellectuals and urban revolutionaries, on one side ; and the urban bourgeoisie, the State functionaries, the landowners, and the upper strata of the peasantry on the other. The skilled-labour elements—and the Labour Party generally—were paralysed by division.

Involved in the struggle was a conflict which had profound consequences—that between the I.R.B.—which under DEVOY's influence was pro-Treaty—and the majority section of the I.R.A. which was anti-Treaty. The resulting dissipation of the moral authority of the " Fenian " body told heavily on the side of disintegration and disillusioned-pessimism in the years that followed.

The Civil War and the Six Counties

The formal cause of the CIVIL WAR was the refusal of a majority section of the I.R.A., led by RORY O'CONNOR and LIAM MELLOWS, to submit to the authority of the Free State Government. Its real cause was the *fact of* PARTITION ; and the response of the Six-County Government to the Treaty.

When the terms of the Treaty were made public, Orange zealots fastened on the terms of the Boundary Clause to raise a scare. The " inner ring " had private assurances, from their die-hard confederates in England, that all would be well ; but it was " good politics " to let the zealots of " No Popery " work up as much excitement as they could.

A law was passed by the Northern Ireland Parliament imposing severe penalties for possessing fire-arms without a licence ; and upon membership of any " seditious " association. A new category of full-time Special Constables was established and equipped ; the number of the " occasional " Specials was increased. Any member of an Orange Lodge, or Unionist Association, could get an arms-licence for the asking ; no Catholic could get one in any circumstances. Merely applying for one was a ground for his arrest and detention " on suspicion ".

The ground was prepared for a pogrom by a search of the Catholic quarter of Belfast ostensibly for concealed arms. As a result of previous *pogroms* the quarter was densely overcrowded. Families were living in sheds, and in shacks improvised in back-gardens, and on every spot of waste ground—as well as in halls and church crypts. When the Specials had satisfied themselves that the quarter was destitute of means of defence, the word was given. "Patriotic" Orange mobs marched in with revolvers, rifles and machine-guns and set to work to destroy the entire quarter.

The Catholics fought back as well as they could. A party of young Protestant-Socialists beat off a murderous attack upon a convent (which had been fired) and helped to extinguish the flames. A few I.R.A. men from surrounding districts fought their way in to take part in the defence. Then the military were called in to *fire upon the I.R.A.* The military, however, quelled the riot, temporarily ; but as often as the soldiers retired riot broke out again—and again ! With brazen effrontery Orange apologists blamed the whole trouble upon "*Sinn Fein*" *gunmen.*

When the riots finally died down, it was estimated that another 9,000 Catholics had been driven from their work, and the number rendered homeless had been increased to 23,000. Altogether between June 21st, 1920, and June 21st, 1922, 428 had been killed and 1,766 wounded.

A reprisal, which excited much "horror" in the Tory press, was the shooting—on his own doorstep in London, by two Irish ex-servicemen—of Sir HENRY WILSON, Chief of the Imperial General Staff, and *Chief Military Adviser* to the Government of Northern Ireland. Wilson was generally believed to have instigated the *pogroms* from the first.

The actual occasion of the Civil War between the Free Staters and the Republicans was the resolve of RORY O'CONNOR to lead the I.R.A. into the Six Counties for a war of reprisals.

O'Connor had taken possession of the FOUR COURTS

in Dublin as his headquarters and had begun to commandeer lorries for his raid upon Belfast. The English Government, alarmed at what might happen, urged the Free State Government to dislodge the " anarchists". Finally MICHAEL COLLINS, now Commander in Chief of the Free State Army, at 4 a.m. on June 28th, 1922, began the bombardment of the Four Courts with artillery lent by the English Government.

The civil war between the GRIFFITH-COLLINS *Free State Government* forces, and the " *irregular* " I.R.A. led by DE VALERA, as *President of the Irish Republic*, was fought with intense bitterness on both sides ; and by men who had become largely dehumanised by the prolonged struggle with the Black-and-Tans. The Free State Government had the advantage, in that its army consisted mainly of trained ex-servicemen, and they had unlimited supplies of arms and ammunition. The Republicans suffered the disability of the lack of any real popular support. A tragic aspect of the struggle was the large number of men, distinguished in the Anglo-Irish War, who were killed either in action, by execution, or " trying to escape ". COLLINS, LIAM LYNCH, RORY O'CONNOR, MELLOWS, CATHAL BRUGHA and ERSKINE CHILDERS are among this number.

At noon, on April 30th, 1923, the Republican Chief of Staff ordered the cessation of offensive operations. On May 24th, this was followed by an order to *Cease Fire*, to conceal all arms and ammunition, and disperse. There was no formal surrender. But the civil war was at an end. Attempts to revive it which have been made from time to time have found no popular backing ; except, occasionally, from the exasperated minority in the Six Counties.

The struggle when transferred by DE VALERA to the plane of political contest met with much greater success.

Partition Consummated

When the civil war ended the Free State Government, now headed by W. T. COSGRAVE—Arthur Griffith had died suddenly, shortly after Collins had been killed in action—made approaches for the appointment of a Boundary Commission.

The Northern Ireland Government refused to consider the question. The English Government eventually appointed a representative and nominated one for the Six Counties. These two, with a representative of the Free State, constituted a BOUNDARY COMMISSION.

After a great parade of " investigation " the Commission let it be known that " by a majority " it had decided to act on two principles (1) Northern Ireland had been established for " so long " that changes were undesirable ; (2) nothing should be done to *worsen the economic position* of Northern Ireland. In short, the Treaty-stipulated consideration, " the wishes of the inhabitants ", was to be ignored ; and the net outcome would be that the Boundary would be altered, if at all, to *add* territory and population to Northern Ireland.

Even the British Government was staggered by this exhibition of brass-faced Orange bias ; accordingly it seized the chance to drive a bargain with the Free State Government, which included the cancellation of the Boundary Clause altogether.

Thus in 1925 Partition was finally consummated.

CHAPTER THIRTY-FOUR

ECONOMIC WAR : CONCLUSIONS TO DATE

EAMON DE VALERA returned to power in 1932, and at once opened a struggle to remove, as far as could be done without precipitating a war, all the constitutional and financial ties binding Ireland to England. This policy was replied to by an ECONOMIC WAR, which was ended in 1938 by an AGREEMENT, conceding all De Valera's claims except the vital ones of (1) undoing the *Partition* ; and (2) recognising *Ireland's Independence*.

The refusal to concede these vital points was the ultimate cause of the *Neutrality* of *Eire* during World War II ; the need to concede these demands—and so to complete the negation of the English Conquest of Ireland—is proved by the whole course of the history surveyed in this book.

De Valera Returns to Power

In 1927, DE VALERA and the REPUBLICANS abandoned their attitude of doctrinaire refusal to "recognise" the Irish Free State and took, under protest, the Oath, and their seats in the *Dáil*. A rump of Republicans (claiming to be the original *Dáil*, the old I.R.A., and *Sinn Fein*) refused to support De Valera in this course. He accordingly, with his supporters, founded a new party, the FIANNA FÁIL (" Soldiers of Destiny ") and by persistent propaganda, from the standpoint of the urban and rural petit-bourgeoisie, secured, in 1932, a majority position in the *Dáil*.

On becoming Premier he at once notified the English Government that he intended to abolish the *Oath of Allegiance* and to withhold payment of the ANNUITIES due to the Land Commissioners under the various

Land Purchase Acts (1880-1909). The English Government said nothing about the Oath ; but said a lot about the annuities (really the instalments due annually as the purchase price of their holdings from the tenants). The Dominions Secretary of the National Government, J. H. THOMAS, announced the imposition of special duties on Irish imports into Britain. It was confidently believed that this would so cripple the trade of the Free State that it would be forced to surrender in six months. Actually the " war " lasted for nearly six years, and in that interval more damage was done to the trade of England than to that of the Free State.

The ECONOMIC WAR enabled De Valera to institute a protective system to foster the growth of new industries in the (mainly agricultural) Irish Free State ; which growth would, in some measure, compensate for the loss of the industrial area separated from it by Partition.

In January, 1935, the economic war was tempered by concessions, which modified the import duties, on both sides, for the benefit of English exporters of *coal* and Irish exporters of *cattle*. Finally the economic war was ended by the AGREEMENTS OF 1938, negotiated by Neville Chamberlain. The Irish Free State (now *Eire*) paid £10 million in final settlement of all claims of a financial character ; and, in return, received a concession of the ports and naval depots retained in English control under the Treaty of 1921-2. The constitutional questions outstanding were not mentioned in the Agreement ; and while *Eire* statesmen are entitled to claim that " silence gives consent " the fact remains that the *Eire* constitution of 1936 has never been formally approved (or denounced) by England.

England's constitutional position is weak, here, since by the STATUTE OF WESTMINSTER (1931) every Dominion of the British Empire has the right to alter its constitution at will ; and the exercise of this right by "Northern Ireland " was at once accepted by the English Govern-

ment.*   Under this Statute " Dominion status " implied
co-equality, legislative independence, and " free association "   with   the   British   Commonwealth—which,
incidentally, carries with it the right of *dissociation,
including the right to remain neutral in a war waged by
England.*

De Valera began in 1932 by abolishing the Oath of
Allegiance to the King.   Then at the first opportunity
he got rid of the Governor-Generalship by appointing
a party supporter (*Donald Buckley*, who led a contingent
from Maynooth which fought its way into Dublin in
Easter Week) on the understanding that he would do
nothing whatever in his official capacity.

Then in 1937 a new Constitution was adopted which
declared Ireland a "*sovereign, independent and democratic
state*", under the name *Eire*. Its territory was declared to
be the whole of Ireland ; but the application of the Constitution was limited, temporarily, to the twenty-six
counties of the Free State.   It included no Governor-
General ; and no reference to the Crown or the
" Commonwealth of Nations " (which is Labour Party
humbug for British Empire).   Under this Constitution
an *Uachtaran* (President) is elected every seven years by
direct vote. There are two chambers, a *Dáil* and a Senate,
and the *Dáil* appoints (through the President) a *Taoiseach*
(" Tee-shock ") or Prime Minister who appoints his
ministers, not more than two of whom may be members
of the Senate.   Eamon De Valera has held the office of
Taoiseach ever since.

The tacit acceptance of this Constitution by Neville
Chamberlain and the English Government—while it
might conceal an ulterior motive—was and is a tacit

---

* *Dominion Status :*   Neither *Eire* nor Northern Ireland can be described
as a " Dominion " of the British Empire without qualification. The *Eire*
Government's official view is that it is a " republic *externally associated* with "
the British Empire, while Northern Ireland is officially a special self-governing
" part of the United Kingdom".   Nonetheless, they are both in effect
" Dominions".

recognition, at any rate, that the Irish people claim the right to establish a sovereign, independent State, and that the exercise of that right is obstructed and frustrated by the existence of the Six-County state of "Northern Ireland".

The Evil of Partition

That Partition is an evil—that it was inflicted upon Ireland expressly to thwart the *national* aspirations of the Irish people—we have in this book abundantly proved. Forced to abandon the Act of Union—and "Protestant Ascendancy"—the ruling class of England retorted by *re-establishing the Pale in a new geographical location.*

The excuse for Partition was the pretence that the "Protestants" of N.E. Ulster might be penalised and discriminated against by a Catholic majority. That this was a pure pretence is proved by the abandonment to the Catholic majority of the Twenty-Six Counties of a 6 per cent Protestant minority ; and by the enforced inclusion in "Northern Ireland" of a 33 per cent. Catholic minority which has been insultingly and injuriously discriminated against ever since.

There are many things in the constitution and practice of *Eire* which deserve drastic condemnation from the standpoint of (say) James Connolly, Patrick Pearse, or Theobald Wolfe Tone. But they are matched and surpassed at their worst by the gerrymandered representation and the all-but Fascist administration of Northern Ireland.

Even if this were not so, the war-situation and its outcome shows how very much the enemies of the people of England and of their true interests have been those ruling classes who, the better to be able to exploit the people, have for nearly eight centuries sought to destroy Irish Nationality and to hold Ireland in permanent subjection, directly or indirectly.

On the ground that the English workers can never

be free while they consent to the holding of the Irish people in subjection, it is our case that Partition must be ended to make possible free and fraternal co-operation between England and Ireland.

A *free* Ireland would have taken its rightful place in the Liberation War of Humanity as a matter of course. A partitioned and insulted Ireland was morally forced to occupy the less honourable, but necessitated, position of neutral.

To End Partition

Englishmen, during the war, paid in added peril for the crimes committed in Ireland by the rulers of England (and Ireland) for nearly 800 years. But for that evil legacy—for which every honourable Englishman recognises the obligation to make reparation—we could have counted on the invaluable aid a free and united Ireland could give. We must pay our debt—if only to earn, thereby, the right to applaud, as fellow-fighters for Freedom, the men whose deeds and struggles are recorded in this book.

Partition—a crime and an insult in one—was imposed from England. In England the work of undoing Partition must be, and will be, begun.

Partition was imposed by the rulers of England to serve their class ends. The common people of England, impelled by their class needs, must struggle to end Partition as part of the process of winning their own emancipation.

Partition has established vested interests, on either side of its dividing line. It is reinforced on either side by a mass of inculcated prejudices. Because of that it is not possible to end Partition in a merely formal fashion by a simple repeal of the laws which instituted " Northern Ireland ". It must be ended by the common agreement of all parties concerned—the COMMON PEOPLE in the Six Counties, the Twenty-Six, and in England.

The English democracy has the duty, as well as the privilege, of so cultivating the friendship of the common people on either side of the Boundary that this concrete embodiment of an evil past will fall before the combined assault of the three democracies operating in concert.

Only so shall we fittingly conclude the history set out herein with a return to the beginning on a higher plane—the plane of triumphant democratic advance.

In this effort we can, and will, realise the prophecy of *James Connolly* :

"In *our* movement North and South will again clasp hands, and again it will be demonstrated, as in '98, that the pressure of a common exploitation will make enthusiastic rebels out of a Protestant working-class, enthusiastic champions of civil and religious liberty out of Catholics, and out of both a united Socialist democracy."

And we can make *Patrick Pearse's* words also come true :

"*Let no man be mistaken as to who will be Lord in Ireland, when Ireland is free. The People will be Lord and Master.*"

—— The End ——

INDEX

F

G